SACRAMENTO PUBLIC LIBRARY

SO-ATJ-049

CENTRAL LIBRARY

JAN − 8 1991

RACE and HISTORY

Also by John Hope Franklin

As Author

The Free Negro in North Carolina, 1790–1860
From Slavery to Freedom: A History of Negro Americans
The Militant South, 1800–1860
Reconstruction After the Civil War
The Emancipation Proclamation
Land of the Free
(with John Caughey and Ernest May)
Illustrated History of Black Americans
(with the editors of Time-Life Books)
A Southern Odyssey: Travelers in the Antebellum North
Racial Equality in America
George Washington Williams: A Biography

As Editor

The Civil War Diary of James T. Ayers
Albion Tourgée, *A Fool's Errand*
T. W. Higginson, *Army Life in a Black Regiment*
Three Negro Classics
The Negro in the Twentieth Century
(with Isadore Starr)
Color and Race
W. E. B. Du Bois, *The Suppression of the African Slave Trade*
Reminiscences of an Active Life: The Autobiography of John R. Lynch
Black Leaders of the 20th Century
(with August Meier)
Harlan Davidson American History Series
(with A. S. Eisenstadt), twenty-five volumes
Negro American Biographies and Autobiographies, seven volumes

RACE and HISTORY

Selected Essays

1938–1988

JOHN HOPE FRANKLIN

Louisiana State University Press

Baton Rouge and London

Copyright © 1989 by
Louisiana State University Press
All rights reserved
Manufactured in the United States of America
First printing

98 97 96 95 94 93 92 91 90 89   5 4 3 2 1

Designer: Albert Crochet
Typeface: Linotron Trump Mediaeval
Typesetter: The Composing Room of Michigan, Inc.
Printer and Binder: Thomson-Shore, Inc.

LIBRARY OF CONGRESS CATALOGING-IN-PUBLICATION DATA

Franklin, John Hope, 1915–
    [Essays.   Selections]
    Race and History. Selected essays, 1938–1988.
    p.   cm.
    Bibliography: p.
    Includes index.
    ISBN 0-8071-1547-9 (alk. paper)
    1. Afro-Americans—Historiography.   2. United States—Race
relations—Historiography.   3. Historiography—United States.
I. Title.
E175.5.F73A25   1989
973'.0496073—dc20   89-32613
                                                                CIP

The paper in this book meets the guidelines for permanence
and durability of the Committee on Production Guidelines for Book
Longevity of the Council on Library Resources.⊖

For Margaret Fitzsimmons
In Appreciation for Twenty-five Years of
Rewarding Collaboration

Contents

Preface

The essays in this volume represent historical writing that extends over the last half-century. The earliest one appeared in the *New England Quarterly* in 1938, and the most recent one was delivered as the Charles Homer Haskins Lecture before the American Council of Learned Societies in the spring of 1988. Those fifty years were momentous by any standard—marked by three major wars, numerous civil conflicts, colonial upheavals in Asia and Africa, and tumultuous struggles for racial equality in the United States and elsewhere. There was the temptation, on more than one occasion, to turn one's attention exclusively to the great contemporary issues, to offer possible solutions for intractable human problems, to urge consistency between the nation's professions and its practices, and to join in the civil rights struggle in various parts of the country.

Under the circumstances, therefore, it was difficult to remain professionally committed to historical research, writing, and teaching. Antebellum free Negroes and the militant white southerners who dogged their tracks seemed somehow quite remote from current struggles. And yet what they did in the 1850s was obviously very relevant to what their descendants faced in the 1950s. On one occasion, in 1968, I confronted this interesting intellectual conundrum in an essay, "The Dilemma of the American Negro Scholar," that appears in this volume. I recognized then, as I do now, that while a black scholar has a clear responsibility to join in improving the society in which he lives, he must understand the difference between hard-hitting advocacy on the one hand and the highest standards of scholarship on the other. If the scholar engages in both activities he must make it clear which role he is playing at any given time. Even so, as my father often said about the practice of law, historical scholarship is a jealous mistress who is loath to share her suitor with anyone else.

For the young scholar, appropriately impatient with the slow pace of change in a society that seemed reluctant to make equality a universal attribute, activism was most attractive. Signing protests, joining the Selma marchers, and demonstrating against the evils of racism were ways in which the black

ix

historian could make common cause with fellow sufferers. There were, however, other ways to bear witness that utilized the professional skills I had acquired. I could provide background and context for the problems of the day when, for example, at the end of my year's professorship at Cambridge University, I served as commentator for the British Broadcasting Corporation in its program explaining to British viewers the August, 1963, March on Washington. Or, I could serve as an expert witness in legal actions to achieve equality, as I did in *Lyman Johnson* v. *The University of Kentucky* in 1949.

Using one's skills to influence public policy seemed to be a satisfactory middle ground between an ivory tower posture of isolation and disengagement and a posture of passionate advocacy that too often deserted the canons of scholarship. Thus, with several historians, political scientists, sociologists, and psychologists, I joined the nonlegal research staff of the NAACP Legal Defense Fund in 1953 to assist in the preparation of the brief in *Brown* v. *The Board of Education*. In 1988, several historians presented a brief as friends of the Court when the United States Supreme Court heard arguments in *Brenda Patterson* v. *The McLean Credit Union*. In it we set forth our view that the Civil Rights Act of 1866 was intended to bar racial discrimination in the private as well as the public sector. And historians remain active in showing through their research how the black vote has regularly been diluted and thus rendered powerless in at-large elections in many counties and municipalities throughout the country.

If the historian can have the satisfaction of influencing public policy, as one essay in this volume argues, perhaps it will be sufficient to encourage him also to continue to work on less urgent subjects. Even topics having to do with historiography—the American Revolution, Abraham Lincoln, Reconstruction, and the Civil Rights Act of 1875—while perhaps less urgent than some current public policy matters, remain topical and even relevant in any honest quest for a better social order. This is what provides enormous satisfaction to this historian who seeks to mine the various quarries of the past in the belief that good history is a good foundation for a better present and future.

Over the last fifty years I have become indebted to more people than I can name or even remember. I am especially grateful to my publishers as well as several editors of journals who have graciously granted permission to publish essays in this volume, versions of which previously appeared elsewhere. Then, there are my many teachers, colleagues, and friends, and, of course, countless students who have taught me much and have shared with me their wisdom, patience, and refreshing enthusiasm for exploring the unknown. My sons Whit and Bouna have brought me respectively the refreshing New World impatience and enthusiasm for change and the resilience and adaptability of an Old World culture. My wife of forty-eight years read my first essay when it was published two years before we were married and since that time has been a source of inspiration, encouragement, and loving criticism. I am grateful to all of them.

The dedication of this volume to Margaret Fitzsimmons is an expression of my appreciation, esteem, and affection. For one-half of the time represented by these essays, she has worked with me at the University of Chicago, at the National Humanities Center, at Duke University, and in historical archives. She has been an excellent secretary, a resourceful personal assistant, a friendly critic, and an extraordinarily able editor. Since this is for her birthday, she has had no part in the production of this volume which, for the volume's sake, is a pity. Thus, I must relieve her as well as all others from any responsibility for its shortcomings. Happily, Beverly Jarrett, my editor at the LSU Press, and her colleagues have worked admirably to do Margaret's work as well as their own on this volume, for which I shall be ever grateful.

John Hope Franklin

May 29, 1989

RACE and HISTORY

PART I

The Profession of History

Early in my career I took quite seriously the position that writing and teaching history was not only an exciting and rewarding vocation, it was also a noble profession. To pursue it diligently involved a commitment to seeking the facts and interpreting them responsibly. Another worthy objective was to stimulate the study of history by innovative approaches and methods. This is what led me to take my University of Chicago seminar to North Carolina in 1967 to do research in the libraries and manuscript collections there. It was an unforgettable experience for teacher and students alike. Out of it came several articles and books by members of the seminar that earned for them an enhanced reputation and a wide readership.

The professional historian can make no just claim to a monopoly of the field. Indeed, some of the great works of history have been written by persons who have been labeled lay historians. They have shown through their prizewinning books that the distinction between them and the so-called professional historian is, at best, unclear. One great boon to popularizing history, moreover, has been its use by the media, especially motion pictures and television. Neither the professional historian nor the lay historian nor the media is exempt from observing the canons of the discipline. At the outset, the pioneer in the motion picture field set an example that could not have been worse. *The Birth of a Nation*, based on the Reconstruction novels of Thomas Dixon and brought to the screen by D. W. Griffith in 1915, is an example of the transgression of the canons with utter abandon. *The South During Reconstruction* by E. Merton Coulter is an example of a similar transgression by a distinguished professional historian. The film and the Coulter volume both played on the anxieties, fears, and prejudices of white southerners, which I have sought to point out in essays on each of them.

Afro-American history, which was formally launched as a serious field of study in 1915 by Carter G. Woodson, had its most significant growth in the decades following World War II. It attracted numerous able scholars, white and black, as well as many students of both races. It was an important factor in the civil rights struggle, in the drive for curriculum revision in secondary and

1

higher education, and in establishing linkages among participants in the African diaspora. I was both participant in and observer of these developments. From time to time I expressed my own opinions about the phenomenon as represented in three essays on the subject reprinted here.

I have never ceased to be fascinated by the place that history occupies in the southern ethos. Time and place were the twin ingredients that fueled the southern imagination and provided the setting for what whites of the region proudly called southern civilization. They wrote their own history to explain and justify the idiosyncrasies of their institutions and their policies. Over the years, however, the study of southern history has attracted northerners as well as blacks from the South and the North, for not even southern whites could keep such a fascinating area of intellectual inquiry as their exclusive domain. As one kind of southerner I have always insisted on studying and writing about the entire South and commenting on it as I did in "As for Our History."

Archival Odyssey: Taking Students
to the Sources

A few years ago I was walking along the banks of the Neckar in the lovely university town of Tübingen. There was a great commotion on the river, as scores of university students, in boats and along the banks, were engaged in some sort of game that involved their ducking each other. I was completely absorbed in trying to understand just what they were up to; and I did not notice another observer who had taken up a position at my side. He was a local citizen, although I would never have guessed it from his impeccable English. He said, almost casually, "They enjoy the summers here. There is nothing like the Neckar for summer water sports. But soon, they will be leaving for Munich and Freiburg. The skiing is better there during the winter months."

I did not know that European students were quite that mobile; and I was thoroughly unprepared to discover that summer and winter sports were a major factor in their movements. Perhaps I had been too much influenced by the romantic picture of the medieval student who did, indeed, move but only in order to work with some great professor whose fame drew students to him. I was even aware that towns had founded universities with a view to attracting students. In 1442 the Board of Twelve Wise Men and twenty-four citizens of Ferrara urged the establishment of a university because "strangers will flock thither from various remote regions, and many scholars will stay here, live upon our bread and wine, and purchase of us clothing and other necessities for human existence, will leave their money in our city, and will not depart hence without great gain for all of us." It seemed a bit excessive that students should move from one place to another because of the physical attractions; and frankly I hoped that my companion for

Reprinted from *The American Archivist*, Volume 32, Number 4 (October, 1969) by permission of the Society of American Archivists.

the moment, there on the banks of the Neckar, was at least half-facetious in what he said.

Such ruminations put me in a mood to consider the mobility of university students in the United States. Actually, I said to myself, they do not move very much. There are the usual exchange programs, ranging from a week to a semester, when students of one race, class, or religion do a bit of sampling of another race, class, or religion. Several universities in the Midwest and elsewhere have entered into agreements that facilitate the movement of their students from one member campus to another. Then, there are the junior years abroad, about most of which I should like to say absolutely nothing. Thanks, however, to the rigidity of university structures and matriculation regulations in the United States and thanks, perhaps to an even greater degree, to the regulations by athletic associations regarding the movement of undergraduate athletes, students in this country do not move very much and seldom do so to benefit from the presence of a scholar on another campus.

And yet, among our students, especially our graduate students, who are serious about more than the weekend athletic events and the winter carnival week, it is possible to generate a measure of real enthusiasm for going after truth, even if that means going to some remote place merely to work in an archives or a library. A few years ago I had an opportunity to put this general proposition to a test. When I was visiting the South Carolina Archives, Charles Lee engaged me in conversation about the richness of the archival sources in his state and elsewhere. In the stacks he pointed to an entire wall of manuscript boxes bearing on a well-known and highly controversial period in South Carolina history. He observed that no scholars had yet examined any of them. Then looking at me somewhat condescendingly, he said, "Why have your students engage in a tug of war over two or three pages of manuscripts, perhaps one newspaper, and *Appleton's Annual Cyclopædia* as they attempt to write seminar papers up there in Chicago, when each of them could have his own wall of manuscripts down here."

My first reaction bordered on outrage. How dare anyone speak disparagingly of the university and the library that I love. "This sounds like a Proper Bostonian," I said to myself, "remarking on the library resources of Reno, Nevada." Then, I remembered that Charles Lee, an alumnus of the University of Chicago, did, indeed, know something about the University of Chicago Library. Even more important, I recognized in his remarks a most valuable suggestion that could greatly contribute to the success of my graduate seminar. The more I thought of it the more I saw its great possibilities. Soon, I had resolved to give my seminar students a bit of mobility by sending them to the sources. Better still, I would go with them. By this time I had begun to regard it as a wonderful idea; and I wanted to claim it as my own. I could not, for it was the property of Charles Lee.

For this first venture in taking the students to the sources, I decided on North Carolina rather than South Carolina. There were two primary considerations that influenced my decision. In the first place I was much more familiar with the archives of North Carolina. I had done much of the research for my own doctoral dissertation in the State Archives of North Carolina, and for the next eight years while I was resident in the state I worked there regularly. I believed that my students would derive more benefit in an experimental situation where I was secure in my own knowledge of the institution in which they were working. I also appreciated the fact that with Duke University and the University of North Carolina nearby, the students would have an opportunity to work in the rich manuscript collections of those two universities. The second consideration was that since the seminar was to be on the Reconstruction era and since no major work on Reconstruction in North Carolina had been published since 1914—as contrasted to several important works in recent years for South Carolina—we would have what would amount to a "wide open field" in selecting North Carolina.

In the autumn quarter 1966 I announced that my seminar for the winter quarter would be on the history of Reconstruction in North Carolina and that the eight members of the seminar would spend two weeks in North Carolina working in the sources. Within a few days the seminar was closed, for eight students had indicated by their qualifications and personal interviews that they would benefit from the experience. I had already received assurances from the university that although it could not underwrite the seminar, it would be willing to bear the expenses of any qualified student who would be unable to go for financial reasons. The university also indicated that it would be pleased to finance the photoduplication of all materials that the students found useful but that they did not want to consume valuable time in copying by hand.

Once the students had signed up, I began to confer with them individually and collectively long before the beginning of the quarter in which the seminar was to be held. I encouraged them to read as widely as they could on the general problem of Reconstruction in North Carolina and to come to some decision, as early as possible, about a possible topic on which they would like to work. By the middle of December, all of the students had selected tentative topics and they had gone as far as possible in the reading of secondary materials. Indeed, during the Christmas holidays several students had pursued their topics in New York and Washington as well as Chicago. It was an impressive introduction to a seminar that officially had not yet begun.

Meanwhile I had proceeded with the arrangements for the trip to North Carolina. Since the term began the first week in January, I thought that it would be best if we remained in Chicago for the first three weeks of the term. This would give the students ample time not only to complete the preliminary work connected with their own seminar topics but also to get a good start in the other courses in which they were enrolled. First, there was the problem of transportation. It has never failed to awe this child of the Depression that virtually all the members of the seminar had cars; and it was merely a problem of choosing which two cars we would use for the trip. As there were two women and five men (one student dropped out at the last minute because he could not resist a $10,000 job that was offered him), we decided that one of the women should take her car and one of the men should take his. Second—and this is related to the matter of transportation—North Carolina State University offered to house the men students at a rate that was tempting even to one who might have to commute to Chicago to his job. St. Augustine's College made a similarly attractive offer to house the women students. The women who lived at St. Augustine's could transport themselves to the archives, and the men could do the same in the faithful Volkswagen bus of one of the students.

The North Carolina archivist and the director of the State Department of Archives and History were delighted that we had decided to visit them during the final week in January and the first week in February, 1967. I sent them the tentative topics on which the students had decided, and the archivists assured me that they would give the matter their attention and would be prepared to make suggestions upon our arrival. I also sent the topics to the curators of the manuscript collections at Duke and the University of North Carolina and received similar responses. Indeed, the curators at the universities offered to keep their manuscript collections open during the evenings and on weekends to accommodate our students. (I hope that this did not set a precedent that has proved inconvenient to our hospitable friends at these institutions.)

During those exciting three weeks of the term before we departed for North Carolina, I met regularly with the members of the seminar. We refined the topics, continued our reading, and prepared ourselves in every way to make certain that we would spend the two weeks in North Carolina most profitably. We had sessions on Joseph G. Hamilton's *Reconstruction in North Carolina.* We discussed every article that had been published in the *North Carolina Historical Review.* We reviewed the published guides to the manuscript collections of the State Archives, the University of North Carolina, and Duke University. Even before we departed for the Tarheel State, the students had begun to feel that they were real authorities on Reconstruction in North Carolina.

It was only now and then that I recognized the fact that they were not yet the authorities that they wanted to be. In the lull in our conversations about the Negro Convention of 1865 or the Kirk-Holden War, one of the students would say, "Please tell us something about the climate in Raleigh in late January. What kind of clothing should we take, and is it all right if we take our golf clubs." Then, I would assume the full authority of my years of experience, deplore the ignorance of my students and add, somewhat impatiently,

> It is a pity that you know nothing of the climate of this state. North Carolina is not in the tropics. It is located in the upper South, where the weather in late January is likely to be harsh and raw. Kindly take ear muffs, storm coats, and snowshoes. I can only hope that you will fare better than I did during those eight bleak, cold winters I spent in the state.

Some students grumbled that they were more interested in the Reconstruction of Florida and wished that we had selected that state.

I did not travel with the students but flew down on the day of their arrival. They met me at the airport on a balmy Sunday afternoon. My plane was late owing to a snowstorm in Chicago. The students were also late in arriving to meet me at the Raleigh-Durham airport because they had been out to a golf course watching a number of matches in which the participants had been attired in shorts. I shall never again be so certain about the weather in North Carolina or even in Antarctica!

At the beginning of our first working day we spent the morning consulting with the staff of the North Carolina State Department of Archives and History. Christopher Crittenden, the director, and H. G. Jones, the archivist, brought together the members of their staff who had informed themselves about relevant materials on each of the topics on which the students were working. For several hours all of us exchanged notes and observations about the research problems, with the students asking literally hundreds of questions and the staff making literally hundreds of suggestions about sources and approaches. This was the first of several such seminars with the staff, and I venture to say that this part of the seminar was one of the most valuable experiences that any group of students could possibly have. Our friends at Chapel Hill and Durham offered the kind of cooperation we were receiving at Raleigh. As a class we also met several evenings each week during the two weeks that we were in North Carolina. We usually ate lunch and dinner together. These regular associations gave us an opportunity to exchange materials, discuss problems that arose, and suggest to each other possible ways of approaching the next stage of the research.

Under the circumstances it was not long before the students knew quite well what was involved in getting to the heart of their problems, and quite early I began to detect an air of confidence and a feeling of self-satisfaction among them. One student, working on "The Reception of the Fourteenth Amendment in North Carolina," began to talk quite confidently about the inadequacy of the treatment of the subject by Hamilton. Another student, who was concerned with agricultural recovery in postwar North Carolina, complained that no historian, with the exception of him of course, had done justice to agricultural developments in the piedmont and in the western part of the state and that the Carolina *Western Democrat*, a newspaper of Mecklenburg County, had been tragically overlooked by students of the period. On the second day of our visit I asked the student who was working on "Race Relations in Raleigh, 1865–1866" how he was getting along. After reviewing the auspicious beginnings of the career of Jim Crow in the jails and cemeteries of Raleigh in 1866, he replied, "I'm doing fine, but Professor Vann Woodward isn't doing very well!"

This self-confidence and self-esteem on the part of the students—rapidly becoming authorities—were bolstered considerably by the local attention that they received. On the third day of our visit the Raleigh *Times* devoted half a page, with pictures, to an article entitled "Chicago Students Sift North Carolina Historical Documents." Before the end of the week, the piece had appeared in more than a score of afternoon daily newspapers in North Carolina. There were other reporters and other articles, and one of my unanticipated duties was to protect the students from journalists who wanted to do feature stories

8

on them. Then, there was the luncheon with Lieutenant Governor Robert Scott, who later became the governor of North Carolina. A measure of the effect of this heady experience was to be seen shortly, when a student was overheard saying, "Did you hear what I told Bob Scott about his state's educational needs?"

While the students were busy with their own research, their professor remained busy not only protecting them from reporters but also performing other duties as impressario and "fixer." He was called upon to make speeches at Shaw University and St. Augustine's College. He addressed the members of the archives staff on "What the Teaching Historian Looks for in a State Historical Agency." He found it necessary to talk with various local citizens who had been impressed with the newspaper articles that continued to appear. In one case he succeeded in convincing one woman that the state archives was the place for the papers of a member of her family who had been prominent during the Reconstruction era. He even had to give a talk about his own research before a group of graduate students from neighboring institutions at a dinner graciously arranged by Jones and Crittenden.

These were insignificant tasks when one compares them with the great rewards that such an experience provided. As I look back on it, I should say that the opportunity afforded the students of going "beyond the water's edge" to confront significant materials that formed the bases for meaningful and even important papers was worth every effort that was put into the undertaking. The members of the seminar made useful and lasting contacts that are still proving valuable with the archival and library staffs and with other graduate students. The students came away from the experience of the fifteen days more absorbed in their subjects than they had ever been before, for the concentration of many hours each day on one topic was a new experience for virtually all of them. Now they were real professionals; and they knew it. If one had any doubt about this he had merely to witness the conduct of these neophyte professionals upon their return to the University of Chicago. The recounting of an African safari and the display of the trophies could hardly have been more exciting. And if that was a bit hard to take at times, one can observe that the effect on the poor, underprivileged students who did not make the trip was humbling if not humiliating. If the privileged seven were a bit difficult to live with, the hundred or so who remained behind were infinitely more sober and even more teachable.

The Birth of a Nation:
Propaganda as History

The fact that certain scholars specialize in studying the past does not mean that the past as an area of serious inquiry is beyond the reach of the layman with even the most modest intellectual and professional equipment. One must respect the efforts of anyone who seeks to understand the past; but it does not follow that one must respect or accept the findings of all who inquire into the past. Nor does it follow that the curiosity seekers of one brand or another can speak for those who by training and commitment devote their major attention to a study of the past. The decades and centuries that have receded from contemporary view are too important to all of us to leave their study to those who do not bring to the task all the skills available and present their findings with a clear understanding of what history means to the present and to the future.

The study of the past may mean many things to many people. For some it means that the effort to reconstruct what actually happened in an earlier era demands an honesty and integrity that elevate the study of history to a noble enterprise. For some it means that the search for a usable past provides instruction that may help to avoid the errors of their forefathers. It is not necessary to enumerate each of the many uses of the past, but it is worth noting that not all such quests are characterized by a search for the truth. Some of the most diligent would-be historians have sought out those historical episodes that support some contemporary axe they have to grind. Others look for ways to justify the social and public policy that they and like-minded persons advocate. Others even use the past to hold up to public scorn and ridicule those who are the object of their own prejudices.

The era of Reconstruction after the Civil War is an excellent exam-

Reprinted from *The Massachusetts Review,* © 1979 The Massachusetts Review, Inc.

ple of a period that attracts historians—laymen and professionals alike—who seek historical explanations for certain contemporary social and political problems. And Thomas Dixon, Jr., is a peerless example of a historian—in his case a layman—who has mined the era of Reconstruction to seek a historical justification for his own social attitudes and who has exerted as much influence on current opinions of Reconstruction as any historian, lay or professional. Born in 1864 in a farmhouse near Shelby, North Carolina, Dixon was eight years old when he accompanied an uncle to a session of the state legislature in South Carolina where he saw in that body "ninety-four Negroes, seven native scalawags [white South Carolina Republicans] and twenty-three white men [presumably carpetbaggers from the North]." The impression on young Dixon of blacks and unworthy whites sitting in the seats of the mighty was a lasting one and ostensibly had a profound influence on his future career.[1]

Dixon's Reconstruction experience was not unlike that which he had in 1887 when he heard Justin D. Fulton speak in Boston's Tremont Temple on "The Southern Problem." He was so outraged at Fulton's strictures against the South, based on a visit of six months, that he interrupted the distinguished minister midway through his lecture to denounce his assertions as "false and biased." It was on this occasion that Dixon decided to tell the world what he knew about the South firsthand; and thus he began seriously to study the Civil War and Reconstruction.[2]

The road that led Dixon to write about the Reconstruction era took him on a long and eventful journey. It led to Wake Forest College, where he was a superior student and leading debater. Then, for a brief sojourn he was at the Johns Hopkins University, where he became friendly with a graduate student, Woodrow Wilson, with whom he would later exchange favors. At the age of twenty young Dixon was a one-term member of the North Carolina legislature, which he quit because he was sickened by the conduct of the politicians whom he called "the prostitutes of the masses." Incidentally, the number of black members of the assembly was so small in 1884 that they could not possibly have been the cause of Dixon's disillusionment. Successively, this restless and talented young man became an actor, lawyer, clergyman, essayist, and lecturer. None of these pursuits satisfied Thomas Dixon as long as he was consumed with the desire to "set the record straight," as he would put it, regarding Reconstruction. Consequently, he forsook his other activities and proceeded to write the first volume of his Recon-

11

struction trilogy. He called it *The Leopard's Spots: A Romance of the White Man's Burden.* The title was derived from the biblical question "Can the Ethiopian change his skin, or the leopard his spots?"

Dixon sent his first novel to his old Raleigh, North Carolina, friend, Walter Hines Page, then a partner in the publishing house, Doubleday, Page and Company. Page accepted it immediately and optimistically ordered a first printing of fifteen thousand copies. The success of the work when it appeared in 1903 was instantaneous. Within a few months more than one hundred thousand copies had been sold, and arrangements made for numerous foreign translations. Highly touted as a general history of the racial problem in the South and especially in North Carolina from 1885 to 1900, *The Leopard's Spots* established Dixon as an authority whom many were inclined to take seriously. His "luxuriant imagination" gave him the power to create "human characters that live and love and suffer before your eyes," a critic in the Chicago *Record-Herald* exclaimed.[3] If there were those who were adversely critical—and there were—their voices could scarcely be heard above the din of almost universal praise.

Fame and fortune merely stimulated Dixon to greater accomplishments. He was in constant demand as a lecturer and writer; and soon his tall, commanding figure was on the platform in many parts of the country, constantly pressing his case as if in an adversary relationship with his audience. Within a few years he was ready to begin the second of his works on the Reconstruction, and thirty days after he began the writing he completed *The Clansman; An Historical Romance of the Ku Klux Klan.* Two years later, in July, 1907, he finished the last of the volumes in the Reconstruction trilogy, which appeared under the title *The Traitor: A Story of the Rise and Fall of the Invisible Empire.*

The great success of *The Clansman* as a novel caused Dixon to consider its possibilities as a drama. In a matter of months, in 1905, Dixon had converted his second Reconstruction novel into a dramatic play whose script won the praise of Secretary of State John Hay and of Albert Bigelow Paine, who was to become the literary executor of Mark Twain. When the play went on tour, it was acclaimed as "The Greatest Play of the South . . . A Daring Thrilling Romance of the Ku Klux Klan . . ." and it drew enormous crowds even though some critics thought it a bit excessive in its strictures against blacks and the way in which it aroused emotions and animosities that many hoped were abating. But *The Clansman* remained as thrilling on the stage as it had been as a best-selling novel.

On a voyage from Europe in 1912, Dixon, proud of what he had accomplished, began once more to think seriously about his future. By that time he had completed his trilogy on Reconstruction as well as a trilogy on socialism. *The Clansman* had been a success on the stage, and everywhere he was acclaimed as a near-genius. He began to wonder if he should return to acting, but he rejected such a career as being too prosaic. Likewise, he rejected the idea that he should remain a playwright on the thoroughly defensible ground that the endless repetition of plot and scene before relatively small audiences was not a very effective medium for the dissemination of ideas. Books, likewise, were limited in their appeal, and although Dixon would continue to write them, they would never claim all of his attention.

By this time, however, there was a new medium, called "motion pictures," just becoming known. This novel method of communication lured Dixon "like the words of a vaguely-heard song," as his biographer put it. If this new medium, still scorned by most actors, most religious groups, and many "respectable" people, could be dignified by some great statement—like a historically vital story—would it not be the means of reaching and influencing millions of people? This could be an exciting new venture, and this adventuresome man answered his own question in the affirmative.

In the months following his return from Europe, Dixon tried to persuade some producer in the infant motion picture industry to take on his scenario of *The Clansman,* but none would accept the offer. The movies were popular only as low comedies, light farce, and short action sequences with little plot. All the producers whom Dixon approached insisted that *The Clansman* was too long, too serious, and too controversial. Finally, late in 1913, Dixon met Harry E. Aitken, the head of a small company, and through him he met David W. Griffith who had enough daring and imagination to turn from his one-reel productions at least to consider the possibility of producing a large work like *The Clansman.* When Griffith's own company, the Epoch Producing Corporation, was unable to pay Dixon the ten thousand dollars he asked for his work, the author had to content himself by accepting a 25 percent interest in the picture. Armed with Dixon's blessings and thousands of his suggestions, Griffith set out for Hollywood to find a cast and to proceed with production. The actual filming occupied nine weeks, between July and October, 1914.

Prior to this time the motion picture had been composed of a series of stilted poses taken at random distances and tagged together with little continuity. The motion, not the play, was the thing. Griffith now introduced principles of shooting that were to make the motion picture a new and important art form. "His camera became a living human eye, peering into faces of joy and grief, ranging over great vistas of time and space, and resolving the whole into a meaning flux, which created a sense of dramatic unity and rhythm to the story."[4] It was this living human eye that gave the Reconstruction story a new dimension.

It has been suggested that the film was more Griffith than Dixon. This is patently not the case. To be sure, Griffith was from Kentucky, and he had a certain sympathy for the southern cause. And in the flush of success, Dixon would say, on opening night between the acts, that none but the son of a Confederate soldier could have directed the film.[5] But Griffith's knowledge of history was scant, and he was much too occupied with the technical aspects of filming the picture to interpose his views regarding its content. Even a casual comparison of the texts of *The Leopard's Spots* and *The Clansman* with the film itself will convince one that *Birth of a Nation* is pure Dixon, all Dixon!

When the twelve-reel drama was completed, Joseph Carl Breil composed a musical score for it that was essentially adaptations from Negro folk songs and passages from Wagner's *Rienzi* and *Die Walküre*, and Bellini's *Norma*. In February, 1915, there were private showings in Los Angeles and New York. Dixon first saw the film at the New York showing. He sat in the balcony alone, fearing that he would be hooted and jeered by the seventy-odd people on the first floor. There was no such likelihood. Dixon said that his own experience of seeing the film was "uncanny." "When the last scene had faded," he later recounted, "I wondered vaguely if the emotions that had strangled me were purely personal. I hesitated to go down to the little group in the lobby and hear their comments. I descended slowly, cautiously, only to be greeted by the loudest uproar I had ever heard from seventy-five people." It was at that time that Dixon shouted to Griffith across the auditorium and exclaimed that *The Clansman* was too tame a title for such a powerful story. "It should be called 'The Birth of a Nation,'" he exclaimed.[6]

There is a great deal of overlap in the characters and plots of the works in the Dixon Reconstruction trilogy, but *Birth of a Nation* draws more heavily on *The Clansman* than on the others. The first part of the film introduces the Stoneman brothers, Phil and Tod, from Pennsylvania, who are visiting their school friends, the Cameron brothers, in Piedmont, South Carolina. They are the sons of Austin Stoneman, a member of Congress. Phil falls in love with Margaret Cameron, while

Ben Cameron falls in love with Elsie Stoneman. When the war erupts, the Stonemans return north to join the Union Army while the Camerons enter the Confederate Army. During the war the two younger Cameron brothers and Tod Stoneman are killed. Ben Cameron is wounded and is nursed by Elsie Stoneman as he lies a prisoner of Phil Stoneman in Washington. Meanwhile, Elsie and Phil's father, Austin Stoneman—in real life Thaddeus Stevens, the North's most unreconcilable radical—is busy urging southern blacks to rise up against the southern whites. Dixon does not fail to make the most of the fact that Stoneman has a mulatto housekeeper, and, because of Stoneman's power as leader of Congress and the alleged intimacy of Stoneman and his housekeeper, Dixon in *The Clansman* dubs her "The First Lady of the Land."

As the story of Reconstruction unfolds there is, of course, much corruption, much black presumption and arrogance, much humiliation of whites by black troops, and much looting and lawlessness. In order to avenge the wrongs perpetrated against his people, Ben Cameron becomes the leader of the Ku Klux Klan. It is not in time, however, to save his younger sister from the advances of Gus, a Negro roustabout, from whom she escapes by jumping from a cliff to her death. There are other would-be interracial trysts. When Elsie Stoneman asks Silas Lynch, a leader in the Black League, to save her brother Phil from the Negro militia that had besieged him in a log cabin, Lynch demands that Elsie marry him. The situation is resolved when the clansmen, under the leadership of Ben Cameron, put the black militia to flight, free Elsie from Lynch, and kill Gus. Then, a double wedding takes place between the Stoneman and Cameron families, symbolic of the unification of the North and South. Thus, the long, dark night of Reconstruction ends, and the white people of the South take on an optimistic view of their future as their nation, Phoenix-like, arises from the ashes of war and reconstruction.

The euphoria that Dixon and his friends experienced at the New York theater in February, 1915, was not sufficient to sustain *The Birth of a Nation* in the face of strong opposition from unexpected quarters. Despite strong criticism of his earlier works on Reconstruction, Dixon had been able to cope with it. When *The Leopard's Spots* appeared, Kelly Miller, the Negro dean of Howard University, wrote to Dixon, "Your teachings subvert the foundations of law and established order. You are the high priest of lawlessness, the prophet of anarchy."[7] Sutton E. Griggs, the Arkansas black lawyer, asserted that Dixon "said and did all things which he deemed necessary to leave behind him the greatest heritage of hate the world has ever known."[8] Dixon countered by saying, "My books are hard reading for a Negro, and yet the Negroes, in denouncing them, are unwittingly denouncing one of their best friends."[9]

The opposition to *Birth of a Nation* was more formidable. Oswald Garrison Villard, editor of the New York *Evening Post*, and Moorfield Storey, president of the American Bar Association, were both founders and active leaders in the National Association for the Advancement of Colored People. They were representative of a large number of Americans, black and white, who thought that the film was a travesty against truth as well as an insult to an entire race of people. (Villard called it "improper, immoral, and unjust.")[10] They were determined to prevent the showing of the film and began to work assiduously to bring about its doom. But they had not assayed the resourcefulness of Thomas Dixon, Jr., who was equally determined to secure a nationwide showing of his masterpiece. He proved to be a formidable and, indeed, an invincible adversary.

If the president of the United States should give *his* approval to the film, Dixon thought, perhaps the opposition would be silenced. And so, in February, 1915, Thomas Dixon decided to visit his old schoolmate, Woodrow Wilson, who now occupied the White House. When Dixon called, Wilson was pleased to see his old friend. The two were soon reminiscing about their days at the Johns Hopkins University and about the manner in which Dixon had been instrumental in securing an honorary degree for Wilson at Wake Forest College. When Dixon told Wilson about his new motion picture, Wilson immediately expressed an interest, but indicated that since he was still mourning the death of his wife he could not attend the theater. Wilson then suggested that if Dixon could arrange to show the film in the East Room of the White House he, his family, and members of the cabinet and their families could see it. The president said, "I want you to know, Tom, that I am pleased to do this little thing for you, because a long time ago you took a day out of your busy life to do something for me. It came at a crisis in my career, and greatly helped me. I've always cherished the memory of it."[11]

On February 18, 1915, *The Birth of a Nation* was shown at the White House, and at the end of the showing President Wilson is said to have remarked that "It is like writing history with lightning. And my only regret is that it is all so terribly true."[12]

Dixon's next scheme was to show the film to the members of the Supreme Court. With the help of Secretary of the Navy Josephus Daniels of North Carolina, Dixon secured an appointment with Chief Justice Edward D. White. The chief justice told Dixon that he was not interested in motion pictures, and indicated that the members of the Supreme Court had better ways to spend their time. As Dixon was taking his leave he told the chief justice that the motion picture was the true story of Reconstruction and of the redemption of the South by the Ku Klux Klan. Upon learning this, the chief justice leaned forward in his chair and said, "I was a member of the Klan, sir," and he agreed to see the picture that evening. Not only were members of the Supreme Court at the ballroom of the Raleigh Hotel to see the picture, but many members of the Senate and House of Representatives were also there with their guests.[13]

When opposition to the film persisted, Dixon let it be known that the President, the Supreme Court, and the Congress had seen the film and liked it. When this was confirmed by a call to the White House, the censors in New York withdrew their objection and the film opened there on March 3, 1915, and played for forty-seven weeks at the Liberty Theatre. Although the picture showed to huge audiences in New York and in every city and hamlet across the country, there was always great opposition to it. In New York, Rabbi Stephen Wise, a member of the city's censorship board, called *Birth of a Nation* an "indescribably foul and loathsome libel on a race of human beings. . . . The Board of Censors which allowed this exhibition to go on is stupid or worse. I regret I am a member."[14] In Boston a crowd of five hundred persons, including firebrands such as William Monroe Trotter, demonstrated on the grounds of the state capitol, demanding that the governor take steps to ban the film.[15] A bill to that end was rushed through the lower house of the legislature only to be found unconstitutional by the judiciary committee of the upper house.

The president of Harvard University said that the film perverted white ideals. Jane Addams, the founder of Hull House, was greatly disturbed over the picture and wrote vigorously against it.[16] Booker T. Washington denounced the film in the newspapers.[17] Branches of the NAACP protested its showing in cities across the nation. But the film was seldom suppressed anywhere, and the reviews by drama critics were almost universally favorable. Burns Mantle said that there was an "element of excitement that swept a sophisticated audience like a prairie fire in a high wind." Hector Turnbull of the New York *Tribune* called it a "spectacular drama" with "thrills piled upon thrills."[18] But Francis Hackett's review in the *New Republic* conceded that as a spectacle "it is stupendous," but its author was a yellow journalist because he distorted the facts. The film, Hackett insisted, was aggressively vicious and defamatory. "It is spiritual assassination."[19] That may well be, Dixon seemed to think, but to the charges that he had falsified history, Dixon offered a reward of one thousand dollars to anyone who could prove one historical inaccuracy in the story.

I do not know of any person's having proved to Dixon's satisfaction that there were any inaccuracies in the film. I do know that many critics besides Hackett, convinced that it was filled with distortions, half-truths, and outright falsifications, challenged the truth of *Birth of a Nation*. Francis J. Grimké, distinguished Negro minister in Washington, published a pamphlet entitled "Fighting a Vicious Film" that was a virtual line-by-line refutation of the Dixon-Griffith work. *Crisis* magazine, the official organ of the NAACP, ran a series of monthly reports under the heading "Fighting Race Calumny."[20] The film soon became the object of scathing criticism in mass meetings held by Negro religious, educational, and civic groups across the nation. The only concession that Dixon made after the film had been running for several months, was to add a reel on the industrial work being done by blacks at Hampton Institute in Virginia. And for cooperating with Dixon in this undertaking, the white president of Hampton was bitterly criticized by the same blacks and whites who had so severely criticized the film.

It is not at all difficult to find inaccuracies and distortions in *Birth of a Nation*. Ostensibly a firsthand account of the events that transpired between 1865 and 1877, it could hardly have been firsthand when one recalls that Dixon was one year old when Reconstruction began and only thirteen when the last federal troops were withdrawn from the South in 1877. That was one reason, though not the principal reason, for Dixon's failure to include anything on Reconstruction in the South between 1865 and 1867, when not one black man had the vote, when all southern whites except the top Confederate leaders were in charge of all southern state governments, and when white southerners enacted laws designed to maintain a social and economic order that was barely distinguishable from the antebellum period. There is not a shred of evidence to support the film's depiction of blacks as impudent, vengeful, or malicious in their conduct toward whites. As pointed out by Francis B. Simkins, a southern white historian who specialized in

Reconstruction in South Carolina where most of *Birth of a Nation* takes place, freedmen manifested virtually no hostility toward former masters.[21] The evidence is overwhelming, although not necessarily commendable, that the vast majority of freedmen worked energetically and peacefully on their former masters' plantations during the entire period of Reconstruction.[22]

The film makes a great deal of the alleged disorderliness, ignorance, and mendacity of the blacks in the South Carolina legislature. It also depicts Silas Lynch, the black lieutenant governor, as an audacious, arrogant, cheap politician whose only interest in life was to marry the blonde daughter of Austin Stoneman, the prototype of Thaddeus Stevens, Pennsylvania's Radical leader in Congress. It did not fit Dixon's scheme of things to acknowledge that the most important black political leader in South Carolina was Francis Cordozo, a graduate of Glasgow University, or that blacks were never in control of the machinery of government in the state. Nor did it matter to Dixon that the two black lieutenant governors of South Carolina during Reconstruction were Richard Gleaves, a Pennsylvania businessman who enjoyed a reputation as an excellent president of the senate, and Alonzo Ransier, a shipping clerk in antebellum Charleston who was never accused of dishonesty, arrogance, or of harboring any antipathy toward whites. Which of these men, the only two available, did Dixon use as a model for his Silas Lynch? In any case, there was no black lieutenant governor in the closing years of Reconstruction when Dixon gloats over black lieutenant governor Silas Lynch being killed by the Ku Klux Klan for making advances to blonde Elsie Stoneman.[23]

If southern blacks had a competitor for the most degraded and depraved place in *Birth of a Nation* it was Austin Stoneman, a very thin disguise for Thaddeus Stevens of Pennsylvania. As the member of Congress most deeply committed to racial equality, Stevens was the most hated northerner in the South. Dixon was so determined to use Thaddeus Stevens for his purposes that he committed every possible violence to the facts of Stevens' life. First, he presented Stoneman (Stevens) as a widower, though Stevens was never married. This was necessary in order to provide Stoneman with a son and daughter. That would set the stage for a North-South reconciliation through the double wedding of his son and daughter with two young southerners. This, in turn, was necessary in order to make Stoneman's conversion to southern principles complete when his black protegé sought to marry his daughter.

Secondly, Dixon presented Stoneman (still Stevens) as being intimate with his black housekeeper, although there is no evidence to support it except that they lived in the same house. For the ultimate proof, Dixon could have had Lydia Brown become pregnant by Stoneman, as actually happened in some other instances of intimacies between white leaders and their black "friends." Apparently, this would have interfered with some of the other contrivances. Finally, Dixon was not content until he had Stoneman traveling to South Carolina at the climax of Reconstruction in order to experience the ultimate humiliation both from the black lieutenant governor Silas Lynch, who attempted to marry his daughter, and from the Ku Klux Klan, who rescued his daughter from Lynch.

It seems unnecessary to add that Thaddeus Stevens never went to South Carolina and had, indeed, died in 1868, when Dixon was four years old and several years before the high drama of South Carolina Reconstruction actually began.[24] Even so, Thomas Dixon could write as follows: "I drew of old Thaddeus Stevens the first full length portrait of history. I showed him to be, what he was, the greatest and the vilest man who ever trod the halls of the American Congress." This was followed by his customary challenge: "I dare my critic to come out . . . and put his finger on a single word, line, sentence, paragraph, page, or chapter in 'The Clansman' in which I had done Thad Stevens an injustice."[25]

Were it not for other considerations *Birth of a Nation* would be celebrated—and properly so—as the instrument that ushered the world into the era of the modern motion picture, a truly revolutionary medium of communication. Mantle called the picture "wonderful"; to Charles Darnton, Griffith's work was "big and fine"; while the New York *Times* called it an "impressive new illustration of the scope of the motion picture camera."[26] There were, however, other considerations. By his own admission Dixon's motives were not to discover the truth but to find a means by which to make a case for the South that, regardless of the facts (one is tempted to say, in spite of the facts), would commend itself to the rest of the country. "The real purpose back of my film," Dixon wrote in May, 1915, to Joseph Tumulty, Woodrow Wilson's secretary, "was to revolutionize Northern sentiments by a presentation of history that would transform every man in my audience into a good Democrat! . . . Every man who comes out of one of our theatres is a Southern partisan for life." A few months later he wrote President Wilson, "This play is transforming the entire population of the North and West into sympathetic Southern voters. There will never be an issue of your segregation policy."[27]

Thus, Thomas Woodrow Wilson, twenty-eighth president of the United States and a professionally trained historian, lent the prestige of his high office and the hospitality of the Executive Mansion to promote this unseemly piece of propaganda as history. Dixon was never interested in the truth in history. He was interested in "selling" a particular promotion piece as history. That in itself is not the supreme tragedy, bad as it is. The supreme tragedy is that in *The Clansman* and in *Birth of a Nation*, Thomas Dixon succeeded in using a powerful and wonderful new instrument of communication to perpetuate a cruel hoax on the American people that has come distressingly close to being permanent.

In the same year, 1915, that *Birth of a Nation* was showing to millions across the United States, the Ku Klux Klan was reborn. When the film opened in Atlanta that fall, William J. Simmons, who had considered a Klan revival for several years, sprang into action. He gathered together nearly two score men, including two members of the original Klan of 1866 and the speaker of the Georgia legislature. They agreed to found the order, and Simmons picked Thanksgiving eve for the formal ceremonies. As the film opened in Atlanta, a local paper carried Simmons' announcement next to the advertisement of the movie. It was an announcement of the founding of "The World's greatest Secret, Patriotic, Fraternal, Beneficiary Order." With an assist from *Birth of a Nation*, the new Ku Klux Klan, a "High Class order of men of Intelligence and Order," was launched.[28] It would spread all across the South and into the North and West in the 1920s and spread terror among Jews and Catholics as well as among blacks.

In the fall and winter of 1915–1916, thousands of southerners thrilled to the stirring scenes of *Birth of a Nation*. "Men who once wore gray uniforms, white sheets and red shirts wept, yelled, whooped, cheered—and on one occasion even shot up the screen in a valiant effort to save Flora Cameron from her black pursuer."[29] They were ripe for enlistment in the new Ku Klux Klan. Thus, *Birth of a Nation* was the midwife in the rebirth of the most vicious terrorist organization in the history of the United States.

When Dixon was writing *The Clansman*, several others were actively competing with him for the title as the most uncompromising racist writer to appear on the American scene. In 1900 Charles Carroll published *The Negro a Beast*, a scurrilous attack on the nature and

21

immorality of blacks that was expanded two years later in his *The Tempter of Eve; or The Criminality of Man's Social, Political and Religious Equality with the Negro.* In 1902 William P. Calhoun continued the attack in *The Caucasian and the Negro in the United States.* In 1907, two years after Dixon's *The Clansman* appeared, Robert W. Schufeldt published *The Negro, a Menace to American Civilization.*

These, however, were mere books, as *The Clansman* was; and Dixon had already concluded that books were limited in their appeal. The diabolical genius of Dixon lay in his embracing the new medium, the motion picture, and thus using that medium to persuade and even to convince millions of white Americans, even those who could not read books, that his case against Negro Americans was valid and irrefutable. It was not merely that illiterate and unthinking Americans were convinced by Dixon's propaganda. It was also that vast numbers of white Americans, searching for a rationale for their own predilections and prejudices, seized on Dixon's propaganda, by his own admission propaganda designed to win sympathy for the southern cause, and transformed it into history as the gospel truth.

As one reads *The Tragic Era,* published in 1929 by Claude Bowers, surely one of the country's most respected journalist-historians, one is impressed if not awed by its faithful adherence to the case as argued in *Birth of a Nation.* It is all there—the vicious vindictiveness of Thaddeus Stevens, the corruptibility of every black legislator, and the nobility of the Ku Klux Klan in redeeming a white civilization threatened with black rule. It was the scum of northern society that inflamed "the Negro's egotism," said Bowers, "and soon the lustful assaults began. Rape is the foul daughter of Reconstruction," he exclaimed. And even Dixon must have been forced to concede that an inflammatory book like *The Tragic Era,* selected by the prestigious Literary Guild, was in a position to wield enormous influence. *The Tragic Era* remained the most widely read book on Reconstruction for more than a generation, thus perpetuating the positions taken in *Birth of a Nation.*

If one seeks a more recent Dixonesque treatment, he can read *The South During Reconstruction,* published in 1948 by E. Merton Coulter, the Regents Professor of History at the University of Georgia and the first president of the Southern Historical Association. Once again, it is all there—the unwashed, drunken, corrupt black legislators; the innocent disfranchised whites; and the resort to desperate measures by the Klan in order to save the South from complete disaster. There are, moreover, Alistair Cooke's book and television programs that, even in their polish and sophistication, follow, to an incredible degree, the argument set forth in *Birth of a Nation*. Pick up almost any elementary or secondary textbook in American history used in our schools and you will discover much about corruption, white oppression by blacks, and the overthrow of Reconstruction by the socially responsible and morally impeccable whites in the South. You will *not* find there as you will *not* find in Bowers, Coulter, or Cooke and certainly not in *Birth of a Nation* anything about the oppression of freedmen by southern whites, the reign of southern white terror that followed the close of the Civil War, the persistence of white majority rule even during Radical Reconstruction, and the establishment of the first public schools and other social institutions during the period.

Obviously, one cannot place all the blame for the current view of Reconstruction on *Birth of a Nation*. There were too many others who shared Dixon's views when he wrote and too many who have held to those views since that time. As an eloquent statement of the position of most white southerners, using a new and increasingly influential medium of communication, and as an instrument that deliberately and successfully undertook to use propaganda as history, the influence of *Birth of a Nation* on the current view of Reconstruction has been greater than any other single force. There have been many revivals of *Birth of a Nation* and through them the main arguments Dixon set forth have remained alive. The film is shown in many places today as a period piece. It has achieved the status of an antique and its value is supposed to be in what it tells us about the evolution of the technique of film making. But as one sits in a darkened hall viewing the period piece as this writer recently did, one is a bit perplexed by the nervous laughter and scattered applause as the Klan begins its night ride. One can only surmise—and hope—that these reactions are to *Birth of a Nation* as a period piece and not to *Birth of a Nation* as a powerful instrument in promoting propaganda as history.

Whither Reconstruction
Historiography?

Professor E. Merton Coulter's *The South During Reconstruction, 1865–1877*[1] is widely considered a significant contribution to Reconstruction historiography. For a generation, now, students of American history have been turning to cooperative historical writing in the effort to cope with the growing body of source materials that defy satisfactory and comprehensive treatment by a single author. The first major effort to write a cooperative history of the South was undertaken in 1909 by Julian A. C. Chandler and others.[2] This present effort, *A History of the South*, is under the editorship of Professor Coulter and Professor Wendell H. Stephenson and is being sponsored by the Louisiana State University Press, its publisher, and the Littlefield Fund for Southern History of the University of Texas. Its contributors are among the South's most distinguished historians, and its ten volumes will cover the period from 1607 to 1946.

Ellis Merton Coulter, a professor of history at the University of Georgia, is the author of many works on southern history. His *Civil War and Readjustment in Kentucky*[3] is regarded as the definitive work on that subject, while his *College Life in the Old South*[4] is unique in the field of southern educational history. His fellow historians have recognized his contributions on numerous occasions, and he has served as the president of the Agricultural History Society and of the Southern Historical Association. *The South During Reconstruction* has been widely reviewed and, for the most part, the chorus of praise has contained few reservations. Writing in the New York *Times*, James G. Randall said, "Taking a difficult subject, one of the South's most distinguished historians has subjected it to fresh investigation, and has

Reprinted by permission from *The Journal of Negro Education*, Volume XVII, Number 4 (Fall, 1948). Copyright 1948 The Journal of Negro Education.

come through with a competent, well-documented, and readable treatment."[5] Paul Hutchinson wrote in the *Christian Century*, "This is not the first time that the history of the reconstruction period has been written. Yet rarely has the story been told with more wealth of incident and historical integrity. The fact that a southern historian can write with so little partisanship or passion is another proof that time is a great healer."[6]

The praise of Professor Coulter's new work was as great in the professional journals as in the lay periodicals. In a leading journal, Wirt Armistead Cate indicated that there was some evidence of faulty perspective and interpretation, but he added that the "study sets a high standard for the forthcoming volumes. . . . Though sometimes drawn too exclusively from Southern sources, the documentation is accurate, and it is unlikely that future historians will materially alter the author's basic conclusions."[7] J. G. de Roulhac Hamilton, a well-known historian of the Reconstruction, wrote, "The study—a tremendously difficult task—is well done throughout, and covers the case as effectively as is possible in a volume of this length. Its historical quality and its new approach make it a significant contribution, and too high praise cannot be given the author's calm and dispassionate treatment of the whole subject." In conclusion, he stated, "The work is a consummation devoutly to be praised."[8] Frank L. Owsley endorsed the volume with the following comment: "The author, by the large-scale use of contemporary southern newspapers, periodicals, and personal letters and biographical material, has been able to catch the reactions of the southern white people to reconstruction. Often, of course, this gives the book a sharp and bitter tone, which must not be confused with the author's outlook; there are few historians today whose approach is more impartial and unemotional than Coulter's."[9]

One of the few reviewers who took serious exception to the construction of the volume and some of the author's conclusions was Allan Nevins. Among other things he was not satisfied with the treatment of the Ku Klux Klan, or with the treatment of the Negro, or with the author's discussion of why the white southerners were not left free to guide the section's destinies. Admitting that a "just treatment of this crowded and chaotic period makes heavy demands upon any writer's scholarship, judgment, and literary skill," Professor Nevins concluded that "Mr. Coulter's book ably meets most of these demands."[10]

Because of the great significance of *The South During Reconstruction* it deserves a more extensive and critical examination than it has received. The kind of analysis which Professor Nevins undertook needs to be extended with a view to seeing if, finally, the definitive study of the region during these fateful years has been written. It is an extremely controversial period in which journalists, novelists, and historians have labored almost ceaselessly. Persons representing every conceivable point of view have examined one or several phases of it, while many monographs on special problems have appeared. A new and exhaustive study of the period has been greatly needed for many years. If this work proposes to answer that need, it deserves a serious examination in the light of the best canons of historical research and writing.

Coulter approaches his task with the point of view that, in addition to politics, there are many phases of everyday life in the South during Reconstruction that deserve consideration. He has, perhaps, given more attention to urban growth, recreation, and culture than has any other student of the period. While he thereby seeks to broaden the base of the Reconstruction story he is not inclined to reexamine certain other phases of it in the light of recent studies. He contends that "there can be no sensible departure from the well-known facts of the Reconstruction program as it was applied to the South. No amount of revision can write away the grievous mistakes made in this abnormal period of American history" (p. xi). With hardly more than a shrug of his shoulder, the author, thus, swept aside the findings of several worthy studies, including those by Howard K. Beale, Francis B. Simkins, R. H. Woody, Horace Mann Bond, Vernon Wharton, W. E. B. Du Bois, and Roger W. Shugg.[11] The question that immediately arises is, "What are the well-known facts of Reconstruction?" Are they the facts on which the Reconstruction historians of the early part of this century based their conclusions? Has not the intervening generation of scholarly activity provided any alteration in the view of the "dean" of the historians of the Reconstruction who described life in the South at the height of the Radical period as "a social and political system in which all the forces that made for civilization were dominated by a mass of barbarous freedmen"?[12] Are the well-known facts to be gained from those historians who have treated the Reconstruction as a "melodrama involving wild-eyed conspirators whose acts are best described in red flashes upon a canvas"?[13] Is it not possible that time has not only served to "heal" feelings of hurt, but also to provide the serious student with information and perspective with which to reinterpret the period?

The author asserts that he has "chosen to write this volume in the atmosphere and spirit of the times here portrayed rather than to measure the South of Reconstruction by present-day standards" (p. xi). As commendable as such an effort is, it has limitations and dangers that are extremely difficult to overcome. Every serious historian seeks to re-create the period in which he writes. He must be conscious, however, of the complexity of any event or set of circumstances and of the danger of focusing attention on certain events to the exclusion of others that might have some significant bearing. In his effort to write in the spirit and atmosphere of the period the author is not relieved of the responsibility of seeking to determine, by all of the acceptable principles of internal criticism, the nature of that atmosphere and the forces that created it. There is, moreover, a grave danger of the author's injecting his point of view or misconstructing the period when he is not satisfied with permitting the characters to speak for themselves and feels called upon to explain and, perhaps, to extend their feelings. For example, in describing the South Carolina Convention, in which Negroes sat, Coulter quotes a northern newspaperman as saying that it was "barbarism overwhelming civilization by physical force" and "a wonder and a shame to modern civilization." Then, out of quotations, the author declares, "A black parliament representing a white constituency—the only example in all history!" (p. 148). Even if it is not pertinent to inquire into the logic of one who is alarmed because Negroes, who, incidentally, constituted a considerable proportion of the population, were in the legislature "representing a white constituency," it is of considerable importance to know if the sentiments represent the views of the newspaperman or those of the author of *The South During Reconstruction*, or both.[14] There is no way of knowing where the atmosphere of that period ends and the atmosphere of this period begins.

In another statement, which is an important expression of the point of view of the author, he asserts, "The Civil War was not worth its cost. . . . What good the war produced would have come with time in an orderly way; the bad would not have come at all" (p. 1). Since the proof that the good would have come at some future date must, of necessity, be inconclusive it seems to be out of the range of an historian to make such an unsupported prediction. What is more important, however, is that such a point of view falls so far outside the framework of the basic ideology of America, that it might be regarded as a fundamental compromise with freedom. By the same token it could be argued that eventually the American colonies would have become free without a war, or that eventually the Kaiser's schemes to dominate Europe would have gone to his grave with him. But such a point of view has little appreciation for the moral implications of slavery and freedom, of subjugation and independence. It would seem to represent a basic compromise with the American concept of freedom, and there seems to have been no more justification for compromising in 1861 than there was in 1775, 1917, or 1941.

Coulter, seeking to write in the atmosphere and spirit of the times, seems especially partial to those sources that create a particular kind of atmosphere. The atmosphere is one in which federal troops stride over the South with a merciless vengeance, irresponsible Negroes exhibit a complete lack of restraint in their new freedom, and southern whites writhe under the heel of Negro-Scalawag-Carpetbag rule. Thus, southern periodicals such as the Macon *American Union*, the Charleston *Courier*, and *De Bow's Review* are quoted extensively not only for atmosphere but for statistical information and accounts of incidents in which there might be another side. There is a good deal of reliance, too, on the pronouncements of such works as James Pike's *The Prostrate State* and Myrta Avery's *Dixie After the War*, which are difficult to equal in their bias in behalf of the South's cause and their vituperation with respect to the Negro during the period.

While the work by Professor Coulter reflects an extensive use of source materials, there is no indication of his having approximated an exhaustion of the available materials, many of which have scarcely been used by students of the period and which might contain some very important but not well-known facts. The records of contemporary articulate Negroes are almost completely ignored. The author writes contemptuously of Negro conventions, but he gives no evidence of having examined the minutes of the conventions. While the accounts in the southern newspapers might convey the atmosphere of the whites as they reacted to the conventions, it would only be fair to seek to create the atmosphere of the conventions themselves if, as Coulter claims, he sought to discover what the aspirations of the Negroes were (p. xi).[15]

In a similar manner the biographies and autobiographies of Negroes were overlooked, their innumerable public and private utterances are ignored; and there is no use of the reports of Negro officeholders. The reports of federal, state, and local officials might have been used to balance, if not to neutralize, the criticisms of these same officials by southern newspapers. If judgment is to be passed on the Freedmen's Bureau, it would seem that some consideration might have been given to the numerous reports made by the bureau and its officials. Certainly, the official reports, even if Coulter should undertake to impeach their validity, should receive as much attention with respect to the work of the Freedmen's Bureau as, say, the Atlanta *Daily Opinion* or the Little Rock *Weekly Arkansas Gazette.*[16]

While Coulter seeks to portray the period of the Reconstruction by letting the sources speak for themselves, wherever possible, he takes the opportunity, on occasions, to test the validity of the sources to determine whether they are impeachable. That is a commendable exercise of the function of historical criticism. It is altogether possible, however, to violate that function when only those sources that do not support one's point of view are subjected to impeachment. After the close of the Civil War several persons visited the South to study conditions and reported their findings to the president. Among them were Carl Schurz, Benjamin C. Truman, General U. S. Grant, and Harvey M. Watterson. All except Schurz found little or no feeling of hostility and thought that the South was ready for restoration. Coulter obviously took serious exception to the findings of Schurz, and, therefore, before commenting on Schurz's observations he undertook to impeach his character and discredit him altogether. He described him as a "reformer to the extent of revolutionist, German-born, and lacking a common sense produced by American upbringing" (p. 27). Even if one overlooked Coulter's obviously subjective appraisal of Schurz and concluded that the German-born American was unfit to make a fair study of the South, what of the other observers? They escape with no discussion of their qualities or qualifications whatever. It was enough for the author to refer to Truman as "the President's New England secretary," to describe Watterson as the "father of 'Marse Henry,' the famous newspaper editor," and to say nothing at all of General Grant (p. 28). If Schurz was so incapable of making critical and objective observations in the South, is not there a bare possibility that, for example, Grant's ability to study conditions might be seriously challenged?

It is so easy, in the handling of sources, to present a picture that, at best, is only a half-truth. In describing the Negroes in the Reconstruction conventions and legislatures, Coulter cites none of the several references that make favorable comments regarding the conduct of the freedmen. He is content to quote the Atlanta *Weekly Opinion*'s description of a Negro in the following manner: "The arrogant presumption, ignorance, bullyism and impertinence of this Negro, is becoming intolerable" (p. 134). Of the South Carolina House in 1873 the best that Coulter could say was that "the Negro legislators were of all shades, from the lightest mulattoes to the blackest negroids, fresh from the kitchen and the field, in clothing ranging from secondhand black frock coats to the 'coarse and dirty garments of the field'" (p. 147). More important than their varied shades, it would seem, were their varied backgrounds. Some were former field hands, while others were college and university graduates. The Negro speaker of the house at that time has been described by the closest students of South Carolina Reconstruction as "one of the most creditable lawyers of the state for his age."[17] The comment of the Charleston *Daily News* regarding the South Carolina convention of 1868 was that "beyond all question, the best men in the convention are the colored members. Considering the influences under which they were called together, and their imperfect acquaintance with parliamentary law, they have displayed, for the most part, remarkable moderation and dignity."[18] Although Coulter relied heavily on Edward King's account of conditions in the South and refers to it as "particularly valuable" (p. 398), perhaps he did not find King's description of Negro leaders in the South Carolina legislature "particularly valuable." It serves, however, to point up another side of the picture. In part, King said, "The President of the Senate and the Speaker of the House, both colored, were elegant and accomplished men, highly educated, who would have creditably presided over any commonwealth's legislative assembly."[19]

In the effort to show how grievously the South had been wounded by the war and its aftermath, Coulter presented a table entitled "Per Capita Wealth of Former Slave States compared with that of Northern and Middle Western States, 1860–1880." It shows that Louisiana, for example, had fallen from the second position in 1860 to the thirty-seventh in 1880 and that South Carolina had moved from third in the earlier year to forty-fifth twenty years later. He reminds the reader that "the change in the status of the Negroes produced an important part of the decline. It not only destroyed over a billion dollars worth of personal property in slaves, but also added the poverty-stricken Negroes to the population on which per capita wealth was reckoned" (pp. 192–93).

One wonders what value the table is, since admittedly it presents an abnormal picture with respect to southern wealth. It should be remembered that in 1860 the South had every advantage in the reckoning of per capita wealth, since Negro slaves were valued but not counted. The author's remarks, moreover, do not take into consideration the tremendous accumulation of capital wealth in the North that resulted from the economic revolution. There would have been a considerable change in the rank of southern states even if they had kept their slaves.

The author's inclination to indict and discredit factors making for the improvement of the status of Negroes led him, on occasion, to make generalizations that do not seem to be supported by the evidence he presents. In describing the work of the Freedmen's Bureau courts, he says, "They took up all matters relating to freedmen and if a white man were concerned especially in the matter of contracts the Negro usually came out winner" (p. 79). This is such a sweeping generalization that it is most unfortunate that the author did not feel called upon to support it with careful and adequate documentation. While perhaps no exhaustive study has been made of the operation of the courts, the reports of the assistant commissioners of the bureau in the several states and the study of the bureau by Paul S. Peirce would seem to afford more authoritative and complete information than the southern newspapers which the author cited. In a similar generalization the author asserts that "education was, in fact, a fad which soon lost its novelty for the majority of Negroes" (p. 86). Since some attendance figures are available it would have been appropriate for the author to have introduced them in support of his contention. Even if attendance declined, as it did in some places, it was not always because of the lack of interest. Other factors were the lack of schools, which Coulter mentioned, the preoccupation with economic survival, and the open hostility, in some places, to Negroes attending school.

Perhaps the most serious and grievous offense that an historian can commit is either to misquote or to distort his sources. Here, again, the offense stems, in all probability, from an overweening desire to produce illustrations to support a particular point of view. While this anxiety might understandably lead one to misinterpret a source, it should never become so ungovernable as to cause a student striving for objectivity to misquote or to distort a source. Yet, Coulter appears to have succumbed to the temptation to misquote some of his sources, presumably in order that they might fit into the picture he was seeking to draw. In discussing the educational situation in Louisiana, the author states, "An observer of the scene in Louisiana [Edward King] found that the superintendent of education, a mulatto, was *so ignorant and careless of his duties*[20] that he did not know how many schools were in his state" (p. 323). This is a clear-cut distortion of the observer's statement. The following is the statement by King as it appears in his account of his travels:

> The present condition of the educational system in Louisiana is encouraging although disfigured from evils which arise from the political disorganization. The State superintendent of education, at the time of my visit was a mulatto gentleman of evident culture, seeming, indeed, quite up to the measure of his task, if he only had the means to perform it. He could not tell me how many schools were in operation in the State; nor how much the increase had been since the war. *There was, he explained, the greatest difficulty in procuring returns from the interior districts, even the annual reports being forwarded tardily, or sometimes not at all.*[21]

There seems to be no justification whatever in Coulter's representing King as having found that the superintendent was "ignorant and careless."[22]

Once again, in Coulter's discussion of crop productivity after the Civil War, Edward King is made to provide an unfair share of the evidence to support a conclusion that the author had reached. Coulter says, "A careful observer, after traveling through the South in 1873 and 1874, concluded that plantations were producing only from one third to a half of their ante-bellum crops" (p. 95). The actual statement by King was not based on a general conclusion that he had reached regarding productivity over the entire South. Rather, it was merely his report of what he had found on *one* plantation, Clairmont, in Louisiana. He said, "On this Clairmont, in 1860, the owner raised 1,000 bales of cotton and 8,000 bushels of corn; now he raises about 500 bales, and hardly any corn."[23]

Another northern traveler whose observations have been taken out of context and distorted was Sidney Andrews who visited the South shortly after the war's end. Coulter says, "A Northerner traveling in the South in the summer of 1865 [Sidney Andrews] was convinced that 'the race is, on a large scale, ignorantly sacrificing its own good for the husks of vagabondage'" (pp. 50–51). The impression is thus conveyed that Andrews was writing that Negroes in general were unwise in abandoning the plantations and going away to search for a better life. It is an erroneous impression. Andrews was speaking of a particular section of *one* state. In part, he says, "I know very well that every white man, woman, and child in the whole State [of Georgia] is ready to swear that every negro is worse off now than before he was freed. I accept no such evidence; but hundreds of conversations with negroes of every class in at least a dozen towns of this section [Central Georgia] have convinced me that the race is, on a large scale, ignorantly sacrificing its own material good for the husks of vagabondage."[24] Andrews shows that he was not willing to generalize this statement with respect to all Negroes when he added, "In South Carolina, as I have already said, where slavery reached its lowest estate, it was not possible for the negro to make his condition worse by striking out for himself. There was scarcely more than a choice between two evils, and he chose that which promised him the most independence."[25] Here, then, are examples of Coulter's misrepresenting and distorting his sources in a manner that seems, indeed, unusual for a serious scholar who writes about a period in which the facts are allegedly so well known as to need no alteration or revision.

Not only should the historian's conclusions be based on adequate and reliable evidence, but they should also reflect a judiciousness in keeping with the temperament of one disciplined in objectivity and preciseness. Yet, the observation of Nevins that the author has done less than justice to the record of the Negro in Congress and in state offices is merely a suggestion of the limits to which Coulter has gone in his rather systematic effort to discredit the Negro in almost all phases of life during the Reconstruction. Perhaps his discussion of "the fundamental character of the Negro" (p. 95) is justified on the grounds that there prevailed, during the period, the belief that Negroes had a fundamental character peculiar to them. One gets the impression, from other remarks by Coulter, that he, too, subscribes to the view that Negroes possessed certain inherent traits. The view led him to make some generalizations regarding Negro character and conduct that are as injudicious as they are tenuous. The author makes the extravagant claim that "as a race they [Negroes] were spendthrift and gullible" and adds, as if it were an afterthought, "though some were amenable to the advice to save their money" (p. 49). These spendthrift Negroes had, even according to Coulter, put almost $20,000,000 into one banking system, the Freedmen's Savings and Trust Company, by 1874 (p. 88) and, despite considerable opposition, had acquired 586,664 acres of land in Georgia by 1880 (p. 112).

Coulter's delineation of the character of Negroes even extended to a statement regarding their cleanliness. He said, "Unfortunately for the Negroes freedom meant the loss of certain attentions which they received in slavery, designed to keep them healthy and clean and to prolong their lives. Freed from restraint 'since dis time come,' they tended to become slovenly and careless of their health and cleanliness" (p. 55). While it is extremely difficult to imagine the antebellum planters setting up rules and practices of personal hygiene to which slaves had to conform, it is even more difficult to imagine that the whites of the South possessed all the habits of personal hygiene while the Negroes had none. Indeed, it would seem that the observations of one of the travelers whom Coulter frequently quotes, but not on this subject, were perhaps more accurate. On the subject of cleanliness in the South Sidney Andrews said, "The importance of soap and water as elements in civilization have been much ignored or overlooked. I am thoroughly satisfied that if the people of this state [South Carolina], with all their belongings and surroundings—except such as would be damaged by water—could be thoroughly washed once a week, a year would show a very material advance toward civilization." Andrews, who traveled extensively in the postwar South, made no reference to any particular race.[26]

Another characteristic which Coulter ascribes to Negroes is excessive emotionalism, especially with regard to religion.[27] He says, "Being by nature highly emotional and excitable and now unrestrained by the hand of former masters, they carried their religious exercises to extreme lengths, both in time and content." There follows a description of their services in which the author is as unrestrained as the subjects of his discussion. There is no need to discuss here Coulter's subjective statement with respect to the emotional and excitable nature of Negroes. Although it might be the topic for a discussion *during* the Reconstruction period, it would hardly seem to merit consideration today, in the light of the findings of students of human nature. Nor is there any point in discussing the characteristics of Negro religious exercises. Close students of rural and primitive religions know how remarkably similar they were to the exercises of whites.[28] Indeed, it would be difficult to find in the accounts of Negro religious meetings any that would surpass those of the whites in the period. Simkins and Woody made a proper analysis of the situation in one state when they said, "The religious practices of the Negroes seldom got beyond an application of the imagery of the Bible to the culture which the race had acquired in South Carolina. Their religion was as native and as orthodox as that of the white Methodist and Baptist."[29]

Another indictment of Negroes by Coulter was for their alleged addiction to alcoholic beverages. He says, "The greatest difficulty the South had in handling its liquor problem related to the control of drinking by Negroes. . . . With little experience of self-control they would spend their last piece of money for a drink of whisky, and they would break in and steal this article before all else" (p. 336). It need only be said that there is no reason why this generalization, which excludes whites from censure, should be uncritically accepted. There is, moreover, some basis for disagreement with Coulter. Other authorities have contended that the Negro's "taste for strong drink was not so avid as that of the whites." They also pointed out that white "farmers spent their money as readily for drink as they did for family necessities." "A prosecuting officer asserted that drinking was much less a cause of crime among the blacks than among the whites. 'Drinking,' he added, 'is not a very prevalent crime among Negroes.' "[30] Drinking was a serious problem among all groups during the Reconstruction period. It must be described in such a manner if the proper atmosphere of the period is to be recreated.[31]

The manner of Coulter's impeachment of the character of individual Negroes reflects, further, an injudicious temperament. For example, Henry M. Turner is the special object of the ire and invective of the author. On one occasion he is described as "Georgia's *nègre terrible*" (p. 60). Later he is referred to as "ubiquitous preacher, politician, and crook" (p. 98). An unnamed carpetbagger is quoted as having characterized him as "a licentious robber and counterfeiter, a vulgar blackguard, a sacrilegious profaner of God's name, and a most consummate hypocrite" (p. 146). Nowhere is there any specific evidence to show why this man who became bishop of the A.M.E. Church and chancellor of Morris Brown College was regarded by Coulter as a "crook." The only occasion on which the author permitted Turner to escape his merciless attack was when Turner spoke out against the hated labor agent who was attempting to lure Negroes off the plantation. To Coulter, Turner was, on this occasion, a "special advisor for his flock in Georgia," who "did valiant service in quieting the stirring freedmen" (p. 99).

The height of injudiciousness is reached by Coulter when he says that after the collapse of the Reconstruction in South Carolina "high colored officials returned to their old positions of streetsweepers, waiters, and field hands" (p. 373). The post-Reconstruction careers of the

South Carolina leaders simply do not bear out this fanciful assertion. Francis Cardozo, the state treasurer in South Carolina at the time of the "overthrow," moved to Washington where he became an auditor in the post office department. Later he became the principal of a high school and remained a man of influence and prestige until his death. Robert Smalls, who was in Congress in 1876, remained there until 1879. He returned to Congress in 1881 for three terms. When he retired from Congress he became collector of the Port of Beaufort where, with the exception of Cleveland's second term, he remained until 1913. R. H. Cain, who was in Congress, remained there until 1879. In the following year he was elected bishop of the A.M.E. Church and held that position until his death in 1887. Robert B. Elliott, who had been in Congress earlier in the period and who lost the race for attorney general in 1876, became a special agent of the treasury department in New Orleans. Later he resumed the practice of the law and remained active in his profession until his death in 1884. Joseph H. Rainey, who served in Congress for five terms, was replaced by a Democrat in 1877. He was then employed for four years by the treasury department. Beginning in 1881 he conducted a banking and brokerage business for five years in Washington. He died in 1887.[32] This does not exhaust the list, nor is this to deny that some Negro leaders became menial workers after 1877.[33] It merely calls attention to the fact that Coulter's assertion was extravagant and injudicious.

It does not appear that Coulter's discussion of the Black Codes is either sufficiently extensive or critical. It cannot be gainsaid that an examination and understanding of the Black Codes are essential to an understanding of the early part of the Reconstruction period. Yet, there is nowhere any extensive discussion of the provisions of the Codes. Some provisions are given in a footnote (pp. 39–40), but the textual discussion is largely a defense of the laws passed in the period before the Radicals took charge. Coulter says, "There can be no doubt that the fundamental purpose in the minds of the lawmakers was to advance the fortunes of the Negroes rather than retard them or try to push them back into slavery" (p. 38). In a cursory discussion the author defended the exclusion of Negroes from jury service and criticized as "poor logic" the exclusion of Negro testimony in a case where a white person was the defendant. He explained, "No law could force a jury to believe Negro testimony, but at times it might be valuable in establishing facts, and by allowing it where Negroes were defendants it actually gave Negroes greater protection than whites" (p. 39). Then, Coulter blandly brushes the Black Codes aside with the statement "Whatever anyone might have thought, the question was in fact academic, for they were never actually put into effect" (p. 40).

The question of the Black Codes was not merely academic for at least two significant reasons. In the first place they reflect, better than dozens of statements of sentiment or feeling, the actual attitude of the southern leaders toward Negroes at the end of the war.[34] Perhaps they did not intend to push Negroes back into slavery, but in South Carolina, where employment opportunities were legally proscribed and where Negro farm workers could not leave the premises without the express permission of their "masters," who had the privilege of "moderately" whipping servants under eighteen, it was close to antebellum relationships. In Mississippi, where Negroes were prevented from renting or leasing farm lands and where they were given less than two months to find a home and employment or suffer penalties, Negroes could hardly be described as enjoying freedom.[35] There were southern contemporaries who severely criticized the Black Codes, and it is surprising to find an historian today whose views are more tolerant of the Codes than "the best thought of the state" of Mississippi at that time.[36]

The Black Codes, moreover, *were* enforced in some places. In Jackson and in Hinds County, Mississippi, for example, "the Act that required freedmen without a yearly contract to secure licenses was rigidly enforced." "In Vicksburg as late as March, 1868, more than 60 Negroes were arbitrarily arrested and thrown into jail on the charge of vagrancy."[37] Coulter offers no proof that the Codes were not enforced except to assert that the Freedmen's Bureau and the United States Army prevented their enforcement. Yet, it is certainly one of the well-known facts of the period that neither the bureau nor the army was always successful in enforcing their own orders.[38]

With respect to the acquisition of land by Negroes, Coulter says, "Most whites favored Negro ownership of land if they got it in a legal way. . . . The statement, often retailed, that Southerners did not want the Negro to own land, and that they successfully kept him from it to a large extent, is based on very slight fact. Land for sale was so plentiful and so cheap that it would have been practically impossible to deny the sale of it to a Negro who could pay for it. In most cases where a planter refused to sell land to a Negro, it turned out that the Negro wanted a choice spot in the midst of the plantation, or was making some other unreasonable demand which would have been as quickly denied to a white man" (p. 111). It must be remembered that the laws enacted by the southern whites immediately after the war so proscribed Negroes that it was almost impossible for them to secure employment by which they could gain the means to purchase land, however cheap. But there was also opposition to the sale of land to Negroes. Coulter himself admits it when he says that the poor whites, "fearing the competition of Negro landowners . . . threatened planters who would sell or rent land to them" (p. 164). Perhaps there is still another reason, provided by Coulter, why whites were opposed to Negroes owning land. He says, "There was a certain political significance in a Negro's owning land. As long as he was a laborer his employer could hold an uncomfortable and restraining hand over him when he cast his ballot" (p. 111). Wharton says that a white landowner who would make arrangements to sell a tract of land to a Negro "brought on himself the enmity of his fellows."[39] It is to be remembered that, in Mississippi, the first state legislature after the end of the war enacted a law prohibiting the sale of farm land to Negroes. It did not go into effect, but it doubtless illustrates the attitude that many planters continued to hold. A northern observer noticed in 1865 that in the upper part of the Charleston District "the planters are quietly holding meetings at which they pass resolutions not to sell land to Negroes. . . . In Beaufort District they not only refuse to sell land to Negroes, but also refuse to rent it to them; and many black men have been told that they would be shot if they leased land and undertook to work for themselves."[40]

When Coulter describes Radical Reconstruction as having a "glimmering resemblance to the latter cults of Fascism and Nazism" (p. 114), he is no longer even attempting to create the atmosphere of the period under study, but is measuring conditions by present day standards, a procedure which, at the outset, he denied to himself (p. xi). While there seems to be nothing wrong with such a procedure, under the circumstances, it does open up the opportunity to examine his contention that Radical Reconstruction was fascistic. It might be contended, and with considerable logic, that the antebellum South had an even greater "glimmering resemblance to the later cults of Fascism and Nazism." There were, indeed, many of the elements: an oppressed race; the great and continuing drive for *Lebensraum;* the annihilation of almost every vestige of free thought and free speech; and the enthusiastic glorification of the martial spirit. Perhaps, then, the North, enjoying a more favorable ideological position, may be regarded as accomplishing an overthrow of "nazism" and what Professor Coulter sees as a forerunner of the twentieth-century "cults" was, instead, the "denazification process" in which a firm and, at times, unreasonable stand was taken by the victor. At any rate, the mere suggestion by the author presents many possibilities for the reinterpretation of the period.

On the basis of the preceding discussion it is not too much to say that one can take serious exception to *The South During Reconstruction* on several specific grounds. First of all, the author's point of view may be challenged in rejecting most of the so-called revisionist findings and in confusing his own attitudes with those of contemporaries under the claim of writing in the spirit and atmosphere of the period. In the second place, he has handled some of his sources in a manner not in keeping with the best canons of the discipline when he selected his materials from sources that supported his point of view while over-looking others that might have shed considerable, though different, light on the period; when he generalized from inadequate sources; and when he distorted some sources and took others out of context. In the third place, some of his conclusions seemed lacking in judiciousness and objectivity when he described many phases of Negro life in sweeping and unsupported generalities that do not stand up under careful examination; when he failed to discuss critically and exhaustively so crucial a matter as the Black Codes; and when he revealed an inconsistent as well as a tenuous position in his discussion of Negro landowning.

The South During Reconstruction suffered not only from the weaknesses previously discussed, but it left much to be desired in other respects. Briefly, it would seem that it was necessary for the author to have remembered more frequently that Reconstruction was a national problem, although his main attention was properly focused on the South. The war's aftermath was seen and felt all over the nation, and the South was not immune to the forces and circumstances operating outside the region. There were the economic forces, many of which originated in New York or Boston but which exerted considerable influence in many southern communities.[41] There were the constitutional and political aspects, centering in the struggle between the president and Congress, which had more to do with the outcome of Reconstruction than meets the eye of the casual observer. There were, also, the social aspects, which were tied up not only with the movement to elevate the conditions of working men in the South but were a part of the intercontinental revolutionary movement to improve the conditions of working classes in many lands.

One would have welcomed a more adequate discussion of the results of Reconstruction. It should not be sufficient merely to describe the celebrations attending "redemption." To what extent was the South economically and physically rehabilitated by the end of Reconstruction? How was the school system functioning and who had assumed responsibility for promoting the education of the South's youth? What was the significance of the Reconstruction constitutions for democracy in the South? There is a palpable connection between the answers to these questions and a final evaluation of the period under study.

This work by Professor Coulter is another chapter, if not a milestone, in Reconstruction historiography. It is as valuable in the history of history as it is in the history of the Reconstruction. The questionable historiographical practices employed by the author and his summary rejection of historians whose findings fail to support his views lead one to ask, "In what direction is Reconstruction historiography moving?" It is to be hoped that those who continue to study the Reconstruction, regardless of their point of view, will not summarily reject or accept this work in an uncritical manner. Rather, it is to be hoped that they will use it, both its polemics and its history, for the advancement of Reconstruction historiography.

The New Negro
History

During the last two decades some significant changes have taken place in the writing, teaching, and study of the history of the Negro in the United States. On almost every side there has been a remarkable growth of interest in the history of the Negro. Of equal importance has been the modification of the approaches of those who have participated in writing the history. It is not necessary to evaluate precisely the impact of these developments to state, at the outset, that they have great relevance to any understanding of the rapidly unfolding developments in human relations in the United States.

In discussing the history of a people one must distinguish between what has *actually* happened and what those who have written the history have *said* has happened. So far as the *actual* history of the American Negro is concerned, there is nothing particularly new about it. It is an exciting story, a remarkable story. It is the story of slavery and freedom, humanity and inhumanity, democracy and its denial. It is tragedy and triumph, suffering and compassion, sadness and joy. The *actual* history of the Negro is David Walker in 1828 calling on his people to throw off the shackles of slavery by any means at their command. It is Robert Smalls in 1863 delivering a Confederate vessel into the hands of United States forces. It is Booker T. Washington electrifying a southern audience and hammering out a program of accommodation and adjustment in a section inflamed by racial intolerance. It is W. E. B. Du Bois providing intellectual inspiration to a despairing people and charting the course for the future. It is Thurgood Marshall calling on the Supreme Court to strike down the pernicious and un-American doctrine of "separate but equal." It is all these things and

Originally published in the *Crisis* (February, 1977). Reprinted by permission.

more, emblazoned on the national record to be seen by all who would care to look.

But Negro history is more than the exertions of Negroes in their behalf. It is Governor James Henry Hammond of South Carolina declaring that slavery is the best thing that has ever happened to the Negro people. It is Roger B. Taney denying freedom to Dred Scott. It is Abraham Lincoln issuing the Emancipation Proclamation. It is Joel and Arthur Springarn working to organize the National Association for the Advancement of Colored People. It is the United States Supreme Court striking down segregated public schools. It is White Citizens Councils, aptly called the "uptown Ku Klux Klan," stoning Autherine Lucy at the University of Alabama. It is Walter George, President Eisenhower's special representative to the NATO countries, leading the Senate fight to discredit the Supreme Court decision. Thus, Negro history is more than the overt actions of Negroes. It is also America's treatment of the Negro. It is the impact of forces and events affecting the lives of Negroes in countless ways.

These things are and have been; and no amount of dishonesty in the writing of history, no amount of specious propaganda designed to distort and misrepresent, can ever change them. These things do not constitute the "new" Negro history. They are new only in the sense that today's events are different from yesterday's; and every passing era during the past three centuries has witnessed a new stage in the struggle for freedom and human equality in the United States.

But it is all too clear that what has actually happened is one thing, and what has been described by writers of history as having happened is quite another thing. The changes that have occurred in the writing of the history of the Negro are as significant and, in some ways, even more dramatic than the very events themselves that the writers have sought to describe.

A century ago one of the South's most distinguished scientists, in discussing diseases peculiar to the Negro, wrote a lengthy treatise on drapetomania, a malady that gave Negroes a compulsion to run away. He showed, to the apparent satisfaction of his many readers, that whenever Negroes disappeared from the plantation it was not because they were unhappy or dissatisfied but because they were afflicted with a dread disease that forced them to run away. This was, he argued, a historical fact, running back into the history of the Negroes for centuries. This and many similar fantastic claims became a part of the *written* history of the Negro in the United States. At about the same time and, indeed, for many ensuing decades, a host of writers described Negroes as happy with their lot as slaves; and they claimed that to emancipate them would not only be a tragedy but un-Christian as well. In the generation following the Civil War several historians expressed the greatest grief that Negroes had been emancipated, for, they argued, it would only be a matter of time—a few decades at the most—and all Negroes would disappear. History, they claimed, clearly demonstrated that Negroes could not survive as free men.

Even the so-called scientific historians showed little inclination to use the materials of history for any purpose other than to support their own predilections, prejudices, and earlier commitments. Thus, they wrote at length about the childish nature of Negroes as displayed during slavery, their cowardice and ineffectiveness during the Civil War, and their barbarity and prodigality after emancipation. Even in the present century and *even in our own time* these historians have, with remarkable effectiveness, described the Negro as a beast, have worked assiduously to justify and even to glorify Negro slavery, and have described the period since emancipation as one of unmitigated woe for Negroes and of inconvenience for whites.

The effect of this kind of written history has been not only far-reaching but deadly. It has provided the historical justification for the whole complex of mischievous and pernicious laws designed to create and maintain an unbridgeable gulf between Negroes and whites. It was the basis for a query put to a Negro by a white woman, "refined and educated," in Montgomery, Alabama, a few years ago. When she asked, in all seriousness, if it were possible for a Negro with no admixture of white blood to learn anything in college, the Negro was reminded of the child who had horrible nightmares because he had seen too many murder mysteries on television. He began his reply by suggesting that she had been reading too many fairy stories parading under the guise of "authentic histories." And the deadly effects of such propaganda have been spread in all directions, pervading northern communities and even countries abroad. The effects could be seen a few months ago in Heidelberg when a German was moved to observe that the American denazification program in his country not only permitted American white supremacy doctrines to flourish but, in some instances, encouraged such doctrines.

Negroes generally have not had any illusions about the distortions of their history, and they have not been unduly influenced by them. Those who have been articulate have consistently and bitterly resented the systematic efforts to misrepresent their role in history or to deny them membership in the human family, to say nothing of first-class American citizenship. When John Russwurm issued the first Negro newspaper in 1827 he touched on this point when he said, "We wish to plead for our cause. Too long have others spoken for us. Too long has the public been deceived by misrepresentations, in things which concern us dearly. . . . We form a spoke in the human wheel, and it is necessary that we should understand our dependence on the different parts, and theirs on us, in order to perform our part with propriety." In 1851, when William C. Nell brought out his history of Negroes in the Revolution and the War of 1812, he declared, "I yield to no one in appreciating the propriety and pertinency of every *effort*, on the part of colored Americans, in *all* pursuits, which, as members of the human family, it becomes them to share in."

The baleful effects of the propaganda of history on the one hand and what one historian has aptly called "the conspiracy of silence" on the other were deeply understood by George Washington Williams who devoted many years to research and writing and published in 1883 the first serious history of the Negro in the United States. "Not as a blind panegyrist of my race," he asserted, "nor as a partisan apologist, but for a love for *'the truth of history'* I have striven to record the truth. . . . My whole aim has been to write a thoroughly trustworthy history; and what I have written, if it have no other merit, is reliable." Williams was painfully aware that too many of the histories published in his own day fell far short of reliability where Negroes were concerned. And he knew all too well the uses to which distorted history and irresponsible propaganda were put in the establishment of second-class citizenship for Negroes. He was determined to combat them with weapons of indisputable truth. His success for the period in which he worked was nothing short of phenomenal.

It was an appreciation such as Nell and Williams had that caused Dr. Carter G. Woodson to found the Association for the Study of Negro Life and History more than forty years ago. The work of Dr. Woodson and the Association in those early years may be regarded as launching the era of "The New Negro History." Dr. Woodson and his associates went about the task of exploding the myths of Negro history and of putting the Negro in his rightful place in the history of this country. And they did it with as much precision and system as those who sought to tear the Negro out of any meaningful context of American history. This was no small undertaking. By the time Dr. Woodson began his work, the system of second-class citizenship, with its trappings of segregation and disfranchisement, was functioning effectively. It had, moreover, been buttressed by the sanctions of respectable religious and political institutions. And it had received the blessings of a great body of intellectual rationalizations.

The story of the work of Dr. Woodson and the Association is well known and does not need to be recounted here. It should be recalled, however, that the problem of restoring the Negro to his proper place in the nation's history was attacked on a wide front. Recognizing the indisputable fact that the distortion of Negro history prevailed at every level of society and in almost every facet of American life, Woodson proceeded to correct the defects at these numerous points. His own scholarly books and monographs and the works of several others, including W. E. B. Du Bois, provided the grist for the Negro history mill. The *Journal of Negro History* projected the new approach to every part of the world where history was seriously studied. The Association and its branches proceeded to carry out a campaign at the grass-roots to revise the role of Negro history in the minds of the most ordinary laymen of the community. The *Negro History Bulletin* extended the new Negro history into the lower grades in the schools. Negro History Week popularized Negro history in a variety of ways.

This was, perhaps, the most far-reaching and ambitious effort to rewrite history that has ever been attempted in this country. But it was more than an attempt to rewrite history. It was a remarkable attempt to rehabilitate a whole people—to explode racial myths, to establish a secure and respectable place for the Negro in the evolution of the American social order, to develop self-respect and self-esteem among those who had been subjected to the greatest indignities known in the Western world. Finally, it was a valiant attempt to force America to keep faith with herself, to remind her that truth is more praiseworthy than power, and that justice and equality, long the stated policy of this nation, should apply to all its citizens and *even* to the writing of history.

But the most significant intellectual result of the work of Dr. Woodson and the movement he founded lies in the impact on the writing of American history in general and on the writing of the history of the

Negro in particular. Within the last two decades there has been a most profound and salutary change in the whole approach to the history of human relations in the United States. In the process the new Negro history has indeed come into its own.

It would be foolhardy to the point of creating a new myth to suggest that the Woodson movement enjoys exclusive responsibility for the new Negro history. This is a phenomenon caused by many factors, among which Dr. Woodson and the work of the Association for the Study of Negro Life and History are significant and primary. The legal and political drive for first-class citizenship is another factor. The remarkable changes in the economic and social conditions among Negroes are another. The work in the other social sciences in exploding numerous racial myths is another. Then, one must recognize the powerful effect of two world wars and the significant improvement in the status of peoples of color throughout the world. There is, also, the sense of guilt shared by many white Americans for three centuries of injustice and inhumanity in their treatment of Negroes. Finally, there is the factor of time. The passing of the years has removed the people of this country from the period when the race question was dealt with in the bloodiest terms; and these years have given Americans a new perspective from which to view the Negro and his role in American history. These and perhaps many other factors have brought forth this new Negro history.

Stimulated by the numerous forces that have been at work over the past generation, the writing of the history of the Negro in the United States has come into its own. In quantitative terms alone the results have been most impressive. White and Negro historians, northern and southern historians, Japanese and Dutch historians have turned their attention to the study of the history of the Negro in the United States. And they have produced an enormous quantity of studies of various aspects of Negro life. In books, monographs, learned journals, popular magazines, and newspapers they have shared with the world their findings regarding the American Negro's past. Within the past decade no less than a half-dozen general histories of the Negro have appeared, compared with only one during the preceding twenty-five years. Every major historical association in this country in the past ten years has given considerable attention to subjects related to Negro history at its annual meetings. Newspapers, North and South, run feature stories on some phase of the history of the Negro, and several of the mass circulation magazines have featured the history of the Negro in recent years.

For the first time in the history of the United States, there is a striking resemblance between what historians are writing and what has actually happened in the history of the American Negro. A northern white historian has laid bare the sordid details of slavery and has described it as the barbaric institution that it actually was. Another has described with telling effectiveness the numerous revolts of Negroes against slavery. A southern white historian, after making due public apology for having once called Negroes "darkies," has proceeded to prove that during the Civil War slaves did everything possible to betray their masters and destroy the institution of slavery. Another has written with remarkable understanding and insight and has produced perhaps the best account in print of the Negro during the Reconstruction of a southern state. One Negro historian has proved conclusively that Negroes did not have their freedom handed to them but fought for it with blood, sweat, and tears. Another, writing about the late nineteenth century, has described with vivid detail how even in the North there was no real desire to promote freedom and equality and how even the respectable elements of society joined in the general program of degrading the Negro. Historians of both races and both sections have contributed to establishing the fact that avarice and vice, honesty and virtue, and other human qualities are biracial; and that far from being men of unsullied virtue, those who have inveighed against the Negro have themselves frequently been villainous and hypocritical.

The new Negro history, then, is the literary and intellectual movement that seeks to achieve the same justice in history that is sought in other spheres. Moreover, it gives strength and support to the other efforts that today seek equality and freedom. To be sure, it has had to continue to struggle against those who persist in distorting history, for these latter elements have by no means given up their fight. But the new Negro history says to America that its rich heritage is the result of the struggles of all its peoples, playing the roles that conditions and circumstances have permitted them to play. These roles cannot be evaluated in terms of race. Rather, they must be judged in terms of their effect on the realization of the great American dream. In this context the role of the Negro in America is not only significant in itself but central in the task of fulfilling the nation's true destiny. This is the message of the new Negro history, and it is being carried forth with great effectiveness by an increasing number of able messengers.

No one can properly evaluate the influence of history on the minds of men. But one can say that through the ages history has been an important instrument in shaping the course of human affairs. It gave to Prussians that appreciation for the military prowess by which they were known for centuries. It has given to Americans a deep appreciation for the historic foundations of democratic principles. It has given to Negroes a sense of self-esteem and self-respect that has sustained them in their darkest hours. The future function of the new Negro history is even more important. It can and, in time, will provide *all America* with a lesson in the wastefulness, nay, the wickedness of human exploitation and injustice that have characterized too much of this nation's past. This is a lesson that must be learned if we are to survive and if we are to win the respect and admiration of the other peoples of the world. The new Negro history also provides all America with an inspiring lesson in human potentialities and a profound basis on which to build a better America. It is to be hoped that neither this great lesson nor this great inspiration will be lost in the years that lie ahead.

On the Evolution of Scholarship
in Afro-American History

Every generation has the opportunity to write its own history, and indeed it is obliged to do so. Only in that way can it provide its contemporaries with the materials vital to understanding the present and to planning strategies for coping with the future. Only in that way can it fulfill its obligation to pass on to posterity the accumulated knowledge and wisdom of the past, which, after all, give substance and direction for the continuity of civilization.

According to my calculation, there have been four generations of scholarship—of unequal length—in Afro-American history. The first generation began auspiciously with the publication in 1882 of the two-volume *History of the Negro Race in America* by George Washington Williams and ended around 1909 with the publication of Booker T. Washington's *Story of the Negro*. Although it is difficult to characterize this first period of serious scholarship in the field, it is safe to say that the primary concern of the writers was to explain the process of adjustment Afro-Americans made to conditions in the United States. Whether it was the aggressive integrationism of George Washington Williams or the mild accommodationism of Booker T. Washington, the common objective of the writers of this period was to define and describe the role of Afro-Americans in the life of the nation. They by no means shared the same view of the past or the same way of writing history; they delineated the epic of Afro-American history in the manner that their talents and training permitted. They wrought as well as they could; and they wrought well.

There were no trained, professional historians among them, with

Originally published in *The State of Afro-American History: Past, Present, and Future,* ed. Darlene Clark Hine (Baton Rouge: Louisiana State University Press), © 1986 by Louisiana State University Press.

the exception of W. E. B. Du Bois, who deserted the field shortly after he entered it. As he roamed across the fields of history, sociology, anthropology, political science, education, and literature, Du Bois became one of the few people ever who could be considered truly qualified in the broad field of Afro-American studies. Likewise, it is impossible to confine Du Bois to one generation. His life spanned three generations, and he made contributions to each of them. Others of the first generation were able, industrious, and well focused. They were historians more interested in espousing the causes of human beings than in adhering strictly to the canons of history. They provided panoramic, even pictorial views of Afro-Americans from the earliest times to the present. They wrote of "The Progress of the Race," "A New Negro for a New Century," and "The Remarkable Advancement of the American Negro." As one of them said, in commenting on post–Civil War Afro-Americans, "Starting in the most humble way, with limited intelligence and exceedingly circumscribed knowledge . . . they have gone on from year to year accumulating a little until the savings, as represented by their property, have built churches, erected schools, paid teachers and preachers, and greatly improved the home and home life." Obviously their concern was with adjustment, adaptation, and the compatibility of Afro-Americans with the white world in which they were compelled to live.

The second generation was marked by no special fanfare until the publication of Du Bois' *The Negro* in 1915, the founding of the Association for the Study of Negro Life and History also in 1915, the launching of the *Journal of Negro History* in 1916, and the publication in 1922 of Carter G. Woodson's *The Negro in Our History*. Woodson was the dominant figure of the period. He was not only the leading historian but also the principal founder of the association, editor of the *Journal*, and executive director of the Associated Publishers. He gathered around him a circle of highly trained younger historians whose research he directed and whose writings he published in the *Journal of Negro History* and under the imprint of the Associated Publishers. Monographs on labor, education, Reconstruction, art, music, and other aspects of Afro-American life appeared in steady succession, calling to the attention of the larger community the role of Afro-Americans, more specifically the contributions they had made to the development of the United States. The articles and monographs reflected prodigious research and zeal in pursuing the truth that had *not* been the hallmark of much of the so-called scientific historical writing produced in university seminars in this country some years earlier.

Woodson provided the intellectual and practical leadership of the second generation. With his strong sense of commitment, he offered the spirit and enthusiasm of a pioneer, a discoverer. He even provided the principal theme for the period when he said—in his writings and on numerous occasions—that it was his objective and that of his colleagues "to save and publish the records of the Negro, that the race may not become a negligible factor in the thought of the world." Nor should the record of Afro-Americans become a negligible factor in their own thought, Woodson contended. Thus he began doing everything possible to keep the history of Afro-Americans before them and before the larger community as well. Every annual meeting of the Association for the Study of Negro Life and History had several sessions devoted to the teaching of Afro-American history in the elementary and secondary schools. In 1926 Woodson began the annual observance of Negro History Week to raise the consciousness of Afro-Americans regarding their own worth and to draw the attention of others to what Afro-Americans had contributed to American civilization. Shortly thereafter he launched the *Negro History Bulletin*, a magazine for students, teachers, and the general public. Forty years before this country began to observe History Day, there was Negro History Week. Fifty years after the beginning of the *Negro History Bulletin*, the American Historical Association was still wrestling with the idea of a popular history magazine for students and the general public.

The second generation of Afro-American historical scholarship was coming to a close some years before Woodson's death in 1950. Perhaps a convenient place to mark the beginning of the third generation is with the appearance in 1935 of W. E. B. Du Bois' *Black Reconstruction*. Although Du Bois had gone to some length to disassociate himself from efforts toward racial integration when he left the NAACP the previous year, *Black Reconstruction* reflected little of the separatist sentiment that characterized some of his other writings in 1934 and 1935. In his book on Reconstruction, as the subtitle indicates, he was interested in "the part which black folk played in the attempt to reconstruct democracy in America." In this attempt Du Bois saw merit in blacks and whites working together, espousing the same causes, voting together, and promoting the same candidates. If his book lacked the scholarship of *The Suppression of the African Slave Trade*, which had appeared forty years earlier in 1896, it achieved a level of original interpretation seldom if ever matched by the most profound students of history.

The third generation of Afro-American historical scholarship spanned, roughly, a twenty-five-year period that ended with the close of the 1960s. Most of the members of this generation were, like Du Bois, interested in the role that Afro-Americans had played in the nation's history. Their training was similar to that of the second generation, but their interests were different. They looked less to Afro-American achievements and more to the interactions of blacks with whites, and more to the frequent antagonisms than to the rare moments of genuine cooperation. They tended to see Afro-American history in a larger context, insisting that any event that affected the status of Afro-Americans was a part of Afro-American history even if no Afro-Americans were directly involved. Mississippi's Theodore Bilbo, reading Rayford Logan's *What the Negro Wants* (1944) to his colleagues in the United States Senate and interpreting it for their benefit, was as much a part of Afro-American history as was Heman Sweatt's seeking admission to the University of Texas Law School.

The third generation experienced the fire and brimstone of World War II. Its predicament was not one that Adolf Hitler created but one created by the racial bigotry within their own government and in the American community in general. While all Afro-Americans were exposed to this special brand of racial perversion in the form of eloquent, if shallow, pronouncements against worldwide racism, Afro-American historians were especially sensitive to the persistent hypocrisy of the United States from the colonial years right down to World War II. Small wonder that they had difficulty maintaining a semblance of balance in the face of studied racial discrimination and humiliation. One of them declared that the United States government was "guilty of catering to the ideals of white supremacy." Another called on the United States to "address herself to the unfinished business of democracy," adding somewhat threateningly that "time was of the essence." If anyone doubts the impatience and anger of Afro-American historians during those years, he or she should examine the proceedings of the annual meetings of the Association for the Study of Negro Life and History or follow the activities of the historians themselves.

A salient feature of this generation was the increasing number of white historians working in the field. Some years earlier the second generation of historians had indicated that there were numerous areas in which work needed to be done. White historians entered the field to share in the work. One of them published the first extensive study of slavery in almost forty years and another wrote an elaborate work on the antislavery movement. Still another presented the first critical examination of Negro thought in the late nineteenth century. Interestingly enough, hostile white critics called these white historians "neo-abolitionists." Others worked on Afro-Americans in the antebellum North, Afro-American intellectual history, racial discrimination in education, and Afro-Americans in urban settings. Meanwhile, university professors began to assign dissertation topics in Afro-American history to white as well as Afro-American students. Whites also participated in the annual meetings of the Association for the Study of Negro Life and History and contributed to the *Journal of Negro History*. By the end of the 1960s Afro-American history was no longer the exclusive domain of Afro-Americans.

I believe that Carter G. Woodson would have been pleased with this involvement of white historians in the third generation of scholarship. When he founded the *Journal of Negro History* in 1916, he invited white scholars to sit on the editorial board and to contribute articles. He was, nevertheless, a man of shrewd insights, and I am not suggesting for a moment that he would have approved of or even tolerated whites of the third generation whose motives were more political than scholarly. Even so, he would have welcomed papers for publication in the *Journal of Negro History*, whether submitted by whites or blacks, so long as they were the product of rigorous scholarship and were not contaminated by the venom of racial bias. I knew him well and spent many hours with him each year between 1940 and 1950, when he died. He would have been appalled at the bickering that enveloped the association in the 1960s over the question of whether white historians should be permitted to participate in the work of the association. He had always insisted that men and women should be judged strictly on the basis of their work and not on the basis of their race or the color of their skin.

In the fourth generation, which began around 1970, there emerged the largest and perhaps the best-trained group of historians of Afro-America that had ever appeared. The Afro-Americans in the group were trained, as were the white historians, in graduate centers in every part of the country, in contrast to those of the third generation, who had been trained at three or four universities in the East and Midwest. No area of inquiry escaped their attention. They worked on the colonial period, the era of Reconstruction, and the twentieth century. They examined slavery, the Afro-American family, and antebellum free blacks. Their range was wide, and they brought education, cultural, and military subjects, among many others, under their scrutiny.

These new approaches as well as the accelerated intensity in the study of Afro-American history were greatly stimulated by the drive for equality that had already begun in the third period. In their insistence that they be accorded equal treatment in every respect, Afro-Americans summoned the history of the United States to their side. They had been here from the beginning, they argued, and had done more than their share in making the country rich and great. Since history validated their claims, it was important that the entire nation should become familiar with the facts of Afro-American history. Consequently, it should be studied more intensely, written about more extensively, and taught more vigorously. Institutions of higher education came under pressure to add courses in Afro-American history and related fields and to employ specialists in the field. Responses were varied. One dean at a leading predominantly white university said that he had no objection to a course in Afro-American history, but it would be difficult in view of the fact that there was not sufficient subject matter to occupy the teachers and students for a *whole* semester. Another rushed out and persuaded one of the leaders in the black community, who happened to be a Baptist minister, to teach a course in Afro-American history. Despite the intellectual, educational, and political considerations affecting their decisions, many colleges and universities incorporated courses in Afro-American history into their curricula.

It was the frenetic quality of the concerns of university administrators that cast doubts on their interest in maintaining high academic standards in the area of Afro-American studies. As students intensified their demands for courses in this area, university officials seemed more interested in mollifying students than in enriching the curriculum with courses taught by well-trained professors who maintained high standards. The results were that some courses were staffed by persons whose familiarity with what they taught was minimal and whose approach tended to confirm the views of the dean who thought there was not sufficient subject matter in Afro-American history to span an entire semester.

It is nothing short of marvelous that under the circumstances scholarship in Afro-American history moved to a new high level of achievement. Some claimed that those who taught were not doing the researching and writing and, thus, were not adding to the body of knowledge that was needed in order to satisfy our doubting dean. That was true, to some extent, but it was no less true in, say, diplomatic, cultural, intellectual, or economic history. There have always been more purveyors than creators of knowledge in all fields, and there is nothing fundamentally wrong with this, I suppose. We who teach *and* do research and write tend to think that the dual activity is more healthy intellectually, but that is a matter of opinion. What is remarkable in the field of Afro-American history is not that there were so many teachers who did not write but that there were so many who did.

Perhaps it was because scholars in the field of Afro-American history saw so many opportunities to reinterpret their field that such a large number of them were engaged in researching and writing. There was zeal, even passion, in much that they wrote, for they were anxious to correct all the errors and misinterpretations of earlier historians. Thus, they undertook to reinterpret not only the racist historians of an earlier day but the Afro-American historians of an earlier generation as well. There was not always the grace and charity and certainly not the gratitude that one might expect of persons whose work almost invariably rested on the work of their intellectual godfathers. That, however, was relatively unimportant, especially if the work they produced was of the highest quality and made a solid contribution to the scholarship of Afro-American history. This was true often enough that one could blush more often in pride than in sorrow.

Some writing, nevertheless, was stimulated by publishers who were anxious to take advantage of a growing market. Under pressure from their agents and editors, some scholars produced works that had the sole merit of having been written with more than deliberate speed. When the speed was not great enough to produce "instant" books, publishers prevailed on some scholars to anthologize the writings of others. Some of the products were of great merit, bringing together as they did the best writings of some of the leaders in the field. Some of the products, however, were excellent illustrations of how scholars and scholarship can be corrupted by the prospect of monetary gain. Many anthologies were literally thrown together, without any thought being given to arrangement or organization and without any introduction, interpretation, or connective tissue. The only thing that one can say of such works is that they were not alone in the nature and extent of their compromise with intellectual integrity. Lecturers could be just as bad or worse. One recalls how in the early 1970s one of the "authoritative" lecturers in Afro-American history broke an engagement at a leading western university and simply informed them by telegram that he had been offered more money to lecture at another institution. Perhaps more common were "instant" professors, black and white, who rushed into the field to make a quick reputation as well as a quick buck. Unhappily, college and university administrators did not display the same skill in detecting the charlatans in this field that they did in some other fields. Thus, the field often suffered from the presence of so-called authorities whose abilities were no higher than their motives.

At this point one must not dwell on defects of scholarship or even the character of the scholars. Time will take care of such matters, without even so much as a suggestion from us as to how we should like to settle them. Instead, we could better serve the present *and* the future by attempting, as historians, to take lessons from the last century, using them to make certain that this generation will make significant improvements over what preceding generations had to offer.

In his *History of the Negro Race in America* (1882), George Washington Williams was extremely critical of Frederick Douglass for various positions he took on slavery and freedom in the years before the Civil War. We could excoriate Williams, as did his contemporaries, but that would be unfair without at least first understanding Williams' impatience with a political party that had betrayed not only the freedmen but Frederick Douglass, their chosen spokesman, as well. Likewise, one could be extremely critical of Carter G. Woodson's preoccupation with the achievements of Afro-Americans, but one should remember that Woodson was hurling historical brickbats at those who had said that Afro-Americans had achieved nothing at all. One could likewise be extremely critical of the historians of the third generation for their preoccupation with what may be called "mainstream history." In the process, some claim, they neglected some cherished attributes of Afro-American life and history, such as race pride and cultural nationalism. Such claims overlook the important fact that the historians of the third generation were compelled by circumstances to fight for the integration of Afro-American history into the mainstream of the nation's history. Their fight to integrate Afro-American history into the mainstream was a part of the fight by Afro-American students to break into the graduate departments of history in every predominantly white university in the southern states and in many such institutions outside the South. It was also a part of the fight of Afro-

Americans to gain admission to the mainstream of American life—for the vote, for equal treatment, for equal opportunity, for their rights as Americans. They pursued that course in order to be able to refute those, including our favorite dean—our favorite whipping boy, incidentally—who argued that Afro-Americans had little or no history. They also did so in order to support their argument that Afro-American history should be recognized as a centerpiece—an adornment, if you will—of the history of the United States.

The excoriations and strictures heaped on one generation of Afro-American historians by succeeding generations could better be spent on more constructive pursuits. Better trained and with better means of communication, they could, for example, seek to tell us more than we already know about malingering and sabotage among slaves. They could devote more attention to writing vignettes if not full biographies of hundreds of important Afro-Americans, the remembrance and recognition of whom are endangered by neglect and the passage of time. They could devote some of their energies to helping us understand how it is, in a country committed to the dignity of man, that so much energy has been spent throughout its history to maintain the proposition that Afro-Americans have no dignity and, therefore, are not deserving of respect. Thomas Jefferson argued it when he likened Afro-Americans to the orangutan. Fourth-generation historians of Afro-America have come close to arguing it by claiming that slaves, as a whole, were not only content but were imbued with the Protestant work ethic that gave them a sense of commitment to what they were doing. No area of intellectual endeavor needs such stumbling blocks to truth, whether it comes out of the eighteenth century or out of the last quarter of the twentieth century.

The implications of all of this for the teaching of Afro-American history are profound, to say the least. As a relatively new field, at least only recently recognized as a respectable field of intellectual endeavor, it is alive and vibrant. This is why it can easily attract and excite a large number of graduate and undergraduate students. It provides, moreover, a very important context in which much, if not the whole, of the history of the United States can be taught and studied. It also provides an important context in which much of the history of the United States can be reexamined and rewritten. In its unique position as one of the most recent areas of intellectual inquiry, it invites the attention of those who genuinely seek new avenues for solving some of the nation's most difficult historical problems. And, if it is a valid area of intellectual inquiry, it cannot be segregated by sex, religion, or race. Historians must be judged by what they do, not by how they look.

I like to think that it was more than opportunism that increased the offerings in Afro-American history in the colleges and universities across the land. I like to believe that it was more than the excitement of the late 1960s that provided new opportunities to teach and learn Afro-American history. I prefer to entertain the thought that in addition to those other considerations there was the valid interconnection between the history of a people and their drive for first-class citizenship. The quest for their history, lost and strayed, was a quest in which black and white alike could and did participate, as both teachers and writers of history. The drive for first-class citizenship was a drive whose immediate benefit could be enjoyed only by those who had been denied it or by those others who at least truly understood the loathsome nature that such denial represented.

Some members of the fourth generation, no doubt, will regard this sentiment as optimistic if not maudlin. I would be the first to say that there is some of both in it. I would only add that when one begins a poem, a hymn, a short story, or even a history, one must be optimistic about its completion and about what it seeks to teach. If one believes in the power of his own words and in the words of others, one must also hope and believe that the world will be a better place by our having spoken or written those words.

"As for Our History"

Our poetry is our lives," boasted William Lowndes Yancey on the eve of the Civil War; "our fiction will come when truth has ceased to satisfy us; and as for our history, we have made about all that has glorified the United States." Yancey's historical allusions were well calculated for his campaign to "fire the Southern heart," for the sectional crisis was creating in the South of the 1850s a historical consciousness that would long remain both acute and polemical. Inventing and glorifying a fictitious historical South, a pliant Southern Clio furnished one of the weapons that enabled Yancey's forces of sectional chauvinism to "precipitate the cotton states into a revolution."[1] The myth did not die with the crisis that produced it, for the succeeding experiences of defeat and humiliation made it even more a psychological necessity to southerners. For a hundred years southern historians found the dream so warm, the truth so cold, that they were slow to construct for the South an image of itself that was true to the reality of its past or relevant to its changing circumstances.

Before the 1850s the South had been too much a "bundle of contrasting and conflicting interests, classes, and values"[2] to see itself as an entity, historical or contemporary; and its people had shown little interest in history of any kind. During the colonial period the writing of history, along with other literary activities, had been discouraged by the preoccupation with survival, the lack of leisure, the absence of a large literate population, and the southerner's apparent preference for action over contemplation. But the South had shared in the burst of national pride that accompanied the American Revolution and mounted steadily during the early decades of the nineteenth century;

Originally published in *The Southerner as American*, ed. Charles G. Sellers (Chapel Hill: University of North Carolina Press, 1960). Reprinted by permission.

and a few southerners had expressed their American nationalism in historical writings. David Ramsay's influential *History of the American Revolution*, published in 1789, was the most notable early product of this impulse; and as late as 1841 a Virginian, George Tucker, could write an impressive *History of the United States* that showed little sectional bias.

By and large, however, southerners left historical writing to Americans in other sections, and what histories they did produce were for the most part histories of individual states. These state histories[3] revealed almost no consciousness of the South as a distinctive section. Rather, each claimed for its state a larger contribution to the nation's liberal Revolutionary tradition. Reading them along with their northern counterparts, one is struck by "how much good will was shown." Localistic only in their spirit of competition with other states, the southern state historians were essentially nationalistic in that they competed for national honors; and they uniformly recognized that the honors were to be awarded according to a standard that "had been fixed by the national ideal."[4] Indeed, some southerners conceded the claims to primacy staked out by the more active New England historians. "The Yankee is the man, who first hung out the banner of liberty . . . and determined to be free," wrote William Gilmore Simms in 1830; while as late as 1854 the eminent Virginia historian, Hugh Blair Grigsby, contrasted his state's beginnings at Jamestown unfavorably with the "grand and noble achievement" of the pilgrims.[5]

Yet by the 1840s the South was beginning to view its past in a less national spirit. The southern states were asserting their historical claims more stridently, and some southerners were rejecting altogether the liberal national tradition as the theme of their history. Virginians, for example, began to argue that royalist refugees from Cromwellian England had given their commonwealth its distinctive tone. This cavalier thesis was propagated by politicians, literary men, and publicists, against the opposition of Virginia's abler historians, for it arose not from new historical knowledge, but from the exigencies of the mounting sectional controversy.[6]

During these years the pressures of sectional conflict were causing southerners to minimize the physiographic variations within their section, the differences in the economic and social status of the people, and the several disagreements in political allegiances and philosophies. Committed to perpetuating a system of servitude increasingly condemned by the rest of the Western world, southern whites began to think of themselves as having a set of common values, common problems, common dangers, and common aspirations that set them apart from other Americans. Inevitably they came to believe also that they had a common and distinctive history.

The shrewder southern leaders perceived, moreover, that history could be a major weapon in the sectional struggle. By demonstrating their section's glorious past and common dangers and destiny, southern historians could help forge the unity that was indispensable, whether to maintain the South's position within the American Union, or to prepare the way for separate nationhood.[7] Consequently the late 1840s and 1850s witnessed a gradual but decided shift from a history that asserted the various southern states' peculiar contributions to the American tradition, to a history that asserted the South's difference from and superiority over the North.

This shift was facilitated by a growing sectional feeling among northern historians, whose "breach of faith" shocked southerners out of their historical complacency and inactivity. In their effort to demonstrate the immoralities and deficiencies of the southern way of life, northern writers and speakers began to say that the South's contribution to the growth of the nation had been negligible. In 1847, for example, Lorenzo Sabine of Massachusetts brought out his *American Loyalists*, the first comprehensive treatment of those colonists who supported England during the War for Independence. He argued that Loyalist sentiment was so strong in the South that the section's contribution to the winning of independence was extremely limited and, on the whole, without effect. "South Carolina, with a Northern army to assist her could not, or would not, preserve her own capital," Sabine concluded.[8]

If Sabine had deliberately planned it, he could not have wounded southerners more deeply or evoked from them a more spirited retaliation. They regarded his book as a part of a dark northern design to impugn their loyalty, their integrity, and their way of life. It could not be ignored any more than the attacks of the abolitionists; and for the next ten years they refuted it in the press, on the platform, on the floor of the Congress, and anywhere they could find an audience.[9] Even more significant than the immediate, vehement reaction to the Sabine thesis was the way in which it convinced a section, daily growing more conscious of its minority status in the Union, that it must write its own history of the Revolution and of everything else.

Three years before the Sabine volume appeared, William Gilmore

Simms had argued that South Carolina needed no written history. "It is already deeply engraven on the everlasting monuments of the nation," he said. "It is around us, a living trophy upon all our hills. It is within us, an undying memory in all our hearts. It is a record which no fortune can obliterate—inseparable from all that is great and glorious in the work of the Revolution."[10] Within a year after Sabine's assault Simms had changed his mind about the writing of the history of his state and of the South. He had become convinced that the men of the section would have to assume the task, for their history was being written "by superficial and corrupt historians, who are quite numerous in our country and who abuse the confidence of the reader."[11] One of the South's leading firebrands, Lawrence M. Keitt, agreed and added that South Carolina should "gather together the Records of her History, and put them beyond the reach of flame and casualty."[12] In the late fifties William Porcher Miles rejoiced to see in the South a "disposition, at last, beginning to manifest itself, to recall and perpetuate . . . the glorious memories" of the past.[13]

The argument over the South's role in the struggle for independence did not result in a victory for the South, but it did teach southerners the importance of writing their history in order, from their point of view, to keep it straight. The numerous historical societies that had come into existence in several southern states in the 1830s and 1840s as scarcely more than social organizations now began to enlarge their activities. Anniversaries of battles and other historic events became the occasions for reviewing the South's peculiar contributions to the history of the nation.[14] Virginia paid homage to her George Washington, "who had led an earlier crusade for independence; Maryland recalled her heroes in Randall's stirring stanzas; Carolina cherished the cult of Calhoun; Louisiana pointed to her proud Creole heritage."[15] By 1860 a student of southern history could declare in all earnestness: "The Southern States were settled and governed, in a great measure . . . by and under the direction of persons belonging to the blood and race of the reigning family, and belong to that stock recognized as CAVA-LIERS. . . . The Southern people come from that race . . . to whom law and order, obedience and command, are convertible terms, and who do command, the world over."[16]

The student of history in the antebellum South was, therefore, more concerned with supporting the position his section was taking than he was with the precise accuracy of the facts. In fanning the flames of southern nationalism the historian—whether he was an accomplished man of letters like William Gilmore Simms or a shrewd lawyer-planter-amateur historian like David F. Jamison—contributed much to the feeling of homogeneity and unity. Although this meant ignoring the religious, ethnic, and cultural differences among the peoples of the South or creating myths about them, it was a task that had to be performed. With few exceptions southern historians performed it zealously and faithfully.[17]

The South's historians served the cause of southern nationalism with more lasting effect than did its armies. Having failed to establish a separate nation and having gone down to defeat on the field of battle, southerners in the period after the Civil War turned their attention to their own past with a concentration so great that the cult of history became a permanent and important ingredient of the southern culture. Through monuments, patriotic societies, songs, verses, memorial celebrations, and informal reminiscences, they kept before southern youth the glorious yesteryear when the South stood on the threshold of greatness. Especially did they seek to explain and justify their past actions to their contemporaries and to posterity through historical writings. Southerners must win with the pen what they had failed to win with the sword.

In the second issue of his *Southern Review* Alfred Taylor Bledsoe showed his profound respect for history in general and the history of his beloved South in particular. He especially appreciated its importance in binding a people together; and he made it clear that it must not be neglected in the South. In part, he said: "The world is too apt to forget its heroes whose efforts have not been crowned with visible success, and its martyrs whose sufferings have been borne in obscurity. 'They failed,' is too often the verdict that discrowns them of their well-worn laurels. . . . Must it be so with these. . . . If we could forget the blackened ruins of Vicksburg, Fredericksburg or Columbia, the track of desolation, the rapine and the carnage, still, of the deeds of our heroic brothers, of the lessons and legacy of their life and death, there can be no forgetfulness."[18]

Thus the writing of history became an act of sectional allegiance and devotion. Many of the leaders of the secession movement and officials of the Confederacy published their memoirs or histories of the southern cause, relying confidently on the observation of Benjamin H. Hill that the greatest resource the South had was history—"impartial, and unpassioned, un-office-seeking history."[19] Several of them organized, in 1869, the Southern Historical Society, which collected and preserved the records of the Confederacy and published articles in the *Southern Magazine* and later in its own publication, the *Southern Historical Society Papers.* In other publications such as *The Land We Love, Field and Fireside,* and the *Southern Review,* southerners depicted the sunnier aspects of antebellum life, the righteousness of the South's position in secession and war, and the horrors of Reconstruction. So well tailored was this cult of the Lost Cause to the emotional needs of the rank and file of southern whites that the section's Bourbon politicians took it up and made it the panoply under which they promoted their incongruous but eminently practical program of economic and political reconciliation with the North.

Yet some of the most ardent devotees of the Lost Cause remained dissatisfied with the work of the post–Civil War generation of southern historians. Too many historical societies and magazines had begun with a burst of enthusiasm, only to die within a few months or years. Too many of the memoirs and sketches that told the South's story were undeniably mediocre. "There is no true history of the South," Thomas Nelson Page complained in 1892. "In a few years there will be no South to demand a history." This was all the more regrettable from Page's point of view, for no civilization as unique had existed "since the dawn of history, as potent in its influence, and yet no chronicle of it has been made by any but the hand of hostility."[20]

While Page complained primarily about the quantity of southern historical writing, a few southerners began to complain about its quality, and to realize that southern history could receive no intellectual recognition as long as it remained merely reminiscent, uncritical, and self-pitying. "No man with instincts for accuracy can be satisfied with our statement of our own case," John Spencer Bassett told his students and colleagues at Trinity College in 1897. The Confederate Brigadier-General school of historians who, having fought bravely with their swords, were now "tempted to make asses of themselves with the pen," had convinced Bassett that southern historians needed other qualifications than their Confederate experience and devotion to the Lost Cause. The student of southern history must, like any scholar, "know how to weigh evidence; he must have the scientific spirit for facts, he must have the clear light of truth." But Bassett saw little prospect of rapid improvement, for any southern historian who departed from the traditional view would be "denounced as a traitor and mercenary defiler of his Birthplace."[21]

Despite Bassett's pessimism, the scholarly ideals he voiced were just about to transform the writing of southern history. Bassett was only one of a number of capable, energetic young southerners who had begun entering the seminars of Herbert Baxter Adams at the Johns Hopkins University, William Archibald Dunning at Columbia, and the great masters at the European universities, to acquire the skills and techniques of the new scientific history. By the first decade of the twentieth century they were publishing numerous studies on southern history, and a remarkable flowering of southern historiography was under way. Professors at some of the leading southern colleges and universities began to concentrate on the section's history, and some northern universities engaged southern scholars and encouraged them to offer courses and do research on the South's past.[22] Southern states established archives and historical commissions; and state and local historical societies were revitalized. In these years of reviving American nationalism, the history-conscious South was claiming a conspicuous place in the national movement to develop a scientific historiography.

Yet the sincere aspirations to scientific method of this first generation of professional southern historians failed to result in the scientific, or completely unbiased and objective, history at which they aimed. There could be no more eloquent evidence of the continuing power of the South's mythology than the curious mixtures of science, polemics, folklore, and fantasy that these scholars produced under the impression that they were being scientific. Almost invariably they concentrated on two aspects of southern history: the heyday of slavery and the period of the Civil War and Reconstruction. These were the two heroic ages of southern history; one was the age of the apex of a glorious civilization, the other the age of a tragic but glorious defeat.

These histories were dominated by inherited sectional prejudices and assumptions of which the authors seemed largely unaware. One of the most distinguished historians of slavery rhapsodized that the plantation was a "parish, or perhaps a chapel of ease," and that it was "a matrimonial bureau, something of a harem perhaps, a copious nursery, and a divorce court."[23] One of the most influential of the historians of Reconstruction described the first results of the Ku Klux Klan movement as "good" since, as he insisted, it "quieted the Negroes, made life and property safer, gave protection to women, stopped burnings . . . and started the whites on the way to gain political supremacy."[24] Readers of these histories could draw the inference that slavery was a positive good, since whites were free and Negroes were slaves, and that Reconstruction was an unmitigated evil, since many whites were without the vote and most Negroes had the vote.

Shot through with an uncritical and unrealistic judgment of some of the facts and ignoring many other facts, these histories did not provide the basis for a mature understanding of the South and its problems. More seriously, they gave the white South the intellectual justification for its determination not to yield on many important points, especially in its treatment of the Negro, that set it apart from the rest of the nation. Claiming as they did to be "scientific" and "impartial," the new southern historians even helped persuade many nonsoutherners that through the years the South had been treated unjustly, that its own course of action had been substantially right, and that its racial attitudes should be condoned if not imitated.

At the same time, however, these pioneer professional historians strengthened the cult of history in the South and established scientific ideals and methods that paved the way for sounder historical writing. Some of them did try to rise above their prejudices, and an occasional Bassett succeeded. Most important, by trying to write history as others were writing it, they sought to emphasize the fact that they were Americans writing about the South, just as other Americans were writing about the West or North. They differed from their predecessors in their willingness to concede that the past was really irretrievably gone; and although they cast longing eyes over their shoulders they were resigned to the reality of being a part of the United States. It is not without significance, therefore, that when they brought out their first great collaborative history of the section, they gave it the title *The South in the Building of the Nation.*[25]

Since Bassett's death more than twenty-five years ago, the standards of scholarly objectivity so warmly avowed but so imperfectly realized by his generation have steadily, if with painful slowness, gained headway among southern historians. The process has been accelerated within the present generation, as the new focus of national attention on the South and its problems has forced the section to reexamine its position within the nation. Perhaps the new introspection has also been stimulated by the indisputable findings of the social sciences that have branded as a hoax some of the long-held southern views regarding race. Court decisions adverse to these southern views have underlined the urgency of this reexamination; and increasing pressures, social and economic, have made it imperative for the South to take another look at itself.

It was inevitable that in any new stock-taking the South would look at its past. For a section where the cult of history is so deeply imbedded and where the past looms so large in the present, no critical evaluation of its position would be complete without a careful examination of its heritage. There could have been no more propitious moment for enlarging the role of history in understanding the South than the recent years. Historical scholarship has reached a maturity and respectability that gave its findings greater credence and wider acceptance than at any previous period. The opportunities for research have been greatly broadened by the physical improvement of local and state libraries and archives and the employment of trained personnel.[26] Finally, there has emerged a new generation of scholars who have escaped the most traumatic effects of the nineteenth-century experience.

The study of the South's history has been nationalized in much the same way that its other problems have been. Northerners with no particular brief for John Brown are studying the South. Southerners with no defense of slavery or the fire-eaters are among the most zealous students of the new history of the South. Negroes with no feeling of inadequacy are examining various phases of the South's history and are writing about whites as well as about Negroes.

The range of problems being fruitfully explored by these contemporary historians as they seek new insight into the South's past is most impressive. It runs the gamut of the section's experience, from the earliest colonial days to the present, from agriculture to industry, from intricate political and economic problems to complex social and intellectual developments.[27] The new skills and resources of the historical profession are currently being used to study the back country of the colonial South and the South's role in the American Revolution. Historians are reexamining with meticulous care the institution of slavery and the structure of society in the antebellum South. They are studying the many ramifications of the Reconstruction, including the Freedmen's Bureau, Negro officeholding, the Ku Klux Klan, and the Union League. They are giving attention to the history of civil rights, disfranchisement, the rise of cities, the growth of industry, and the labor movement. It may be said, in fact, that hardly any significant phase or aspect of the South's history is escaping the scrutiny of today's historians.[28]

As impressive as the range and scope of the historical problems under consideration is the approach of the historians themselves. They appear to possess at least the normal amount of skepticism and disinterestedness, and they seem to lack the excessive preconceptions and presuppositions that have perpetuated so many myths about the South. Most of them do not appear to be studying the South to prove a point or to take sides. They seem to be reasonably free of the acrimony that has beclouded so much of the South's history and rendered it polemical and unscientific. Their approaches are seldom merely iconoclastic, for most of them recognize the distinctiveness and validity of a southernism that springs from the physiographic, ethnic, and experiential factors peculiar to the region. At least some of them are more interested in understanding the South's past than in merely tolerating it.[29] At least some of them recognize the complete uselessness of either condemning or defending the South. At the same time they seem to appreciate the value of critically examining and analyzing its history with a view to understanding more clearly the relationship between the past and the present as well as between the South and the rest of the country.

One would be contributing a new myth to the South's historiography if he asserted that all historians of the South shared these views and employed these new approaches. There are still some who, with strong commitments to the old order or with vested interests in long-held points of view, have escaped entirely the spirit of the new southern historical scholarship. These, however, seem to be decreasing in numbers and influence. They who once constituted such a confident majority may soon be, as Bassett once was, a voice crying in the wilderness.

The new research in southern history is already yielding much in the way of broad and significant results for the section. Where a healthy skepticism, an indefatigable zeal, and a truly scientific approach are employed, they frequently result in facts and interpretations that demand a revision of some long-held view of southern history. Even as the process is under way one can see some significant revisions taking place. Recent studies of the antebellum social structure, for example, have made it clear that the vast majority of southern whites owned no slaves and had no hope of owning slaves.[30] This incontrovertible fact has, of course, only slowly made headway in popular thinking against the more attractive, exotic view, sustained in historical fiction, that slavery provided an idyllic existence for all or most southern whites. But as southern whites come to understand slavery as an institution that materially benefited a very small segment of the southern population, they may be freed from personal involvement in the defense not only of the Old South's defunct "peculiar institution," but also its surviving corollary, the doctrine of white superiority.

Other recent research in southern history has shown that southerners answered Lincoln's attempted relief of Sumter with gunfire because of, among other things, their long tradition of individualism, carried to the point of lawlessness, and because of a continuing fascination with military show. Goaded almost into a persecution complex on the score of their inordinate racism, southerners could boast only so long of their military prowess—could repress only for a time some further expression of their ardent expansionism—before giving explosive expression to their sensitivity. Southern historians have found it easy to glorify the explosion without reflecting on its cause.

Not long ago a young southern white historian showed conclusively that during the Civil War the loyalty of slaves to their masters was the exception rather than the rule.[31] Even more recently a young Negro historian has described in detail the role of the nearly 200,000 Negroes who fought on the side of the Union in that war.[32] When more white southerners learn these facts and accept them, they will gain an insight into the views and aspirations of Negroes that should materially lessen the empty assertions that they "understand" Negroes.

In recent years we have learned that corruption during Reconstruction was not only biracial but also bipartisan.[33] Even more recently a southern white historian has adduced convincing evidence that the corruption of the Reconstruction period continued unabated after the southern whites had thrown Negroes and carpetbaggers out and "redeemed" their states.[34] As this view becomes accepted for the cold historical truth that it is, it will perhaps be possible for the South to modify its view of the Reconstruction. As the section comes to realize that some of its own white sons were guilty of the same things it has denounced in others, it may even adopt the view that integrity, like blackguardism, is not the monopoly of a particular race or party and that there are more valid standards by which to judge a people than race and party.

No one can say with certainty just what influence historical conceptions have had on the minds of men, nor can one accurately predict the impact of such conceptions on human relations in the future. But historical traditions have controlled the attitudes and conduct of peoples too often to permit a denial that history has been an important instrument in shaping human affairs. History gave to the Prussians a tradition of military prowess that influenced European affairs profoundly for more than a century. It has given to Americans an almost eerie sense of national virtue and destiny, as well as a deep attachment to their historically grounded democratic institutions.

Nowhere in the United States, however, has the cult of history flourished as it has flourished in the South. Nowhere are the consequences of a historical tradition more apparent, for from its history the South derived the image of itself that has in large measure governed its reactions to successive changes and challenges. If the South has often reacted churlishly and shortsightedly, the fault does not lie with history itself, but with a distorted historical tradition of which even the South's historians have been victims, but which only they can correct.

Thus it may be fortunate that the cult of history still flourishes in the South, as can be seen in the generous public support of its historical activities, in the vitality of its historical societies, and in the rich variety of its historical publications. The historians themselves—northern and southern, Negro and white—are at last shaking off the blinders fashioned by the Yanceys of the 1850s and the events of the 1860s and 1870s.

The southern past unearthed by recent scholarship deserves a long hard look from all southerners, for it reveals a section that has been continuously both southern and American and a people who rushed upon tragedy by making virtues of their vices. Only as the South understands what it has been can it come to know itself well enough to value and preserve the valuable in both its southernism and its Americanism, while discarding the attitudes and habits so long and so fatefully perpetuated by a false history.

PART II

The Practice of History

These essays are examples of what I have done in the practice of my craft. I believe that the historian should engage in research and present findings that are new or that at least throw some new light on old materials. He should be willing to make broad generalizations and examine long-range trends. Finally, he should be willing to share with others his reflections that are the result of extensive study, perhaps over a long period of time.

My field of concentration has been the South, where I have studied intensively the two great racial groups, black and white, the principal actors in the drama of southern history. (Even before most of them were expelled from the South by Andrew Jackson, native Americans played only a limited role in the region.) At times during my studies the focus was on free Negroes and those slaves who were virtually free. At other times I gave attention to the relationship of slavery to certain attributes of white southerners, such as their apparent predisposition toward militancy. I was also interested in the expansionist tendencies of southerners, which also seemed related in some ways to slavery. These forays into various aspects of southern history had as their principal objective a better understanding of the entire South and all of its people.

I continued to have interests outside the South, especially where historical events and forces deeply affected the status of Negro Americans. Several years before the Kerner Commission reported that the United States was moving toward two societies "one black, one white—separate and unequal," I undertook to describe this national social tragedy in an essay originally presented at a conference called by the American Academy of Arts and Sciences. My position, set forth in "Two Worlds of Race," placed the phenomenon in its historical setting and argued that it had its roots in the early seventeenth century and had flourished for the ensuing three centuries. This same phenomenon was illustrated in the piece on the Civil Rights Act of 1875 in which I pointed out that racial discrimination in the post–Civil War years was as prevalent in New York and Chicago as in New Orleans and Charleston.

In anticipation of the bicentennial of the American Revolution I looked at

71

the two worlds of race in the late eighteenth century and saw that the founding fathers were not at all ready or willing to extend to blacks, slave and free, the privileges or opportunities or even rights for which they were fighting in their war with Britain. Thus, even in our finest hours the matter of race has compelled Americans to take notice of the paradoxes and inconsistencies in their own society.

When the Chicago Historical Society observed the 150th anniversary of the birth of Abraham Lincoln in 1959, I was invited to speak. Recently it had been revealed that President Dwight Eisenhower's chief of staff, Sherman Adams, had received several favors, including a vicuna coat, from a person who was seen by some as attempting to influence some public policies or decisions. I thought that it would be interesting to see how Lincoln dealt with such matters. It soon became clear to me that public morality in 1864 was quite different from what it was in 1959.

Slaves Virtually Free in
Antebellum North Carolina

The treatment of Negro slaves in the antebellum South has been the subject of considerable discussion among students of history for many years. Points of difference in the matter have ranged all the way from the contentions of the apologists that the slave system was one of genuine paternal benevolence to the arguments of the antagonists who insisted that almost every southern plantation was a place where humanity ended and barbarism began.[1] Too often, the sweeping generalizations which the contenders have set forth have been based on more passion than fact; and they have frequently overlooked the opportunity to bolster their points of view with supporting evidence, of which there is an abundance on both sides. The evidence on either side can hardly be conclusive, however, for the fact is that the treatment of slaves in the antebellum South had almost as many variations as there were slaveholders. The attitudes of whites toward Negro slaves and the policies that were the results of those attitudes were determined in a large measure by the social, economic, and political conditions in a given area.[2] These conditions were, in turn, affected by a large number of personal considerations that grew out of the master-slave relationship. Although the black codes were stringent in every part of the South, especially in the period immediately preceding the Civil War, the treatment of slaves by groups or individuals was at such marked variance with the law that many Negroes enjoyed virtual freedom.

In observing a group whose status was only technically that of slaves, one must be careful not to slip into the rather enticing pitfall of making hasty generalizations regarding the treatment of slaves. The mass of evidence on the other side of the picture is just as imposing—

Originally appeared in the *Journal of Negro History*, Volume XXVIII (July, 1943). Reprinted by permission.

perhaps even more so—and upon sober reflection, the student of history can enjoy the consolation that comes from the knowledge that every institution has its lights and its shadows. It is enough, here, to realize that in the face of an abundance of restrictive legislation, there were many slaveholders who, for one reason or another, had sufficient humanity within themselves to treat their human chattel as human beings. In the state of North Carolina, the number of masters who treated their slaves in such a manner was always considerable, and some of the reasons for such an attitude are not difficult to discover.

North Carolina was never one of the chief slaveholding states. Her slaves were considerably fewer than those of her neighbor states of Virginia, South Carolina, and Georgia. As a matter of fact, 67 percent of the slaveholding families held fewer than ten slaves in 1860, while 72 percent of North Carolina's families had no slaves at all.[3] On the whole, the state was one of yeomen and small slaveholders. In the absence of a large number of great plantations, one can be certain that there was also a smaller degree of the impersonal relationships that breed suspicion and distrust. Since many masters in antebellum North Carolina worked side by side with their slaves, they felt that they *knew* them and had the problem of discipline well in hand. When the slaveholder clamored for more restrictive legislation, it was for the purpose of bringing his neighbor's slaves under the surveillance of the law rather than his own. Under these circumstances, it is not difficult to conceive of a situation in which many slaveholders refused to enforce thc law in regard to their own slaves, which resulted in a general laxity of law enforcement over a large area.

By the beginning of the eighteenth century, there was to be found in North Carolina a large number of persons whose social background, political philosophy, and religious teachings served to weaken their beliefs in the efficacy or the righteousness of the peculiar institution. Hard-working Scotch-Irish yeomen of the West and the piedmont and Quakers and Moravians of the central counties were not very enthusiastic about slavery. And although some of them owned slaves, they were moving rather rapidly into the category of antislavery proponents or slaveholders who permitted their wards to go virtually free.

Long before the beginning of the nineteenth century, North Carolina had a set of laws concerning the treatment of Negro slaves. Beginning in 1715, the lords proprietors and the general assembly had begun to establish rules governing slaves within the colony, and by the time of the Revolution, the black code had been completed. The injunction against slaves traveling without passes,[4] the laws concerning the places and conditions under which Negroes could have meetings,[5] and the severe penalties attached to the laws against enticing slaves to leave their masters[6] were all safeguards against possible insurrections. Even more effective precautions were the laws against the possession of weapons by Negroes,[7] and the penalty of death for "consulting, advising or conspiring to rebel, or make insurrection."[8] The establishment of patrols from the very beginning, moreover, served to insure the enforcement, at times at least, of the laws that were being enacted.

In the first half of the nineteenth century, North Carolina found herself in a situation that almost demanded a more stringent black code. Her neighbors were passing legislation affecting slaves at such a rate as to embarrass her proslavery politicos.[9] The restrictive legislation in neighboring states, moreover, had the effect of driving a large number of slaves out of Virginia, South Carolina, and Georgia into the Old North State with the result that the jails of North Carolina were, at times, literally filled with runaway slaves from outside the state.[10] By 1826 the effective work of the twenty-three branches of the North Carolina Manumission Society brought to the attention of North Carolinians the fact that the system of slavery was being undermined from within.[11] In the same year, an attack on the institution came from outside the state. The legislature of Vermont transmitted a resolution to the North Carolina general assembly stating that "slavery is an evil to be deprecated by a free and enlightened people" and offered its cooperation in "any measures which may be adopted by the general government for its abolition in the United States."[12] So infuriated were the governor and the assembly of North Carolina that legislation was passed more carefully regulating the militia and patrols and circumscribing even further the activities of slaves.[13]

The appearance of David Walker's *Appeal in Four Articles* in North Carolina in 1829 aroused the deepest fears in the hearts of North Carolina slaveholders. Walker, a North Carolina free Negro living in Massachusetts, denounced the institution with such bitter invectives that his *Appeal* proved to be one of the most powerful antislavery tracts written by any of the enemies of the institution.[14] He predicted that a Negro would rise to lead his people out of bondage and called on all Negroes, slave and free, to fight against the institution with all the vigor that they could summon. Reaction against the Walker pamphlet on the part of North Carolina officials was immediate and positive. A law against the circulation of books and papers that tended to "excite insurrection, conspiracy or resistance in the slaves or free Negroes" was passed at the next session of the legislature.[15] Another law was passed which prohibited "all persons from teaching slaves to read and write, the use of figures excepted."[16]

By 1830 the laws concerning manumission had become something of a dead letter and were rather generally disregarded. The clause in the enactment of 1796 requiring proof of meritorious services in the case of emancipated slaves was not enforced, and the county courts granted almost all applications for freedom without making the slightest investigations.[17] The increase of free Negroes in every part of the state[18] and the provocations by such individuals and groups as David Walker and the Vermont legislature caused the passage of a law, in 1830, carefully regulating the manumission of Negro slaves. In part, the law said,

> Any inhabitant of this State, desirous to emancipate a slave or slaves, shall file a petition in writing in some one of the Superior Courts of this State, setting forth . . . the name, sex, and age of each slave intended to be emancipated, and praying permission to emancipate the same; and the Court . . . shall grant the prayer . . . on the following conditions, and not otherwise, viz, That the petitioner shall show that he has given public notice of his intention to file such petition at the court house of the county, and in the State Gazette for at least six weeks before the hearing of such petition; and that the petitioner shall enter into bond, with two securities . . . payable to the Governor . . . in the sum of one thousand dollars for each slave named in the petition, conditioned that the slave or slaves shall honestly and correctly demean him, her, or themselves . . . and that within ninety days shall leave the State of North Carolina and never afterwards come within the same.

In another section, the law made it valid, with certain qualifications, "for any person by his or her last will and testament, to direct and authorize his or her executors to cause to be emancipated any slave or slaves, pursuant to this act." It further provided that slaves over fifty years old could be emancipated for meritorious services which, incidentally, had to consist "in more than general performance of duty."[19]

Although the number of free Negroes continued to increase after the passage of the manumission law of 1830,[20] it can be said with reasonable certainty that some slaveholders declined to accept the conditions set forth in the law. The bond of $1,000 required for every slave to be emancipated was an obstacle of considerable magnitude. Often, too, either the master or the slave, or both, refused to accept the condition of emancipation that required almost immediate, and certainly permanent, removal from the state. Finally, the fact that slaves could not be emancipated for meritorious services until they were past fifty years of age worked such hardship on the prospective freedman that he might have reasonably refused freedom at his advanced age. Under such circumstances, it is safe to say that when manumission was desired on the part of the master, but where the obstacles were practically prohibitive, the master relaxed his control on the slave and allowed him to go virtually free.

It may be said, moreover, that the supreme court of North Carolina was always hostile to that part of the law of 1830 which permitted masters to free their slaves in their wills. In a case that came before the court in 1848, that body declared that the slave, George Washington, could not be emancipated by the will of his mistress.[21] Again in 1860, the court declared void that part of a will which sought to free the descendants of slaves that were kept within the state.[22] These opinions, adverse to the wishes of slaveholders desiring to free their slaves, had the effect of increasing the number of slaves virtually free.

Up to 1830, North Carolinians found little legal difficulty in setting their slaves free, if for economic or benevolent reasons they decided to do so. After the passage of the manumission law of that year, however, they found that the manumission of Negro slaves was not just a matter of going through perfunctory proceedings. The superior courts were not nearly as lax as the county courts had been, and not infrequently those tribunals saw fit to reject the applications of would-be emancipators and sent them scurrying off to some other tribunal for more liberal consideration. The records for the period after 1830 abound in requests by slaveholders that the state legislature pass special acts of emancipation. In the petitions, they often make it quite clear that the slaves were already virtually free, and they were only seeking legal approbation of a *fait accompli.*

In 1838 a most interesting case of a slave virtually free came to the attention of the North Carolina general assembly. The owners of the woman slave were a white couple seventy-eight years old, who had taken the slave when she was an infant and had reared her "as though she were their own flesh and blood, they being deprived of those common pledges of love and affection of parents, and . . . said adopted coloured child became as near and dear to your petitioners as if she was burned of their bodies." The county court of Wilkes had set the girl free several years earlier, and she had "married a white man by the name of Joshua Cook, who is of a respectable family and now has four children by the Said Cook. Since that time," the owners asserted, "doubts has arose in the minds of professional men that said court did not possess the power according to the laws now in force."[23] The owners, therefore, wanted the slave set free by the state legislature. The petitioners said that they could send the slave to a free state where she could retain her freedom, but they were old and infirm and had no other slaves who would pay the same attention as their adopted colored child. "She is obedient and affectionate and to sever the ties of parent and child is more than your petitioners could forego without great pain and affliction . . . and pray that your honorable body . . . pass a law to emancipate and set free their adopted child . . . and her four children."[24]

The foregoing petition was apparently convincing to the assembly, for after the Committee on Propositions and Grievances recommended the passage of a bill containing the necessary provisions, both the house and the senate passed it; and it became law on December 17, 1838.[25] There can be little doubt that in this instance, Caroline Cook, the slave in question, had been virtually free for many years before the passage of the bill of emancipation.

One practice that was fairly common among would-be emancipators was to give their slaves to their friends in their wills and stipulate that the slaves be held in nominal bondage only. In 1844 a slaveholder by the name of Query of Mecklenburg County conveyed to Richard Peoples a Negro woman and her child and $600 and later gave him twelve acres of land. When Query died intestate, it was brought out in the proceedings that he had transferred the slave and the property with the understanding that Peoples was not to free the slave, but to provide for her "protection, comfort and happiness." When the case came before the supreme court of the state, Mr. Chief Justice Ruffin took the point of view that that part of the will which dealt with the disposition of the slaves was contrary to the laws providing for emancipation. "There could scarcely be a plainer case of *quasi* emancipation, in violation and fraud of the law; for the family is only required to maintain themselves, and the authority to be exercised is that, not of owners, but of parents." He, therefore, declared that portion of the will invalid and granted relief to the plaintiffs.[26]

Another case involving a similar set of circumstances was one which came to the supreme court from Caswell County in 1854. In his last will, N. P. Thomas conveyed his slaves to Nathaniel J. Palmer and provided a suitable home for them. When it appeared that they could not receive the benefits of the will as long as they remained in the state, the slaves moved to Ohio. The supreme court, in a decision declaring the will void, said,

> It is against the public policy . . . to allow negroes to remain among us in a qualified state of slavery. [Chief Justice Ruffin took the point of view that slaves might return as soon as the litigation was concluded satisfactorily.] Slaves who have the care and protection of a master, have houses provided for them, and a fund set apart for their support and maintenance, so that they can have the control of their own time, and may work or not . . . necessarily become objects of envy to those who continue to look upon them as fellow slaves.[27]

The chief justice concluded by saying that no will that gave slaves such wide freedom could be valid.

Another practice of testators was to provide that their slaves be given opportunity to hire out their own time. When Jeremiah Dunlap died in 1856, his will provided that certain of his Negroes given to his nephew, John Ingram, be permitted to "enjoy the proceeds of their labor in all respects in as full and ample a manner as the laws of the State will permit, and that they may have a sufficient portion of my land in the Patterson tract for making their support." Here again, the supreme court ruled against the testator, stating that such a bequest was one for emancipation and therefore not in agreement with the laws of the state.[28]

Slaves were sometimes permitted to select their own masters. At times, these virtually free slaves carried an affidavit with them giving them such authority. In 1823 Sam Boney possessed such authority. His affidavit read,

> The bearer Sam Boney has leave to look for a purchaser his price is Three hundred and twenty-five dollars.
>
> Thomas Smith[29]

At other times, testators made such provisions in their wills. In 1852 a slaveholder said in his will,

> I desire that my two negroes, A. and S. shall continue to labor for the benefit of my estate for 3 years after my death, or pay the sum of seven hundred and fifty dollars. At the expiration of that time . . . I desire that they be permitted to select their masters; and do authorize and empower my executor to sell them . . . to such person or persons . . . at a nominal price . . . my intention being to have them kindly treated and properly taken care of, for the remainder of their lives.

The supreme court decided that this provision of the will was void and that "if the negroes chose to remain in the State, it would be the duty of the executor to sell them *as slaves.*"[30] Thus, even though several liberal North Carolinians sought to give their slaves virtual freedom, the highest tribunal of the state stood in their way at almost every turn.

One group that was continuously seeking to alleviate the conditions of slaves in antebellum North Carolina was the Society of Friends. In 1776 they began to improve the lot of the slaves when the yearly meeting appointed a committee to aid Friends in emancipating their slaves.[31] When the North Carolina Manumission Society was organized in 1816, Quakers of that state were among its most influential charter members.[32] Whenever they could, they would set their slaves free; but when legislation as well as public sentiment stood out against the emancipation of slaves, members of the Society of Friends began to work on the problem of how they could reconcile the law with the dictates of their innermost consciences.

The story of the activities of the Quakers in connection with the question of slavery is one of the most interesting of the antebellum period. Their troubles began in 1796 when the legislature passed a law making it unlawful for any religious society to purchase or hold real estate exceeding 2,000 acres or in value £200 per year. Upon the advice of a young attorney, William Gaston, that there was nothing in the act that could be construed as a prohibition of the acquisition of personal property, the Quakers began to acquire slaves and either to set them free or hold them in a state of quasi-freedom.[33]

As the Quakers began to buy up slaves and set them free, North Carolina slaveholders became alarmed at the rapid increase in the number of free Negroes and began to register their protests in various quarters. In several instances, the Quakers, fearing that the newly freed Negroes would be taken up or run out of the state, took them up themselves and either kept them or sold them to other Friends in order to prevent any trouble.[34]

Some North Carolinians began to protest the right of Quakers to hold slaves. They took the point of view that since the enslavement of human beings ran counter to the religious principles of the Society of Friends, the Quakers who held slaves were not doing so in good faith. When, in 1827, the Quaker Society of Contentnea acquired slaves from William Dickinson, the right of such acquisition was questioned in the courts of the state. When the case came before the supreme court, that body decided against the Society. The words of Mr. Chief Justice Taylor are most revealing and deserve extensive quotation:

When Quakers hold slaves, nothing but the name is wanting to render it at once a complete emancipation; the trustees are but nominally the owners and it is merely colorable to talk of future emancipation by law, for as none can be set free but for meritorious services the idea that a collection of them will perform such services . . . is quite chimerical.

The chief justice then laid down the general principle underlying his attitude toward the Society in question:

It is true that an individual may purchase a slave for gratitude, or affection and afford him such an indulgence as to preclude all notion of profit. The right of acquiring property and of disposing of it in any way consistently with law is one of the primary rights which every member of society enjoys. But when the law invests individuals or societies with a political character and personality entirely distinct from their natural capacity, it may also restrain them in the acquisition or uses of property. Our law allows the trustees to hold them for the benefit of the society, whereas in truth they hold them for the benefit of the slaves themselves, and only in the name of the society.

He left no doubt as to his own attitude toward the intentions of the Society and of the implications of such practices when he said,

Numerous collections of slaves, having nothing but the name, and working for their own benefit, in view and under the continual observance of others who are compelled to labor for their owners, would naturally excite in the latter discontent with their condition, encourage idleness and disobedience, and lead possibly in the course of human events to the most calamitous of all contests, a bellum servile.[35]

The decision of the court is valuable here, not only because it represents a struggle between two opposing points of view in the matter of the treatment of slaves, but also because of the impression which the court had of the attitude of the Quakers toward the institution. The chief justice, and obviously a majority of his colleagues, felt that slaves in the hands of Quakers were virtually free and that such a state of things would have a most deleterious effect upon the institution in general.

The decision of the court in 1827, far-reaching though it may have been in its effect on the program of the Society of Friends, did not altogether prevent the acquisition of slaves by Quakers. This delicate matter again came before the supreme court in 1833. Joshua White questioned the validity of a will that conveyed slaves to the trustees of a Quaker Society. The supreme court said that if by the will, the testator intended to confer on the slaves the right of free men, while they were nominally held in bondage, it was inoperative. But, Mr. Chief Justice Ruffin added, "when the Society has had the slaves for three years . . . the detinue [suit to recover them] cannot be successful, notwithstanding the society considers slavery as sinful and holds the slaves for the purpose of giving them advantages of freemen."[36] Thus, if no action was taken against the acquisition of slaves by a Quaker Society within a period of three years, the slaves were not recoverable and could go on living in the state of virtual freedom which the Quakers were wont to grant them.

One of the most famous cases involving the transfer of slaves of Quakers is that of *Newlin* v. *Freeman,* which was decided by the supreme court in 1841. Mrs. Sarah Freeman, a German-born citizen of North Carolina, acquired considerable real and personal property during the lifetime of her first husband. They decided, before his death, to emancipate their slaves; but the law of 1830 made manumission so difficult that she decided to seek some other way out. She therefore decided to leave them to "some steady old Quaker who would not have slaves." When her second husband, Richard Freeman, found that she had made such a disposition in her will, he entered a *caveat* to prevent her will from being executed. He took the position that she could not dispose of her real and personal property without his consent. In the lower court the jury held that the disposition of slaves and other personal property by Mrs. Freeman was lawful, but that she could not dispose of her real property without the consent of her husband. The supreme court upheld the decision. By this time, the liberal and sympathetic William Gaston, who had on several occasions acted as counsel for the Quakers, was sitting on the supreme court and wrote the decision. In part, he said, "We are of the opinion . . . that the law has been fairly expounded and correctly administered upon the trial."[37]

The acquisition of slaves by North Carolina Quakers went on with varying degrees of enthusiasm down to the end of the antebellum period. By 1814 more than 350 Negroes had been transferred to Quaker agents. In 1822 alone, 113 slaves were taken over by Quakers.[38] Although there are no figures for the period after 1830, the court litigations, the increased difficulty in manumitting slaves, and the continued persistence of Quakers in the effort to improve the lot of the Negro seem to confirm the point of view that the Society of Friends continued to hold some slaves. The activities of the Quakers in this connection were not inspired by any determination to circumvent the laws of the state or to nullify them. Instead, they acquired slaves for the express purpose either of setting them free or sending them to some land where they could obtain their freedom. Their continued cooperation with the North Carolina Manumission Society and the American Colonization Society demonstrates their interest in setting up a colony to which Negroes could be sent. Of course, they met growing obstacles, of an economic, political, and social nature, to the colonization plan; and toward the end of the period they found it practically impossible to carry out the program effectively.[39] Meanwhile, the Negroes who were under the care of the Quakers received the rudiments of education, enjoyed relaxed rules regarding their movements, and often hired out their own time. In other words, they enjoyed virtual freedom.

Another group which held slaves in what often amounted to a state of virtual freedom was the free Negroes themselves. Naturally, there are numerous cases on record of free Negroes who held slaves for economic gain.[40] There seems to be little doubt, however, that the majority of free Negroes held their slaves benevolently, and, therefore, granted them virtual freedom. There are many examples of free Negroes having purchased relatives or friends to ease their lot. Many of them manumitted such slaves.[41] When the laws against manumission were made more exacting and when the legislature declined to pass special acts granting emancipation, free Negroes experienced considerable difficulty in setting free their human chattel. Thus, Lila Abshur continued to hold title to her father when the legislature acted unfavorably on her petition to emancipate him.[42]

Free Negro husbands, wives, mothers, and fathers often purchased their loved ones and, in turn, sought to emancipate them. When they failed the number of slaves virtually free was thereby increased. In 1840 Phillis Dennis, a free Negro, presented petition to the legislature asking for the emancipation of her husband, whom she had purchased in 1834. She said that she was an invalid and had no relatives except slaves. She then said, "The petitioner represents . . . That her husband has always treated her with great affection and tenderness both in sickness and in health and as a return therefor and for the reason that she has no heir to inherit her property . . . she is induced to petition . . . for an act emancipating her said husband, the said Joseph Dennis." Accompanying the petition were various documents signed by citizens of Fayetteville asserting the good character of the woman and her slave husband and declaring him to be a "mechanic of consider able skill." Despite the plea of the petitioner and nearly fifty respectable citizens of Fayetteville, the house rejected a bill to emancipate Dennis on December 12, 1840, and it never reached the senate.[43] There can be little doubt that Dennis, although technically still in the bonds of slavery, enjoyed virtual freedom.

When Polydore Johnston, a free Negro, asked the legislature to emancipate his children, to whom he held title, a heated debate ensued; and by a vote of seventy-one to forty-one, the house refused to act favorably on the petition.[44]

The nature of the freedom which some slaves enjoyed deserves some discussion. Some enjoyed almost unrestricted movement. Others enjoyed the opportunity to establish their economic independence. Still others, through education afforded them by their masters, were able to throw off the shackles of ignorance which bound them in a world of intellectual darkness. Some enjoyed all these aspects of freedom and even more. Sam Morphis, the slave of James Newlin, a Quaker of Alamance County, is a good example of a person in bondage enjoying freedom of movement and freedom in work. Morphis was a hack driver in Chapel Hill and a waiter at the University of North Carolina. Although he lived with Newlin, the latter apparently had little to do with his movements or activities. In his various jobs about the campus, he ingratiated himself into the favor of the students and teachers, and earned a fair livelihood. His popularity was attested to by the fact that 309 students, the president of the university, and several members of the faculty sent petitions to the legislature asking that Newlin's request that he be given permission to emancipate Morphis be granted. When the legislature refused to comply with the request of Newlin, the small college town accepted once again the popular slave who enjoyed virtual freedom.[45]

Jerry, the slave of Honorable D. M. Barringer, prominent lawyer and diplomat, enjoyed considerable freedom before he was finally emancipated in 1854. Mr. Barringer took him to Europe, where he remained for fourteen years as a "universal favorite." He traveled with Mr. Barringer on his trips to Washington and the East and, although he enjoyed complete freedom of movement, conducted himself in a very creditable manner. On one occasion, when Jerry was strolling alone about New York, he stepped into a business house, where "some North Carolina brokers were shaving the paper money of their State." He took gold from his pocket and redeemed the paper at its full value, for the honor of his native state.[46] Freedom was no new thing to Jerry when the house of commons by a division of ninety-four to seventeen voted to emancipate him.[47]

By a law passed in the colonial period, slaves were forbidden to carry firearms. Exceptions were frequently made to this law, and in such cases, slaves were granted a privilege that was ordinarily reserved for free men. In 1808 the Craven County Court entered the following statement in its minutes: "Negro Jerry property of David Pearce is permitted to carry a gun on his master's plantation, the said David complying with the acts in such cases provided."[48] In the following year, the court records the fact that John C. Stanley, wealthy free Negro of New Bern, could permit one of his slaves to carry a gun "on the lands and plantations of said John C. Stanley."[49] While the carrying of a gun may not loom large as an evidence of freedom, it can hardly be disputed that it was a privilege ordinarily reserved for free men in the antebellum period.

Among certain individuals and groups, especially the Quakers, there was a considerable amount of sentiment in favor of giving the slaves the rudiments of an education. Very early in the history of North Carolina, the followers of George Fox became actively engaged in the education of the Negro. By 1731 some of the North Carolina slaves, under the tutelage of members of the Society of Friends, could read and write.[50] Thereafter, household servants were generally given the rudiments of an English education. In 1816 the North Carolina Quakers opened a school for Negroes which was to run two days a week for three months. "Men were to attend until they could read, write and cypher as far as the rule of three, and . . . females to read and write." In 1821 the slaveholders in the vicinity of New Garden were induced to allow slaves to attend Sunday School where they learned to spell, but when many nonparticipating slaveholders became alarmed over the possible consequences of such an undertaking, the practice was discontinued.[51] Although this undoubtedly checked the zeal with which North Carolina Quakers prosecuted their plans to raise the intellectual level among the slaves, it did not stop their activities altogether. Wm. Forster, a Quaker missionary from England, visited North Carolina in 1825, and made the following observation concerning his brethren:

> In the meeting for discipline, I endeavored to be faithful, and was favoured to feel some relief, especially in my concern to encourage Friends to greater diligence in educating the black children under their care, giving them an opportunity of hearing the Scriptures read, and bringing them

constantly to meetings. They have no less than 500 individuals of that description under the care of trustees appointed by the Yearly Meeting; to all intents and purposes in the eye of the law, they stand as slaveholders, but there seems no help for it; the existing laws of . . . North Carolina do not allow of indiscriminate manumission. . . . I am very sorry to say that very little attention appears to have been paid to their education; but I think Friends are beginning to feel the necessity of exerting themselves a little more in this great duty.[52]

Among the other sects interested in the education of Negro slaves in antebellum North Carolina, the Presbyterians figured prominently. Regarding their activities in this area, Dr. Woodson says, "Despite the fact that Southern Methodists and Presbyterians generally ceased to have much antislavery ardor, there continued still in the western slave states, and in the mountains of Virginia and North Carolina, a goodly number of these churchmen who suffered no diminution of interest in the enlightenment of Negroes."[53] As late as 1851, the committee on the state of the Presbyterian Church in North Carolina could make the following observation regarding the religious and educational life of Negroes under their care:

> We are encouraged by the good attendance and the means of grace gener-
> ally reported; by the fact that prayer-meetings are generally kept up in our
> congregations; that Sabbath schools and Bible classes are sustained in most
> of our churches . . . that increased attention is given to their instruction;
> that opposition . . . is maintained against intemperance, and against the
> causes tending to its prevelance [sic].[54]

Although sentiment against granting slaves more of the privileges of free men was fairly general in the decade immediately preceding the Civil War, it is notable that in 1855 a goodly number of the citizens of North Carolina submitted a petition to the general assembly asking for a revision of the slave code as it affected education and marriage. In part, they proposed, "That the laws which prohibit the instruction of slaves and free colored persons, by teaching them to read the Bible and other good books, be repealed." Turning to the matter of marriage, they said:

> 1. That it behooves us as Christian people to establish the institution of
> matrimony among our slaves, with all its legal obligations and guarantees
> as to its duration between the parties. 2. That under no circumstances
> should masters be permitted to disregard these natural and sacred ties of
> relationship among their slaves, or between slaves belonging to different
> Masters.

The memorialists admitted that they proposed "some radical changes in the law of slavery" but contended that these changes were demanded by "our common Christianity, by public morality, and by the common weal of the whole South."[55] Although this proposal did not find its way into the statutes of North Carolina, it indicates, as few documents do, the extent to which a number of North Carolinians were willing to go—in the hectic days of sectional controversy—in the direction of granting their slaves the privileges of free men.

If one would seek specific examples of slaves who enjoyed virtual freedom, they are not difficult to find. The records of North Carolina are literally filled with the accounts of slaves whose bondage was hardly more than nominal. Two examples, the lives of George Moses Horton and Julius Melbourn, have become classic in the history of antebellum North Carolina.

George Moses Horton was the slave of Jack Horton, a farmer of Chatham, who "treated him very kindly." He was generally engaged in working on his master's farm, cultivating crops of corn and wheat. Whenever Horton wished to do so, he was permitted to "hire his own time," paying his master fifty cents a day. On such occasions, he would go to Chapel Hill and write poetry and love letters for the students at the university. His charge was twenty-five and fifty cents per item, depending on the palpable ardor of the suitor. "His love letters were quite eloquent and often, it is said, not only touched but captured the fair hearts for which they pleaded." Some of his poems are well known, due to the publication of two volumes of verse, the first in 1829 and the second after the war.[56] It is believed, however, that the following poem—a good example of his literary efforts—has not been previously published:

"The Pleasures of a College Life"

With tears I leave these academic bowers
And cease to cull the scientific flowers,
With tears I hail the fair succeeding train
And take my exit with a breast of pain.
The "Fresh" may trace these wonders as they smile
The stream of sciences like the river Nile,
Reflection of mutual beauties as it flows
Which all the charms of "college life" disclose.
This sacred current as it runs refines
Whilst Byron sings and Shakespeare's "mirror shines."
First like a garden flower did I rise

When on the college bloom I cast my eyes.
I strove to emulate each smiling gem
Resolved to wear the classic Diadem,
But when the Freshman garden [illegible] was gone
Around me spread a vast extension lawn.
'Twas there the muse of college life begun
Beneath the rays of erudition's sun,
When study drew the mystic forms down
And like the lamp of nature with renown.
Then first—I heard the Epic thunder roll
And Homer's lightning darted through my soul.
Hard was the task to trace each devious line
Through Locke and Newton bid me soar and shine.
I sank beneath the heat of Franklin's blaze
And struck the notes of philosophic praise,
With timid thoughts I strove the best to stand
Reclining on a cultivated land
Which often spread beneath a college bower
And thus invoked the intellectual shower.
E'en that fond sin on whose stately crown
The smile of Courts and States shall shed renown,
Now far above the noise of country strife
I frown upon the gloom of rustick life.[57]

While the above lines, obviously written for a senior at the university, are hardly more than doggerel, they reveal a smattering of information that came either from rather extensive reading or more or less constant association with individuals who studied a wide variety of subjects. "The Pleasures of a College Life," like other poems of George Moses Horton, reflect the life of a person who enjoyed privileges altogether inconsistent with his slave status.

One of the most notable examples of a slave who enjoyed virtual freedom is that of Julius Melbourn, whose name is now almost unknown even to students of the period. Born a slave in 1790 on a plantation near Raleigh, he was bought, at five years of age, by a British naval official's wealthy widow who lived in Raleigh. Under Mrs. Melbourn, Julius was well provided for and received a good English education. She had an excellent library to which he had free access. When he was ten years old, he was sent to a "select school" near Raleigh, but on account of the African blood in his veins, he was not permitted to remain. Upon his return to the home of Mrs. Melbourn, Julius obtained instructions from a Methodist minister, who was a regular visitor in the Melbourn home. During his leisure time, of which he had a sufficient amount,

Julius studied in the Melbourn library and prepared his lessons for the minister's inspection. In this way, he secured an education comparable to that which Mrs. Melbourn's son was receiving at the "select school."[58]

When Mrs. Melbourn's only son was slain in a duel—said to have been fought concerning his mother's having reared a Negro as a gentleman—Julius was emancipated and made the sole heir to the estate of $20,000.[59] The progress that Melbourn made after freedom was due largely to the training he received and the privileges he enjoyed when he was still a slave. If the accounts of the flogging of slaves and of their numerous privations at the hands of their masters represent one extreme in the treatment of slaves, the life of Julius Melbourn, who enjoyed virtual freedom at the hands of his benevolent mistress, represents the other.

Opposition to the practice of granting virtual freedom to slaves was as incessant, if not as vehement, in North Carolina as it was in other states of the antebellum South. It is interesting to observe, here, that many examples of virtual freedom—or, at least, the semblance of it— may be inferred from the very opposition to the practice which arose. As early as 1785, the lawmakers of North Carolina evinced considerable concern over the conduct of slaves virtually free, and in an enactment of that year they revealed a number of facts that shed much light on this class of persons:

> And whereas there are many slaves in the said towns, who contrary to law have houses of their own, or are permitted to reside in the outhouses or kitchens of divers of the inhabitants, or in the houses of free negroes, mulattos, persons of mixed blood and others, and work and labour for themselves in several trades and occupations . . . Be it enacted . . . That no slaves shall be permitted to exercise any trade or occupation in the said towns [of Wilmington, Washington, Edenton and Fayetteville] without a certificate from the owner.[60]

At the beginning of the militant period of the slave controversy, the members of the North Carolina legislature were still showing some concern over the activities of slaves virtually free. Their concern, at this time, was doubtless occasioned by several requests from citizens that additional legislation further restricting their movements be enacted. The citizens of Sampson, Bladen, New Hanover, and Duplin counties asserted:

> That our own slaves are become almost uncontrolable. They go and come when and where they pleas, and if an Attempt is made to Correct them they

Immediately fly to the Woods and there Continue for months and years committing grievous depredations on our Cattle, hogs and Sheep, and many other things, and as patrols are of no use on Account of the danger they Subject themselves to and their Property. Not long Since three patrols two of which for executing their duty had their dwelling and other houses burnt down and the Other his fodder Stacks burnt.[61]

If these protestations were all based on facts, it is clear that some slaves, against the will of their masters, were actively engaged in the effort to obtain virtual freedom. The legislature took the advice of the petitioners and passed the following law:

And be it . . . enacted . . . That it shall not be lawful for any slaves to go at large as a freeman, exercising his or her own discretion in the employment of his or her time; nor shall it be lawful for any slave to keep house to him or herself as a free person, exercising the like discretion in the employment of his or her own time; and in case the owner of any slave shall consent or connive at the commission of such offense, he or she so offending shall be subject to indictment, and on conviction shall be fined in the discretion of the court. . . . *Provided* that nothing shall be construed to prevent any person permitting his or her slave or slaves to live or keep house upon his or her land for the purpose of attending to the business of his or her master or mistress.[62]

In the above enactment, even the exception made at the end of the law suggests that there were slaves in North Carolina—some with and some without their master's permission—who enjoyed virtual freedom.

One other example of protestation reveals the state of virtual freedom which some slaves enjoyed. In a letter to the editor of a Warrenton paper, Michael Collins said,

I wish through your paper to drop a few thoughts to the Citizens of Warrenton and its vicinity. . . . First we will take a view of the vilage on the Sabath day. . . . What do we behold, we see the streets lined with ox waggons and carts, loded with cotten, hay, fodder, cole, wood, etc. We also see negroes going from house to House along the streets with their basks of Ducks, Chickens, eggs, potatoes, peas, rice, and onions, and to my astonishment they seldom fail to sell all of those articles before they leave town, and that too whether they have a permit from their master or not. What is the most dreadful thing [is that] after disposing of their produce we see them assemble around and in front of houses in town where the bottles of rum, whiskey, and brandy is handed out to them, by the way of windows and back doors, perhaps to the amt. of the produce sold by them; what is the next appearance that presents itself the afternoon of the same day we behold the streets infested with drunken negroes stagering from side to side and they pay no respect to person.[63]

90

That such a condition could have existed at any time in antebellum North Carolina suggests a laxity in the enforcement of the slave code that, of itself, made for the rise of a group of slaves who were almost completely beyond the pale of regimentation.

Thus, it can be seen that within the framework of the peculiar institution, there were innumerable variations and exceptions to the code that was accepted as the very symbol, as well as the means of the enforcement, of a uniform system of regulating the lives of the slaves. The variations and exceptions were not infrequently made by the masters themselves, who, for reasons of benevolence or economic necessity, found it desirable to grant to their human chattel an amount of freedom inconsistent with their legal status. It was not out of the question, however, for the slave himself to force society to accept him as an individual who was entitled to enjoy a state of existence that amounted to virtual freedom.

Slavery and the
Martial South

When southern sectionalism emerged as a powerful force in the third decade of the nineteenth century, the aggressive belligerency of the people of the South became one of their outstanding attributes. In their relationships among themselves and with others, accusations, threats, and challenges were a part of the general conduct; while duels, fights, and other forms of violence became almost as common as the most ordinary pursuits of daily life. The atmosphere of the entire South seemed charged with a martial spirit; and pugnacity achieved a respectability, even among the upper classes, that doomed any moves toward gentility and mutual understanding. There were, perhaps, many factors that contributed to this martial spirit, and there were many aspects of life in the South that reflected its numerous manifestations. Among them were the conditions of frontier living, the Indian danger, the strong attachment of the people to military organizations, and the widespread preparedness movement in the two decades preceding the Civil War. Few of them, however, had the profound effect that slavery had both in shaping the martial tradition of the South and in illustrating the ways that the spirit of belligerency could manifest itself.

Slavery was not only a central feature in southern commercial agriculture; it was also a major factor in the development of those traits of southern character that produced a domineering spirit and a will to fight to defend its position. Thomas Jefferson recognized and deplored this condition as early as 1782. In his *Notes on Virginia* he observed that the whole relationship between master and slave was a "perpetual exercise of the most boisterous passions, the most unremitting despotism on the one part; and degrading submissions on the other." What

Originally published in the *Journal of Negro History*, Volume XXXVII (January, 1952). Reprinted by permission.

was even worse, Jefferson continued, the slave owner's child learns to imitate it. Seeing the parent storm, the child "catches the lineaments of wrath, puts on the same airs in the circle of smaller slaves, gives loose to the worst of passions, and thus nursed, educated, and daily exercised in tyranny, cannot but be stamped by it with odious peculiarities."[1]

These views were not confined to the period of the Enlightenment. Countless observers of a later day saw what Jefferson had seen, and were of the view that slavery had a most deleterious effect on the owners and their children. Captain Basil Hall reported in 1828 that even the slave owners themselves lamented the "evil influence" that slavery was having on the character of their children. It was a curious and instructive fact, he declared, that the slaves themselves delighted in "encouraging 'young master' or even 'young mistress' to play the tyrant over them!"[2] Tocqueville made some significant remarks regarding the effect of slavery on the character of the master. In part, he said:

> The citizen of the Southern states becomes a sort of domestic dictator from infancy; the first notion he acquires in life is, that he was born to command, and the first habit he contracts is that of ruling without resistance. His education tends, then, to give him the character of a haughty and hasty man,—irascible, violent, ardent in his desires, impatient of obstacles but easily discouraged if he cannot succeed in his first attempt.[3]

When James S. Buckingham visited Columbia, South Carolina, in 1839 he saw the same thing. White children of four to seven years of age played about the streets under the care of Negro boys and girls but little older than themselves, the mode, he thought, by which parents evaded the responsibility of looking after their children. "But the little whites soon learn their own superiority, and make great progress in the art of tormenting and abusing their black guardians; laying, thus, in their very first steps in life, the foundations of that irascible temper and ungovernable self-will, which characterize nearly all the white inhabitants of the Slave States."[4]

Fanny Kemble saw in slavery an even greater evil in this connection than Buckingham, if such were possible. She was greatly disturbed over what her oldest child's superior position was doing to the child. She saw with dismay how the little girl's "swarthy worshippers . . . sprang to obey her little gestures of command. She said something about a swing, and in less than five minutes head man Frank had erected it for her, and a dozen young slaves were ready to swing little 'missus'; think of learning to rule despotically your fellow-creatures before the first lesson of self-government has been well spelt over!" Miss Kemble said that the habit of command developed so early among southerners seemed to give them a certain self-possession and ease. This, she believed, was rather superficial, and upon closer observation the vices of the social system would become apparent. The "haughty, over-bearing irritability, effeminate indolence, reckless extravagancy, and a union of profligacy and cruelty" of the slaveholders were the "immediate result of their irresponsible power over their dependents." This became apparent upon intimate acquaintance with southern character, she asserted.[5]

That slavery tended to create a reign of tyranny in the South was no mere abolitionist prattle. It was the considered judgment of some responsible southerners, from the eighteenth to the twentieth centuries, that a powerful sociopolitical absolutism was a significant consequence of the institution of slavery. In the debate on the question of the importation of slaves, Colonel George Mason of Virginia told the Federal Convention in 1787 that slaves produced "a most pernicious effect on manners" and that every master was a "born petty tyrant."[6] The description of slavery by Ulrich B. Phillips was along a similar line. In part, Phillips said:

> The actual regime was one of government not by laws but by men. In fact each slave was under a paternalistic despotism, a despotism in the majority of cases benevolent but in some cases harsh and oppressive, a despotism resented and resisted by some . . . but borne with lightheartedness, submission and affection by a huge number of blacks.[7]

How much benevolence there was in the despotism, or whether there was any benevolence at all depended on the individual master and his relationship with his slave or slaves. What is important is that the system provided the despot with almost unlimited prerogatives and with ample opportunities for their extensive abuse. The owner had an unlimited amount of personal authority over his slaves as long as the slaves were guilty of no flagrant violations of the rights of other whites or of the feebly enforced laws of the state. For all practical purposes the master was the source of law on the plantation; and, in the infrequent instances when he resorted to the law of the state to invoke his right over his human property, its interpretation and enforcement were at his hands. If, then, the government of the plantation was not by laws, but by men, the stability of such an institution rested on the use of force, or the threat to use it. If owners felt that slavery could be sustained by force and violence against the slave or against the free men who challenged it, they had no qualms about resorting to force and violence.

The planter was forced to regard arms as a necessary adjunct to the machinery of control. The lash might be used generously or sparingly, depending on the temperament of the master and the tractability of the slave. There was always the possibility, moreover, of resorting to more deadly weapons. If the slave resisted the "mild" discipline of the lash or undertook to return blow for blow, how else could the master maintain his complete authority except through the use of, or the threat to use, the weapons whose possession was forever denied the slave?

Going about armed with knives and guns became the daily habit of many masters and overseers. And if the armed conquerors, in moments of anger, sometimes turned their weapons against each other, it was no more than was to be expected among an aggregation of armed men. The rule of tyranny by which they lived naturally fostered an independence and self-sufficiency—one is tempted to call it an individual sovereignty—that would, on occasion, burst out in all its fury in their quarrels with each other.

If the relationship between master and slave was that of a superior and a subordinate, a despot or tyrant and a powerless subject, or an armed victor and a vanquished foe, it can almost be described as a state of war. At least it is possible to recognize the martial spirit that pervaded the entire plantation atmosphere. The conduct of the master toward the slave was determined by rules and considerations not unlike those that characterized a military situation. Slaves enjoyed no well-defined body of rights; for their infractions there was summary punishment; and there was, of course, no appeal. As Richard Hildreth pointed out in a vigorous antislavery tract, the plantation might be viewed "as the seat of a little camp, which overawes and keeps in subjection the surrounding peasantry." The master was in a position to claim and exercise over his slaves all the rights that he, as a warrior, could exercise over a vanquished foe.[8] Hildreth's rather apt analogy found its counterpart in a statement by a New Orleans editor who declared that "every plantation is a small military establishment or ought to be."

Thus, the connection between slavery and the martial spirit was apparent and was almost universally recognized by friend and foe of southern civilization. If the observer were an implacable foe like Charles Sumner, he could see only the totally bad effects of the martial spirit growing out of slavery. To Sumner the result was criminal distortion of the values and notions regarding the fighting spirit. Thus in the South, the swagger of the bully was called chivalry; a swiftness to quarrel was regarded as courage; the bludgeon was adopted as a substitute for argument; and assassination was lifted to a fine art.[9] If the observer were an apologetic friend like the Mississippi planter H. S. Fulkerson, he could be proud of the fact that southerners had been bred under the influences of the institution of slavery, "which, with its admitted evil, was calculated to foster the martial spirit and give force of character."[10]

The slave was never so completely subjugated as to allay all fears that he would make a desperate, bloody attempt to destroy the institution to which he was bound. Fear and apprehension were relative matters in the antebellum South; but they were always present. If the slaves seemed satisfied and did not appear to be up to some deviltry, such as running away or revolting, the fears, while still present, were not easily discernible. But if there was even the slightest rumor of an uprising, the entire countryside was not only terrified, but the alarm was sounded. All whites—loyal Negroes, too—were expected to do their share to prevent death and destruction from stalking through the land and to restore the natural foe to his natural condition.

The kind of dread fear that prevailed even in periods of relative calm greatly impressed Frederick Law Olmsted during his visit to the lower Mississippi valley in 1856. At the place where he secured accommodations for the night, his roommate, a southern white, insisted on barricading the door of the rather small, windowless room. He explained that he would not feel safe if the door were left open. "'You don't know,' he said, 'there may be runaways around.' He then drew two small revolvers, hitherto concealed under his clothing, and began to examine the caps. He certainly was a nervous man," Olmsted concluded, "perhaps a mad man."[11]

Southern slaveholders could never be quite certain that they had established unquestioned control over their slaves. A moment's relaxation always raised new fears, like those of the night watchman who awoke with a start, wondering how long he had been asleep. The better judgment insisted on the strictest vigilance, with no relaxation. This policy was the only one consistent with the maintenance of the institution. As one southerner pointed out, a policy of carelessly widening the sphere of freedom for the slave "would have virtually destroyed the institution. The policy pursued by the slave states was consistent with the *fact of* slavery, and it was an inexorable necessity that the policy should be maintained."[12]

The responsibility for maintaining control rested, first of all, on the shoulders of the owner and his staff. Neither the laws of the state nor those imposed by the slaveholder himself were of any avail unless they were enforced by the plantation constabulary. The importance of the owner's role was indicated by Judge Thomas Ruffin of the North Carolina Supreme Court who said, "The power of the master must be absolute, to render the submission of the slave perfect."[13] The owner, his overseer—if he had one—and other subordinates were dedicated to the task of maintaining the kind of discipline that would preserve the institution. Such a policy called for action resembling a declaration of war on the slaves. An overseer told Olmsted that if a slave resisted a white man's chastisement, he should be killed. On one occasion, a slave whom he was about to whip struck him in the head with a hoe. The overseer "parried the blow with his whip, and drawing a pistol tried to shoot him, but the pistol missing fire he rushed in and knocked him down with the butt of it."[14] While deadly weapons might be used in disciplining slaves only in extreme cases or by singularly cruel masters and overseers, such instruments were, nevertheless, a part of the pattern of control which even the mildest owners did not entirely overlook.

Despite the fact that the plantation sought to be self-sufficient and succeeded in many respects, the maintenance of a stable institution of slavery was so important that owners early sought the cooperation of the entire community. This cooperation took the form of the patrol, which became an established institution in most areas of the South at an early date. There were many variations in the size and organization of the patrol. Rather typical was the South Carolina patrol that was established by law in 1690. The law set up patrol detachments of ten men under the captain of a militia company. All white men were eligible for patrol service. In 1819 all white males over eighteen were made liable for patrol duty, the nonslaveholders being excused from duty upon reaching the age of forty-five.[15]

The patrol was to ride its "beat at night for the purpose of apprehending any and all Negroes who were not in their proper places." Alabama empowered its patrols

to enter, in a peaceable manner, upon any plantation; to enter by force if necessary, all Negro cabins or quarters, kitchens and out-houses, and to apprehend all slaves who may there be found, not belonging to the plantation or household, without a pass from their owner or overseer; or strolling from place to place, without authority.[16]

There were variations in the disposition of offenders taken up by patrols. If the violators were free Negroes or runaways, they were to be taken before a justice of the peace. If they were slaves, temporarily away from their master's plantation, they were to be summarily punished by a whipping, not to exceed thirty-nine lashes.[17]

The patrol system was essentially a military agency, and it tended to strengthen the position of the military in the southern community. In most instances there was a substantial connection between the patrol and the militia, either through control of one by the other or through identity of personnel. In South Carolina, for example, the patrol system was early merged into the militia organization, "making it a part of the military system, and devolving upon the military authority its arrangement and maintenance."[18] In Mississippi the structure of the patrol was but an "adaptation of the militia to the control of slaves."[19] Under such circumstances the patrol system appeared to be an arm of the military.

Nor was the military support of slavery confined to plantations. In the towns and cities, where slaves frequently enjoyed a measure of freedom seldom conceded to persons of that status in rural areas, there was considerable military protection of the whites from the possible dangers inherent in such an arrangement. When Captain Basil Hall visited Richmond in 1828, he thought that the sentinel marching in front of the capitol building was part of an honor guard for the legislature. His guide corrected this impression by pointing out that the soldier was part of a guard to keep order among the Negroes.

> "It is necessary," he continued, "or at all events it is customary in these states to have a small guard always under arms; there are only fifty men here. It is in consequence of the nature of our coloured population; but it is done more as a preventive check than anything else—it keeps all thoughts of insurrection out of the heads of the slaves, and so gives confidence to those persons amongst us who may be timorous."[20]

The sight of this guard at the capitol "had almost the startling effect of an apparition" on William Chambers when he visited Richmond in 1853. It was the first time that he had seen a bayonet in the United States, and it "suggested the unpleasant reflection, that the large infusion of slaves in the composition of society was not unattended with danger."[21]

Charleston likewise felt the need for special guards to keep order among the slaves. In 1839 the city constructed a guard house for the military on the important corner of Meeting and Broad streets. Strategically located across from the city hall, the court house, and St. Michael's Church, it housed soldiers whose "chief duty was to watch and crush any attempt at insurrection by the slaves!"[22] When Benwell, the English traveler, visited the city several years later, he arrived during an Independence Day celebration. His first impression was that "a sense of happiness and security reigned in the assembled multitude." But he found this to be "a notion quite fallacious" upon observing troops stationed at the guard house and sentinels pacing in front of the building, "as if in preparation or in expectation of a foe." Each evening at nine o'clock the roll of drums at the guard house announced the departure of the patrol, armed with muskets and bayonets, to make its rounds through the Negro quarters.[23]

As early as 1787 a militia company patrolled the streets of Savannah. The group, composed of a commanding officer, a sergeant, a corporal, and fifteen privates, was under orders to mount guard each evening at eight o'clock at the court house and patrol the outskirts of the town. During the spring months they were to patrol throughout the night. The guard was instructed to be particularly careful not to offend persons walking the streets in a peaceable manner, "but to challenge with Decency."[24] Seventy years later, with the state of Mississippi well populated, Natchez was facing her problem of law and order among the slaves in much the same way that Savannah had done. The citizens of that growing town were pleased that the Christmas holidays of 1856 had passed off without incident. They were quick to credit the proper persons for this good fortune: the "careful and prescient mayor who had taken the precaution to double the night guard" and "the voluntary military companies" which had been unusually on the alert to see that there was no disorder among the slaves.[25]

The South's greatest nightmare was the fear of slave uprisings; and one of the most vigorous agitations of her martial spirit was in evidence whenever this fear was activated by even the slightest rumor of revolt. Fear easily and frequently mounted to an uncontrollable alarm in which the conduct of some citizens could hardly be described as sober or responsible. "We regard our Negroes as 'JACOBINS' of the country," Edwin C. Holland of Charleston declared in 1822. The whites should always be on their guard against them, and although there was no reason to fear any permanent effects from insurrectionary activities, they "should be watched with an eye of steady and unremitted observation. . . . Let it never be forgotten, that our Negroes are freely the JACOBINS of the country; that they are the ANARCHISTS and the DOMESTIC ENEMY; the COMMON ENEMY OF CIVILIZED SOCIETY, and the BARBARIANS WHO WOULD, IF THEY COULD BECOME THE DESTROYERS OF OUR RACE."[26]

The farmer who told Olmsted of how the fear of revolts completely terrified some Alabama whites suggests either the extent of fear or the impact of fear upon the mind. The farmer said that when he was a boy "folks was dreadful frightened about the niggers. I remember they built pens in the woods," he continued, "where they could hide, and Christmas time they went and got into the pens, 'fraid the niggers was risin'. . . . I remember the same thing when we was in South Carolina . . . we had all our things put in bags, so we could tote 'em, if we heerd they was comin' our way."[27] This does not seem to have been the usual reaction of whites to threats of slave insurrections. To be sure, such grave eventualities threw them into a veritable paroxysm of fear, but they moved swiftly and with determination to put up a joint defense against the common foe. Committees of safety would spring into existence with little prior notice, and all available military resources would be mobilized for immediate action. These were not the times to entrust the lives of the citizens to the ordinary protective agencies of government. If a community or a state had any effective military force, this was the time for its deployment. Military patrols and guards were alerted, and volunteer troops and regular militia were called into service. It was a tense martial air that these groups created. For all practical purposes, moreover, even the civil law of the community tended to break down in the face of the emergency, while something akin to martial law, with its arbitrary searches and seizures and its summary trials and executions, prevailed until the danger had passed.

When Gabriel attempted to revolt in Richmond in 1800 the Light Infantry Blues were called into immediate service, the Public Guard was organized and drilled to help avert the calamity, and Governor Monroe instructed every militia commander in the state to be ready to answer the call to duty.[28] In 1822, when Charleston was thrown into a panic by rumors of Vesey's plot, all kinds of military groups were called into service. A person unfamiliar with the problem might well have thought that such extensive mobilization was for the purpose of meeting some powerful foreign foe. The Neck Rangers, the Charleston Riflemen, the Light Infantry, and the Corps of Hussars were only some of the established military organizations called up. A special city guard of one hundred and fifty men was provided for Charleston. The cry for reinforcement by federal troops was answered before the danger had completely subsided.[29]

The attempted revolt of Nat Turner in 1831 brought military assistance to Southampton County, Virginia, not only from the governor of the state, but from neighboring North Carolina counties, and from the federal government.[30] Indeed, more troops reached Southampton County than were needed or could be accommodated.[31] With artillery companies and a field piece from Fort Monroe, detachments of men from the warships *Warren* and *Natchez*, and hundreds of volunteers and militiamen converging on the place, there was every suggestion of an impending battle on a rather large scale.[32]

There was a strong show of military force not only when the large-scale plots like those of Gabriel, Vessey, and Turner were uncovered, but also whenever there was any suggestion or intimation of insurrection, however slight. The rumor of revolt in Louisiana in January, 1811, caused Governor Claiborne to call out the militia. A contingent of four hundred militiamen and sixty federal troops left Baton Rouge for the reported scene of action.[33] Two years later the Virginia militia was ordered out to quell a suspected revolt in Lancaster.[34] In 1816 the South Carolina militia took summary action against a group of Negroes suspected of subversive activities.[35] The militia of Onslow County, North Carolina, was so tense during a "Negro hunt" in 1821 that its two detachments mistook each other for the Negro incendiaries and their exchange of fire caused considerable damage.[36] Alabama pressed its militia into service in 1841 to search for slave outlaws and to put down rumored uprisings.[37]

Few antebellum years were completely free of the rumors of slave revolts; and, consequently, there were few years when the South was free of at least some mobilization of its military strength. Agitation for stronger defenses against slave depredations was almost constant, with some leaders advocating a state of continuous preparation for the dreaded day of insurrection. Governor Robert Hayne of South Carolina told the legislature, "A state of military preparation must always be with us, a state of perfect domestic security. A period of profound peace and consequent apathy may expose us to the danger of domestic insurrection."[38] The editor of a New Orleans daily called for armed vigilance, adding that "the times are at least urgent for the exercise of the most watchful vigilance over the conduct of slaves and free colored persons."[39]

Slavery strengthened the military tradition in the South not only because owners found it desirable and, at times, necessary to build up a fighting force to keep the slaves under control, but also because they felt compelled to oppose outside attacks with a militant rationale of the institution. As the abolitionists began to attack slavery, the leaders of the South evolved a defense of slavery that was as full of fight as a state militia called out to quell a slave uprising. They began to restate the theory of social organization that prevailed in the South, and out of it came a racism that could find congenial reception only in an emotion-charged, militant, unreasoning atmosphere. They vigorously rejected the principles of liberty and equality, and one of them, Thomas Cooper, said that talk about the rights of man was a "great deal of nonsense. . . . We say that man is born free, and equal to every other man. Nothing can be more untrue: no human being ever was, now is, or ever will be born free."[40] They also rejected political democracy. "An unmixed democracy," said one Mississippian, "is capricious and unstable, and unless arrested by the hand of despotism, leads to anarchy . . . as much of the aristocracy of England as would have been retained in America would have leavened the mass and purified the whole."[41]

The South's society, as described by its proponents, was to rest on the inequality of men in law and economics. Slavery was a positive good. South Carolina's James H. Hammond said that slavery was "the greatest of all blessings which a kind providence has bestowed upon the South."[42] It gave to the white man the only basis on which he could do something for a group of hopelessly inferior human beings. The view of the inferiority of the Negro was organized into a body of systematic thought by the scientists and social scientists of the South and out of it emerged a doctrine of racial superiority that justified any kind of control that the owner established and maintained over the slave. The racial basis of slavery gave southern leaders an effective means of solidifying the economically divergent elements among the whites. At the same time, it strengthened the ardor with which most white southerners were willing to fight to preserve slavery. The sharp cleavage between slavery and freedom was made even sharper by the factor of race. All slaves belonged to a degraded, "inferior" race; and, by the same token, all whites, however wretched some of them might be, were superior. In a society where race was so important, the whites at the lowest rung could satisfy themselves because they could identify themselves with the most privileged of the community. "Color alone is here the badge of distinction, the true mark of aristocracy," said Thomas Dew, "and all who are white are equal in spite of the variety of occupation."[43]

White southerners were, thus, among the first people of the world to develop a militant race superiority. As in other parts of the world where such a notion evolved, these frontier aristocrats sought support for their position by developing a common bond with the less privileged. The obvious basis was race, and outside the white race there was to be found no favor from God, no honor or respect from man. By the time that Europeans were reading Gobineau's *Inequality of Human Races* southerners were reading Cartwright's *Slavery in the Light of Ethnology.* In admitting all whites of the South into the pseudonobility of race, Cartwright won their enthusiastic support in the struggle to preserve the integrity and honor of *the* race. This was a concept of social organization worth fighting for, and the white people of the South entered upon the grim task of exterminating persons and ideas hostile to their way of life.

This state of affairs and the anxiety accompanying it transformed the South into an armed camp. One seeking military activity did not have to wait for war with Britain or Mexico. He could find it in the regular campaign against the subversion of slavery. He could go with General Youngblood to annihilate a group of suspected slaves in South Carolina, or with Brigadier General Wade Hampton in the march from Baton Rouge to an infected plantation in St. John the Baptist Parish. The citadels, sentries, "grape-shotted cannon," and alerted minute men became familiar and integral parts of the southern scene and came to be regarded by many as indispensable for the preservation of the "cornerstone" of southern civilization. It would seem, then, that the South's first Armageddon was with her own slaves.

The Southern Expansionists
of 1846

The decade of the 1840s witnessed a remarkable growth in expansionist sentiment in the United States.[1] For years restless Americans, their voracious appetite for land whetted by the acquisition of Louisiana, had hoped to extend their territorial possessions in many directions. But their efforts had fallen far short of the mark. They got nothing from the second war with England; the annexation of Florida was certainly not satisfying; and the long struggle to remove the Seminoles was humiliating to say the least. The numerous efforts to acquire Texas had ended in failure, while the hope of securing Canada and California had become little more than an idle dream. Prospects suddenly became brighter in the early 1840s. Texas gave clear indications that she preferred annexation to independence or to some subordinate arrangement with a European power. California and, perhaps, other parts of Mexico now seemed within reach. And if Canada could not be taken in one stroke, at least all of Oregon might be wrested from Britain upon the termination of the treaty of joint occupation.

The motivations for expansion had increased in number and complexity with the passing years. Among the principal ones was the desire to push Britain out of the Northwest and generally to frustrate the machinations of European powers. There was widespread fear of British designs in the New World; and an English foothold in Oregon could, in all probability, jeopardize American settlements there.[2] There was, moreover, the steady deterioration of the relations of the United States with Mexico. For years they had been unsatisfactory, and the entrance of the Republic of Texas into the picture merely aggravated the situation at a time when many southerners were casting

Originally published in *Journal of Southern History*, Volume XXV (August, 1959). Copyright © 1959 by the Southern Historical Association. Reprinted by permission of the Managing Editor.

covetous eyes on the new republic and other territories still under the Mexican flag.[3] Then, too, there were the vague dreams of an empire of continental proportions, made more attractive by the desire to extend Protestant Christianity and Anglo-Saxon institutions and to enlarge the area of American commercial and industrial domination. To these must be added the feverish race between the slave states and free states to bring in new territories that would strengthen their respective positions. These were the major considerations that created an urgency regarding expansion in the middle forties.

Beneath the movement and giving it emotional and intellectual content was the agitation for expansion that came from many quarters, including the South. The expansionist views of many southerners were represented by Richard Hawes, the Kentucky Whig, who told Calhoun in 1844 that it should be the policy of this country to own "all the cotton lands of North America if we can."[4] In the House of Representatives an Alabama Democrat, James Belser, asserted that it was impossible to limit the area of freedom, "the area of the Anglo-Saxon race." In the Senate William Merrick of Maryland declared that the question of the annexation of Texas was "a subject which concerned the fate of empires, and which was to effect, for weal or for wo, through ages yet to come, millions of the Anglo-Saxon race."[5] While visiting California in 1845 a Calhoun correspondent said, "We only want the Flag of the United States and a good lot of Yankees, and you would soon see the immense natural riches of the Country developed and her commerce in a flourishing condition. To see that Flag planted here would be most Acceptable to the Sons of Uncle Sam, and by no means repugnant to the native population."[6] The editor of the Richmond *Enquirer* rejoiced that the Whig *American Review* had come out boldly for California in 1846. He had no fear of extending the area of freedom, he asserted, for he was satisfied that "a federative system of free republics like our own, is capable of almost indefinite expansion, without disadvantage."[7]

The extent of the expansionist fever in 1846 can be seen in the resolution of Senator David Yulee of Florida proposing that the president open negotiations with Spain with a view to purchasing Cuba.[8] In the first weeks of the Mexican War a Charleston friend described to Calhoun a fantastic scheme launched by southerners for the acquisition of all Mexico. Some years earlier, he said, an undisclosed number of southerners had taken an oath to enlist in the conquest of Mexico. Each person was to do everything possible to bring into the cause every man who would make a good soldier, to hold himself in readiness, and to report to any place he was summoned for the purpose of carrying out the scheme.[9] Meanwhile, the sentiment for acquiring Oregon up to 54° 40' had gained currency during the first year of Polk's administration. Views supporting the occupation of Oregon ranged from the lusty expansionist aims of the venerable John Quincy Adams to the noisy demands of young Andrew Johnson.[10]

There was, however, no unanimity regarding either the area into which the United States should expand or whether it should expand at all. Even in the South for instance, there was some sentiment against expansion. Meredith Gentry of Tennessee told the House of Representatives that he saw no reason for contaminating American institutions by expanding into new areas. "If England were to propose to cede Canada to this Government to-morrow in my humble judgment, it would be unwise to accept the cession," and if Mexico asked to be annexed, she, too, should be rebuffed.[11] Men like Alexander Stephens and John Calhoun had such grave doubts about the validity of the American title to Oregon that they felt it would be extremely rash to press any claims above 49°. Meanwhile, they frowned on any involvement with Mexico, even though victory there would surely lead to the acquisition of new territory.[12]

On the question of expansion, party considerations loomed important in 1846. The Democrats had won the presidential election of 1844, and even if "Fifty-four Forty or Fight" was not their slogan, expansionist sentiment within the party was strong.[13] But conservative southern members of the party, gratified over the annexation of Texas, were not as enthusiastic about "reannexing" Oregon as they might have been, and their northern colleagues chided them for it. This led Jefferson Davis, among other southerners, to speak for the section. He defended the South's desire to get Texas by declaring that this was in the national interest. While he did not want to do anything to precipitate a war with Britain, he wished to preserve the whole of Oregon for the United States.[14] As the Democrats argued among themselves about whether to demand all of Oregon, southern Whigs showed little enthusiasm for the project.[15] Many northern Whigs, with their growing antislavery radicalism, hoped that Oregon would be acquired to offset the mounting strength of the slave power.[16]

The lukewarm-to-indifferent attitude of many southerners toward Oregon in 1846 was enough to raise suspicions regarding their lack of interest in territories into which slavery could not expand. On December 18, 1845, Ohio's William Allen, chairman of the Senate Committee on Foreign Relations, introduced a resolution authorizing the president to give formal notice to England of the termination of the joint occupation of Oregon. This was the first of a number of resolutions, of varying degrees of bellicosity, hinting that if England did not withdraw from Oregon she would be driven out. Some expansionists were indeed rash in their statements and resolutions. And it is not surprising that resolutions for the occupation of Oregon were enthusiastically supported by the antislavery leaders in Congress.

Southern leaders in Congress who had little or no enthusiasm for Oregon were much too astute to oppose it on the obvious ground that eventually Oregon would enter the Union as one or several free states. These men, to whom a duel was commonplace, who had fought Indians incessantly and bitterly, some of whom had agitated for war against England in 1812, suddenly became the leading peacemakers of the country. In his notable speech of March 16 against giving notice unless it proposed negotiation and compromise, Calhoun rather feebly asserted that he was for Oregon. He hastened to add, however, that because the time was improper to insist on all of it, he favored compromise to avert war. He painted a vivid picture of the terrible destruction that war would bring. He spoke of the great mission of the people of the United States to occupy the entire continent and asserted that war would impede this high mission. He insisted that he wanted Oregon as much as Texas, but the latter was being secured without endangering peace. The only possible way to obtain Oregon was through patient negotiation, which an "all or none" attitude would make impossible.[17]

Calhoun received generous support in his position from southerners on both sides of the aisle. Alexander Barrow, the Whig senator from Louisiana, said he was certain war would result if the United States adopted an uncompromising position on Oregon. He was equally certain that public sentiment was not prepared for war with England. He hoped that the government would not be ashamed to do what the people demanded, and would enter into negotiations leading to an amicable settlement.[18] Whig Senator William Archer of Virginia asserted that he did not believe that the United States had a clear title to 54° 40', but he thought it would be unstatesmanlike and undiplomatic to be intransigent. Other southerners followed Calhoun's lead, including men of great prestige like George McDuffie of South Carolina, Joseph Chalmers of Mississippi, and John Berrien of Georgia.[19]

Some of the leading Democratic and Whig organs of the South were as opposed to a firm stand for all of Oregon as were Calhoun and his supporters. Even in Polk's own state there was considerable opposition to an uncompromising position on Oregon. The Memphis *Enquirer* was highly critical of Senator Allen for introducing the resolution to give notice and expressed the fear that the administration policy might lead to war.[20] In January, 1846, the Nashville *Republican Banner*, a Whig newspaper, warned the administration to be cautious about Oregon. It denounced John Quincy Adams and the others who insisted on 54° 40' and praised Calhoun for his moderation. Later in the year the paper expressed the fear that the pressure to acquire Oregon was largely an abolitionist plot, since Adams, Joshua Giddings, and other abolitionist congressmen were so anxious for the territory.[21] In Charleston the *Mercury* asserted that "never was there a greater mistake than to suppose that the feeling of the nation is in favor of a war for Oregon, so long as our national honor is not involved." After most of the speeches for and against notice had been made in Congress the *Mercury* insisted that the 54° 40' pretension was the result of "shallow ignorance. . . . Our just *claims* are limited by the latitude of 49; and with such a basis for adjustment, there can be neither war nor cause of war. Substantially we must have it; and we will have it."[22]

A partially neglected consideration that influenced some southern opposition to drastic action in Oregon was the South's interest in a relaxed trade and antislavery policy for England. As early as 1841 Duff Green went to England to promote a policy of free trade, arguing that the American West's interest in Oregon would cool if England would be willing to negotiate a treaty for the admission of American grain. If England dropped her campaign against slavery *and* repealed her Corn Laws, the West would be more kindly disposed to England; and the South, which purchased a good deal of Western produce, would benefit from lower grain prices as well as from a softer British antislavery policy.[23] In his endeavors Green undoubtedly spoke for Calhoun, McDuffie, and other southerners who supported a compromise with England on the Oregon question.

Still, despite the great prestige and the eloquent arguments for peace of men like Calhoun and papers like the *Mercury*, they did not speak for the entire South. Even while Senator Chalmers was declaring that the people of Mississippi favored conciliation and compromise up to 49°, the legislators of his state were adopting a resolution supporting the claim of the United States up to 54° 40' and praising the president's stand, which was "marked up by a spirit of liberal concession, firmness, patriotism, and signal ability."[24] Nor did the equivocal position of Senators Berrien and Colquitt of Georgia represent the views of all their constituents. After Polk declared that the title of the United States to Oregon was "clear and unquestionable," one of Howell Cobb's friends wrote him that the message had stimulated the mountain folk around Clarksville, Georgia, to thought and discussion. "Every one understands, or thinks he understands, all about the Oregon question," he said. "I heard a crowd on Christmas, not one of whom knew on which side of the Rocky Mountains Oregon was, swear they would support and fight for Polk *all over the world*, that he was right, and we would have Oregon and thrash the British into the bargain."[25] Southerners like these, inured to the hard life, quick to defend themselves, and ever willing to fight any nation large or small, would have rejected the olive branch that was being proffered so generously by their more conservative representatives in the Congress.

Southerners who favored unqualified expansion were not mere voices crying in the mountains and desolate countrysides of their section. They had an impressive group of able young men as their spokesmen in Congress—largely in the House. There were about twenty men in Congress who represented what may be termed the hard core of southern expansionism. They came from every state of the South with the exception of South Carolina, where the Calhoun intransigence seemed pervasive. Twelve were serving their first terms in the Congress in 1846, and four had been elected for the second time. Thus only four can be regarded as veteran congressmen. Most of them were under forty years of age. The elder statesman of the group was Seaborn Jones, a fifty-eight-year-old lawyer from Columbus, Georgia. The other member beyond the half-century mark was Sam Houston, who at fifty-three had just taken his seat as one of the first senators from Texas.

These southern spokesmen for expansion seemed bound by neither the conservative traditions of Congress nor the vested interests of the section from which they came. Largely small-town lawyers and farmers, their only loyalties seemed to be to party and country. All of them except Henry Hilliard of Alabama were Democrats who took much more seriously than some of the older members the avowed expansionist commitments of the party. These older members irritated some of the "true" expansionists in the party like Howell Cobb, who went so far as to say that the southerners who did not stand upon the great question of Oregon "as *some of us* did" were responsible for "alienating the good feelings of many of our northern and western democrats and thereby rendering the harmonious and united action of the party more difficult than it would have been."[26] No voices in the country spoke out more clearly or vigorously in behalf of the fulfillment of the American dream of empire than these young "War Hawks" of 1846.

The southern expansionists thought that President Polk's description of the American title to Oregon as "clear and unquestionable" was modest and conciliatory. They spoke with great familiarity of the American claims, based on discovery, exploration, and settlement; and none of them entertained the slightest doubt as to the validity of the American title. "Oregon is *ours*," thirty-four-year-old Representative Henry Bedinger of Virginia cried. "Every acre, every poor rood of it— and we must and *will* have it. . . . This great territory is of such immense value and importance to this Union, that we would deserve to be regarded as idiots by the civilized world, if we should suffer any portion of it to be wrested from us by any power upon earth."[27]

Lucien Chase of Clarksville, Tennessee, twenty-nine years old and serving his first term in the House, asserted that the United States had the "sole and indisputable right from 42° to 54° 40'." It would be humiliating as well as dangerous, he said, for the country to surrender any portion of it.[28] The young Greeneville, Tennessee, tailor, Andrew Johnson, said that he was for the whole of Oregon up to 54° 40' "and for enough on the other side to *deaden the timber* on beyond, that we may know where the line is."[29]

Several of the southern expansionists insisted that the people of the country would not tolerate any concession on a matter so clear and unmistakable as America's claim to Oregon. Edmund Dargan from Mobile said that the people had been taught to believe "that the whole of Oregon is ours." The people of Alabama, he declared, took the position that all of Oregon belonged to the United States, and they were determined to maintain their rights by not yielding one inch. Senator Ambrose Sevier of Arkansas also doubted that the people would accept a compromise short of 54° 40'. "They were words that had sunk deep into the hearts of the people, and before the summer was over, they would become so deeply impressed as not to be erased." They would, therefore, go to any lengths to save Oregon. Jacob Thompson, the former schoolmaster from Pontotoc, Mississippi, asserted that the claim of the United States was better than Britain's and that the people of this country were demanding action. It was idle for members of the Congress to say they were for Oregon "and yet do nothing towards asserting our rights."[30]

The sentiments of "Manifest Destiny" uttered by these southern expansionists were as strong as those of any expansionists of any period in the nation's history. The southerners deftly coupled the historic mission of the nation with the immense economic and military importance of the territory they sought, thus appealing to the realists as well as the idealists. It was Robert M. T. Hunter, one of the few veteran congressmen among the southern expansionists, who was sufficiently practical and astute to develop this argument. "There is no man with an American heart in his bosom," he declared, "who could be insensible to the prospect of planting our flag and our settlements upon the shores of the Pacific. There is no such bosom which would not swell . . . at the prospect of the influence, commercial, political, and military, which we should derive from a position on the shores of Oregon and California." The possession of Oregon would place the Union in a position of "impregnable strength and stable greatness, with one arm on the Atlantic sea and the other on the Pacific shore, ready to strike in either direction with a rapidity and an efficiency not to be rivalled by any nation on the earth."[31] Henry Hilliard predicted that after the nation had established her exclusive rights in Oregon, a profitable trade with China and numerous other benefits would accrue from such an acquisition; "then would be fulfilled that vision which had wrapt and filled the mind of Nunez as he gazed over the placid waves of the Pacific."[32]

Some southern expansionists apparently thought it unnecessary to emphasize the great value of Oregon but merely to declare that it was the destiny of the United States to rule all of North America. Representative Seaborn Jones declared that the flag of the United States must "ultimately float everywhere over this continent." In the same vein Henry Bedinger said that he hoped that "the 'American eagle' would take its onward flight, unresisted and unopposed, to the rich regions of Oregon." Henry S. Clarke of Washington, North Carolina, regarded Oregon as "our own soil, our own patrimony," and thought that it would be wonderful to see the American flag float over the mountains of Oregon, for "mountainous countries are the nurseries of freemen."[33]

Insinuations by northerners that the people of the South were not really interested in acquiring Oregon deeply wounded the feelings of the southern expansionists. Although they came from a section whose animosity toward the North was mounting steadily, they spoke for expansion as nationalists, not sectionalists. The northern jibes were directed at the southern pacificators, of course, but the expansionists also took offense and were quick to defend their constituency. To those northerners who said that the South did not want to risk war with England because of its disastrous consequences for the South, Jacob Thompson of Mississippi admitted that there was no section that would feel more heavily the weight of war.

> Yet this indiscriminate assault upon the South was unworthy of the gentlemen; this assumption that it was a sectional question—that it was a northern question—was ridiculous and absurd. . . . Gentlemen should remember that there may be differences of opinion between individuals from different sections of the Union; but, as regards the South, they have never been actuated by any such narrow and contracted considerations.[34]

This was, of course, an overstatement of the case. Likewise, Henry Bedinger objected to the gratuitous insults of the northerners and assured them that southern honor and southern integrity would stand by them in the hour of need. Howell Cobb could never regard Oregon as a sectional question and looked forward to the day when "not a British flag floats on an American breeze; that not a British subject treads on American soil."[35]

Regarding the prospect of war with Britain over Oregon, the southern expansionists thought it peculiarly unbecoming for some of their southern colleagues to assume the role of peacemakers when national honor and integrity were involved. Young James C. Dobbin of Fayetteville, North Carolina, refused to be frightened by the assertion that the resolution to terminate joint occupation was a war measure.

"This incessant alarm-shout of war, war, war, shall not deter me from voting to give this notice, when I entertain the sincere conviction that national honor demands it . . . good policy demands it . . . justice to our adventurous pioneers in Oregon demands it." He did not expect war, but if it did come, "our best fortifications will be found in the noble hearts of our patriotic countrymen; our best preparation, to let the people understand their rights."[36]

Andrew Johnson said that he was not afraid of the British lion.

> Let him but growl, let him assume a menacing attitude, and on some lofty peak in Oregon . . . the armor-bearer of Jupiter will be found. . . . The British lion will be descried in the distance, if he shall dare approach, and if he shall moor to our shore, he will descend from his elevated position, and . . . strike terror to his heart, and cause him . . . to retreat, with the

reeking blood dripping from his mane, from a soil that he has dared to pollute by his impious tread.[37]

The southern expansionists tried to convince their opponents that the best way to avoid war was to take a firm stand against Britain.[38] Seaborn Jones insisted that England would not dare go to war to defend Oregon. If she did, Ireland would rebel, Canada would strike for her liberty, and British commerce would be ruined. If British leaders were shortsighted enough to start a war, the United States would be victorious. Archibald Yell of Arkansas could not see why anyone feared England. "We have whipped her twice, and we can whip her again," he exclaimed inaccurately but confidently. Yell's colleague from Arkansas, Senator Ambrose Sevier, said that the people of Arkansas would go to war rather than lose any of Oregon. They were a warlike people, he asserted, who gave guns to their children for playthings![39]

It was Sam Houston who topped off the argument for the "War Hawks." Deprecating the compromise as a position that would merely make Britain more aggressive and unreasonable, Houston contended that the peacemakers had exaggerated the evils of war. War certainly had its virtues, such as "draining off the restless and dissatisfied portion of the population, who might be killed off with benefit to the remainder; and also the effect it had in disciplining the habits of men into subordination to the rules of order."[40]

When the Oregon treaty was ratified in June, 1846, settling the boundary at 49°, the score of southern expansionists who led the drive to place the boundary at 54° 40' could view with satisfaction their valiant struggle. There were some southerners, such as Robert Toombs of Georgia and L. H. Sims of Missouri, who had spoken out for all of Oregon but who were finally won over to a policy of compromise. The "hard core" southern expansionists stood their ground and seemed proud of what they had done. They had given about as much support for all of Oregon as any southerners had given for Texas. Their consciences were clear, for they had acted as "Manifest Destiny" Americans, not as narrow-minded sectionalists. But they never seemed to realize that they had almost no chance for success. In the highest quarters there were always serious doubts about the validity of the American claim north of 49°, and the official contentions of the two governments never took serious cognizance of the American claim in that area. President Polk, moreover, doubtless took that into consideration when he offered in the spring of 1846 to settle at 49°.

There were other considerations that made it unthinkable to hold out for a more favorable settlement than 49°. The impending repeal of the Corn Laws indicated to the Washington government that it would be folly to risk alienating a country whose new trade policy would mean so much to the American farmers. Then, too, the deterioration of relations with Mexico made it highly desirable that the difficulties with England be settled promptly and amicably.[41] Certainly, experienced men like Calhoun and McDuffie, despite their awkward position in the administration, exerted effective pressure on Polk not to pursue a course of action that would increase the complexities and difficulties of United States foreign relations and of the southern cotton planters.[42] Finally, the southern expansionists had joined their northern and western colleagues in contending for something in which not even the Oregon pioneers were interested. In 1846 there were only eight American settlers north of the Columbia River, and there seemed to be no immediate prospect of an increase. They preferred to remain in the Willamette Valley, by far the most attractive portion of Oregon. It was, therefore, inaccurate to declare that the Oregon settlers were merely waiting for American action before moving into the territory up to 54° 40'.[43]

In participating in the unsuccessful struggle to secure Oregon up to 54° 40' the southern expansionists of 1846 represented American "Manifest Destiny" at its best. Their southern colleagues who had been enthusiastic for Texas revealed a strong sectional bias in dragging their feet so noticeably when the Oregon question arose. Some of them doubtless agreed with Robert Toombs who said that he did not care a "fig about *any* of Oregon. . . . I don't want a foot of Oregon or an acre of any other country, especially without 'niggers.' These are some of my reasons for my course which don't appear in print."[44] Many of the pro-Oregon northerners indicated clearly that they regarded the Oregon question as a sectional matter when they castigated southerners who did not support it and by declaring gleefully that it would be a new area of freedom. Only the southern expansionists seemed to transcend sectional lines by contending for a territory whose acquisition they deemed to be in the national interest.

Too, the southern expansionists described more accurately and honestly than did the southern peacemakers the views of their constituents when they insisted that the southern people did not deprecate war. And they were closer to the truth than their northern critics when they declared that the southern people would fight to extend the nation's possessions in any direction. They did not have the opportunity to prove the point in regard to Oregon, but they did when the Mexican crisis arose. Some southern peacemakers like Calhoun and Berrien had no enthusiasm for the Mexican war, and some expansionists like Cobb thought that the United States should have been fighting England instead of Mexico.[45] But the southern expansionists had done their job well. They filled the common people of the South with a desire to defend the national honor, and when Zachary Taylor's troops were fired on near Matamoros in early May, 1846, southerners felt the national honor had been impugned. They would do in Mexico what they did not have the chance to do in Oregon.

The Enforcement of the Civil
Rights Act of 1875

Few bills, if any, have had a longer legislative history in the Congress of the United States than the Civil Rights Act of 1875. From the time that Charles Sumner of Massachusetts first introduced it in the Senate in 1870 until it was passed by both houses and signed by the president almost five years later, the bill was subjected to endless scrutiny and debate. Its supporters argued that the bill was necessary to protect the rights of all citizens against class and caste prejudice. They insisted that it did no more than provide a federal guarantee of the rights that citizens were supposed to enjoy on the basis of common law. The opponents called it an unconstitutional attempt to legislate social equality and an unenforceable and unmitigated evil. It was, moreover, impolitic, for it would "vex white men, North and South," and it would "expose the black man to more persecution. He is going too fast. He needs time and patience." Despite the fact that the bill's author had long since died and that there were no supporters to match the ardor of Sumner, the bill passed the House by a vote of 162 to 99 and the Senate by a vote of 38 to 26, becoming law on March 1, 1875.[1] It was the final triumph of a Republican majority of doubtful motives that would, within a few days, be superseded by an anti-civil rights Democratic majority.

The "great fundamental principles" that the bill proposed to enact into law were that "all persons within the jurisdiction of the United States shall be entitled to the full and equal enjoyment of the accommodations, advantages, facilities, and privileges of inns, public conveyances on land or water, theaters, and other places of public amusement," and that such enjoyment should be subject "only to the conditions and limitations established by law, and applicable alike to

Originally published in *Prologue*, Volume VI (Winter, 1974). Reprinted by permission.

citizens of every race and color, regardless of any previous condition of servitude." Another provision was that "no citizen possessing all other qualifications which are or may be prescribed by law shall be disqualified for service as grand or petit juror in any court of the United States, or of any State, on account of race, color, or previous condition of servitude."

Persons found guilty of violating the act—by denying to any citizen the enjoyment of the accommodations it described or by aiding or inciting such denial—would, for every offense, "forfeit and pay the sum of five hundred dollars to the person aggrieved thereby, to be recovered in any action of debt, with full costs; and shall also, for every such offense, be deemed guilty of a misdemeanor, and, upon conviction thereof, shall be fined not less than five hundred nor more than one thousand dollars, or shall be imprisoned not less than thirty days nor more than one year."

The act placed direct responsibility for enforcement on the federal courts and their officers. District and circuit courts of the United States were to have cognizance of all crimes and offenses against the statute. "And the district attorneys, marshals, and deputy marshals of the United States, and commissioners appointed by the circuit and territorial courts" were specifically authorized and required to institute proceedings against "every person who shall violate the provisions of this act, and cause him to be arrested and imprisoned or bailed . . . for trial before such court of the United States . . . as by law has cognizance of the offense." District attorneys were obligated to prosecute such proceedings to their termination. Any district attorney who willfully failed to institute and prosecute the required proceedings was to pay the sum of five hundred dollars to the person aggrieved and was to be fined not less than one thousand nor more than five thousand dollars.[2]

From the very beginning, the prospects for effective enforcement of the new measure were not bright. President Grant made no comment about the bill either at the time that he signed it or in subsequent messages to Congress or in other public statements. Members of Congress had little to say about the bill after it had passed. At least one member attempted to soften the blow by minimizing its possible effects. Representative Benjamin Butler, who had a significant part in bringing about the bill's passage as well as in deleting the provision that would have desegregated schools, sought to allay the fears of a friend. In a letter to Robert Harlan of Cincinnati, Butler said that the bill did not give Negroes the right to go into a drinking saloon and that he was very glad it did not. "I am willing to concede, as a friend to the colored man, that the white race may have at least this one superior privilege . . . and I never shall do anything to interfere with the exercise of that high and distinctive privilege."[3]

If people in high places were somewhat diffident about speaking out, the general public was not. The New York *Times*, which had vigorously opposed the bill from the beginning, insisted that it was unconstitutional and, what was more, that it could not be enforced. White southerners, the newspaper argued, would close their businesses rather than comply with the provisions of the act. There would be little trouble in the North, the paper predicted, largely because the blacks are in so great a minority that "they will hardly deem it prudent to force themselves into first-class hotels or restaurants. . . . As a rule, the negroes in this part of the country are quiet, inoffensive people who live for and to themselves, and have no desire to intrude where they are not welcome. In the South, however, there are many colored men and women who delight in 'scenes' and cheap notoriety."[4]

There were, however, Negroes in the South and also in the North who were prepared to intrude where they were not welcome in order to test the efficacy of the new legislation. On the day after it was signed into law, several Negroes in Richmond visited "various restaurants, including the bar room at the Exchange Hotel, and in one instance a barber shop, and demanded to be waited upon. They were refused in every instance and ordered out." A Negro couple in New Orleans attempted to occupy a stateroom on a steamboat plying the Mississippi River between that city and a landing on the Red River and were refused. In Chicago two Negroes demanded seats in the dress circle of the McVickers Theater; and although the ticket taker offered them seats elsewhere they persisted in their demands, "and there being no alternative, in they went. Except for their color," one reporter observed, "they would not have been noticed, for they behaved with becoming propriety." During the month after the passage of the bill the New York *Times* was embarrassed to report that in New York "an intelligent and respectable-appearing colored man" accompanied by a friend attempted to gain admission to the parquet of Booth's Theater but was not admitted because of his color and was told to go to the upper circle, whereupon he left.[5]

Between 1875 and 1877 blacks in all parts of the country were seeking to enjoy the privileges granted in the new law and were demanding that the government of the United States enforce it. In Wilmington, North Carolina, a Negro demanded that a saloonkeeper be arrested for refusing to sell him liquor.[6] Two Negro women in Galveston, Texas, sought admission to the parquet of the Tremont Opera House and were refused.[7] In Winona, Minnesota, several Negroes sought to indict by grand jury persons who had denied them accommodations.[8] A similar complaint was brought in San Francisco, and in Philadelphia a Negro woman brought action against the Mt. Moriah Cemetery Association for refusing to permit burial of her husband in a plot they had purchased.[9] Neither observers on the sidelines nor federal officials could claim that the Civil Rights Act failed to command the attention of possible beneficiaries.

The determination of blacks to enjoy their civil rights was at least matched by the spirited and vigorous resistance offered by whites in all parts of the country. Immediately upon learning of the act being passed the proprietor of the Park Hotel in Baltimore closed his house to the public "to escape incurring the [act's] penalties." In Chattanooga, Tennessee, two hotels surrendered their licenses as public places and became private boardinghouses.[10] Resistance in Virginia took several forms. In Alexandria on March 2, the two principal hotels canceled their licenses and closed. Proprietors of saloons in various parts of the state posted notices that the price of a drink would be $5.00, with liberal discounts to friends. Presumably, the proprietors had no Negro friends. During the same week that the act was passed a member of the state legislature in Richmond introduced a bill "to punish parties creating disturbances in hotels, theaters, and other places of amusement." And to prevent white friends or light-skinned Negroes from purchasing theater tickets and passing them on to their darker brothers, the proposed bill provided that such tickets should be marked "not transferable, to be used only by the original purchaser."[11] This was the kind of resistance that caused a reporter to observe some six months later that the Civil Rights Act had been "a dead letter in Virginia apparently for some time."[12]

Elsewhere the resistance was as intense if not as imaginative as that in Virginia. In New York a Negro was put out of a confectioner's shop when he sought to order a dish of ice cream.[13] The Baltimore and Ohio Railroad Company held its ground against eighteen blacks who wanted to ride from Rockville to Washington in a car occupied by whites.[14] There were numerous other instances in which railroad conductors steadfastly refused to permit blacks to ride in the first-class cars with white passengers, even when they presented first-class tickets.[15] The Philadelphia proprietor of Bingham House refused to give a Negro minister any accommodations in the hotel. A white guest offered to share his room with the Negro, but the proprietor would not permit him to do so. The minister then sat in the lobby for the entire night and saw eighteen whites receive accommodations.[16]

There can be no doubt that the pressures of Negroes who sought early and effective enforcement of the Civil Rights Act and the stern resistance of the whites had much to do with the desire of U.S. district attorneys and marshals for some instructions from Washington. One Tennessee judge observed, "The severe penalties imposed by this law upon prosecuting attorneys and other officials will, we are advised, be attempted to be enforced, should the grand jury fail to indict, in the assumption that their action will be controlled by such officers unless the Court acts."[17] As Negroes made their complaints, U.S. attorneys began to act. They could do nothing, however, until they were fully informed of the provisions of the law; and the office of the Department of Justice in Washington was remarkably derelict in providing attorneys in the field with copies of the act. The attorney general, George H. Williams of Oregon, was in the final months of his tenure—he would resign in May, 1875—and he might well have been preoccupied with other matters. But he sent out no special instructions regarding the new act, although during March, 1875, he sent out three circulars to U.S. attorneys and marshals. One dealt with an "act regulating fees and costs and for other purposes"; another dealt with recommendations for pardons; and a third contained copies of an "act to provide for reductions of terms of sentence of United States prisoners."[18] One might assume that the new civil rights law was at least as important as one regulating fees and costs.

U.S. attorneys were obliged, therefore, to send special and urgent requests to the attorney general for copies of the new statute. "Please send me without delay a duly certified copy of the 'Civil Rights Bill' as it exists as a law," the U.S. attorney for western Tennessee wrote. "I desire it for use in court and am anxious that it be forwarded as early as possible."[19] "Complaint is made under the civil rights law," wrote the U.S. attorney for the southern district of Ohio. "Please send me copies of the law."[20] The U.S. attorney for Georgia complained that he was unable to draw an indictment for several aggrieved parties because he had not seen a copy of the law. "Will you please send me a copy of the Law known as the 'Civil Rights Bill' recently passed."[21] Before the end of the first month after the bill's passage similar requests were forwarded to Attorney General Williams by U.S. attorneys in Chicago, Savannah, Raleigh, New Orleans, and San Francisco. The U.S. attorney for California seemed especially anxious, for he wrote, "Can I be furnished with a certified copy of the law previous to its appearing in book form. If not I will be compelled to defer any prosecutions under it till the session laws are received in the usual way."[22]

It was, of course, the responsibility of the secretary of state to furnish certified copies of newly enacted legislation, but the interest of the office of the attorney general in this critical piece of legislation can hardly be denied. Despite the fact that the attorney general himself routinely distributed other acts of Congress to U.S. attorneys without being solicited, he nevertheless referred their requests for copies of this act to the secretary of state. Later, as the requests increased, he complied with some of them directly.[23] The disposition of others of these requests is not clear, however. The endorsement on the request from the U.S. attorney in Atlanta merely indicates that the letter was "filed"; and one wonders if the attorney ever saw a copy of the statute before the session laws were printed and distributed.[24]

Specific requests for instructions and interpretations regarding the Civil Rights Act came into the office of the attorney general from federal officials in the field and from others. A member of a legal debating society in Cincinnati queried the attorney general on whether the law "contemplated and can be so construed as to include drinking saloons, and other places of public resort in its provisions." "Some of us," the correspondent continued, "are of the opinion that the preamble to the law, and the word 'Inns' which in the English sense also includes drinking places brings all eating and drinking saloons and their proprietors within the provisions of the civil rights law."[25] The attorney general replied courteously that "under the laws creating the office of Attorney General he is precluded from giving opinions except upon the call of the President or the head of one of the Executive Departments of the Government."[26] In 1879 the collector of customs at Natchez, Mississippi, informed the attorney general that Negroes constantly complained to him that steamboat officers refused to carry them "even after they tender them the amount of passage money demanded." The collector wanted to know if any law of Congress made the officer liable for so refusing. The attorney general referred the collector to the Civil Rights Act of 1875, which, he observed, "makes such refusal an offense to which considerable penalty attaches, and provides the method by which a prosecution for the penalty or for damages to the party entitled can be pursued."[27] Attorney General Charles Devens appears, on the surface, to have been a bit more willing to discuss the Civil Rights Act than his predecessor, Attorney General Williams. But neither Devens nor any of the other four attorneys general who succeeded Williams during the life of the act exerted any more influence than Williams in seeking its enforcement.[28]

Even without encouragement or specific instructions from the attorneys general, the U.S. attorneys gave evidence of some diligence in the prosecution of civil rights cases, if only to escape the penalties of the law. In April, 1875, when a black, William R. Davis, was refused admission to a New York theater, he called on Assistant U.S. Attorney Purdy and requested him to issue a warrant for the arrest of the ticket seller. That evening Davis went to the theater with the chief deputy marshal, pointed out the offender, and the marshal arrested him. When the case came before the U.S. commissioner, the assistant district attorney appeared for the government. The counsel for the defense refused to disclose what the nature of his defense would be; and the assistant U.S. attorney said, "It is imperatively required by the law that the District Attorney shall diligently prosecute all cases arising under it, under penalty of civil and criminal prosecution, in the event of failure." Amid laughter, the commissioner said, "I guess no one will question your zealous attention to duty."[29] Several days later, when the case was argued, the assistant U.S. attorney sought a ruling from the commissioner regarding the law's constitutionality but the commissioner declined to make such a ruling. The grand jury, to whom the case was remanded, was not impressed that the Negro had a case; and it presented no bill against the defendant.[30]

In the Philadelphia hotel sit-in case in 1876, both U.S. Attorney Valentine and his assistant, Hazlehurst, participated in the prosecution. They argued successfully that the act was constitutional and that the defendant, in refusing a room to a prospective guest who was a traveler, "because of color," was guilty "in the manner and form as he stands indicted." In charging the jury Judge John Cadwalader said, "The case appears to the court to be proved." The jury then found the defendant guilty.[31] When eighteen blacks brought suit against the Baltimore and Ohio Railroad Company in 1876, charging that the company assigned them to a separate car that they insisted was inferior, the U.S. attorney, Archibald Stirling, Jr., joined the attorney for the plaintiffs in pressing the civil action. On the basis of a charge by Judge

William F. Giles, the jury brought in a decision for the defendant, whereupon the U.S. attorney said he would reserve an exception to the ruling and appeal it to the U.S. Supreme Court.[32] Although Congress had deleted the provision for schools from the 1875 bill, the U.S. attorney for the southern district of Ohio sought to prosecute a township in Clermont County, Ohio, for excluding Negro children from the school nearest their home. The jury found for the defendant, presumably on the ground that in traveling five miles to the school designated for them the Negroes were placed at no material disadvantage with respect to their white neighbors.[33]

Blacks who were aggrieved did not hesitate to involve federal officials, including U.S. attorneys, in their efforts to secure redress. In Ottawa, Kansas, a Negro, Smith L. Rogers, was refused a haircut in a white barbershop; and he went to Topeka to consult with the U.S. attorney, J. R. Hallowell. Finding the chief attorney absent, Rogers consulted with the assistant, who promised to refer the matter to Hallowell. When Rogers did not receive a reply as promptly as he thought he should, he dispatched a letter to the attorney general of the United States, who, of course, referred the matter to Hallowell. By that time, however, Rogers had the reply that he certainly did not wish to receive. Hallowell wrote, "After an examination of your case as presented by you to my assistant . . . and in your letter heretofore received, I am of the opinion that while the conduct of the parties who refused to wait on you on account of your color was reprehensible and unbecoming a citizen of Kansas or of the United States, yet I know of no law of the United States which would make them criminally liable for such refusal."[34] Thus, barbershops were added to Butler's saloons as places "of superior privilege" on which blacks could not trespass.

Since U.S. attorneys were not obliged to participate in civil rights cases, when the aggrieved party brought a civil action against the alleged offender to recover the $500 provided for in the law, they must have been relieved whenever such action was brought. And the amount was so attractive that many aggrieved blacks seemed to prefer to bring civil action. Indeed, one of the early criticisms of the statute was that "shyster lawyers" would make a business of sending Negroes into places of public accommodation with the hope that they would be refused service, thus giving them an opportunity to collect damages, which would be divided between the plaintiff and the lawyer.[35] In many parts of the country Negroes took their complaints to the U.S. commissioners or U.S. attorneys; and it is not too much to conclude that when they subsequently brought civil suits, they did so after consultation with or even upon advice from federal officials.

William R. Davis, the business agent for the Negro paper *The Progressive American*, had an opportunity to observe the attitude of the U.S. attorney's office in New York toward criminal charges against alleged offenders. On the morning of November 22, 1879, an octoroon woman who was a friend of Davis purchased two tickets to a matinee performance at the New York Grand Opera House. That afternoon, when they presented themselves for admission, they were barred by the ticket taker who told them that their tickets were not valid. Then Davis hired a young white boy to purchase two tickets for him and gave him ten cents for his trouble. With the newly purchased tickets Davis and his lightskinned friend once again sought admission. She gained entrance, but Davis was stopped. When he insisted on entering, he was evicted by the police. The following day Davis took up the matter of denial of his civil rights with Assistant U.S. District Attorney Fiero, who advised Davis that he could secure "all the vindication his rights required by beginning a civil suit in the United States District Court, the civil penalty recoverable being $500." Davis was by now an old hand at civil rights cases. He had lost a case against Booth's Theater during the first weeks after the law was passed. At this point, he would not be denied the full legal assistance of the government of the United States—if he could get it. Of the assistant district attorney it must be said that he argued the case for Davis with great energy, and when the court divided on the question of the guilt of the defendant, the U.S. attorney sent it on to the U.S. Supreme Court. This became one of the cases to be decided in 1883.[36]

The role of the judiciary, especially in the months just after the act was passed, was crucial in determining the manner and the zeal with which it was enforced, if, indeed, it was to be enforced at all. And the ever-present question of the constitutionality of the act was a temptation—even to a U.S. commissioner, to say nothing of a district or circuit court judge—to issue an opinion on the weighty question, thereby becoming a participant in the final decision-making process. Not many judges took the rather modest position of Robert Dick of the western district of North Carolina who, in April, 1875, declined to rule on the question of constitutionality. In answer to the grand jury's question as to whether or not the act was constitutional, he said, "The constitutionality of the Civil Rights bill has been asserted by the deliberate action of Congress, composed of many able lawyers and wise and enlightened statesmen, and it would be very presumptuous in me, collaterally and without argument, to decide differently upon a question which that body carefully considered and acted upon under the solemn sanction of official obligation."[37] Some judges were content to assume that the statute was constitutional and merely to pass judgment on the facts in the case. Others seemed almost anxious to comment on its constitutionality. In either case, the effect of their opinions, or even of their charges to the jury, on the enforcement of the act was extremely important.

One of the earliest judicial opinions regarding the law's constitutionality was given on June 8, 1875, by Judge R. R. Nelson of the U.S. District Court of Minnesota. In response to a request made by a grand jury regarding a case it was considering, Nelson referred to the doctrine of implied powers set forth in 1819 by Chief Justice John Marshall in *McCulloch* v. *Maryland*. "If the opinion in that case," Judge Nelson said, "correctly represents the extent of Congressional legislation, the power of Congress can be exerted directly to put down all outrage or discrimination on the part of individuals when the motive originates only in race or color. . . . The law in my opinion is constitutional."[38] Several months later its constitutionality was upheld by Judge Alexander Rives of the U.S. District Court for the Western District of Virginia. The U.S. attorney, "deeming it a matter of interest," dispatched a message to the attorney general as soon as the opinion was rendered.[39]

While it is difficult to assess the effect of favorable decisions in civil rights cases beyond the specific cases themselves, some judges left no doubt that they would not be lenient with those found guilty of violations. In his charge to the grand jury, Judge Morrill of the U.S. District Court for the Eastern District of Texas reviewed the Civil Rights Act and expressed the opinion that "all persons have a legal right to have board and lodgings at inns, transportation on steamers, railroads, or stages, and entrance in theatres." On the basis of this view, the manager of the Tremont Opera House in Galveston was fined $500 for refusing two Negro women seats in the parquet of the theater. When the editor of the Galveston *News* criticized the construction Judge Morrill placed on the act in his ruling, the outraged judge ordered the marshal to bring the editor into court and have him show cause why he should not be held in contempt. Through his attorney the editor immediately apologized and said that "no disrespect was intended, nor was any attempt to influence the ruling or bring the court into disrepute intended."[40]

After the first two years, few judges were hearing cases arising under the act; but in 1882 a judge for the circuit court in the southern district of Ohio made it quite clear that the act should be enforced. The case involved a Negro woman with a round trip first-class ticket traveling with her husband and sick child from Lexington to Cincinnati. As she attempted to go into the ladies' car, she was stopped by the brakeman. When the conductor upheld the brakeman's action, the woman got off and returned later by another route. In his opinion Judge Swing said, "In the eye of the law we all stand now upon the same footing. . . . Whatever the social relations of life may be, before the law we all stand upon the broad plane of equality. And this company was bound to provide for this colored woman precisely such accommodations, in every respect, as were provided for white women." The jury brought in a verdict for the plaintiff and awarded her $1,000 damages.[41]

There can be little doubt that adverse judicial opinions or criticisms of the act tended to discourage enforcement; and many such views were expressed during the life of the act. Several judges, for example, refused to interpret it as covering places of accommodation or amusement that it did not specifically mention. For example, in North Carolina, U.S. Commissioner E. H. McQuigg dismissed one civil rights case in March, 1875, on the ground that the act did not apply to saloons.[42] In June, 1875, U.S. Commissioner Betts of New York, without asking the name of the complainant or of the person against whom he desired to enter the complaint, refused to grant a warrant, on the ground that the law did not extend to ice cream parlors.[43]

Some judges did not hesitate to declare the act unconstitutional and even to chastise Congress for its presumption. Judge Halmor H. Emmons, ruling in the Circuit Court of the Western District of Tennessee, said in the month the act was passed that Congress had no right, under the Thirteenth or Fourteenth Amendment or otherwise, "to declare it a crime for any individuals to deny to negroes the full and equal enjoyment of accommodations . . . of the theaters and inns of a state."[44] In May, 1875, Judge Brook of the eastern district of North Carolina charged the jury that the criminal features of the statute "in which they as a Grand Jury were alone interested," were unconstitutional. During the same week Judge Dick charged the grand jury of the western district of North Carolina that "a citizen of the United States, under the broad Constitution of this country can go to any portion of it and exercise all the immunities which by his freedom he possesses, but no law, human or divine, can compel a hotch-potch of citizens; all that is necessary are suitable comforts, and every inn-keeper has a right to exercise his privilege as to where he shall place his guests, convenience and comfort being all that is required, and no law can say all men shall be equal socially."[45]

What Judge Dick seemed to suggest was that while an innkeeper might be expected to provide reasonably equal accommodations for all travelers, he was not obliged to provide precisely the same accommodations. In a case before the district court for the Western District of Texas in 1877, Judge Thomas H. Duval was much more explicit on the question of separate but equal accommodations. In part, he said, "If there are two cars equally fit and appropriate, in all respects, for use of white female passengers and for colored female passengers, there is no offence of denying a colored female passenger entrance to one and requiring her to ride in the other."[46] Such an interpretation of the law, however, presented new opportunities for its evasion. When a Negro woman, traveling on a steamboat from Savannah to Palatka, Florida, in 1878 sought first-class accommodations, the purser refused, saying that the upper deck was reserved for whites. She then brought him into court and accused him of violating the Civil Rights Act. The purser pleaded that she was noisy and boisterous while on board. In deciding against the Negro woman, Judge John Erskine admitted that common law required carriers to be open to all, but he insisted that the owner could make rules to preserve order and decorum. He added, somewhat lamely, that it was all right for officials of the steamboat to keep blacks and whites separate, since the accommodations were substantially equal. He said nothing about the desirability of separating this allegedly boisterous Negro passenger from the more decorous Negro passengers, if, indeed, the owner's rules were for the purpose of preserving order and decorum.[47]

Thus, there were sharp differences among federal judges regarding the question of constitutionality. Some assumed the act to be constitutional, while others were quite uncertain of that. On the other hand, some denied that their courts had jurisdiction to rule on such matters, while others declared, with considerable feeling, that the law was unconstitutional. Some merely nullified the effect of the law by declaring that its requirements had been satisfied when separate but substantially equal accommodations were provided. The situation became so confused and the chances of relief under the act so uncertain that there is small wonder that after 1877 the number of complaints declined significantly. Perhaps an even more important explanation for the decline in cases arising under the act was the preoccupation of federal officials with securing a ruling by the Supreme Court.

Very soon after passage of the act, judges in lower courts and other interested persons began to focus their attention on the Supreme Court with the hope that it would soon rule on the law's constitutionality. In July, 1875, Judge Halmor H. Emmons, who in March had declared the act unconstitutional, inquired of the attorney general whether the Supreme Court had before it any case involving its constitutionality. The attorney general replied that no such case was before the Court.[48] It was to be only a matter of months, however, before such cases would be on the docket of the high court.

The first case arose in Kansas. In October, 1875, one Murray Stanley of Topeka, Kansas, refused to serve supper to a Negro who came to his inn. The grand jury indicted Stanley for conduct in violation of an act of Congress and "against the peace and dignity of the United States." In June of the following year, after a good deal of legal maneuvering on both sides, the judges of the U.S. circuit court in Kansas divided in their opinion. They agreed, with much pleasure it would appear, to send the case to the Supreme Court.[49]

At about the same time another civil rights case reached the Court from California. It involved the denial of a seat to a Negro in the dress circle of Maguire's New Theatre in San Francisco. The defendant, Michael Ryan, filed a demurrer to the charge that he had violated the law and challenged both the substance and form of the information that had been presented. The circuit court sustained him and dismissed the case. The U.S. attorney sent the record of the case to the Supreme Court, where it was filed October 14, 1876.[50] In transmitting the case to the attorney general, the U.S. attorney for California was almost apologetic. He observed that this was merely "one of a large number of cases which I am compelled under heavy penalties to bring."[51] Thus, eighteen months after it was passed, the Supreme Court had before it two cases involving the Civil Rights Act. It would be seven years, however, before the Court disposed of these and similar cases.

In subsequent years other civil rights cases came to the Supreme Court. The Court received one from Missouri in 1877 involving the denial of a room to a Negro at an inn in Jefferson City. A case involving the eviction of a Negro woman from the ladies' car in Tennessee reached the Court in 1880. In the same year William R. Davis, the Negro who had been denied a seat at the New York Grand Opera, placed his case before the Court.[52] The judges of the lower courts were most cooperative in facilitating appeals to the Supreme Court in each of these cases. At the level of the circuit court, the judges—two in number—were quite conveniently divided; and the consistency of the division suggests that this was a technique by which the circuit judges were pleased to send the cases on to the Court, since there was no danger of their being reversed.

The opening of each term of the Court, beginning in 1876, caused a buildup of anxiety regarding possible decisions in the civil rights cases. The closing of each term, with no decision on the cases, brought a corresponding amount of disappointment to the legal profession and to the general public. The reason for the delay is not clear. It may be that the Court was waiting for a variety of cases; but it had a rich variety by 1880. However, the reason for the delay is not relevant to this discussion. At the same time, the fact that there was inordinate delay is quite relevant. It was well known throughout the country that the Supreme Court began to consider its first civil rights case in 1876. There can be no doubt that lawyers, judges, and even the public tended to suspend activity in the area of civil rights, hoping that the matter would soon be settled once and for all by the nation's highest tribunal. In 1879 Judge Gresham took a civil rights case under advisement and said that he would not rule in the matter because of an impending decision by the Supreme Court. In reply to an inquiry from the U.S. attorney for Indiana, the attorney general informed him that the Court would, perhaps, reach the Kansas civil rights case "in a month or two."[53]

During the next four years the attorney general was besieged with requests for information regarding pending civil rights cases. In March, 1880, he wrote the U.S. attorney in New York that the civil rights cases "have remained unacted upon."[54] In the following month he speculated that the cases would be decided by the Supreme Court "at a very early day of its next term, in October next."[55] To the U.S. attorney at Nashville, Tennessee, who was interested in one of the cases, he wrote in November, 1880, that he would move to have it advanced so that it could be argued with the other cases.[56] But the cases were not argued during that term.[57] A year later, the attorney general's office had to report that "nothing had been said at this term about these cases."[58]

For another two years the nation waited. Finally, in October, 1883, the Supreme Court declared that Congress had no power to pass laws regulating the conduct and transactions of individuals unless it was clothed with direct and plenary powers of legislation over a whole

subject, such as foreign or interstate commerce, commerce with Indian tribes, the coinage of money, the establishment of post offices and
post roads, or declaring war. "But where a subject is not submitted to
the general legislative power of Congress, but is only submitted
thereto for the purpose of rendering effective some prohibition against
particular state legislation or state action in reference to that subject,
the power given is limited to its object, and any legislation by Congress
in the matter must necessarily be corrective in its character." Mr.
Justice Bradley said that the Civil Rights Act was not corrective, but
primary and direct and, therefore, unconstitutional. The wrongful acts
of an individual, unsupported by state authority in the shape of laws,
customs, judicial, or executive proceedings, were "simply a private
wrong, or a crime of that individual." Redress or relief must be sought
from the state, not from the federal government.[59]

During the days following the decision, numerous citizens expressed their views regarding its wisdom and its justice. None was
more eloquent or passionate than Frederick Douglass, by far the outstanding Negro leader of the time. Before a protest meeting held in
Washington on October 22, 1883, he expressed deepest regret that the
Court had seen fit to strike down the law. "When it has taken its place
upon the statute book," he said, "and has remained there for nearly a
decade, and the country has largely assented to it, you will agree with
me that the reasons for declaring such a law unconstitutional and void
should be strong, irresistible, and absolutely conclusive."[60] These remarks struck a high note that was more eloquent than accurate. He
could hardly have proved that the country had "largely assented" to the
act. Much more hard-headed and realistic were the comments of the
white editor of an Arkansas newspaper who said, "While public opinion decrees that whites and blacks shall not enjoy the social relations
of equality the Civil Rights Act of 1875 pronounces the latter entitled
to, no such measure can be enforced, even though pronounced constitutional a thousand times. Society decides for itself what is and
what is not social equality. The statutes cannot decide it. At all events,
they cannot be enforced in this regard against public sentiment."[61]

The Civil Rights Act was never effectively enforced; but the reasons
were a bit more complex than those suggested by the Arkansas editor.
From the day it was introduced in 1870 until it was declared unconstitutional thirteen years later, it was bitterly assailed by its numerous
enemies and only lamely defended by its dwindling number of friends.
In the South it found no general support, except among blacks, while in

the North the opponents seemed to be at least as numerous as support-ers. The air of controversy that surrounded its enactment continued to dog it all its life; and there could have been little chance for effective enforcement when the status of the group it was designed to benefit was generally deteriorating. A Mississippi editor said in the year it was passed that any effort to inculcate in the Negro the great truths that mankind has discovered "but tends to bestialize his nature and by obfuscating his little brain unfits him for the duties assigned him as a hewer of wood and drawer of water. The effort makes him a demon of wild, fanatical destruction and consigns him to the fatal shot of the white man."[62] Two years after the act was passed, one of the most respected editors of the North made a final pronouncement on the Negro when he said flatly and unequivocally, "Henceforth, the nation as a nation will have nothing more to do with him."[63] This was not a climate that was congenial to the enforcement of equal rights for Negroes.

Surely the lukewarm-to-indifferent attitude of the federal officials toward the Civil Rights Act had much to do with the manner in which it was indifferently enforced. When the attorney general did not feel obliged even to provide his subordinates with copies of the act and when the greatest pressure on U.S. attorneys and marshals arose from the fact that dereliction on their part might be costly, there was no reason to expect vigorous enforcement. There was, moreover, the un-settling effect that the numerous adverse decisions of the lower courts had on enforcement. Neither federal officials nor the general public of a particular judicial district could muster much enthusiasm for the law or even respect for it when judges excoriated not only the law but the lawmakers as well. Finally, the unconscionable six-year delay by the Supreme Court itself merely created a state of suspense during which both the white public and federal officials felt that they could ignore the law with impunity. Long before the act was struck down by the Court it had become a casualty in the war waged by white su-premacists who were determined to make certain that the freedom of the Negro, forged out of an earlier war, would be most carefully proscribed.

The Two Worlds of Race:
A Historical View

Measured by universal standards the history of the United States is indeed brief. But during the brief span of three and one-half centuries of colonial and national history Americans developed traditions and prejudices which created the two worlds of race in modern America. From the time that Africans were brought as indentured servants to the mainland of English America in 1619, the enormous task of rationalizing and justifying the forced labor of peoples on the basis of racial differences was begun; and even after legal slavery was ended, the notion of racial differences persisted as a basis for maintaining segregation and discrimination. At the same time, the effort to establish a more healthy basis for the new world social order was begun, thus launching the continuing battle between the two worlds of race, on the one hand, and the world of equality and complete human fellowship, on the other.

For a century before the American Revolution the status of Negroes in the English colonies had become fixed at a low point that distinguished them from all other persons who had been held in temporary bondage. By the middle of the eighteenth century, laws governing Negroes denied to them certain basic rights that were conceded to others. They were permitted no independence of thought, no opportunity to improve their minds or their talents or to worship freely, no right to marry and enjoy the conventional family relationships, no right to own or dispose of property, and no protection against miscarriages of justice or cruel and unreasonable punishments. They were outside the pale of the laws that protected ordinary humans. In most places they were to be governed, as the South Carolina code of 1712 expressed it, by special laws "as may restrain the disorders, rapines,

Originally published in *Daedalus*, Vol. XCIV, No. 4 (Fall, 1965), pp. 899–920. Reprinted by permission of *Daedalus: Journal of the American Academy of Arts and Sciences*.

and inhumanity to which they are naturally prone and inclined." A separate world for them had been established by law and custom. Its dimensions and the conduct of its inhabitants were determined by those living in a quite different world.

By the time that the colonists took up arms against their mother country in order to secure their independence, the world of Negro slavery had become deeply entrenched and the idea of Negro inferiority well established. But the dilemmas inherent in such a situation were a source of constant embarrassment. "It always appeared a most iniquitous scheme to me," Mrs. John Adams wrote her husband in 1774, "to fight ourselves for what we are daily robbing and plundering from those who have as good a right to freedom as we have." There were others who shared her views, but they were unable to wield much influence. When the fighting began General George Washington issued an order to recruiting officers that they were not to enlist "any deserter from the ministerial army, nor any stroller, negro, or vagabond, or person suspected of being an enemy to the liberty of America nor any under eighteen years of age." In classifying Negroes with the dregs of society, traitors, and children, Washington made it clear that Negroes, slave or free, were not to enjoy the high privilege of fighting for political independence. He would change that order later, but only after it became clear that Negroes were enlisting with the "ministerial army" in droves in order to secure their own freedom. In changing his policy if not his views, Washington availed himself of the services of more than five thousand Negroes who took up arms against England.[1]

Many Americans besides Mrs. Adams were struck by the inconsistency of their stand during the War for Independence, and they were not averse to making moves to emancipate the slaves. Quakers and other religious groups organized antislavery societies, while numerous individuals manumitted their slaves. In the years following the close of the war most of the states of the East made provisions for the gradual emancipation of slaves. In the South, meanwhile, the antislavery societies were unable to effect programs of statewide emancipation. When the southerners came to the Constitutional Convention in 1787 they succeeded in winning some representation on the basis of slavery, in securing federal support for the capture and rendition of fugitive slaves, and in preventing the closing of the slave trade before 1808.

Even where the sentiment favoring emancipation was pronounced, it was seldom accompanied by a view that Negroes were the equals of whites and should become a part of one family of Americans. Jefferson, for example, was opposed to slavery; and if he could have had his way, he would have condemned it in the Declaration of Independence. It did not follow, however, that he believed Negroes to be the equals of whites. He did not want to "degrade a whole race of men from the work in the scale of beings which their Creator may *perhaps* have given them. . . . I advance it therefore, as a suspicion only, that the blacks, whether originally a distinct race, or made distinct by time and circumstance, are inferior to the whites in the endowment both of body and mind." It is entirely possible that Jefferson's later association with the extraordinarily able Negro astronomer and mathematician, Benjamin Banneker, resulted in some modification of his views. After reading a copy of Banneker's almanac, Jefferson told him that it was "a document to which your whole race had a right for its justifications against the doubts which have been entertained of them."[2]

In communities such as Philadelphia and New York, where the climate was more favorably disposed to the idea of Negro equality than in Jefferson's Virginia, few concessions were made, except by a limited number of Quakers and their associates. Indeed, the white citizens in the "City of Brotherly Love" contributed substantially to the perpetuation of two distinct worlds of race. In the 1780s, the white Methodists permitted Negroes to worship with them, provided the Negroes sat in a designated place in the balcony. On one occasion, when the Negro worshippers occupied the front rows of the balcony, from which they had been excluded, the officials pulled them from their knees during prayer and evicted them from the church. Thus, in the early days of the republic and in the place where the republic was founded, Negroes had a definite "place" in which they were expected at all times to remain. The white Methodists of New York had much the same attitude toward their Negro fellows. Soon, there were separate Negro churches in these and other communities. Baptists were very much the same. In 1809 thirteen Negro members of a white Baptist church in Philadelphia were dismissed, and they formed a church of their own. Thus, the earliest Negro religious institutions emerged as the result of the rejection by white communicants of their darker fellow worshippers. Soon there would be other institutions—schools, newspapers, benevolent societies—to serve those who lived in a world apart.

Those Americans who conceded the importance of education for Negroes tended to favor some particular type of education that would be in keeping with their lowly station in life. In 1794, for example, the American Convention of Abolition Societies recommended that

Negroes be instructed in "those mechanic arts which will keep them most constantly employed and, of course, which will less subject them to idleness and debauchery, and thus prepare them for becoming good citizens of the United States." When Anthony Benezet, a dedicated Pennsylvania abolitionist, died in 1784 his will provided that on the death of his wife the proceeds of his estate should be used to assist in the establishment of a school for Negroes. In 1787 the school of which Benezet had dreamed was opened in Philadelphia, where the pupils studied reading, writing, arithmetic, plain accounts, and sewing.

Americans who were at all interested in the education of Negroes regarded it as both natural and normal that Negroes should receive their training in separate schools. As early as 1773 Newport, Rhode Island, had a colored school, maintained by a society of benevolent clergymen of the Anglican church. In 1798 a separate private school for Negro children was established in Boston; and two decades later the city opened its first public primary school for the education of Negro children. Meanwhile, New York had established separate schools, the first one opening its doors in 1790. By 1814 there were several such institutions that were generally designated as the New York African Free Schools.[3]

Thus, in the most liberal section of the country, the general view was that Negroes should be kept out of the mainstream of American life. They were forced to establish and maintain their own religious institutions, which were frequently followed by the establishment of separate benevolent societies. Likewise, if Negroes were to receive any education, it should be special education provided in separate educational institutions. This principle prevailed in most places in the North throughout the period before the Civil War. In some Massachusetts towns, however, Negroes gained admission to schools that had been maintained for whites. But the school committee of Boston refused to admit Negroes, arguing that the natural distinction of the races, which "no legislature, no social customs, can efface renders a promiscuous intermingling in the public schools disadvantageous both to them and to the whites." Separate schools remained in Boston until the Massachusetts legislature in 1855 enacted a law providing that in determining the qualifications of students to be admitted to any public school no distinction should be made on account of the race, color, or religious opinion of the applicant.

Meanwhile, in the southern states, where the vast majority of the Negroes lived, there were no concessions suggesting equal treatment, even among the most liberal elements. One group that would doubtless have regarded itself as liberal on the race question advocated the deportation of Negroes to Africa, especially those who had become free. Since free Negroes "neither enjoyed the immunities of freemen, nor were they subject to the incapacities of slaves," their condition and "unconquerable prejudices" prevented amalgamation with whites, one colonization leader argued. There was, therefore, a "peculiar moral fitness" in restoring them to "the land of their fathers." Men like Henry Clay, Judge Bushrod Washington, and President James Monroe thought that separation—expatriation—was the best thing for Negroes who were or who would become free.[4]

While the colonization scheme was primarily for Negroes who were already free, it won, for a time, a considerable number of sincere enemies of slavery. From the beginning Negroes were bitterly opposed to it, and only infrequently did certain Negro leaders, such as Dr. Martin Delany and the Reverend Henry M. Turner, support the idea. Colonization, however, retained considerable support in the most responsible quarters. As late as the Civil War, President Lincoln urged Congress to adopt a plan to colonize Negroes, as the only workable solution to the race problem in the United States. Whether the advocates of colonization wanted merely to prevent the contamination of slavery by free Negroes or whether they actually regarded it as the just and honorable thing to do, they represented an important element in the population that rejected the idea of the Negro's assimilation into the mainstream of American life.

Thus, within fifty years after the Declaration of Independence was written, the institution of slavery, which received only a temporary reversal during the Revolutionary era, contributed greatly to the emergence of the two worlds of race in the United States. The natural rights philosophy appeared to have little effect on those who became committed, more and more, to seeking a rationalization for slavery. The search was apparently so successful that even in areas where slavery was declining, the support for maintaining two worlds of race was strong. Since the Negro church and school emerged in northern communities where slavery was dying, it may be said that the free society believed almost as strongly in racial separation as it did in racial freedom.

The generation preceding the outbreak of the Civil War witnessed the development of a set of defenses of slavery that became the basis for much of the racist doctrine to which some Americans have subscribed from then to the present time. The idea of the inferiority of the Negro enjoyed wide acceptance among southerners of all classes and among many northerners. It was an important ingredient in the theory of society promulgated by southern thinkers and leaders. It was organized into a body of systematic thought by the scientists and social scientists of the South, out of which emerged a doctrine of racial superiority that justified any kind of control over the slave. In 1826 Dr. Thomas Cooper said that he had not the slightest doubt that Negroes were an "inferior variety of the human species; and not capable of the same improvement as the whites." Dr. S. C. Cartwright of the University of Louisiana insisted that the capacities of the Negro adult for learning were equal to those of a white infant; and the Negro could properly perform certain physiological functions only when under the control of white men. Because of the Negro's inferiority, liberty and republican institutions were not only unsuited to his temperament, but actually inimical to his well-being and happiness.

Like racists in other parts of the world, southerners sought support for their ideology by developing a common bond with the less privileged. The obvious basis was race; and outside the white race there was to be found no favor from God, no honor or respect from man. By the time that Europeans were reading Gobineau's *Inequality of Races*, southerners were reading Cartwright's *Slavery in the Light of Ethnology*. In admitting all whites into the pseudo-nobility of race, Cartwright won their enthusiastic support in the struggle to preserve the integrity and honor of *the* race. Professor Thomas R. Dew of the College of William and Mary comforted the lower-class whites by indicating that they could identify with the most privileged and affluent of the community. In the South, he said, "no white man feels such inferiority of rank as to be unworthy of association with those around him. Color alone is here the badge of distinction, the true mark of aristocracy, and all who are white are equal in spite of the variety of occupation."[5]

Many northerners were not without their own racist views and policies in the turbulent decades before the Civil War. Some, as Professor Louis Filler has observed, displayed a hatred of Negroes that gave them a sense of superiority and an outlet for their frustrations. Others cared nothing one way or the other about Negroes and demanded only that they be kept separate.[6] Even some of the abolitionists themselves were ambivalent on the question of Negro equality. More than one antislavery society was agitated by the suggestion that Negroes be invited to join. Some members thought it reasonable for them to attend, but not to be put on an "equality with ourselves." The New York abolitionist Lewis Tappan admitted "that when the subject of acting out our profound principles in treating men irrespective of color is discussed heat is always produced."[7]

In the final years before the beginning of the Civil War, the view that the Negro was different, even inferior, was widely held in the United States. Leaders in both major parties subscribed to the view, while the more extreme racists deplored any suggestion that the Negro could ever prosper as a free man. At Peoria, Illinois, in October, 1854, Abraham Lincoln asked what stand the opponents of slavery should take regarding Negroes. "Free them, and make them politically and socially, our equals? My own feelings will not admit of this; and if mine would, we well know that those of the great mass of white people will not. Whether this feeling accords with justice and sound judgment, is not the sole question, if indeed, it is any part of it. A universal feeling, whether well or ill founded, cannot be safely disregarded. We cannot, then, make them equals."

The Lincoln statement was forthright, and it doubtless represented the views of most Americans in the 1850s. Most of those who heard him or read his speech were of the same opinion as he. In later years, the Peoria pronouncement would be used by those who sought to detract from Lincoln's reputation as a champion of the rights of the Negro. In 1964, the White Citizens Councils reprinted portions of the speech in large advertisements in the daily press and insisted that Lincoln shared their views on the desirability of maintaining two distinct worlds of race.

Lincoln could not have overcome the nation's strong predisposition toward racial separation if he had tried. And he did not try very hard. When he called for the enlistment of Negro troops, after issuing the Emancipation Proclamation, he was content not only to set Negroes apart in a unit called "U. S. Colored Troops," but also to have Negro privates receive $10 per month including clothing, while whites of the same rank received $13 per month plus clothing. Only the stubborn refusal of many Negro troops to accept discriminatory pay finally forced Congress to equalize compensation for white and Negro soldiers.[8] The fight for union that became also a fight for freedom never became a fight for equality or for the creation of one racial world.

The Lincoln and Johnson plans for settling the problems of peace and freedom never seriously touched on the concomitant problem of equality. To be sure, in 1864 President Lincoln privately raised with the governor of Louisiana the question of the franchise for a limited number of Negroes, but when the governor ignored the question the president let the matter drop. Johnson raised a similar question in 1866, but he admitted that it was merely to frustrate the design of radical reformers who sought a wider franchise for Negroes. During the two years following Appomattox southern leaders gave not the slightest consideration to permitting any Negroes, regardless of their service to the Union or their education or their property, to share in the political life of their communities. Not only did every southern state refuse to permit Negroes to vote, but they also refused to provide Negroes with any of the educational opportunities that they were providing for the whites.

The early practice of political disfranchisement and of exclusion from public educational facilities helped to determine subsequent policies that the South adopted regarding Negroes. While a few leaders raised their voices against these policies and practices, it was Negroes themselves who made the most eloquent attacks on such discriminations. As early as May, 1865, a group of North Carolina Negroes told President Johnson that some of them had been soldiers and were doing everything possible to learn how to discharge the higher duties of citizenship. "It seems to us that men who are willing on the field of battle to carry the muskets of the Republic, in the days of peace ought to be permitted to carry the ballots; and certainly we cannot understand the justice of denying the elective franchise to men who have been fighting *for* the country, while it is freely given to men who have just returned from *four* years fighting against it." Such pleas fell on deaf ears, however; and it was not until 1867, when Congress was sufficiently outraged by the inhuman black codes, widespread discriminations in the South, and unspeakable forms of violence against Negroes, that new federal legislation sought to correct the evils of the first period of Reconstruction.

The period that we know as Radical Reconstruction had no significant or permanent effect on the status of the Negro in American life. For a period of time, varying from one year to fifteen or twenty years, some Negroes enjoyed the privileges of voting. They gained political ascendancy in a very few communities only temporarily, and they never even began to achieve the status of a ruling class. They made no meaningful steps toward economic independence or even stability; and in no time at all, because of the pressures of the local community and the neglect of the federal government, they were brought under the complete economic subservience of the old ruling class. Organizations such as the Ku Klux Klan were committed to violent action to keep Negroes "in their place" and, having gained respectability through sponsorship by Confederate generals and the like, they proceeded to wreak havoc in the name of white supremacy and protection of white womanhood.[9]

Meanwhile, various forms of segregation and discrimination, developed during the years before the Civil War in order to degrade the half-million free Negroes in the United States, were now applied to the four million Negroes who had become free in 1865. Already the churches and the military were completely segregated. For the most part the schools, even in the North, were separate. In the South segregated schools persisted, even in the places where the radicals made a half-hearted attempt to desegregate them. In 1875 Congress enacted a Civil Rights Act to guarantee the enjoyment of equal rights in carriers and all places of public accommodation and amusement. Even before it became law northern philanthropists succeeded in forcing the deletion of the provision calling for desegregated schools. Soon, because of the massive resistance in the North as well as in the South and the indifferent manner in which the federal government enforced the law, it soon became a dead letter everywhere. When it was declared unconstitutional by the Supreme Court in 1883, there was universal rejoicing, except among the Negroes, one of whom declared that they had been "baptized in ice water."

Neither the Civil War nor the era of Reconstruction made any significant step toward the permanent elimination of racial barriers. The radicals of the post–Civil War years came no closer to the creation of one racial world than the patriots of the Revolutionary years. When Negroes were, for the first time, enrolled in the standing army of the United States, they were placed in separate Negro units. Most of the liberals of the Reconstruction era called for and worked for separate schools for Negroes. Nowhere was there any extensive effort to involve Negroes in the churches and other social institutions of the dominant group. Whatever remained of the old abolitionist fervor, which can hardly be described as unequivocal on the question of true racial equality, was rapidly disappearing. In its place were the sentiments of the businessmen who wanted peace at any price. Those having common railroad interests or crop-marketing interests or investment interests could and did extend their hands across sectional lines and joined in the task of working together for the common good. In such an atmosphere the practice was to accept the realities of two separate worlds of race. Some even subscribed to the view that there were significant economic advantages in maintaining the two worlds of race.

The post-Reconstruction years witnessed a steady deterioration in the status of Negro Americans. These were the years that Professor Rayford Logan has called the "nadir" of the Negro in American life and thought. They were the years when Americans, weary of the crusade that had, for the most part, ended with the outbreak of the Civil War, displayed almost no interest in helping the Negro to achieve equality. The social Darwinists decried the very notion of equality for Negroes, arguing that the lowly place they occupied was natural and normal. The leading literary journals vied with each other in describing Negroes as lazy, idle, improvident, immoral, and criminal.[10] Thomas Dixon's novels *The Clansman* and *The Leopard's Spots* and D. W. Griffith's motion picture *The Birth of a Nation* helped to give Americans a view of the Negro's role in American history that "proved" he was unfit for citizenship, to say nothing of equality. The dictum of William Graham Sumner and his followers that "stateways cannot change folkways" convinced many Americans that legislating equality and creating one great society where race was irrelevant was out of the question.

But many Americans believed that they *could* legislate inequality; and they proceeded to do precisely that. Beginning in 1890, one southern state after another revised the suffrage provisions of its constitution in a manner that made it virtually impossible for Negroes to qualify to vote. The new literacy and "understanding" provisions permitted local registrars to disqualify Negroes while permitting white citizens to qualify. Several states, including Louisiana, North Carolina, and Oklahoma, inserted "grandfather clauses" in their constitutions in order to permit persons, who could not otherwise qualify, to vote if their fathers or grandfathers could vote in 1866. (This was such a flagrant discrimination against Negroes, whose ancestors could not vote in 1866, that the United States Supreme Court in 1915 declared the "grandfather clause" unconstitutional.) Then came the Democratic white primary in 1900 that made it impossible for Negroes to participate in local elections in the South, where, by this time, only the

Democratic party had any appreciable strength. (After more than a generation of assaults on it, the white primary was finally declared unconstitutional in 1944.)

Inequality was legislated in still another way. Beginning in the 1880s, many states, especially but not exclusively in the South, enacted statutes designed to separate the races. After the Civil Rights Act was declared unconstitutional in 1883, state legislatures were emboldened to enact numerous segregation statutes. When the United States Supreme Court, in the case of *Plessy* v. *Ferguson*, set forth the "separate but equal" doctrine in 1896, the decision provided a new stimulus for laws to separate the races and, of course, to discriminate against Negroes. In time, Negroes and whites were separated in the use of schools, churches, cemeteries, drinking fountains, restaurants, and all places of public accommodation and amusement. One state enacted a law providing for the separate warehousing of books used by white and Negro children. Another required the telephone company to provide separate telephone booths for white and Negro customers. In most communities housing was racially separated by law or practice.[11]

Where there was no legislation requiring segregation, local practices filled the void. Contradictions and inconsistencies seemed not to disturb those who sought to maintain racial distinctions at all costs. It mattered not that one drive-in snack bar served Negroes only on the inside, while its competitor across the street served Negroes only on the outside. Both were committed to making racial distinctions; and in communities where practices and mores had the force of law, the distinction was everything. Such practices were greatly strengthened when, in 1913, the federal government adopted policies that segregated the races in its offices as well as in its eating and restroom facilities.

By the time of World War I, Negroes and whites in the South and in parts of the North lived in separate worlds, and the apparatus for keeping the worlds separate was elaborate and complex. Negroes were segregated by law in the public schools of the southern states, while those in the northern ghettos were sent to predominantly Negro schools, except where their numbers were insufficient. Scores of Negro newspapers sprang up to provide news of Negroes that the white press consistently ignored. Negroes were as unwanted in the white churches as they had been in the late eighteenth century; and Negro churches of virtually every denomination were the answer for a people who had accepted the white man's religion even as the white man rejected his religious fellowship.

Taking note of the fact that they had been omitted from any serious consideration by the white historians, Negroes began in earnest to write the history of their own experiences as Americans. There had been Negro historians before the Civil War, but none of them had challenged the white historians' efforts to relegate Negroes to a separate, degraded world. In 1882, however, George Washington Williams published his *History of the Negro Race in America* in order to "give the world more correct ideas about the colored people." He wrote, he said, not "as a partisan apologist, but from a love for the truth of history."[12] Soon there were other historical works by Negroes describing their progress and their contributions and arguing that they deserved to be received into the full fellowship of American citizens.

It was in these post-Reconstruction years that some of the most vigorous efforts were made to destroy the two worlds of race. The desperate pleas of Negro historians were merely the more articulate attempts of Negroes to gain complete acceptance in American life. Scores of Negro organizations joined in the struggle to gain protection and recognition of their rights and to eliminate the more sordid practices that characterized the treatment of the Negro world by the white world. Unhappily, the small number of whites who were committed to racial equality dwindled in the post-Reconstruction years, while government at every level showed no interest in eliminating racial separatism. It seemed that Negro voices were indeed crying in the wilderness, but they carried on their attempts to be heard. In 1890 Negroes from twenty-one states and the District of Columbia met in Chicago and organized the Afro-American League of the United States. They called for more equitable distribution of school funds, fair and impartial trial for accused Negroes, resistance "by all legal and reasonable means" to mob and lynch law, and enjoyment of the franchise by all qualified voters. When a group of young Negro intellectuals, led by W. E. B. Du Bois, met at Niagara Falls, Ontario, in 1905, they made a similar call as they launched their Niagara Movement.

However eloquent their pleas, Negroes alone could make no successful assault on the two worlds of race. They needed help—a great deal of help. It was the bloody race riots in the early years of the twentieth century that shocked civic-mined and socially conscious whites into answering the Negro's pleas for support. Some whites began to take the view that the existence of two societies whose distinction was based solely on race was inimical to the best interests of the entire nation. Soon, they were taking the initiative and in 1909 organized the National Association for the Advancement of Colored People. They assisted the following year in establishing the National Urban League. White attorneys began to stand with Negroes before the United States Supreme Court to challenge the "grandfather clause," local segregation ordinances, and flagrant miscarriages of justice in which Negroes were the victims. The patterns of attack developed during these years were to become invaluable later. Legal action was soon supplemented by picketing, demonstrating, and boycotting, with telling effect particularly in selected northern communities.[13]

The two world wars had a profound effect on the status of Negroes in the United States and did much to mount the attack on the two worlds of race. The decade of World War I witnessed a very significant migration of Negroes. They went in large numbers—perhaps a half-million —from the rural areas of the South to the towns and cities of the South and North. They were especially attracted to the industrial centers of the North. By the thousands they poured into Pittsburgh, Cleveland, and Chicago. Although many were unable to secure employment, others were successful and achieved a standard of living they could not have imagined only a few years earlier. Northern communities were not altogether friendly and hospitable to the newcomers, but the opportunities for education and the enjoyment of political self-respect were greater than they had ever been for these Negroes. Many of them felt that they were entirely justified in their renewed hope that the war would bring about a complete merger of the two worlds of race.

Those who held such high hopes, however, were naïve in the extreme. Already the Ku Klux Klan was being revived—this time in the North as well as in the South. Its leaders were determined to develop a broad program to unite "native-born white Christians for concerted action in the preservation of American institutions and the supremacy of the white race." By the time that the war was over, the Klan was in a position to make capital of the racial animosities that had developed during the conflict itself. Racial conflicts had broken out in many places during the war; and before the conference at Versailles was over race riots in the United States had brought about what can accurately be described as the "long, hot summer" of 1919.

If anything, the military operations which aimed to save the world for democracy merely fixed more permanently the racial separation in the United States. Negro soldiers not only constituted entirely separate fighting units in the United States Army, but, once overseas, were assigned to fighting units with the French Army. Negroes who sought service with the United States Marines or the Air Force were rejected, while the Navy relegated them to menial duties. The reaction of many Negroes was bitter, but most of the leaders, including Du Bois, counseled patience and loyalty. They continued to hope that their show of patriotism would win for them a secure place of acceptance as Americans.

Few Negro Americans could have anticipated the wholesale rejection they experienced at the conclusion of World War I. Returning Negro soldiers were lynched by hanging and burning, even while still in their military uniforms. The Klan warned Negroes that they must respect the rights of the white race "in whose country they are permitted to reside." Racial conflicts swept the country, and neither federal nor state governments seemed interested in effective intervention. The worlds of race were growing farther apart in the postwar decade. Nothing indicated this more clearly than the growth of the Universal Negro Improvement Association, led by Marcus Garvey. From a mere handful of members at the end of the war, the Garvey movement rapidly became the largest secular Negro group ever organized in the United States. Although few Negroes were interested in settling in Africa—the expressed aim of Garvey—they joined the movement by the hundreds of thousands to indicate their resentment of the racial duality that seemed to them to be the central feature of the American social order.[14]

More realistic and hardheaded were the Negroes who were more determined than ever to engage in the most desperate fight of their lives to destroy racism in the United States. As the editor of the *Crisis* said in 1919, "We return from fighting. We return fighting. Make way for Democracy! We saved it in France, and by the Great Jehovah, we will save it in the U.S.A., or know the reason why." This was the spirit of what Alain Locke called "The New Negro." He fought the Democratic white primary, made war on the whites who consigned him to the ghetto, attacked racial discrimination in employment, and pressed for legislation to protect his rights. If he was seldom successful during the postwar decade and the depression, he made it quite clear that he was unalterably opposed to the un-American character of the two worlds of race.

Hope for a new assault on racism was kindled by some of the New Deal policies of Franklin D. Roosevelt. As members of the economically disadvantaged group, Negroes benefited from relief and recovery legislation. Most of it, however, recognized the existence of the two worlds of race and accommodated itself to it. Frequently bread lines and soup kitchens were separated on the basis of race. There was segregation in the employment services, while many new agencies recognized and bowed to Jim Crow. Whenever agencies, such as the Farm Security Administration (FSA), fought segregation and sought to deal with people on the basis of their needs rather than race, they came under the withering fire of the racist critics and seldom escaped alive. Winds of change, however slight, were discernible, and nowhere was this in greater evidence than in the new labor unions. Groups like the Congress of Industrial Organizations, encouraged by the support of the Wagner Labor Relations Act, began to look at manpower resources as a whole and to attack the old racial policies that viewed labor in terms of race.

As World War II approached, Negroes schooled in the experiences of the 1920s and 1930s were unwilling to see the fight against Nazism carried on in the context of an American racist ideology. Some white Americans were likewise uncomfortable in the role of freeing Europe of a racism that still permeated the United States; but it was the Negroes who dramatized American inconsistency by demanding an end to discrimination in employment in defense industries. By threatening to march on Washington in 1941 they forced the president to issue an order forbidding such discrimination. The opposition was loud and strong. Some state governors denounced the order, and some manufacturers skillfully evaded it. But it was a significant step toward the elimination of the two worlds.

During World War II the assault on racism continued. Negroes, more than a million of whom were enlisted in the armed services, bitterly fought discrimination and segregation. The armed services were, for the most part, two quite distinct racial worlds. Some Negro units had white officers, and much of the officer training was desegregated. But it was not until the final months of the war that a deliberate experiment was undertaken to involve Negro and white enlisted men in the same fighting unit. With the success of the experiment and with the warm glow of victory over Nazism as a backdrop, there was greater inclination to recognize the absurdity of maintaining a racially separate military force to protect the freedoms of the country.[15]

During the war there began the greatest migration in the history of Negro Americans. Hundreds of thousands left the South for the industrial centers of the North and West. In those places they met hostility, but they also secured employment in aviation plants, automobile factories, steel mills, and numerous other industries. Their difficulties persisted as they faced problems of housing and adjustment. But they continued to move out of the South in such large numbers that by 1965 one-third of the twenty million Negroes in the United States lived in twelve metropolitan centers of the North and West. The ramifications of such large-scale migration were numerous. The concentration of Negroes in communities where they suffered no political disabilities placed in their hands an enormous amount of political power. Consequently, some of them went to the legislatures, to Congress, and to positions on the judiciary. In turn, this won for them political respect as well as legislation that greatly strengthened their position as citizens.

Following World War II there was a marked acceleration in the war against the two worlds of race in the United States. In 1944 the Supreme Court ruled against segregation in interstate transportation, and three years later it wrote the final chapter in the war against the Democratic white primary. In 1947 the President's Committee on Civil Rights called for the "elimination of segregation, based on race, color, creed, or national origin, from American life."[16] In the following year President Truman asked Congress to establish a permanent Fair Employment Practices Commission. At the same time he took steps to eliminate segregation in the armed services. These moves on the part of the judicial and executive branches of the federal government by no means destroyed the two worlds of race, but they created a more healthy climate in which the government and others could launch an attack on racial separatism.

The attack was greatly strengthened by the new position of world leadership that the United States assumed at the close of the war. Critics of the United States were quick to point to the inconsistencies of an American position that spoke against racism abroad and countenanced it at home. New nations, brown and black, seemed reluctant to follow the lead of a country that adhered to its policy of maintaining two worlds of race—the one identified with the old colonial ruling powers and the other with the colonies now emerging as independent nations. Responsible leaders in the United States saw the weakness of their position, and some of them made new moves to repair it.

Civic and religious groups, some labor organizations, and many individuals from the white community began to join in the effort to destroy segregation and discrimination in American life. There was no danger, after World War II, that Negroes would ever again stand alone in their fight. The older interracial organizations continued, but they were joined by new ones. In addition to the numerous groups that included racial equality in their over-all programs, there were others that made the creation of one racial world their principal objective. Among them were the Congress of Racial Equality, the Southern Christian Leadership Conference, and the Student Non-Violent Coordinating Committee. Those in existence in the 1950s supported the court action that brought about the decision against segregated schools. The more recent ones have taken the lead in pressing for new legislation and in developing new techniques to be used in the war on segregation.

The most powerful direct force in the maintenance of the two worlds of race has been the state and its political subdivisions. In states and communities where racial separation and discrimination are basic to the way of life, the elected officials invariably pledge themselves to the perpetuation of the duality. Indeed, candidates frequently vie with one another in their effort to occupy the most extreme segregationist position possible on the race question. Appointed officials, including the constabulary and, not infrequently, the teachers and school administrators, become auxiliary guardians of the system of racial separation. In such communities Negroes occupy no policy-making positions, exercise no influence over the determination of policy, and are seldom even on the police force. State and local resources, including tax funds, are at the disposal of those who guard the system of segregation and discrimination; and such funds are used to enforce customs as well as laws and to disseminate information in support of the system.

The white community itself acts as a guardian of the segregated system. Schooled in the specious arguments that assert the supremacy of the white race and fearful that a destruction of the system would be harmful to their own position, they not only "go along" with it but, in many cases, enthusiastically support it. Community sanctions are so powerful, moreover, that the independent citizen who would defy the established order would find himself not only ostracized but, worse, the target of economic and political reprisals.

Within the community many self-appointed guardians of white supremacy have emerged at various times. After the Civil War and after

World War I it was the Ku Klux Klan, which has shown surprising strength in recent years. After the desegregation decision of the Supreme Court in 1954 it was the White Citizens Council, which one southern editor has called the "uptown Ku Klux Klan." From time to time since 1865, it has been the political demagogue, who has not only made capital by urging his election as a sure way to maintain the system but has also encouraged the less responsible elements of the community to take the law into their own hands.

Violence, so much a part of American history and particularly of southern history, has been an important factor in maintaining the two worlds of race. Intimidation, terror, lynchings, and riots have, in succession, been the handmaidens of political entities whose officials have been unwilling or unable to put an end to such tactics. Violence drove Negroes from the polls in the 1870s and has kept them away in droves since that time. Lynchings, the spectacular rope and faggot kind or the quiet kind of merely "doing away" with some insubordinate Negro, have served their special purpose by terrorizing whole communities of Negroes. Riots, confined to no section of the country, have demonstrated how explosive the racial situation can be in urban communities burdened with the strain of racial strife.

The heavy hand of history has been a powerful force in the maintenance of a segregated society and, conversely, in the resistance to change. Americans, especially southerners whose devotion to the past is unmatched by that of any others, have summoned history to support their arguments that age-old practices and institutions cannot be changed overnight, that social practices cannot be changed by legislation. Southerners have argued that desegregation would break down long-established customs and bring instability to a social order that, if left alone, would have no serious racial or social disorders. After all, southern whites "know" Negroes; and their knowledge has come from many generations of intimate association and observation, they insist.

White southerners have also summoned history to support them in their resistance to federal legislation designed to secure the civil rights of Negroes. At every level—in local groups, state governments, and in Congress—white southerners have asserted that federal civil rights legislation is an attempt to turn back the clock to the Reconstruction era, when federal intervention, they claim, imposed a harsh and unjust peace.[17] To make effective their argument, they use such emotion-laden phrases as "military occupation," "Negro rule," and "black-out of honest government." Americans other than southerners have been frightened by the southerners' claim that civil rights for Negroes would cause a return to the "evils" of Reconstruction. Insecure in their own knowledge of history, they have accepted the erroneous assertions about the "disaster" of radical rule after the Civil War and the vengeful punishment meted out to the South by the Negro and his white allies. Regardless of the merits of these arguments that seem specious on the face of them—to say nothing of their historical inaccuracy—they have served as effective brakes on the drive to destroy the two worlds of race.

One suspects, however, that racial bigotry has become more expensive in recent years. It is not so easy now as it once was to make political capital out of the race problem, even in the deep South. Local citizens—farmers, laborers, manufacturers—have become a bit weary of the promises of the demagogue that he will preserve the integrity of the races if he is, at the same time, unable to persuade investors to build factories and bring capital to their communities. Some southerners, dependent on tourists, are not certain that their vaunted racial pride is so dear, if it keeps visitors away and brings depression to their economy. The cities that see themselves bypassed by a prospective manufacturer because of their reputation in the field of race relations might have some sober second thoughts about the importance of maintaining their two worlds. In a word, the economics of segregation and discrimination is forcing, in some quarters, a reconsideration of the problem.

It must be added that the existence of the two worlds of race has created forces that cause some Negroes to seek its perpetuation. Some Negro institutions, the product of a dual society, have vested interests in the perpetuation of that society. And Negroes who fear the destruction of their own institutions by desegregation are encouraged by white racists to fight for their maintenance. Even where Negroes have a desire to maintain their institutions because of their honest commitment to the merits of cultural pluralism, the desire becomes a strident struggle for survival in the context of racist forces that seek with a vengeance to destroy such institutions. The firing of a few hundred Negro school teachers by a zealous, racially oriented school board forces some second thoughts on the part of the Negroes regarding the merits of desegregation.

The drive to destroy the two worlds of race has reached a new, dramatic, and somewhat explosive stage in recent years. The forces arrayed in behalf of maintaining these two worlds have been subjected to ceaseless and powerful attacks by the increasing numbers committed to the elimination of racism in American life. Through techniques of demonstrating, picketing, sitting-in, and boycotting they have not only harassed their foes but marshaled their forces. Realizing that another ingredient was needed, they have pressed for new and better laws and the active support of government. At the local and state levels they began to secure legislation in the 1940s to guarantee the civil rights of all, eliminate discrimination in employment, and achieve decent public and private housing for all.

While it is not possible to measure the influence of public opinion in the drive for equality, it can hardly be denied that over the past five or six years public opinion has shown a marked shift toward vigorous support of the civil rights movement. This can be seen in the manner in which the mass-circulation magazines as well as influential newspapers, even in the South, have stepped up their support of specific measures that have as their objective the elimination of at least the worst features of racism. The discussion of the problem of race over radio and television and the use of these media in reporting newsworthy and dramatic events in the world of race undoubtedly have had some impact. If such activities have not brought about the enactment of civil rights legislation, they have doubtless stimulated the public discussion that culminated in such legislation.

The models of city ordinances and state laws and the increased political influence of civil rights advocates stimulated new action on the federal level. Civil rights acts were passed in 1957, 1960, 1964, and 1965—after almost complete federal inactivity in this sphere for more than three-quarters of a century. Strong leadership on the part of the executive and favorable judicial interpretations of old as well as new laws have made it clear that the war against the two worlds of race now enjoys the sanction of the law and its interpreters. In many respects this constitutes the most significant development in the struggle against racism in the present century.

The reading of American history over the past two centuries impresses one with the fact that ambivalence on the crucial question of equality has persisted almost from the beginning. If the term "equal rights for all" has not always meant what it appeared to mean, the inconsistencies and the paradoxes have become increasingly apparent. This is not to say that the view that "equal rights for some" has disappeared or has even ceased to be a threat to the concept of real equality.

It is to say, however, that the voices supporting inequality, while no less strident, have been significantly weakened by the very force of the numbers and elements now seeking to eliminate the two worlds of race.

The Moral Legacy of the
Founding Fathers

As we approach the bicentennial of the independence of the United States, it may not be inappropriate to take advantage of the perspective afforded by these last two centuries. Such a perspective should enable us to understand the distance we have traveled and where we are today.

This stock-taking, as it were, seems unusually desirable, thanks to the recent crises in leadership, in confidence in our political institutions, and in the standards of public morality to which we have paid only a "nodding acquaintance" over the years. As we do so, it is well to remember that criticism does not necessarily imply hostility; and, indeed, the recognition of human weakness suggests no alienation. One thing that becomes painfully clear as we look today at the shattered careers of so many public servants, with their confusion of public service with personal gain, is that we cannot always be certain of the validity or the defensibility of the positions taken by those who claim to be our leaders.

One of the problems that we encounter as we look at our past as well as our present is that we tend to shy away from making judgments or even criticisms of those who occupy the seats of the mighty. To the uninitiated, it seems somehow inappropriate. To the seasoned or cynical politician, it is anathema.

To be sure, we ally ourselves with one political party or another—as we have done since the time of Jefferson and Hamilton—and we have railed against the politics of one party or, now and then, the conduct of party leaders.

On the whole, however, our criticisms have been superficial; and the glass houses we have occupied have, for obvious reasons, prevented

Originally published in the *University of Chicago Magazine*, Vol. XLVII, No. 4 (Spring, 1975); ©1975, *University of Chicago Magazine*, reprinted by permission.

our engaging in all-out strictures against our adversaries. The result has been that we have usually engaged in the most gentle rapping of the knuckles of those who have betrayed their public trust; and seldom have we called our public servants to account in a really serious way.

In the effort to create an "instant history" with which we could live and prosper, our early historians intentionally placed our early national heroes and leaders beyond the pale of criticism. From the time that Benjamin Franklin created his own hero in "Poor Richard" and Mason L. Weems created the cherry tree story about George Washington, it has been virtually impossible to regard our founding fathers as normal, fallible human beings. And this distorted image of them has not only created a gross historical fallacy, but it has also rendered it utterly impossible to deal with our past in terms of the realities that existed at the time. To put it another way, our romanticizing about the history of the late eighteenth century has prevented our recognizing the fact that the founding fathers made serious mistakes that have greatly affected the course of our national history from that time to the present.

In 1974 we observed the bicentennial of the first Continental Congress, called to protest the new trade measures invoked against the colonies by Great Britain and to protest the political and economic measures directed particularly against the colony of Massachusetts. In a sense these measures were, indeed, intolerable as the colonists were forced to house British soldiers stationed in their midst, and Quebec was given political and economic privileges that appeared to be clearly discriminatory against the thirteen colonies.

But were these measures imposed by the British more intolerable than those imposed or, at least, sanctioned by the colonists against their own slaves? And yet, the colonists were outraged that the mother country was denying them their own freedom—the freedom to conduct their trade as they pleased.

It was not that the colonists were unaware of the problem of a much more basic freedom than that for which they were fighting in London. First of all, they knew of the 1772 decision of Lord Mansfield in the Somerset case, in which slavery was outlawed in Britain on the compelling ground that human bondage was "too odious" in England without specific legislation authorizing it. Although the colonists did have the authorization to establish and maintain slavery, Lord Mansfield's strictures against slavery could not have been lost on them altogether.

Secondly, and even more important, the slaves themselves were already pleading for their own freedom even before the first Continental Congress met. In the first six months of 1773 several slaves in Massachusetts submitted petitions to the general court, "praying to be liberated from a State of slavery." In the following year scores of other slaves, denying that they had ever forfeited the blessings of freedom by any compact or agreement to become slaves, asked for their freedom and for some land on which each of them "could sit down quietly under his own fig tree." The legislature of the Massachusetts colony debated the subject of slavery in 1774 and 1775, but voted simply that "the matter now subside."

But the matter would neither die nor subside. As the colonists plunged into war with Great Britain, they were faced with the problem of what to do about Negro slavery. The problem presented itself in the form of urgent questions.

First, should they continue to import slaves? This was a matter of some importance to British slave-trading interests who had built fortunes out of the traffic in human beings and to colonists who feared that new, raw recruits from the West Indies and Africa would be more of a problem than a blessing. Most of the colonies opposed any new importations, and the Continental Congress affirmed the prohibition in April, 1776.

Secondly, should the colonists use black soldiers in their fight against Britain? Although a few were used in the early skirmishes of the war, a pattern of exclusion of blacks had developed by the time that independence was declared. In July, 1775, the policy had been set forth that recruiters were not to enlist any deserter from the British army, "nor any stroller, negro, or vagabond."

Then, late in the year the British welcomed all Negroes willing to join His Majesty's troops, and promised to set them free in return. The colonists were terrified, especially with the prospect of a servile insurrection. And so the Continental Congress shortly reversed its policy and grudgingly admitted blacks into the Continental Army.

The final consideration, as the colonists fought for their own freedom from Britain, was what would be the effect of their revolutionary philosophy on their own slaves. The colonists argued in the Declaration of Independence that they were oppressed; and they wanted their freedom. Thomas Jefferson, in an early draft, went so far as to accuse the king of England of imposing slavery on them; but more "practical" heads prevailed, and that provision was stricken from the Declaration.

Even so, the Declaration said "all men are created equal." "Black men as well as white men?" some wondered. Every man had an inalienable right to "life, liberty, and the pursuit of happiness." "Every black man as well as every white man?" some could well have asked.

How could the colonists make distinctions in their revolutionary philosophy? They either meant that *all* men were created equal or they did not mean it at all. They either meant that *every* man was entitled to life, liberty, and the pursuit of happiness, or they did not mean it at all.

To be sure, some patriots were apparently troubled by the contradictions between their revolutionary philosophy of political freedom and the holding of human beings in bondage. Abigail Adams, the wife of John Adams, admitted that there was something strange about their fighting to achieve and enjoy a status that they daily denied to others. Patrick Henry, who had cried "Give me liberty or give me death," admitted that slavery was "repugnant to humanity"; but it must not have seemed terribly repugnant, for he continued to hold blacks in bondage. So did George Washington and Thomas Jefferson and George Mason and Edmund Randolph and many others who signed the Declaration of Independence or the federal Constitution. They simply would not or could not see how ridiculous their position was.

And where the movement to emancipate the slaves took hold, as in New England and in some of the Middle Atlantic states, slavery was not economically profitable anyway. Consequently, if the patriots in those states were genuinely opposed to slavery, they could afford the luxury of speaking against it. But in both of the Continental Congresses and in the Declaration of Independence the founding fathers failed to take an unequivocal, categorical stand against slavery. Obviously, human bondage and human dignity were not as important to them as their own political and economic independence.

The founding fathers were not only compelled to live with their own inconsistency but they also had to stand convicted before the very humble group which they excluded from their political and social fellowship. In 1777 a group of Massachusetts blacks told the whites of that state that every principle that impelled America to break with England "pleads stronger than a thousand arguments" against slavery. In 1779 a group of Connecticut slaves petitioned the state for their liberty, declaring that they "groaned" under the burdens and indignities they were required to bear.

In 1781, Paul Cuffe and his brother, two young enterprising blacks, asked Massachusetts to excuse them from the duty of paying taxes, since they "had no influence in the election of those who tax us." And when they refused to pay their taxes, those who had shouted that England's taxation without representation was tyranny, slapped the Cuffe brothers in jail!

Thus, when the colonists emerged victorious from their war with England, they had both their independence *and* their slaves. It seemed to matter so little to most of the patriots that the slaves themselves had eloquently pointed out their inconsistencies or that not a few of the patriots themselves saw and pointed out their own fallacious position. It made no difference that five thousand blacks had joined in the fight for independence, only to discover that *real* freedom did not apply to them. The agencies that forged a national policy against England—the Continental Congresses and the government under the Articles of Confederation—were incapable of forging—or unwilling to forge—a national policy in favor of human freedom.

It was not a propitious way to start a new nation, especially since its professions were so different from its practices and since it presumed to be the model for other new world colonies that would, in time, seek their independence from the tyranny of Europe.

Having achieved their own independence, the patriots exhibited no great anxiety to extend the blessings of liberty to those among them who did not enjoy it. They could not altogether ignore the implications of the revolutionary philosophy, however. As early as 1777 the Massachusetts legislature had under consideration a measure to prohibit "the practice of holding persons in Slavery." Three years later the new constitution of that state declared that "all men are born free and equal." Some doubtless hoped that those high sounding words would mean more in the constitution of Massachusetts than they had meant in the Declaration of Independence.

Her neighbors, however, were more equivocal, with New Hampshire, Connecticut, and Rhode Island vacillating, for one reason or another, until another decade had passed. Although Pennsylvania did abolish slavery in 1780, New York and New Jersey did no better than prepare the groundwork for gradual emancipation at a later date.

One may well be greatly saddened by the thought that the author of the Declaration of Independence and the commander of the Revolutionary army and so many heroes of the Revolution were slaveholders. Even more disheartening, if such is possible, is that those *same* leaders and heroes were not greatly affected by the philosophy of freedom which they espoused. At least they gave no evidence of having been greatly affected by it.

Nor did they show any great magnanimity of spirit, once the war was over and political independence was assured. While northerners debated the questions of how and when they would free their slaves, the institution of human bondage remained as deeply entrenched as ever—from Delaware to Georgia. The only area on which there was national agreement that slavery should be prohibited was the area east of the Mississippi River and north of the Ohio River—the Northwest Territory. The agreement to prohibit slavery in that area, where it did not really exist and where relatively few white settlers lived, posed no great problem and surely it did not reflect a ground swell for liberty.

Meanwhile the prohibition, it should be noted, did not apply to the area south of the Ohio River, where slaveholders were more likely to settle anyway! This clearly shows that the founding fathers were willing to "play" with the serious question of freedom, thus evincing a cynicism that was itself unworthy of statesmanship.

Nor is one uplifted or inspired by the attitude of the founding fathers toward the slave trade, once their independence was secured. In the decade following independence the importation of slaves into the United States actually increased over the previous decade as well as over the decade before the War for Independence began. Far from languishing, the institution of slavery was prospering and growing. In its deliberations between 1781 and 1789 the Congress of the Confederation barely touched on the question of slavery or the slave trade. There was, to be sure, some concern over the capture of slaves; and the Congress gave some attention to a Quaker petition against the trade, but it took no action.

On the whole the nation did not raise a hand against it. The flurry of activity in the states, which led to the prohibition of slave importations in some of them and a temporary cessation of the trade in others, had the effect of misleading many people into thinking that slavery's hold on the nation was weakening.

That this was far from the actual situation became painfully clear when the delegates gathered in Philadelphia in 1787 to write a new constitution. In the discussion over the slave trade only practical and economic considerations held sway. Humane considerations simply were not present. Maryland and Virginia tended to oppose the slave trade simply because they were overstocked and were not anxious to have any large importations into their midst. South Carolina and Georgia, where the death rate in the rice swamps was high and where slaveholders needed new recruits to develop new areas, demanded an open door for slave dealers.

And who rushed to the rescue when South Carolina demanded concessions on the question of the slave trade? It was Oliver Ellsworth of Connecticut, who observed that a provision in the Constitution against the slave trade would be "unjust towards South Carolina and Georgia. Let us not intermeddle," he said. "As population increases, poor laborers will be so plenty as to render slaves useless." It is impossible to conceive that such temporizing on the part of a leading colonist would have been tolerated in the late dispute with England.

Could the new national government that was designed to be strong have *anything* to say regarding slavery and the slave trade in the states? Elbridge Gerry of Massachusetts answered that it could not. It only had to refrain from giving direct sanction to the system.

Perhaps this is the view that seemed to silence the venerable Benjamin Franklin. The oldest and easily one of the most respected members of the Constitutional Convention, Franklin brought with him a strong resolution against the slave trade that had been entrusted to him by the Pennsylvania Abolition Society. Although he was one of the most frequent speakers at the convention, he never introduced the resolution. With faint hearts such as Gerry's and Franklin's there is little wonder that South Carolina and Georgia were able to have their own way in wording the provision that declared that the slave trade could not be prohibited for another twenty years. One need only to look at the slave importation figures between 1788 and 1808 to appreciate how much advantage was taken of this generous reprieve.

The founding fathers did no better when it came to counting slaves for purposes of representation and taxation. Northerners, who regarded slaves as property, insisted that for the purpose of representation they could not be counted as people. Southern slaveholders, while cheerfully admitting that slaves were property, insisted that they were also people and should be counted as such. It is one of the remarkable ironies of the early history of this democracy that the very men who had shouted so loudly that all men were created equal could not now agree on whether or not persons of African descent were men at all.

The irony was compounded when, in the so-called major compromise of the Constitution, the delegates agreed that a slave was three-fifths of a man, meaning that five slaves were to be counted as three persons. The magic of racism can work magic with the human mind.

One wonders whether Catherine Drinker Bowen had this in mind when she called her history of the Constitutional Convention *The Miracle at Philadelphia.*

If slaveholders feared possible insurrections by their slaves, they were no less apprehensive about the day-to-day attrition of the institution caused by slaves running away. They wanted to be certain that the Constitution recognized slaves as property and that it offered protection to that property, especially runaways. Significantly, there was virtually no opposition to the proposal that states give up fugitive slaves to their owners. The slaveowners had already won such sweeping constitutional recognition of slavery that the fugitive slave provision may be regarded as something of an anticlimax. There was, as Roger Sherman of Connecticut pointed out, as much justification for the public seizure and surrendering of a slave as there was for the seizure of a horse. Thus, a slave, who was only three-fifths of a man, was to be regarded in this connection as no more than a horse!

And the Constitution required that slaves who ran away were not to enjoy the freedom that they had won in their own private war for independence, but were to be returned to those who claimed title to them. Consequently, there was a remarkable distinction between fighting for one's political independence, which the patriots expected to win, and did, and fighting for one's freedom from slavery, which these same patriots made certain that the slaves would not win.

At the outset it was observed that we tend to shy away from making criticisms or judgments of those who occupy the seats of the mighty. This is not good either for ourselves or the institutions and way of life we seek to foster. If we would deal with our past in terms of the realities that existed at the time, it becomes necessary for us to deal with our early leaders in their own terms, namely, as frail, fallible human beings, and—at times—utterly indifferent to the great causes they claimed to serve.

We may admire them for many things: their courage and bravery in the military struggle against Britain; their imaginative creativity in forging a new instrument of government; and their matchless service to a cause that captured the imagination of people around the world.

It does not follow, however, that we should admire them for betraying the ideals to which they gave lip service, for speaking eloquently at one moment for the brotherhood of man and in the next moment denying it to their black brothers who fought by their side in their darkest hours of peril, and for degrading the human spirit by equating five black men with three white men or equating a black man with a horse!

We are concerned here not so much for the harm that the founding fathers did to the cause they claimed to serve as for the harm that their moral legacy has done to every generation of their progeny. Having created a tragically flawed revolutionary doctrine and a constitution that did *not* bestow the blessings of liberty on its posterity, the founding fathers set the stage for every succeeding generation of Americans to apologize, compromise, and temporize on those principles of liberty that were supposed to be the very foundation of our system of government and way of life.

That is why the United States was so very apprehensive when Haiti and most of the other Latin American countries sought to wipe out slavery the moment they received their political independence. The consistency of those nations was alien to the view of the United States on the same question.

That is why the United States failed to recognize the existence of the pioneer republics of Haiti and Liberia until this nation was in the throes of a great civil war and sought to "use" these countries for colonizing some blacks. Earlier recognition would have implied an equality in the human family that the United States was unwilling to concede.

That is why this nation tolerated and, indeed, nurtured the cultivation of a racism that has been as insidious as it has been pervasive.

Racial segregation, discrimination, and degradation are no unanticipated accidents in this nation's history. They stem logically and directly from the legacy that the founding fathers bestowed upon contemporary America. The denial of equality in the year of independence led directly to the denial of equality in the era of the bicentennial of independence. The so-called compromises in the Constitution of 1787 led directly to the arguments in our own time that we can compromise equality with impunity and somehow use the Constitution as an instrument to preserve privilege and to foster inequality. It has thus become easy to invoke the spirit of the founding fathers whenever we seek ideological support for the social, political, and economic inequities that have become a part of the American way.

It would be perverse indeed to derive satisfaction from calling attention to the flaws in the character and conduct of the founding fathers. And it would be irresponsible to do so merely to indulge in whimsical iconoclasm. But it would be equally irresponsible in the era of the bicentennial of independence not to use the occasion to examine our past with a view to improving the human condition.

An appropriate beginning, it would seem, would be to celebrate our origins for what they were—to honor the principles of independence for which so many patriots fought and died. It is equally appropriate to be outraged over the manner in which the principles of human freedom and human dignity were denied and debased by those same patriots. Their legacy to us in this regard cannot, under any circumstances, be cherished or celebrated. Rather, this legacy represents a continuing and dismaying problem that requires us all to put forth as much effort to overcome it as the founding fathers did in handing it down to us.

Lincoln and
Public Morality

Shortly before Abraham Lincoln left Springfield for his first inauguration, he dispatched the following message to Isaac Fenno, a wholesale clothing merchant of Boston:

> Your note of the 1st inst., together with a very substantial and handsome overcoat which accompanied it by Express, were duly received by me, and would have been acknowledged sooner but for the multifarious demands upon my time and attention.
>
> Permit me now to thank you sincerely for your elegant and valuable New Year's gift, and the many expressions of personal confidence and regard contained in your letter.

There is no suggestion in Lincoln's letter that the acknowledgment of the overcoat was delayed because of some indecision regarding the propriety of accepting it. Nor is there any indication in this or other expressions of the new president that he did not know precisely what to do about such matters. He was already quite aware of the fact that he would be harassed by demands on his time, strains on his patience, and impositions on his good nature not only by zealous patriots and good citizens but also by persons whose base motives and low morality were all too obvious. It was, perhaps, this very awareness of the pressures to which he would be subjected that sharpened Lincoln's understanding of the limits of propriety *and* morality in dealing with matters related to the public service. But even as his understanding increased, Lincoln must have been impressed with the numerous facets of this question and the necessity for being sensitive to what he doubtless would have called its multifarious implications and ramifications.

The continuing interest of our leading public servants in the question of ethics and morality in the performance of their duties is a

Originally published by the Chicago Historical Society, 1959. Reprinted by permission.

significant fact of life on the American political scene. The first president of the United States was anxious that those who assisted in launching the new government should maintain high standards of decency and honesty. In his farewell address he spoke of morality as one of the indispensable supports of political prosperity and commended to his fellows the view that "virtue or morality is a necessary spring of popular government." More than a century and a half later one of Washington's successors, President Dwight D. Eisenhower, reflected the current national hypersensitivity to the question of public morality when he declared in the summer of 1958 that he would not countenance any deviation of public servants from the strictest adherence to the highest standards of ethics in government. He said, "I expect the highest possible standards not only of conduct but of appearance of conduct."

In the years between the founding of our national government and the present time there have been numerous expressions of concern about the maintenance of high standards of morality in the public service. There have, of course, been many shifts in the standards of public morality as well as shifts in emphasis or focus of attention from one type of conduct to another. And it can almost be said that each generation has set its own standards or has attempted to set them. Certainly, we have witnessed in our own time the pronouncement of a rather unique and excessive position on what we now call "ethics in government." It involves a set of policies that bristle, if they do not sparkle, with their commitment to virtue and goodness. These policies and practices require elected or appointed public servants to sever all their outside business connections, and to sell their stocks, bonds, and other securities. These policies forbid these servants of the people from accepting gifts that have any substantial value. They are barred, of course, from advancing, even by a favorable hint, the interests of their friends or associates even if these persons happen to deserve favorable consideration by their government or even if their government would benefit from such an association.

With such standards of public morality in force we have seen a vice presidential candidate go before the nation and plead not guilty to imputations of a defective character because friends had built up a fund for his discretionary use in his "crusade." We have witnessed a secretary of defense divesting himself of assets and investments accumulated over a lifetime in order to qualify for taking his oath of office. We have seen a presidential assistant literally hounded out of office because he received gifts from a friend for whom he made "imprudent" inquiries in other governmental offices.

It is no easy task to prove that these practices have actually elevated morality in the public service or that they have improved the operations of the government itself. On the face of them they seem rather excessively and superficially virtuous. As one critic recently observed, they indict villains in government and reflect only indirectly or obliquely on the villains with whom they have had or with whom they might have some traffic. To the extent that they presume that public servants with accumulated or inherited fortunes are necessarily and inevitably venal or dishonest and must "do something about their filthy lucre" they are flying in the face of fact and are coming dangerously close to equating poverty with virtue. The logical consequences of such practices are not pleasant to contemplate. In the state of New York, for example, it would involve forcing a Harriman to get rid of his last five railroads before he could become governor. Imagine, if you can, forcing a Rockefeller to bury his fortune in *another* Fort Knox (presumably there would not be room in Fort Knox for *his* gold *and* ours) before taking over the reins of the empire state.

It can be argued that our current policies with respect to morality in the public service have become so excessive on the side of an assumed righteousness and in support of the accepted *forms* of morality that they lose sight of the fundamental aspects of decency and honesty that they claim to promote. It cannot be successfully claimed that they necessarily improve the operations of the government, that they guarantee honesty in government, or that they attract a higher type of person into the public service. One would be hard put to produce concrete evidence that any substantial improvement of the public service has come from what we are pleased to call pristine virtue or, more uncharitably, "hound's tooth" cleanliness. It is not irrelevant to remember that coincidental with the introduction of new, rigorous standards of public morality have come the revelations of numerous practices of public immorality—currently defined—ranging from presenting expensive gifts to persons high in the public service to peddling influence from one public door to another. Small wonder that many citizens, in their overly righteous indignation, have wondered what this government is coming to.

It would seem, though, that this righteous wrath, if it was aroused by reports of the changing of hands of a deep freeze, a pastel mink, an oriental rug, or a vicuna coat, had wasted a good deal of its outrage on the wrong objects. Are such transactions symptomatic of moral depravity in government? Do they reflect the kind of dishonesty and indecency that are destructive of the best interests of the people and of the ends of government? An affirmative answer cannot be a superficial one. Any answer must take into consideration the fact that government on any level is a political machine and that there are enormously complex political considerations that have a legitimate relationship with government. These political considerations, to be sure, are abused at times and they often encourage dishonesty and immorality. This need not be true, however. And before an indictment can be drawn against a person or a practice as immoral from the point of view of the public it must recognize the inescapable fact that government functions in a political context, public servants who are not civil servants are politicians, and the use of political influence to further the ends of government is not only realistic but, under our system, a legitimate pursuit.

No president of the United States has realized more clearly these hard, cold facts of his political life than did Abraham Lincoln. He never forgot that he was the head of a party as well as the head of the government, and he fully appreciated the importance of strengthening his party through the use of the resources of the government. Perhaps no president has been forced to face more critical questions bearing on the problem of ethics in government than Lincoln. Certainly no president up to Lincoln's time had been called upon to make so many decisions that involved the defining of public morality. The years of Lincoln's administration seemed peculiarly filled with problems of ethics in government, many of which were to confound this country from that day to this.

A new party had come to power, and the demands of thousands for patronage were not merely the demands of many politicians emerging from a long drought of little patronage but of a group that, as a group, had *never* tasted the spoils of victory. This was a thirst that was almost unquenchable. How to satisfy it without dislocating and rendering inoperable the very machinery of government was one of the very formidable tasks of President Lincoln in the early months of his administration. By the time he came to office, moreover, the course of secession had become so rampant that it was reasonable to entertain the most serious doubts about the loyalty of hundreds of federal employees. It was not only fair but highly desirable to retain loyal public servants in the interest of promoting national security and building political strength. Disloyalty, however, was of course the epitome of public immorality and could not, in any sense, be countenanced. Lincoln's duty in this regard was clear and unmistakable.

Another problem that arose from the crisis of secession and war was created by the dramatic expansion of the functions of government. There was the enormous increase of the roster of public servants performing innumerable tasks on the civilian and military fronts. There was also the fantastic expansion of the activities of the federal government, accompanied by an unprecedented increase in governmental expenditures. Almost overnight the government came to dominate the market place as it began to purchase every conceivable commodity in connection with its prosecution of the war. And the very volume of the business created opportunities for profiteering, graft, and other forms of corruption hitherto undreamed of. The temptations were as persistent as they were tremendous; and only the stout-hearted with high standards of public morality could resist the opportunities for graft that were to be seen on every hand. The danger here was not merely that dishonesty would consume the available resources of the country but that it would lead to the destruction of the government itself. The danger was a real one, and no one appreciated it more fully than Lincoln himself.

Finally, there were the problems related to the prosecution of the war and to the aims for which it was being fought. If this did not bear directly on such matters as graft and dishonesty, it was no less related to the basic problem of public morality. For it was not only desirable but perhaps even necessary for national survival to discuss honestly and forthrightly the war aims. The risks in misrepresentation or dishonesty were formidable, and any leader who was unwilling to enunciate a position on the critical questions of the day was courting personal and national disaster. Lincoln had no intention of doing either. Too long, even before the secession crisis, he had spoken for Union above all, and if he was committed to an ideal of freedom for all it was to be achieved and maintained in an indestructible union. His unequivocal position in this regard was, in a sense, a measure of his high public morality.

Lincoln approached the numerous problems that involved his personal as well as his public morality with a specific and precise philosophy that was the result of long and serious contemplation as well as experience. His deep belief in honesty in all relations, public and private, was set forth in a lecture in 1850. In denying the popular belief that lawyers were necessarily dishonest, he counseled young lawyers to "resolve to be honest at all events; and if in your own judgment you cannot be an honest lawyer, resolve to be honest without being a lawyer." This remained a ruling passion throughout his life. When observers could make no other favorable comment about him they willingly recognized his honesty. "We have seen it in his face; hopeless honesty—that is all," one remarked after visiting him during his first year in office.

There was more than a hopeless honesty in Lincoln's public philosophy, as even this observer could have discovered had he taken the trouble to look. En route to his first inauguration Lincoln stopped in Philadelphia and pledged himself to follow in the path of the founding fathers who had laid down principles of government that were high in every respect and entirely worthy of emulation. The teachings of those who wrote the Declaration of Independence and the Constitution of the United States were sacred, he asserted. "I shall do nothing inconsistent with the teachings of those holy and most sacred walls," in which the Constitution was written. "May my right hand forget its cunning and my tongue cleave to the roof of my mouth, if ever I prove false to those teachings," he concluded. No "hopeless honesty" here but a vigorous commitment to what he regarded as high principles of decent and good government.

But Lincoln was a practical man, a realist in the best sense of the term. To him good government was a feasible, workable instrument that was expected to function in the hands of human beings whose frailties were legion. This led him to the practice of expediency, "of compromise, of seeing or trying to see everything and neglect nothing for every political decision which he had to make." These decisions, he felt, should not be based on notions of right and wrong, but instead, as Stanley Pargellis has suggested, on ideas of what is good and evil. The true rule, Lincoln declared, in determining whether to embrace or reject anything, "is not whether it have any evil in it but whether it have more of evil than of good. There are few things wholly evil or wholly good." He subscribed to the view that the central idea behind the national political philosophy was the equality of men. But practical man that he was, he doubted that the monstrous evil of slavery could be dealt with summarily. It was an infection that was so deeply imbedded in the national fabric that a violent elimination of it would rend the structure of the nation. This view did not alter his strong opposition to the evil of slavery any more than it altered his opposition to public immorality in general.

Lincoln never lost sight of the fact that the presidency of the United States was a political office and its incumbent was necessarily and inevitably a politician. Consequently he admittedly used his appointive power to reward his political supporters and to strengthen his political position. His guiding principle, he said, was "justice to all," but this maxim did not seem to prevent his functioning as a political-minded public servant in dispensing the patronage. As a member of the state legislature, as a member of Congress, and as president the practice of rewarding the party faithful gained strict adherence from Lincoln. He took his patronage obligation seriously, the historian of his years in Congress tells us, and he cheerfully ran errands for loyal and ambitious constituents. Hundreds of times, when president, he sought employment in some branch of the government for loyal supporters. That he did not altogether escape the practice of nepotism can be seen in his effort to secure employment and other favors for some of his relatives but more frequently for Mrs. Lincoln's kinsmen.

Even in the armed forces there are numerous examples of the manner in which Lincoln used the patronage, at times to gain support for the war from discordant elements and at other times to dissipate dissension or even disloyalty. Powerful Democrats like Nathaniel P. Banks, John A. McClernand, and Benjamin Butler found criticizing the conduct of the war a bit awkward once they had received the presidential favor of high military commissions. The scramble for public office, civil or military, greatly distressed Lincoln and caused him once to declare, while especially exasperated, that the struggle for office as a way to live without work would become a real test of the strength of our institutions. Unpleasant and dangerous as it was, it was something with which the president had to live, and he was willing to do so.

But Lincoln's determination to dispense the patronage justly and effectively led him to keep it in his own hands as much as possible. Thus he did not attempt to conceal his disgust when word came to him that Thurlow Weed was passing the word around that he had the president's authority to dispense the patronage in New York. "I do not believe that you have so claimed," Lincoln wrote Weed, "but still so some men say. On that subject you know all I have said to you is 'justice to all,' and I have said nothing more particular to anyone." He concluded by tersely expressing the hope that Weed would not use his name in the matter.

Justice in the matter of the patronage involved awarding public office on an equitable basis. It also involved the honest discharge of one's duties as well as the fair and discreet use of the power vested in the public servant. In 1864 Lincoln had to remind the postmaster of Philadelphia of these basic principles when it was reported that the postmaster was forcing postal employees under him to vote for a certain candidate for Congress. Lincoln's chagrin was based in part on the fact that the postmaster was supporting the candidate who was opposing Lincoln's choice. There was, however, another more important consideration, Lincoln argued, and it was that "all our friends should have absolute freedom of choice among our friends. My wish, therefore, is that you will do just as you think with your own suffrage . . . and not constrain any of your subordinates to do other than he thinks fit with his."

Likewise, when Lincoln learned that the commissioner of public buildings had caused a bill to be introduced in Congress to remove his office from the Interior Department and enlarge his powers and patronage, Lincoln made his position clear. He said that if Congress wished to make the changes it was certainly free to do so. "What I wish to say," he warned, "is that if the change is made, I do not think I can allow you to retain the office; because that would be encouraging officers to be constantly intriguing, to the detriment of the public interest, in order to profit themselves." The public interest, Lincoln contended, must never be abused or injured regardless of the importance of the patronage and its use for political purposes.

The abuse of the power of public office was a matter about which the president was most sensitive. It was doubtless this fear that made Lincoln reluctant to appoint Simon Cameron secretary of war. Lincoln perhaps would not have done so had not his supporters made such a promise at the Chicago convention and had not he fully appreciated the connection between this appointment and party harmony in the East. "Lincoln's in a fix," Billy Herndon said. "Cameron's appointment to an office in his cabinet bothers him. If Lincoln do appoint Cameron, he gets a fight on his hands, and if he do not he gets a quarrel deep abiding and lasting. Poor Lincoln! God help him."

But Cameron's enemies said that as senator he had been guilty of corruption in obtaining contracts and that if appointed secretary of war he would use the patronage of his office for his own private gain. These matters troubled Lincoln and, in attempting to think them through, he set forth some significant points in his conception of public morality. "I can see no impropriety in his taking contracts or making money out of them," Lincoln argued, "as that is a mere matter of business. There is nothing wrong in this, unless some unfairness or dishonesty is shown, which supposition I have no doubt General Cameron will be able to disprove . . . I shall deal with him fairly, but . . . if the charges against him are proven, he cannot have a seat in my cabinet, as I will not have associated with me one whose character is impeached." Despite the frequency of these charges and despite the vacillation of the president-elect, Lincoln finally went through with the appointment and never ceased to regret it.

The kinds of corruption that had been freely predicted by Cameron's critics permeated the War Department almost from the beginning of Cameron's tenure. And the inefficiency of the secretary, together with a phenomenal expansion of the activities of the office, merely contributed to the growth of every conceivable form of corruption. There was incredible fraud in the construction of fortifications in St. Louis, where the contractors made a profit of at least $111,000 on a contract of $171,000. The purchase of worthless muskets for more than $160,000 and the purchase of pocketless, buttonless, and generally useless uniforms from a famous New York firm are classic and well-known examples of wartime corruption. When the rumors were rife that Cameron was involved in the corruption a delegation called on the president and demanded his removal. "Gentlemen," the president said, "if you want General Cameron removed, you have only to bring me *one proved* case of dishonesty, and I promise you his head. But I assure you that I am not going to act on what seems to me the most unfounded gossip."

When Lincoln did act, by retiring Cameron from the War Department and appointing him to be minister to Russia, he did not do so because of any specific act or acts of corruption committed by Cameron. Rather, it was doubtless Cameron's general inefficiency as well as his embarrassment to the administration by the premature support he gave the proposal to arm the slaves in his first annual report. Even these instances of human frailty did not restrain Lincoln in assuring Cameron, in his letter of dismissal, of his "undiminished confidence," his "affectionate esteem," and his sure expectation that in his Russian post Cameron would be able to render services no less important than those he could render at home. Even so, the House of Representatives passed a resolution condemning "Simon Cameron, late Secretary of War," for adopting a "policy highly injurious to the public service." The resolution criticized Cameron's investing several New York businesses with unrestricted authority to purchase military supplies without any guarantee or security for the faithful performance of their duties.

Lincoln was the first to come to Cameron's defense in this public embarrassment. The president told the members of the House that while the secretary of war fully approved the proceedings "they were not moved nor suggested by himself and that not only the president but all the other heads of departments were at least equally responsible with him for whatever error, wrong, or fault was committed in the premises." Lincoln admitted the irregularity of advancing $2,000,000 of public funds without security to a group of men not in the employ of the United States. But he added that he was not aware that a dollar of it had been lost or wasted; and it was clear that in his own mind the "honesty of his act and the emergency which occasioned it excused its illegality." In this matter, Lincoln was not defending a crony but a principle. It was the principle of the transcendent importance of survival over forms and procedure.

While nothing but the direst national emergency could excuse irregularities in the use of authority, nothing at all, from Lincoln's view, could excuse the abuse of power that was inconsistent with the public good. On one occasion an old friend sought Lincoln's assistance in securing possession of land near Memphis for a woman whose husband was in the Confederate service and on which the claim had already been passed once or twice. The fact that the husband was in the Confederate service did not disturb Lincoln, but the fact that his assistance was being sought as a favor and nothing more irritated him greatly. He was blunt in his reply. "The impropriety of bringing such cases to me, is obvious to anyone who will consider that I could not properly act on any case without understanding it; and that I have neither the means nor time to obtain such understanding."

The pressure on the president to grant personal favors that would be financially rewarding to his friends was "almost incredible," and at times he gave way. In Alexandria, Louisiana, two men turned up with trading permits in the president's handwriting. They were old, personal Springfield friends of Lincoln's. What little cotton they collected was taken away from them by the army and put to military use. Their very appearance in the area, however, with permits signed by Lincoln set many tongues wagging. This was doubtless the exception, the rare occasion when the pressure was unbearable and the president relented. More typical is the instance in 1863 when Lincoln's good friend Representative William Kellogg tried to persuade him to grant a friend a permit to sell ordinary articles of commerce at Helena, Arkansas, and to purchase cotton and other commodities from loyal men. This was a request made to order for Lincoln's complete exasperation, and he did not attempt to conceal from his good friend his utter disgust.

> I think you do not know how embarrassing your request is. Few things are so troublesome to the government as the fierceness with which the profits of trading in cotton [sic] are sought. . . . What can and can not be done, has, for the time been settled, and it seems to me I cannot safely break over it. I know it is thought that one case is not much, but how can I favor one and deny another. . . . The administration would do for you as much as for any other man; and I personally would do some more than for most others, but really I cannot involve myself and the Government as this would do.

Lincoln feared neither the power of money nor a close association with men powerful in the business community. The use of money in politics was, at times, both right and indispensable, he wrote a loyal Kansas supporter in 1860; and there were many times when he wished he had more of it for political and other purposes. In 1848 while in Congress he got a bit more money than the law provided for travel expenses of members of Congress. Instead of reporting, as a basis for reimbursement, the official mileage between Springfield and Washington—780 miles—Lincoln submitted a bill for 1,626 miles, thereby securing almost $700 in excess of the amount provided by law. Lincoln did not regard this as other than a political perquisite in which many members shared. From his point of view neither personal nor public integrity was at stake.

Lincoln did not grab at every dollar that was available, however; and the pattern of his personal attitude toward financial matters emerged from the careful studies made of them by the late Harry Pratt. When a real estate dealer offered to raise $10,000 for Lincoln's personal use in 1861, the president-elect gratefully declined on the ground that he did not need the money at that time. When the president of Springfield's First National Bank offered to sell Lincoln $5,000 worth of paid-up shares in the bank in 1864, Lincoln declined but not because he was personally opposed to the transaction. "I would accept at once, were it not that I fear there might be some impropriety in it, though I do not see that there would. I will think of it a while." The impropriety Lincoln feared was related to the judgment that others might place on his acts. The risk in an election year was not worth it. Lincoln never took up the generous offer, for he was not one to run political risks unnecessarily.

Lincoln, however, was not above accepting support to help finance his political activities, and he was realist enough to know that this financial aid did not come to him out of love. "Do men act without motive?" he had asked when in Congress in 1849. "Did business men commonly go into an expenditure of money which could be of no account to them?" To Lincoln the answers were obvious. Thus, he accepted financial support only when absolutely necessary; and when he did, he was fully aware of the obligations he thus incurred. He refused the offer of $500 from a young Bloomington lawyer in 1858 with the following comment: "I am not so poor as you suppose—don't want any money, don't know how to use money on such occasions— can't do it and never will—though much obliged to you." The campaign against Douglas was much more expensive than Lincoln had anticipated, and when it was over the unsuccessful candidate gladly accepted offers to share in the expenses. It was at this time that Lincoln wrote a friend who had helped him in 1856 that inasmuch as he did not spend all that had been offered he hoped that he could call on his generous friend to assist in liquidating the expenses of the campaign of 1858.

Lincoln seemed genuinely pleased with his associations with big business and with important personages from the business community. He was, for a number of years, an attorney for the Illinois Central Railroad and was understandably depressed when the big line threw its support to Douglas in 1858. He had powerful friends on the New York Central Railroad, and legend has it that he was offered the position of general counsel for the line in 1860. He declined it ostensibly on the ground that it would ruin his family to have an annual income of $10,000. A more likely reason was that by 1860 Lincoln had his eyes fixed squarely on the presidency. As Billy Herndon later complained, his partner was devoting precious little time to the practice of law. The New York Central could not compete with the White House.

Bankers, industrialists, railroad men, and the like moved freely in and out of the White House and in and out of the Lincoln administration. The test to which Lincoln subjected them both as friends and officeholders was the same test to which he subjected others, namely, honesty, decency, and freedom from any desire for personal aggrandizement that would be harmful to the public interest. He not only did not require federal officeholders to relinquish their investments but he did not require them to sever their business connections. During his tenure as secretary of war Cameron remained a large stockholder in the Northern Central Railroad, commonly called "Cameron's Road." Thomas A. Scott became assistant secretary of war but retained his position as vice-president of the Pennsylvania Railroad with which he was constantly making contracts for transporting supplies and soldiers. When John Z. Goodrich became collector of the port at Boston he gave up neither his chairmanship of the Republican party in Massachusetts nor his long connection with a woolen factory. The same could be said for flour manufacturer William B. Thomas, who became the collector at Philadelphia. "Conflict of interest" was a phrase unknown to American politics in the Civil War era; and the rules for the whole range of contacts between government and business were, at best, vaguely and indistinctly articulated.

The Civil War president regarded gifts from citizens as a compliment to him and the office that he occupied. While the gifts he received were, for the most part, of small value, there is no evidence that he would have been troubled by questions of propriety in accepting gifts of greater value. He always took the time to acknowledge with gratitude even the most insignificant token of esteem and to return a compliment to the donor by referring to a pair of socks as "fine, and soft and warm," to a whip as "elegant" and "displaying a perfection of workmanship," to a chair presented by the Shakers as "very comfortable," and to the overcoat as "substantial and handsome." The record of gifts to Lincoln's colleagues and subordinates is not so complete as his own. That the other public servants were the objects of various expressions of generosity and even gratitude cannot be gainsaid. There is, so far as this writer knows, no expression of disapproval on Lincoln's part of gifts either to himself or to others in his administration.

Attempts to peddle influence were inevitable in a government whose functions and responsibilities were increasing more rapidly than the theater of war itself. Trobriand described the army of lobbyists and the like as second only to the army that was in the field. "They were everywhere; in the streets, in the hotels, in the offices, at the Capitol, and in the White House." Lincoln attempted to avoid such pressures as much as possible and to pursue a course of action that was oblivious to their existence. By the very nature of the circumstances, however, he was not always successful; but he never stopped trying. And he did not like indiscriminate influence peddling. To a group of St. Louis businessmen who sought his influence in securing a contract he replied, "As to contracts, and jobs, I understand that, by the law, they are awarded to the best bidders; and if the government agents at St. Louis do differently, it would be good ground to prossecute [*sic*] them upon." Whenever it became clear that friends or foes were attempting to use Lincoln to advance their own interests at the expense of the interest of the public, Lincoln was blunt and uncompromising in his rejection of their entreaties.

Lincoln's view of public morality did not, however, restrain him from using the power of his office to gain positions and other favors for his friends. Over and over again a word dropped here or a note scribbled there would bring the desired results, even when it irritated a Chase or a Bates. To the secretary of the interior he wrote, "Can you, by any possibility, find some place for Judge [Horatio N.] Taft? I shall be greatly obliged if you can and will." To the secretary of war he wrote, "I really wish Jesse W. Fell, of Illinois, to be appointed a paymaster in the Regular Army, at farthest, as early as the first of July 1862. I wish nothing to interfere with this; and I have so written as much as two months ago I think." Again, "I personally wish Jacob R. Freese, of New-Jersey to be appointed a Colonel for a colored regiment—and this regardless of whether he can tell the exact shade of Julius Caesar's hair." He also sought interviews in various departments for friends and others who had been commended to him, and fully expected his own recommendations to be honored. Early in his administration he advised a friend who knew almost nothing about surveying to seek contracts surveying public lands. Lincoln said that a knowledge of surveying was not necessary since his job, which was good for about $50,000, would be to organize parties of professional surveyors. When the friend asked how he would get the contracts, Lincoln replied, "Leave that entirely to me. I'll see that you get the contracts."

Thus spoke and acted the man who, more than any of his predecessors, was called upon to face the difficult problem of public morality. He faced it and dealt with it as a realist rather than as a crusader, as a patriot and politician rather than as a doctrinaire moralist and reformer. The conduct he required of himself and his colleagues was always to act in a way that would promote the public interest. He was less concerned with procedure than with acts that would foster union, victory, and human decency. He was not adverse to using the patronage to build a loyal and powerful political organization, but he had no patience for any abuse of this power and especially its use for purely selfish purposes. He was even willing to use the military patronage to give commissions to ambitious politicians, and although it "saddled the army with some prize incompetents in high places," it was a good investment in national cohesion.

Lincoln was never greatly concerned with irregularities if they were consistent with the public good. On the other hand, he was opposed to any act that was against the public interest. Whenever he brought pressure on the head of one of the departments to grant a favor for one of his friends or supporters, he invariably qualified the request by a condition such as "if it can be done consistently with the public interest" or "if the public interest will admit." For a man who was deeply committed to honesty and decency in government the extension of a favor to a friend or supporter did not trouble him as long as he was convinced that the public good was protected.

Nor was Lincoln frightened by the prospect of having in the government men who had close connections with the business community or who themselves belonged to that community. This was admittedly a matter that required constant surveillance and scrutiny, but that was a responsibility inherent in the public service. It could not be evaded by running businessmen out of government or by forcing them to enter the public service only at the expense of divesting themselves of all their worldly possessions. In a country where both the government and the economy were expanding how could such a group be ignored or treated in any manner that would inhibit their effective service? Lincoln could ill afford to lose their services and he had no intention of doing so. His responsibility was to see to it that members of the business community performed loyally and honestly, and he gladly assumed that responsibility.

Gifts never worried Lincoln. He could not be bought by them, regardless of their value. Likewise, he did not intend that any member of his administration should be affected by gifts or other irregularities in the discharge of his duties. He would not countenance the exertion of any undue and purely selfishly motivated influence on public servants by any person or group. While Lincoln fully recognized the inevitability of the government's doing business with persons representing a wide variety of interests, he never tolerated the peddling of influence that completely ignored the public interest. Pressure from without as well as from within was tolerable so long as it was motivated, at least in part, by an appreciation of the obligation of the public service to perform honestly and with full regard for the general welfare.

In the study of the conduct of his office and in an examination of the principles of public morality to which he adhered with tenacity, Lincoln can be instructive to those of us who seek guidance through today's confusing maze of problems related to ethics in government. One is impressed, first of all, with the absence of any semblance of hypocrisy or any suggestion of a double standard for those in and out of government. Indecency and dishonesty *in* government almost invariably had their counterparts *outside* government, and both were equally obnoxious to Lincoln and might well be to us.

One cannot fail to be persuaded, moreover, by the validity of Lincoln's view that business and government are not necessarily incompatible. His policies and practices suggest to us that it is not only a bit foolish but not necessarily in the public interest to require a man of affluence to take the vow of poverty before he can enter upon his duties as a public servant. Lincoln's hard-headed conduct with regard to the use of the patronage, the acceptance of gifts, and the exertion of influence in high places inevitably suggests that by comparison we not only reflect a measure of immaturity with respect to such matters but that we also suffer from a lack of realism or, worse, from downright hypocrisy as we face similar problems. Most of all, however, and in almost every shred of conduct related even remotely to the question of public morality, Lincoln's own position compels a thorough reexamination of our own attitudes and views of the same problems.

It would be foolish to contend that Lincoln solved all the problems involving public morality that he faced. It cannot be claimed that he had a workable formula for coping with each situation as it arose. It does seem, however, that he had thought through these problems rather carefully; and as he faced them a pattern and philosophy seemed to emerge. There were, of course, numerous instances of shameful immorality in his administration, but they were deviations from the high standards set by Lincoln himself. They were violations both of the pattern and philosophy enunciated by him. The century that separates us from Lincoln's time has neither eradicated nor solved the questions of public morality that plagued Lincoln. In all fairness it is not even clear that the century has provided us with any greater wisdom about such matters than that enjoyed by Lincoln and his contemporaries. As we look back upon Lincoln we can certainly profit by the example of his forthrightness, his honesty, and his realistic approach. This was his wisdom, and in any age, even after the problems have changed, this much is worthy of emulation.

PART III

The Near Great and the Not So Great

Although I had been engaged in historical research and writing for some forty-five years before writing a full-length biography, I always held the view that biography was a very legitimate area of inquiry for the historian. If the subject of a biographical study is a major figure upon whom the records are abundant, the scholar confronts relatively easy tasks of verification as well as discrimination in the selection of sources. If the subject is obscure and relatively unimportant, the biographer is challenged to search out materials on which to base the biography, to find the proper place for the person vis-à-vis others, and to recognize him or her as important for the very fact of perhaps being representative of the nameless millions.

The first article I published in a learned journal dealt with certain aspects of the life of Edward Bellamy, the well-known nineteenth-century writer and socialist. Bellamy's widow, who had made his papers available to me, was so pleased with my article that she said she would ask me to write a life of Bellamy if Arthur Morgan's duties as head of the Tennessee Valley Authority prevented his completing the biography of Bellamy that he had already begun. This was a most flattering compliment extended to a twenty-three-year-old graduate student. Alas, in due course, Morgan found time to resume and complete his biography of Bellamy.

Perhaps I was attracted to biographical writing not only because it provided an opportunity to delineate character and judge the significance of the life, but also because it taxed my imagination as well as my skills as a detective. After I had published a book on free Negroes in North Carolina, I discovered a few scraps of paper bearing on the life of a single free Negro, the kind of materials I unsuccessfully sought when I was writing the book. Following leads that took me to apprentice records, tax rolls, court litigations, and even health records, I was able to reconstruct the life of James Boon. I did a similar thing with the white Civil War recruiter of black soldiers, James T. Ayers, whose diary a student at St. Augustine's College brought to me from his family files where it had been kept since the close of the war. After the diary was published, with notes and an introduction, several of the descendants of Ayers for whom I had been searching for several years emerged to "share" the glory of their newly celebrated ancestor, "Grandpa Ayers."

The Ayers diary and the autobiography of John R. Lynch fulfilled my ambition to do serious editorial work of this sort. During his retirement, after service as speaker of the lower house of the Mississippi legislature, member of Congress, and paymaster in the United States Army, Lynch wrote his autobiography. With the assistance of Loren Schweninger I was able to fill in many of the gaps that had been missing in Lynch's own account of his life, gaps that had persuaded me that even the autobiographer does not know all—or does not care to tell all—about his or her own career.

The life of George Washington Williams remained a major project for more than forty years. There were times when it seemed that the quest for elusive, fugitive materials would never end. There were times, moreover, when some friends and colleagues seemed to think I did not want the quest to end. That was not the case, and the account given here of my efforts over four decades and on three continents to master the details of the life of Williams do, I hope, indicate that I completed the task with all deliberate speed. Michael Lanza, my research assistant for two crucial years, kept the pressure on me and himself to search out the last important details.

Since autobiography is a part of the genre of biography and since it seemed inappropriate for Ayers and Lynch to expose their own words to the readers of this volume, I decided to expose myself. This, incidentally, is the most recent piece of writing to appear in this volume. Each year the American Council of Learned Societies invites a person to deliver an autobiographical lecture on the subject "A Life of Learning." My lecture, delivered April 14, 1988, was the sixth in the series.

Edward Bellamy and the
Nationalist Movement

The Industrial Revolution of the nineteenth century radically re-organized American life; the Civil War cruelly disrupted the economic, political, and social structure; and the Reconstruction brought forth innumerable irritations and social maladjustments. These epoch-making occurrences rendered the last quarter of the century a period replete with new conditions of life. The succession of events gave clear proof of the industrial unrest and economic difficulties that threatened American society. This memorable period in American history presented features that were at once encouraging and discouraging: encouraging because they produced cities that became the industrial centers of the world, cores of action, as it were, from which emanated forces providing life for other areas; discouraging because these same cities failed to provide thousands—no, millions—of their own inhabitants with the bare necessaries of life.

It was to the numerous problems of this modern America that many social philosophers arose to give their attention, by whom, "as a result of incessant and untiring speculation and thought in thousands of directions, numerous remedial systems and theories were suggested."[1] The seventies, eighties, and nineties were a period of many "isms," new creeds, and strange utopias. It was a period which gave a considerable amount of attention to the problem of decreasing the burden resting on the shoulders of the oppressed laborer and the debt-ridden farmer. Whether it was the Knights of Labor, with its program for the reorganization of the workers without regard for trade or vocation, or whether it was Henry George, with his proposal for a single tax, the movement was always in one direction—toward the alleviation of conditions among the poorer classes.

Originally published in the *New England Quarterly*, Vol. XI (December, 1938), pp. 739–72. Reprinted with the permission of the *New England Quarterly*.

For the third time in a remarkably short period, America became agitated by a great excitement, or fluttered by a slight commotion—depending on the point of view of the observer—when a movement developed that bade fair to take its place among the more important expressions of the social ideals of the period. More general in its appeal than the Knights of Labor and less savage in its attack than the single tax movement, the Nationalist movement emerged as another effort, distinctively American, to cope with the problems the American people faced. While all these movements were flavored with traits typically American—imagination, enthusiasm, determination—Nationalism was one of the few which made a conscious effort to reconcile peacefully an unreasonable capitalist class to an embittered laboring class.[2] There is small wonder, then, that its appeal was so extensive and its ideals were believed by so many to be within the realm of possibility.

As the son of a Baptist minister who remained at the same church in Chicopee Falls, Massachusetts, for thirty-five years, Edward Bellamy found himself in a home that taught moderation and consistency.[3] In that small manufacturing village very near Springfield, Bellamy attended the public schools and took advantage of the meager opportunities for educational development which the place offered. After studying literature for a short time at Union College in 1868, he went to Germany, where he studied at Dresden and other centers of learning for almost a year. Though wretched conditions existed among the factory workers of his home town, it was those in Europe who first revealed to Bellamy the injustices of modern society.

> It was in the great cities of Europe and among the hovels of peasantry that my eyes were first fully opened to the extent and consequences of man's inhumanity to man. . . .
> Although it had required the sights of Europe to startle me to a vivid realization of the inferno of poverty beneath our civilization, my eyes having once been opened I had no difficulty in recognizing in America, and even in my own comparatively prosperous village, the same conditions in course of progressive development.[4]

A recognition of these facts caused Bellamy to say in 1871, "The great reforms of the world have hitherto been political rather than social. In their progress, classes privileged by title have been swept away, but classes privileged by wealth remain."[5]

Returning to the United States, Bellamy read law but, though admitted to the bar, he never engaged in actual practice. He was apparently disappointed in the antisocial conduct of some of the lawyers about him, for in 1874 he wrote, "So today the lawyers guard with invisible ranks the money kings, whose group is strangling the modern liberties of America. . . . No men deserve so badly of their fellows as these bull-dogs of the money kings."[6] He then turned his attention first to journalism and finally to literary pursuits.

One of Bellamy's friends and admirers describes him as "in manner quiet, yet observant, modest but perfectly self-poised, with mild and gentle tones, yet full of personality, and vibrating with purposes."[7] Calm and undisturbed at all times, he could take the jeers of the mob philosophically and the praises of his admirers reservedly. A brilliant conversationalist with a commanding presence, though of slight stature, Bellamy was the cynosure of all eyes, even on occasions when he was only a spectator.[8]

While he was not to enunciate a clear philosophy of utopian socialism and a concrete program for the reorganization of society until far into the next decade, by 1874 Bellamy had worked out a fairly clear philosophy of life. In a discourse that has never been published, "The Religion of Solidarity," Bellamy pointed out what seemed to him to be the valuable aspects of human development. He believed in two sides of one's being:

> On the one hand, in the personal life, an atom, a grain of sand on a boundless shore, a bubble on a foam-flecked ocean, a life bearing a proportion to the mass of past, present and future life, so infinitesimal as to defy the imagination. . . . On the other hand is a certain other life, as it were, a spark of infinity, asserting solidarity with all things and all existence, containing the limitations of space and time and all other of the restricting conditions of personality.[9]

He goes on to clarify this abstract reasoning by saying, "As an individual, he [man] finds it a task exceeding his powers to secure satisfactory material conditions for his physical life; as a universal he grasps at a life infinitely larger than the one he so poorly cares for," and in a society, as he was to say later, that so poorly cares for him. Further on, he adds:

> Seeing there is in every being a soul common in nature with all other souls . . . it is easy to understand the origin of that cardinal motive of human life which is a tendency and a striving to absorb or be absorbed in or united with other lives and all life. This passion for losing ourselves in others or for absorbing them into ourselves . . . is the greatest expression of

185

the law of Solidarity. . . . It is the operation of this law in great and low things, in the love of men for women, for each other, for the race . . . and for those great ideas which are the symbols of solidarity that has ever made up the web and woof of human passion.[10]

It is not difficult to see in these passages the development of a point of view that could conceive of a world in which the good of the group is of far greater importance than the good of the individual, and in which mankind's supreme function should be to improve the conditions of living for all. Thus at the age of twenty-four Bellamy had already acquired a social consciousness. Still intricately involved in a system of metaphysics by which he sought to explain the spiritual kinship of all men, it needed only to be translated into the language of the farmer and the factory worker before it could be on the lips of thousands. In the search for the Infinite of which he believed himself to be a part, it was only natural for Bellamy to look upon himself as a part of all mankind. Man must, therefore, desist from the old practice of being inhumane to that which is a part of himself.

Few men, at such an early age, possess so clear a philosophy of life as that expressed in Bellamy's "Religion of Solidarity"; and though he later believed that it was "crude and redundant in style" and contained "obvious defects in ratiocinations, and loose links,"[11] he did not care to alter it in 1887 and he wished to have it read to him when he was about to die. That he had such a high regard for this early effort in the same year that he was writing his greatest work may suggest a close connection between the earlier views and those which he was then expressing.

Upon entering the field of journalism, Bellamy became an editorial writer on the Springfield *Union*, and later he went to New York, where he worked for a few months on the *Evening Post*. More important, however, was his connection with the *Berkshire Courier*, in Great Barrington, Massachusetts. It was at the editor's request that he wrote in 1879 a serial entitled *The Duke of Stockbridge*. Having as its background the Shays Rebellion of 1786, this novel described the struggle between the debtor farmers and their harsh creditors. Bellamy poured out his sympathy on the side of the underprivileged group and condemned the social and economic organization that relegated the great mass of Massachusetts citizens to a position far below that which was enjoyed by the few. Bellamy reminded his readers that, though similar conditions still prevailed, he was not writing of the farmer and laborer of the late nineteenth century. Into the mouth of the hero, he put these words:

> Pretty nearly every rich man has a gang of debtors working for him, trying to work out their debts. If they are idle, if they dispute with him, if they don't let him do what he pleases with them and their families, he sends them to jail. . . . No man can interfere between him and them. . . . And that's why I call them slaves.[12]

When the story was completed, Bellamy refused offers from publishers and determined to delay its appearance until after the publication of *Looking Backward*, "which now had taken pressing shape in his mind."

The greatest value of *The Duke of Stockbridge* in 1879 was not in the sympathetic chord which it struck in many hearts with the Massachusetts farmers of 1786, but in what it did for Edward Bellamy. The intimate research among the documents and family traditions of western Massachusetts, the heavy burden of debts and taxes on the shoulders of the farmers, and the bloody object lesson of the results which may be expected from a society of inequality and suffering served to increase Bellamy's desire to contribute something in the way of a solution.[13]

The works of Bellamy which lay clearly outside the scope of social problems also were not without their influences on his development. *Dr. Heidendoff's Process* and *Miss Ludington's Sister*, both fanciful romances, did a great deal to develop in him an imagination that could envision a society where people lived in peace and contentment. These and other literary experiences helped him to develop an ability to portray a utopia so vividly and convincingly that thousands could believe that it was within the realm of possibility. These developments, coupled with the evolution of a definite social consciousness on the basis of training, experience, and temperament, prepared Edward Bellamy for the great work before him.

Considering the positive attitude Bellamy assumed toward the social ills of the day at a remarkably early age and his unusual facility in expressing any such ideas, one is led to wonder—as he did himself—why he did not write in this vein before 1886. The necessity of solving his own economic problem was undoubtedly the greatest deterrent to any such undertaking. He said, "I had, like others, to fight my way to a place at the world's work-bench where I could make a living."[14] The birth of his two children, a son and a daughter, brought to Edward Bellamy a "new and more solemn meaning" of the problem of life. The necessity of planning and plotting to secure for one's offspring "all the advantages that may give them a better chance than other men's children in the struggle for existence" impressed upon him the inadequacy of the facilities at one's disposal for making a living. With the principle of joining hands with "all other anxious parents in making the world a comfortable place in which to live," he set out to enunciate a workable solution of the social problem.

The two accounts of the genesis of *Looking Backward,* both written by Edward Bellamy, leave the reader somewhat confused. In the one written in 1889, "How I Came to Write 'Looking Backward,'" the author says: "I had, at the outset, no idea of attempting a serious contribution to the movement for social reform. The idea was a mere literary fantasy, a fairy tale of social felicity."[15] In the other, written in 1894, the author says: "According to my best recollection it was in the fall or winter of 1886 that I sat down to my desk with the definite purpose of trying to reason out a method of economic organization by which the republic might guarantee the livelihood and material welfare of its citizens on a basis of equality corresponding to and supplementing their political equality."[16] The point is well established that Bellamy had been planning for some years to write a book dealing with the pressing economic and social problems of the day; and there can be little doubt that the birth of a daughter in March, 1886, served to affect him in the manner described above. The different, and somewhat conflicting, accounts presented in the two articles seem to reflect a confusion of purposes that existed in Bellamy's mind when he began writing in the autumn of the same year.

Looking Backward is an interesting, fictional account of the United States in 2000 A.D. as seen through the eyes of a wealthy young man, Julian West, who fell asleep in 1887 and awakened 113 years later. During complete suspension of activity of his vital organs there had been no deterioration of mind and body, and a perfectly normal young man—born in 1857—awoke to find himself in a completely transformed world, the guest of the retired Doctor Leete, his wife, and his daughter Edith. Through his kind hosts, West became fully acquainted with the principles of national cooperation for the promotion of the general welfare, which was the basis of the new social order.[17]

Upon reaching the age of twenty-one, every person had to choose an occupation or a profession or have it chosen for him. After receiving training in the chosen field, the individual was then employed by the national government to work until he reached the age of forty-five, at which time he was retired. Since everyone had all the material comforts of life, Bellamy felt that there was little opportunity for greed and avarice. The concern and interest in life had definitely shifted from that of making a living to many other activities with which one chiefly occupied himself after retirement. Through the nationalization of industry, man had, for the first time, learned to live.

Since the workers of the United States constituted an industrial army under a form of military discipline, the commander-in-chief of the army was also the commander-in-chief of the industrial army. The president of the United States had to come up through the ranks of the workers. Upon retirement, at the age of forty-five, every worker became eligible for that high office. In order that political chicanery and unfair practices should not be resorted to in the administration of the government, no one was eligible to hold high positions or to participate in elections until after he had retired. To be called on by one's country to serve in some such capacity was the highest possible honor.

Though it is the economic organization of the United States in 2000 A.D. that is most startling to the observer of the nineteenth—or twentieth—century, the far-reaching social consequences are indices of the significance of the changes that had taken place. No phase of life was overlooked in the transforming activities of the economic evolution. Since want and privation had been the causes of crime in the nineteenth century and since these evils no longer existed, the country was practically without crime. The change in the position of women was one of the most complete and revolutionary of all the transformations. In the United States of 2000 A.D. women, as well as men, were members of the industrial army, and left their duties only when motherhood claimed them. An elaborate system of female organization had been set up, a kind of allied force to the army of men. In every conceivable way, women were the equals of men, sitting in the president's cabinet, presiding in court, and managing industrial plants. In fact, Dr. Leete could say, "Women are a very happy race nowadays, as compared with what they ever were before in the world's history, and their power of giving happiness to men has been of course increased in proportion."[18]

Bellamy insisted that making one's living is by no means the chief aim in life. He said, "It is not our labor, but the higher and larger activities which the performance of our task will leave us free to enter upon, that are considered the main business of existence."[19] Everyone looked to his retirement as the beginning of the period in which he would enter upon the full enjoyment of his birthright. Whether one had scientific, artistic, literary, or other interests, he valued leisure and saw in it an opportunity to cultivate special tastes and to enjoy some of the world which he had helped to improve. Indeed, life began at forty-five!

One cannot resist the temptation to indicate some of the more interesting habits of living that were to be found in the "nationalized" United States. Homes were far more comfortable than they had been in the nineteenth century. Public dining rooms, where most people ate, could prepare foods with greater skill and at considerably less expense than was possible in a private home. The ease with which shopping could be done and deliveries made was most attractive. The umbrellas over the sidewalks on rainy days suggest the extent to which the government had gone in providing for the comfort of its citizens. Finally, the telephonic musical programs foretold the unlimited possibilities in a field that had become well exploited by the fourth decade of the twentieth century.

Thus, for the first time, the philosophy of Nationalism was enunciated. Although in form a fanciful romance, Looking Backward was a serious effort to outline what seemed to Edward Bellamy the "next stage in the industrial and social development of humanity."[20] To him, it seemed that certain fundamental principles should be incorporated into a plan of action if civilization were to survive. First, the industries in every country should be nationalized. The industrial army should constitute the working force of the nation. Secondly, economic equality of all citizens, regardless of sex or efficiency, is just as necessary as political equality. Thirdly, through the gradual acquisition of the means of production and distribution, nationalization can come by peaceful, nonrevolutionary methods. Lastly, nationalization must make its appeal to all classes of society.

Looking Backward may accurately be called the textbook of Nationalism. Although numerous articles and one other major work were written by Bellamy, this work remained the standard guide to all who sought to learn of his utopia. Bellamy had never been affiliated with any reform group, nor upon the publication of Looking Backward was he willing to be called a socialist, because of the ambiguousness of the term. Its mildness and the hope for experimentation on a small scale in the beginning serve to label his philosophy as utopian socialism. Bellamy was anxious that his plan of social and economic organization be called Nationalism, because he wished to distinguish it from other and more vague forms of socialism and because it was to proceed by the nationalization of industries. "Socialism," he said, "implies the socializing of industry. This may or may not be based upon the national organism and may or may not imply economic equality. Nationalism is a definition not in the sense of opposition or exclusion, but a precision rendered necessary by a cloud of vague and disputed implications historically attached to the former word."[21]

Under its unique name, Nationalism, this utopian socialism fired the imagination of thousands of readers of *Looking Backward*. The sensation created by the novel was due to "its intrinsic qualities, to a charming style, and to an adroit fashion of presenting . . . the doctrine as after all no more than an enlightened self-interest or wholesale common sense."[22] The wide interest in the doctrines embodied in the book was the signal for a movement whose influence was great—on Bellamy and its adherents alike—and which formed one of the advance guards of liberal thought in the last decade of the nineteenth century.

The first phase of the Nationalist movement is characterized by the establishment of units of propaganda—Nationalist Clubs—and the effort to educate the public along the lines of Nationalism. Before the sales of *Looking Backward* had jumped into the scores of thousands, the idea of projecting some kind of organization was taking form. On June 28, 1888, Cyrus F. Willard of Boston wrote Bellamy, "I have been thinking that it would be a good idea to organize an association to spread the ideas contained in your book. What do you think of it?" Bellamy replied, "Go ahead by all means and do it if you can find anybody to associate with." With this encouragement, Willard and Sylvester Baxter set out to organize a Nationalist Club in Boston. By August, the club was well under way, but the absence of Baxter and the preoccupation of Willard with personal affairs caused the small group to disintegrate. In September, 1888, General A. F. Devereux and several others organized the Boston Bellamy Club, and in the next month the fragments of the first group joined the latter to form the Nationalist Club of Boston.[23] At a meeting on December 8, the constitution and the declaration of principles were adopted. At the election of officers on December 15, 1888, Edward Bellamy was present and was elected first vice-president. By January, the club had fifty active members.

Though the Boston club enjoyed a healthy growth during the winter of 1888–1889, the establishment of clubs in other cities was at first slow. In January, 1889, a group in Washington set up a permanent club with more than thirty members in which "doctors, lawyers, and divines played an active part."[24] The Collectivist League, begun in Chicago in April, 1888, became the Nationalist Club of Illinois in the following February, with a charter from the state of Illinois. Many of its members were lawyers, bank officers, and merchants.[25] On February 12, 1889, a Nationalist Club was organized in the Unity Church parlors in Hartford, Connecticut, and during the next month a constitution similar to that of the Boston organization was adopted.[26] On April 11, 1889, a merchant, a master iron worker, and the city librarian organized a club at Portsmouth, New Hampshire.[27] New York followed with a meeting of Nationalists at Everett House. Among the one hundred active members were Thaddeus B. Wakeman and the ardent socialist Professor Daniel Dē Leon of Columbia University.[28] These organizations kept the spirit of Nationalism alive during the early months of development.

With the publication of the *Nationalist* in May, 1889, the movement assumed a shape and size that compelled the attention of many more people than had previously noticed it. With an official organ, it was possible to crystallize the ideas of Nationalism and to urge cooperative action more vigorously. The price of the monthly publication, ten cents per copy, placed it within the reach of everyone who was at all interested. An account of the organization of the first Nationalist Club of Boston, the publication of its declaration of principles, and an article by Edward Bellamy on "How I Came to Write 'Looking Backward' " seemed to inspire men in various parts of the country, for immediately clubs began springing up.

The summer and autumn of 1889 were a period of rapid organization among the Nationalists. By September, there were clubs at Albany, New York; Cincinnati, Ohio; Springfield, Massachusetts; Independence, Kansas; Lehigh, Iowa; Los Angeles, California; Lynn, Massachusetts; Minneapolis, Minnesota, and a number of other places.[29] The movement had grown so rapidly that the following comment was made in the October *Nationalist:*

> The Nationalist movement is just as strong in California as in Boston. Already on our exchange table were two magazines of the faith—The Commonwealth and the Pacific Monthly—and now comes a weekly magazine from National City in that state bearing the gallant title, Looking Forward. All these are ably edited and evidently in the field to stay.[30]

The editor may well have said that the movement in California was even stronger than that in Boston. The *Pacific Union* of San Francisco reported twenty-three clubs in the process of formation in that state.[31] At Los Angeles, a society of three hundred Nationalists had to find a new meeting place in August, 1889, because more than fifty persons could not get into the crowded hall.[32] By October, 1889, the San Diego club had over one hundred members while the San Francisco club maintained reading rooms that were open each day.[33] Edward Bellamy, being invited to give a series of lectures through the state, "where the people seem to be going into Nationalism *en masse,*" declined because of ill health and because he did not want to lecture on Nationalism for money and "could not afford to do it without it."[34]

By the end of the first year of Nationalism—December, 1889— clubs had also been organized in Brooklyn, New York, and Kansas City, Missouri, and additional ones in California and Massachusetts. The older clubs, meanwhile, had continued to grow. Leaders of the movement were encouraged. One of them said:

> The intelligent and educated are joining. Men and women of wealth, brains and of heart are interested. . . . This movement has reached out and is beginning to unite the farmers with the toilers of the city. It has inspired and is inspiring countless books, magazine articles, editorials and articles in the daily press. We have fifty or more papers and magazines unreservedly advocating Nationalism.[35]

The two hundred and ten thousandth copy of *Looking Backward* was sold in December, 1889, and 69,000 copies of the *Nationalist* had circulated. In 1890, the clubs increased in number and size. In January, there were 44 clubs in fourteen states and the District of Columbia, 16 of which were in California.[36] By May, twenty-two states and the District of Columbia had 110 clubs, 47 of which were in California.[37] And by November, the end of the second year, twenty-seven states and the District of Columbia had 158 clubs, of which 65 were in California and 16 were in New York City.[38] The 165 clubs in February, 1891, mark the high tide of Nationalism so far as the organization of clubs is concerned.

The Nationalists sought to spread their doctrines in many ways. Since the textbook of the movement was a novel, it is not strange that fiction should have become one of the means of spreading their ideas.[39] One of the early efforts was a novel by Albert Ross, *Speaking of Ellen,* the story of how a young girl struggled and organized a group of mills as Nationalist institutions. "That he should have made his third book a plea for Nationalism proves his belief in the takingness of our creed," the *Nationalist* commented. Fiction reached its high point as a medium of spreading the doctrine when Laurence Gronlund wrote a novel, *Our Destiny*, which ran serially in the *Nationalist*.[40]

The organization of the Nationalist Education Association in April, 1890, is another instance of the activity of the Boston Nationalists. Incorporated under the laws of Massachusetts with a capital stock of $10,000, with shares at $25.00, the organization avowed the combined purposes of "publishing the Nationalist and spreading the doctrines of Nationalism." Edward Bellamy was made president of the organization. Members of the board of directors were Anne Whitney, George Ayers, John Storer Cobb, and Henry Austin.[41]

Two other interesting features of propaganda appeared in the columns of the *Nationalist*. In October, 1890, that magazine published a list of available Nationalist speakers which included men and women in Minnesota, Iowa, Michigan, and Massachusetts. Any Nationalist could have his name included as an available speaker by sending fifty cents to the *Nationalist*.[42] In the same issue appeared a price-list of books—called the Nationalist Bookcase—on socialism, taxation, sociology, and related subjects.[43]

The moment that *Looking Backward* instituted the movement that brought forth Nationalism as an organized force, the defenders of the old order emerged and began to make scathing attacks on the Bellamy ideas. In a lengthy article in the *Quarterly Journal of Economics*, Nicholas Gilman opposed the claim of the Boston club that its membership was drawn from the more important elements of society. He said that the names of prominent persons were "plainly conspicuous by their absence. . . . There is but one name on the list which I recognize, or have seen before in any place or in any connection as that of a business man." Gilman declared that the assertion of the president to the effect that mechanics, merchants, and businessmen belonged, needed to be investigated and that many important names had been erroneously connected with the movement.[44] He also described the reasoning of Bellamy as illogical. He insisted that the analogy between the fight for economic independence and that for political independence was extremely inaccurate, since the Revolutionary War seemed to him to be "a war on centralization of power, a war to guarantee freedom of the individual from tyranny by the government." He described Bellamy as "so thoroughly a man of letters rather than an orator of the millennium . . . that his best wishers must desire for him the speediest possible collapse" of Nationalism, which seemed "more amusing than formidable."[45]

The *Forum* for October, 1889, carried an article in which the author, Professor W. T. Harris, attacked the principles of Nationalism. He looked upon Bellamy's program as dangerous and un-American:

All other remedies proposed are mere makeshifts compared with this, if this may be called a remedy. Perhaps rather one should say that others propose reforms, but Mr. Bellamy proposes revolution. They are like physicians who propose to cure the body, while he proposes to get rid of the body altogether.[46]

In another place, Professor Harris said that Bellamy's assumption that in a competitive society the rich grow richer and fewer and the poor grow poorer and more numerous was not based on reliable statistics.[47]

The Nationalists would not permit this attack to go unnoticed, and in a subsequent issue of the *Nationalist*, two adherents pounced upon the critic without mercy. One said:

Professor Harris remarks sententiously: "Real human beings have other needs than food, clothing, and shelter." He seems to forget, however, that these wants must be satisfied *before* any other needs can be considered. Would the professor try to feed the hungry on a lecture entitled, "The Higher Aims of the Concord Philosophy"? . . . Man must have bread before Browning! . . . Two strong currents of thought are converging toward Nationalism—one running through the hearts of the wage-slaves; the other, through the minds and hearts and consciences of clear-headed, men-loving men and women. Does Prof. Harris stand so firm that neither current may sweep him off his feet?[48]

In 1890, the attacks became so numerous that the Nationalists apparently resolved to ignore them and concentrate on the matter of strengthening and extending their organization. One author accused Bellamy of imitating the ideas of Louis Blanc, set forth in his "L'Organisation du Travail."[49] Another characterized Nationalism as a "statue with feet of clay and limbs of iron, and forehead of brass, and crutches of splintered reeds . . . and with a cigar in its lips and a wine-cup in its right hand."[50] This critic, Thomas Wentworth Higginson, pointed out a large number of defects of Nationalism, notable among which were the effort of the movement to place government in the hands of a small and, in all probability, selfish minority and the complete destruction of individual initiative. In the preceding year, Colonel Higginson had said in praise of Bellamy:

When he wrote "Looking Backward" he forgot all art and conscious imagination itself in his eagerness for a new social world; he wrote in a manner beyond himself; and the rise of the "Nationalist" movement is a direct reflection of that book. He has created a band of young proselytes who instead of believing that what he says is too good to be true, believe that it is too good not to be true.[51]

The change in Colonel Higginson's attitude between the time when he made this statement in the *Nationalist* and wrote a poem for Bellamy[52] and the time when he spoke on "Edward Bellamy's Nationalism" before an exclusive Boston audience in 1890 was noticed by Bellamy. In a letter to the Colonel, Bellamy solicited the former's cooperation, remarking that the "impending industrial evolution must be sponsored by men of education and position."[53]

From other quarters came other criticisms, in different words but with the same theme: Nationalism makes for the suppression of the individual, eradicates private philanthropy, and destroys competition. These are the foundation-stones of our society; they must be maintained.[54] Nationalists, however, went on, confident in the belief that they were right and need have no fear of the cries of those who protested against the coming of the millennium.

In April, 1891, the *Nationalist* discontinued publication. Difficulty with finances was the cause. The circulation was never extremely large; and the returns from advertising were almost negligible.[55] The *Nationalist*, however, had served the cause of Nationalism well. A new journal in the field paid it the following tribute: "It has undoubtedly done a work which will make its name historic. . . . It belongs to a list of short-lived periodicals which are immortal."[56] The demise of the *Nationalist* marked the end of the first phase of development and made way for the second, which had already begun and which was characterized by the active participation of Edward Bellamy in the movement and the entrance of Nationalism into the political arena.

At no time after the publication of *Looking Backward* did Bellamy turn his attention to the literary pursuits with which he had previously been occupied. He encouraged the Nationalist movement in many ways: actively participating in the organization of the Nationalist Club of Boston, speaking at various times in the interest of the cause, and contributing to the *Nationalist*. A pen-and-ink portrait of Bellamy in the December, 1889, issue of the *Nationalist* was presented as a Christmas gift to followers throughout the country. The editor was anxious, however, that the people should not idolize Bellamy or confuse him with the movement; for *many* had "fought to bring about the intellectual clarity that has brought forth Nationalism." He said further, "Nor does Bellamy wish to pose . . . as a guide or a leader like Henry George for instance. Bellamy recognizes that this movement is too vast to be led or guided by any one man. He knows that to ensure a permanent and speedy success it needs the patient focalization of many earnest hearts and subtle minds."[57]

Whether the editor of the *Nationalist* was pleased or not, the fact remains that Bellamy *was* the spirit of the movement. At the first anniversary of the organization of the Boston Nationalist Club, Bellamy was the honored guest and principal speaker. The demonstration given him that evening could well have caused the editor of the periodical greater concern.

> The vast audience when he was introduced arose as one man. The men applauded, then broke into a cheer, in which the women were waving their handkerchiefs. . . . As he stood there, the comparatively unknown author of little over a year ago, deep must have been his feeling of satisfaction, if he thought over the part which his brain and hand had played in bringing such an audience together to celebrate the anniversary of Nationalism.[58]

Bellamy's willingness and eagerness to do his share in promoting the Nationalist movement were as great as those of any members of the faith. In reply to Mr. Horace Scudder, editor of the *Atlantic Monthly*, Bellamy rejected an offer to write for the magazine and added:

> Since my eyes have been opened to the evils and perils of our social state and I have begun to cherish a clear hope of better things, I simply "can't get my consent" to write or think of anything else. As a literary man I fear I am a "goner". . . . There is a sense in which I am very sorry for this, for I had much work laid out to do. . . . There is one life which I would like to lead and another which I must lead. If I had only been twins.[59]

Bellamy's health, however, was preventing him from taking as active a part in the movement as he would have liked. He had never been a strong man. As early as 1874, he had suffered a breakdown in health to the extent that he wrote, "I think I have got my death."[60] Several months in the Hawaiian Islands served to strengthen him considerably. In the spring and summer of 1890, a severe attack of influenza prevented his taking over the editorship of the *Nationalist*.

By the beginning of January, 1891, Bellamy had recovered from his illness, but the *Nationalist* was in such dire financial straits that he thought it would be useless to try to salvage it. On January 31, 1891, therefore, appeared the *New Nation*, a weekly newspaper edited by Edward Bellamy and "pledged to all the Nationalistic principles that will be realized in the New Nation." It hoped to criticize the existing industrial system, to give a summary of foreign and domestic news, to present special articles to support the editorial views, and to advocate civil service reform and the nationalization of telephone and telegraph companies, express companies, railroads, and coal mines. One section was devoted to the activities of the Nationalist clubs while another— Nationalist Drift—was devoted to items "indicating the approaching breakup of the present system and the tendency . . . toward complete national cooperation."[61] The appearance of the *New Nation* marks the beginning of a vigorous prosecution by Edward Bellamy of the Nationalist program and of the Nationalists to concentrate on carrying out that program piecemeal.[62]

A feature of the *New Nation* for more than a year was a series of conversations between a Nationalist and some other member of society, in which the former would prove beyond any doubt that Nationalism was the answer to all the ills of the world. In this column, Bellamy addressed the businessman, the teacher, and the laborer, among many others, and urged them to join the movement. He missed no opportunity to use a labor dispute or a bank crisis as an example of what would not happen under Nationalism.

Bellamy looked with approval on any reform that seemed to make way for Nationalism. The passage of the bill in the Texas legislature for the state publication of textbooks was an occasion of rejoicing by the *New Nation*.[63] The journal cheered the fact that the Farmers' Alliance was "spreading in Iowa like hot-cakes."[64] The decision of the Supreme Court upholding the New York law which regulated grain elevators was celebrated as a "Looking Backward victory."[65]

The editor answered a large number of his critics in the columns of the *New Nation*. In February, 1891, the editor of the Boston *Advertiser* asked whether, in keeping with the principles of Nationalism, the officeboy for the *New Nation* was getting as much as the editor. Bellamy answered in the negative and added, "The trouble is with the editor of the Advertiser, who evidently has not had time to read 'Looking Backward' or to find out what the idea of the Nationalists really is." He then pointed out that the new nation could come only gradually, and not until it arrived would all be able to share equally in the returns from industry.[66] When the New York *Sun* described the governor-elect of Texas as a "blatant Bellamyite, a nationalist, and a corporation hater," Bellamy had occasion to pass an opinion on that journal: "To be denounced in such terms by the Sun, which is the most consistent thick and thin champion of the plutocratic movement to be found in this country, is the best possible certificate of character for a reformer."[67]

Though ministers and other religious leaders, in almost every part of the country, actively participated in the Nationalist movement, there were others who violently disapproved of any identification of the doctrines of Bellamy with the teachings of Jesus Christ. Miss Anna Dawes said,

> He nowhere gives . . . any evidence that its relation to the religion of Jesus Christ much concerns him. . . . The Christian is not concerned with the universal reign of happiness, but with the universal reign of holiness. . . . From whatever point of view we consider this new socialism, it does not concern Christianity, since its philosophy is anti-Christian, and its method falls to the ground with its philosophy.[68]

Perhaps Bellamy was too busy to answer this unqualified denunciation of his program, or perhaps he did not care to. During the following year, however, an article appeared in the *New Nation* which, no doubt, expressed his views. The writer said, "So clearly pervasive is the spirit of Nationalism men are often found who unconsciously advocate it. It may be possible that Nationalism is 'God's own method of tempering the body together.' "[69] He urged preachers to become conscious of the social problems and to acknowledge Nationalism as the best solution to them.

> As Nationalists, like the prophets of old, are "interpreters of visions" and "dreamers of dreams" they might be allowed to predict that from the theology now in solution but not yet crystallized, will come a new apprehension of Christ's teachings and the individual features of theology will be supplemented by systematized social features.[70]

Bellamy gave considerable space to the activities of Nationalists in Canada and in England. An account of the speech by the president of the Toronto Nationalist Club before the Y.W.C.A. Guild was carried in the *New Nation*.[71] Later, the journal told of the efforts of the Toronto Nationalists to get the city to operate its own street railway system.[72] The *New Nation* took pride in announcing the appearance of the *Nationalization News*, published in London each month by the English Nationalists, and strongly recommended it to "persons desirous of keeping themselves informed on the progress of Nationalism."[73] A later issue of the journal asserted that Nationalist societies were springing up in various parts of England.[74]

Bellamy's greatest concern, however, was in promoting the program of the Nationalists within the United States. He did not seem to think very highly of the club method, for he gave very little space to news of the clubs.[75] In one of his early articles he had urged the rapid nationalization of utilities and had advised the Nationalists to protest against further grants of franchises to private corporations. It was fitting, therefore, that he should urge this with new vigor in the *New Nation*.

It is interesting to note that the first efforts of the Nationalists to participate in politics came simultaneously in two widely separated areas—California and Rhode Island. The California Nationalists, in April, 1891, did not present a state ticket but restricted their campaign to two of the six congressional districts. Nevertheless, they polled 1.25 percent of the total votes of the state.[76] While the efforts in Rhode Island were not quite so fruitful, their proximity to the nominal seat of Nationalism caused considerable interest to be manifested by Bellamy and the *New Nation*. On March 14, 1891, the *New Nation* presented a copy of the platform of the Rhode Island Nationalists. Among the palliative measures which it advocated were the nationalization of telephone and telegraph companies, railroads, mines, and natural resources, and city control of street cars, waterworks, and power companies.[77] A complete state ticket was presented; and an engineer and a newsdealer, running for the offices of governor and lieutenant-governor respectively, spoke in the interest of the ticket.[78]

In a letter to the Rhode Island Nationalists, Bellamy said,

> The platform is admirable in the clearness with which it shows that Nationalism merely proposes to carry the democratic ideas into business. . . . You have done well to set up your standards so boldly. Whether your success be little or great this year, yours is the party of the future, and to have voted for its first ticket will be a thing that men will be boasting of a few years hence.[79]

This hearty approval is the first evidence of Bellamy's looking toward the organization of a Nationalist party to carry out his aims. Each succeeding issue of the *New Nation* suggests the further conviction of its editor along these lines. Thus, when the People's party entered the political arena, the Nationalist journal welcomed it and promised to be cordial and sympathetic. The *New Nation* said that as citizens, if not as an organization, the Nationalists "will be found to be in sympathy with the new party."[80] In the same issue, the platform of the People's party was printed.[81]

The spring of 1891 marked the beginning of a period of close cooperation between the Populists and the Nationalists. The distinction between the two was insisted upon, however, when Bellamy said, "People will do well to remember that the People's party is not an ideal organization from the standpoint of Nationalism. It is a reform body with its face set against trusts, monopolies, and Wall Street, and as such commands respect."[82]

Bellamy, however, heartily endorsed the Massachusetts Populist ticket, headed by Henry Winn of Malden, and spoke at a large rally of the party in Faneuil Hall in Boston, October 7, 1891.[83] Indeed, his endorsement was practically without qualification when he said, "At last week's election in this state, some 151,000 men voted for a man named Allen, about 5,000 . . . voted for a man named Russell . . . and about 2,000 voted for themselves. It is certainly a great pity that more people did not think enough of themselves to vote for their own interests as represented by the People's party."[84]

As early as March, 1891, the *New Nation* declared that neither tariffs nor silver "but the programme of Nationalism" would be the main issue in the campaign of 1892.[85] This attitude was expressed more frequently and more positively as the 1892 campaign came closer. In February, 1892, the *New Nation* said that it was a "manifest destiny that Nationalism is to be the coming issue. Whether it is to be precipitated by the People's party, no one can tell. That it is to be precipitated, however, in the near future, needs no demonstration."[86] The St. Louis meeting of the Central Committee of the People's party occasioned comment to the effect that the party was "drifting more and more towards Nationalism."[87] The Populist platform was pointed to as the "most effective means . . . of preparing the way for the ultimate triumph of Nationalism."[88] Of the St. Louis meeting, a Michigan Nationalist said, "The disciples of Bellamy were present in large numbers. . . . The People's party is educating the people in Nationalism just as fast as they are ready to receive it."[89]

Indeed, the Nationalists had come to feel that their cause was being sponsored by the Populists and that the issue of 1892 *was* Nationalism. Bellamy, in a speech before the Massachusetts convention of the party, said that the Populists were the only party in the country that had the right to call themselves a national party.[90] The Nationalists went to the Omaha convention and met separately, discussing among themselves methods of carrying propaganda to the people. Their demonstrations and influence were noted by an alarmed gentleman at the adoption of the platform:

> And when that furious and hysterical arraignment of the present times, that incoherent mingling of Jeremiah and Bellamy, the platform, was adopted, the cheers and yells which rose like a tornado from four thousand throats and raged without cessation for thirty-four minutes . . . must have told every quiet, thoughtful witness that there was something at the back of all this turmoil more than the failure of crops or the scarcity of cash.[91]

Mr. Tracy had little doubt as to what was behind this turmoil. He realized that the people had been aroused by a body of thought and a group of men who entertained ideas that he regarded as radical socialism. Even if he did not know that Nationalist propagandists from eighteen states and the District of Columbia were meeting at the Windsor Hotel daily during the Omaha convention, he was conscious of another force of unquestioned potency. "Copies of Looking Backward," he said, "are in every community. Probably every village has at least one man who is a thorough Nationalist, while hundreds of his neighbors are in sympathy with its principles."[92]

Nationalists everywhere seemed to turn to Populism with unrestrained enthusiasm after the Omaha meeting; and though Bellamy was ill during the campaign, he continued to voice his opinions through the *New Nation*. He suggested that the four hundredth anniversary of the discovery of America "should be a season of fasting and prayer, that God may save the great experiment of human liberty from a disastrous ending."[93] During the remainder of the campaign, the *New Nation* supported the Populist candidates as though it were an official organ of the party.

When at last the election was over and General Weaver had polled more than a million votes, the *New Nation* observed:

> We consider the recent democratic national campaign to have been a very valuable preparatory school for a host of voters who are destined within a few years to graduate as full-fledged disciples of Nationalism, which, now partially represented by the People's party, may four and perhaps two years hence be completely represented and embodied either in the platform of that or some other party.[94]

It is possible that the People's party had actually become the party of Bellamy's dreams. Later, he said, "We trust and believe that the leaven of Nationalism, which has thus far proved the preponderating influence in the new party, will continue to exert an increasing power and that in the near future, the People's party will adopt not merely the immediate program, but the ultimate ideal of Nationalism as its own."[95] While anxious to support Populism in every way possible, Bellamy always held out the hope that *some* party would rise that would be completely identified with the Nationalists. The conclusion seems unavoidable that Bellamy looked forward to the organization of a powerful Nationalist party!

The election of 1892 was the high water mark for the Nationalists, as it was for a number of other reform bodies. While it is most difficult to measure its influence, one can be certain that Nationalism was of some consequence. If Populism is to be considered an important third party in the election of 1892, it must be remembered that the Nationalists contributed both ideas and supporters to the cause.

Not a very eventful year for the Nationalists, 1893 was marked by an effort on the part of the adherents to consolidate their forces and formulate a new program for the dissemination of propaganda. In August of that year, the National Committee for Propaganda Work met in Chicago, at which time representatives from twenty-seven states exchanged ideas concerning methods of attack. While many suggestions were made, no concrete program was adopted, and the various groups were left to shift as best they could.[96]

The general business recession accompanying the depression of 1893 and the reaction, for the moment at least, that set in with the inauguration of President Cleveland operated to the disadvantage of the *New Nation*. Though it declared that the days of the depression were "great days for making converts to Nationalism," it would seem that general interest in the movement was declining.[97] On February 3, 1894, the last issue of the *New Nation* appeared. Though it carried a large amount of advertising, its editor stated that from the beginning it had been published at a pecuniary loss.[98] In his farewell editorial, Bellamy said that the publication had "fairly well accomplished the specific purpose for which it was established—to state the philosophy of Nationalism in all its bearings, and to demonstrate its practicability by showing its application to the various necessities and emergencies of the world."

At the demise of the *New Nation*, Bellamy had no regrets about the progress of the movement and believed that there was a bright future ahead. He said that there had been no instance in history when an idea "so revolutionary in character had made such progress within so short a time."[99] He refused to say goodbye to the readers, for he insisted that he would continue to "devote himself with unabated earnestness to the cause and to remain in close touch with its adherents through the fellowship of faith and work."[100] Bellamy's health, however, would permit him to do very little after 1894. Later in that year he published two significant articles.[101] His strength was declining so rapidly that he could hardly do more than try to complete his second great work on Nationalism.

When *Equality* appeared in 1897, Bellamy was ill and had the opportunity neither to answer the critics who assailed it nor to thank those who praised it. It was an effort to develop many of the ideas suggested in *Looking Backward* and to answer questions that had been raised since 1888.[102] One reviewer said that it was a "philosophical essay in dialogue and exposition designed to work out the author's cooperative substitute for the present industrial and political system."[103] Another declared that it was "artistically inferior to anything else he had done."[104] Still another insisted that it was significant because it represented a growing body of people who were disgusted with social conditions.[105] The book was fairly well received, but enjoyed none of the popularity of the volume to which it was a sequel.

Though the *Nationalist* and the *New Nation* had ceased publication, and though the Nationalist clubs had become less active than in earlier times, Bellamy was, in 1898, called a prophet by one writer. The historian John Clark Ridpath regarded Bellamy as one of the gentlest and most humane revolutionists that ever lived and insisted that his spirit would continue in the hearts of the more enlightened. He added, "Had we the courage to clear away sometimes, to lay a new foundation, to bring in a new architecture that shall be consistent with itself and equal to the aspiration of the new age, then we should all become apostles of Edward Bellamy."[106]

To be sure, the movement may have lost its identity, as such, but by 1898 it had assisted in the most important task of spreading the ideas of socialism, in a broad sense, to groups that might otherwise have turned a deaf ear to its principles. One writer said, "Edward Bellamy has certainly given 'the dismal science' its *coup de grace*, and the new political economy, unhampered by the blighting traditions of the old, cannot fail to be productive of the most beneficent results."[107]

With the death of Edward Bellamy on May 22, 1898, the second phase of the Nationalist movement came to a close. Of the state of the movement at this time, it is most difficult to speak. One of its arch antagonists of many years asserted that "very few of the clubs now survive, much diminished in membership and in confidence in the realization of their wisdom."[108] Mr. Gilman failed, however, to weigh the influence the movement had exercised on the new attitude that was developing concerning the role of government in the modern industrial society. Here, it is difficult to make any kind of evaluation; but it is safe to say that the effect of Nationalism was distinct. When one considers that in the decade before the Nationalist movement any demand for the municipalization of local public utilities was a voice crying in a wilderness, he begins to sense the difficulties confronting the reformers in the United States in the 1880s and 1890s. But when one observes that in the late 1890s such propositions were being seriously considered by a large number of governmental units throughout the United States, one cannot resist the force of the argument that the novel that sold a half-million copies within a decade and the movement which resulted from the spread of its ideas must have had some considerable effect.

James Boon, Free Negro Artisan

In sketching the life of a particular personality, the student of history finds himself face to face with some of the most serious and dangerous problems in connection with the reconstruction of the past. There is the danger that the writer may oversimplify the period in which his subject lived and thus mislead his readers into thinking that they can understand all the forces that shaped the history of the period by becoming acquainted with one person. There is the great danger, moreover, of becoming too biased and thereby painting the subject as a hero or a villain when he is neither. One must keep in mind the fact that sweeping generalizations based on the life of one person are neither good history nor good biography. It must be remembered, further, that the same psychological, sociological, and environmental factors that defy reduction to rules and laws in society serve to render almost impossible the establishment of generalizations in the sequence of human movement based on individual performances.

Despite the fact that such an undertaking is fraught with dangers that may prove disastrous to one seeking to sketch the life of a person, there are factors which by their very nature are so persuasive that one is willing to assume the risks involved. So often, the reconstruction of the past is done with such artful evasion of personalities that it is completely and irrevocably dehumanized. After all, the history of a group or a nation is made up of the stories of the lives of its constituents; and so long as one realizes that the individual element in the past is less important than the communal element, it is an acceptable procedure to humanize and enrich our history by studying the personalities that have been a part of the past. This view is not to be in-

Originally published in the *Journal of Negro History*, XXX (April, 1945). Reprinted with the permission of the Association for the Study of Afro-American Life and History, Inc.

terpreted as a surrender to the so-called "great man theory of history." It is merely the assertion of what seems to be an obvious fact, namely, that history can be vitalized and, in some instances, clarified by studying the fortunes of personalities who, in their own way, have helped to make the heart of a group or a nation pulsate.

A study of the life of a free Negro—in this instance, James Boon—has value for several significant reasons. In the first place, it is not common to find sufficient historical materials bearing on the life of a free Negro to reconstruct it to any appreciable degree. Such individuals were generally inarticulate, due often to illiteracy and sometimes to their dissociation from life about them. Their preoccupation with the struggle for survival seldom left time or energy for expressing their views or preserving the records that were a part of their experiences. Like many others, however, of similar political, social, and economic circumstances, the average free Negro kept no records, perhaps because of the feeling that posterity would not concern itself with the fortunes and misfortunes of the "little man." In the second place, one way of studying the relationship of the free Negro to the larger community and of observing the difficulties involved in his struggle is to evaluate the impact of the forces at work on the life of a member of that group. The student of history, however, must resist the temptation to claim that his subject is representative or typical of the group. One must be satisfied with the belief that the forces that affected his subject perhaps affected countless others as well. Finally, the study of the life of a free Negro is of sufficient vitality and humanity to remind one that people—of varying statures, of innumerable races, and of diverse characteristics and circumstances—make up history; and through people one can gain a valuable insight into the forces that shape history.

The parentage and early life of James Boon are somewhat obscure. A later reference to him as a "free born boy of color" suggests that at least his mother was a free Negro, though it sheds no light on the status of his father.[1] He was born in 1808, and there is a great likelihood that he was born in or near Louisburg, North Carolina, where he spent most of his life.[2] Free Negroes were generally immobile in antebellum North Carolina, because of their impecunious circumstances and because the whites did not, as a rule, welcome strange free Negroes into the community. It would have been safe, therefore, for Boon to have remained in the community where he was born.

The earliest record of Boon is the unsavory account of his implications in a fight. In 1825, when he was perhaps seventeen years old, he was ordered to appear before the county court "to answer in an indict-ment . . . against him for involvement in a fight and an affray."[3] On September 15, Boon appeared "and entered his submission whereupon the Court ordered he be fined $5 and costs."[4] The records do not indicate either the circumstances of the fight or the other parties involved.

In 1827 Boon became an apprentice under the law of the previous year which empowered the county court "to bind out the children of free Negroes or mulattoes, where the parent, with whom such children may live does not or shall not habitually employ his or her time in some honest industrious occupation."[5] There is no indication that proof was offered to show that Boon came under the law, and there is no record of parental objection. On June 16, 1827, the following order was entered:

> Ordered that James Boon a boy of Colour about the age of Eighteen years be bound to William Jones untill he arrive at the age of 21 years to learn the Carpenters Trade—the said Jones entering to the Bond according to Law by giving for security James H. Murray who is approved by the Court.[6]

The indenture covering the apprenticeship of Boon is not available, but under the law of 1762 all masters of apprentices were required to provide "Diet, clothes, Lodging, Accommodations, fit and necessary; and teach [their wards]."[7] Boon learned the trade of a carpenter and it is assumed that his treatment by his master was satisfactory to the court; but although the requirement of teaching free Negroes to read and write remained an integral part of North Carolina's apprenticeship law until 1838,[8] Jones did not teach Boon to read or write. In all of the papers where his signatures were required, he signed with the mark of an unlettered person in the presence of witnesses.[9] For James Boon, the inability to read and to write was to prove to be a distinct handicap because of his innumerable business transactions which would doubt-less have been facilitated by at least a rudimentary knowledge of the written language.

Boon remained under the care of William Jones for two years and three months. In 1829, at the September term of the Franklin County Court of Pleas and Quarter Sessions, he requested a release from his apprenticeship. The court granted his prayer and entered the following order in its minutes: "James Boon a boy of Colour who was bound by this Court came before the Court at this term and made it appear that he was twenty-one years of age and was thereupon ordered to be liberated."[10] Thus after twenty-seven months Boon was "graduated" from

North Carolina's apprentice system, the principal educational institution for free Negroes and many whites. In some instances it was not a benevolent system, and not infrequently the wards suffered from various kinds of mistreatment at the hands of their masters. For a goodly number of free Negroes, however, it was an opportunity to learn a skilled trade and to become sufficiently close to one or more white persons to have a sponsor on whom to rely in a more or less hostile community. For James Boon it meant that he had acquired the skill of a carpenter and that he had in William Jones a source of protection and support that was to stand him in good stead in the years that lay ahead. If in twenty-seven months James Boon could become a finished carpenter—as he certainly did—it is perhaps both because he had an ample amount of aptitude and initiative and because his master taught him with considerable diligence and faithfulness. Through the years, Boon was to demonstrate the fact that he had learned his trade well and that he had much for which to thank William Jones.

For several years after his release from his apprenticeship, Boon did odd jobs around Louisburg, building up a reputation as an able and reliable carpenter. It seems that during this period his tasks consisted mainly of making repairs in homes and public places. Already, however, he had made an impression on the leaders in the community. In 1835 he was engaged to make some much-needed repairs on the County Court House, for which he was paid the sum of $21.12.[11]

Boon's ingenuity was not confined to the mere matter of engaging in the trade of carpentry himself, but extended into the field of contracting jobs and hiring others to assist in the execution of them. In 1834 he had secured a job which was too large for him to do, and had engaged two hands to help him. For three weeks, during the summer, Boon and his men worked for Benjamin Avery of Louisburg and secured seventy-five cents per day and board.[12] Boon's serious efforts in the field of setting up a labor pool from which he could draw for his own jobs and out of which he could assign men to others began in 1839. During the next fifteen years, Boon had more than a score of men in his employ. On one occasion he had nine men working for him on one job.[13]

At least three of Boon's assistants were free Negroes, two of whom had come up through the apprenticeship system. One former apprentice was William Dunston who was thirty-one years old when he began to work for Boon in 1838.[14] The other was Boon's brother, Carter Evans, about nine years younger than Boon, who had been the apprentice of Nathaniel Dunn and Simon Williams.[15] Another free Negro,

William Mitchell, appears on the payroll of Boon with Evans in 1839. From that time until about 1855 these three men were the most regularly employed helpers of James Boon.[16] Perhaps the majority of the other employees of Boon were free Negroes, but their status cannot be conclusively established. It is interesting to observe, however, that Boon did not confine his staff of workers to free Negroes; for there are several instances where he hired the slaves of white men to work for him. In 1841 the slave of one Webb was working on one of Boon's jobs in Louisburg.[17] In 1848 Hilley, the slave of B. M. O. Gaines, was working for Boon.[18] W. Y. Collins' slaves, Adam and Granville, worked for Boon thirty-seven days in 1850.[19] While in Raleigh, Boon used George W. Mordecai's slave, Lunsford, for many weeks, and even carried him to Louisburg to work on a job.[20] Boon's use of the slaves of white men indicates both the willingness of the slaveholders to hire their slaves out to anyone who could pay for them and their faith in the integrity of James Boon.

By 1843 Boon owned one slave himself. When and how he acquired the slave is not known. It may have been merely an act of benevolence, as was much of the slaveholding by free Negroes. It must be said, however, that on occasions Boon used his slave boy as chattel. In 1843, 1851, and 1852 the "Negro boy Lewis" was a part of the property which Boon conveyed in deeds of trust to insure the payment of his debts.[21] When the boy was old enough, Boon used him as a laborer on his jobs.

With the manpower that was at Boon's disposal, it is only natural to expect that he could undertake jobs of varying proportions and requiring varying degrees of skills. During the twenty-year period in which Boon was active as a carpenter and contractor in Louisburg, Wilmington, and Raleigh, almost every conceivable type of repair and construction job was undertaken by him and his helpers. He was constantly in demand for repairing doors, padlocks, window sills, and the like.[22] He could undertake such jobs alone or send one of his more reliable workers out on them. Replacing and repairing woodwork in homes was one of Boon's specialties. In 1846 he made extensive repairs in the home of Mrs. Elizabeth Yarbrough in Louisburg.[23] In 1849 he repaired the porch, floors, panels, blinds, and molding in the home of Augustus Lewis.[24]

On the more difficult jobs and those which required rapid work—such as those in public places—Boon used several helpers. He and three workers remodeled the interior of the store of Augustus Lewis and put new shingles on it in less than a week.[25] Among the things

Boon had to do on a job for Ballard, Harris, and Davis were to put new shelves in the store, make new drawers, and put new legs on a display stand.[26] Among the more tedious jobs on which Boon worked were turning stairs, making bedsteads, and the making of benches, chairs, and stools. Of his versatility in the field of working in woods, there can be no doubt.

It seems, also, that Boon did some painting on his jobs. Although his papers contain no bills to debtors for painting jobs done,[27] there are many accounts which indicate that he purchased large quantities of paint and painting equipment; and one is led to the conclusion that he was also a painter. For example, in 1838, he purchased a gallon and a half of chrome green and a paint brush on one occasion and a few days later he purchased a varnish brush and a training brush from the same merchant.[28]

On the job, Boon gave every indication of being a man of superior ability and capacity for direction. The records suggest the fact that once he undertook a given job, he assumed the full responsibility of getting it done. There was hardly any detail that was not attended to by him. In most instances he purchased all the materials that would be needed, and had their cost placed on his account. His papers are filled with accounts of his purchases of building materials from merchants in the town where he worked. On one day in 1845 he purchased $36.25 worth of lumber from A. L. Perry of Louisburg. The principal items included in the list were railings and planks of various dimensions and weatherboarding.[29] Boon kept an account with Patterson and Dent, prominent merchants of Louisburg, and there are many purchases of railing, posts, shelving, and planks.[30] He also purchased new tools from time to time. Among his papers, for example, are the following items purchased on one occasion in 1848: one drawing knife, two chisels, one adze, four files, a plane iron, and two augers.[31] For these tools Boon paid cash.

Having purchased the materials and tools with which to work, Boon often assumed the responsibility of transporting them to the scene of the job and charged the costs to his employer. Sometimes this involved hiring the conveyance, as on the occasion in 1840 when he hired a wagon and a driver from Young Patterson, the clerk of the county court.[32] While working for Augustus Lewis in 1847 and 1849, Boon transported the building materials to the job and charged the cost to Mr. Lewis.[33] Boon may not always have been able to hire the means of conveyance with ease. In 1851 he carried a note from W. D. Powell to

Mrs. Delia Herring which requested that she permit him to use her vehicle. In part, it said: "The boy James Boon wishes to hire some vehicle of you to go to Raleigh. He will I have no doubt take good care of it should you let him have it."[34] For hiring a wagon in 1851, Boon paid $1.25 for the use of it for two and one-half days. There is reason to believe that he took full advantage of the opportunity to make extra money when he hired a wagon to haul the materials to his job. There are several instances, among his papers, where he hauled materials for other people, and at times one gets the impression that he was in the drayage business. In 1837 he hauled eight loads of wood for one Vaughan, for which he was paid $2.04.[35] In 1850 Boon charged one employer $1.75 for hauling logs for one day.[36]

Not only did Boon secure the job, purchase and transport the materials to it, and engage a staff of assistants, but he also collected the wages for all the men who worked on the job. Whenever he presented bills to his employers, they included the wages for the labor of the men whom he had hired to work for him as well as for himself. As the contractor and, presumably, the most skilled person on the job he received the highest pay. Once he had established himself as a reliable artisan, he never received less than $1.25 per day for his labors. The pay of the other men, apparently, depended on their skills and ranged from .50 to $1.00 per day. In 1848 he and William Dunston worked "50 and ¾ days" for William Jeffreys. For that period, Boon collected $76.25 for himself, while he collected for Dunston $50.75, averaging $1.25 and $1.00 per day, respectively. He collected $49.75 for the labor of Thomas Hall for "49 and ¾ days."[37] Boon seemed to have had his men carefully classified according to skills, and the pay which he collected for them indicates the meticulous care with which it was done. For example, on one occasion he collected .78 per day for the work of Henry Dunce and .93¾ per day for the work of Lewis Boothe.[38] On another job, he collected .62½ per day for the work of Henderson Tyler for part of the time and .62⅕ for him for the remainder of the time.[39]

In at least some instances, Boon made a profit from the labor of some of his men. When he was working on a job for one Benjamin Jones he collected .75 per day for the labor of William Mitchell,[40] while the rate of Mitchell's pay which he received from Boon was .69¹⁄₁₀ per day for the same period.[41] In other words, in addition to the pay which he received from his own labors, he sometimes made a profit of several cents per day on his laborers. The justification for such a policy is to be found not only in the fact that Boon apparently took the initiative in securing and managing the jobs, but that in many instances he supported these men during periods of unemployment.[42]

The wages which Boon received for himself were somewhat less than the prevailing wage for carpenters during the period. At the end of the decade of Boon's last years, the average wage for carpenters in North Carolina was $1.56 per day,[43] while there is no record of Boon's having ever received more than $1.25 per day. Boon's lower wages were hardly the result of his inferior workmanship or his willingness to depress the wages of his trade. In all probability, they were the result of the determination of his employers to distinguish between his status as a free Negro and the status of white artisans. Because he was a free Negro, he was forced to satisfy himself with a wage below the prevailing standard. There was general hostility toward free Negro artisans throughout North Carolina,[44] and although there is no record of Boon's becoming the special victim of the ire of the whites, his status as an artisan was doubtless affected by it. There is every reason to believe that as a free Negro he was at a disadvantage not only in the matter of wages, but also as far as jobs themselves were concerned. His lower wages, it seems, are symbolic of his degraded position in society.[45]

Boon's employers were among the most respected men in the communities in which he worked. It appears from the records that he did more work in places of business than in private homes. Much of his work was for merchants from whom he could collect in kind if not in cash. Ballard, Harris, and Davis of Louisburg employed Boon fairly regularly. This was one of the leading businesses in the village.[46] Augustus Lewis, another merchant of Louisburg, employed Boon frequently, while his records also reveal employment by Paterson and Dent, and John G. King and Company, of Louisburg, and D. Cosby and Company, of Raleigh.

Through the years, Boon built up an enviable reputation as a carpenter and businessman, and the recommendations of his employers are the best testimony to his efficiency and general reliability. Boon was shrewd enough, it seems, to request his employers to write a word in his behalf, and many of them complied. This was an especially wise procedure for a free Negro. In a community that was hostile to him the word of a respected white man would go far in the effort to secure work, and in especially difficult circumstances might conceivably serve as a protection for a free Negro. Some of Boon's employers may have refused to write recommendations for him, while others may have written ones which were not favorable. Those that have been preserved, however, are so generally full of praise that it is difficult to conceive of his not having been liked by practically all who employed him. In 1843 N. W. and B. W. Edwards wrote:

> This is to certify that James Boon a coloured man has been at work for me during the last twelve months, during which term his conduct has been of the strictest propriety. I believe him to be an honest straightforward hard working man. In short he is in my opinion a gentleman.[47]

In 1847 Brian Green of Penny Hill, Wake County, North Carolina, gave Boon the following recommendation: "This is to certify that the bearer James Boon has worked for me some two or three months and that He has given me to believe that He is a pretty faithful workman and therefore deserves to be patronized."[48] A semiliterate white man by the name of A. Kornegay not only thought highly of Boon, but was willing to assume the responsibility for his conduct. In 1848 he wrote: "James Boon is a free man and under my protection and wishes to pass about where his business may cale him at eny time unmolested and rec'd fair treatment as a honable free man of culer. I hereby recommend as such."[49] One employer referred to Boon as "an excellent carpenter and a man who has uniformly conducted himself with the utmost propriety."[50] All of the recommendations were without qualification except one which said: "The bearer Jim Boon has been in my Employ for some time and but for liquor would have done very well. he is a good workman."[51]

Despite the fact that Boon was usually highly recommended by his employers, work was not always easy to find. For a man of Boon's energy and initiative, there can be no doubt that periods of unemployment were unbearable. He, therefore, risked molestation and humiliation at the hands of whites by going into strange communities in search of work. Armed with a recommendation from one of his former employers, he left Louisburg in 1839 and went to Littleton, North Carolina. He secured work with the person to whom his communication was addressed.[52] He worked between Littleton and Louisburg for more than two years, and added one more name to his growing list of sponsors. When he finally left Littleton early in 1842 for Halifax, he carried with him the best recommendation that he ever received. In part, it said:

> This will be handed to you by James Boon a free man who has been in my imployment as a carpenter for some time—At his instance and as an act of

justice I write this to say to you or to any other person who may wish to get his services that he is an orderly and well behaved man and attentive to his business. His work is executed better and with more taste than any persons within my knowledge in this section of the country. Should you want his services my impression is you cannot do better than imploy him.[53]

To be sure, this was as much as Boon could have wanted in the way of an introduction, but through it Boon was not able to make satisfactory connections in Halifax. Within a few months he was back in Louisburg, where he remained for several years.

When Boon went to Wilmington early in 1848 in search of work he carried with him not only the usual recommendations, but also several men who had worked with him in Louisburg. His brother, Carter Evans, and several others with whom Boon was associated were already there. It was Evans who urged Boon to come to Wilmington. In a letter written in January, 1848, Evans said:

Dear Brother
I take great Pleasure in wrightting yo a few lines to inform yo that I am well and hope theas few lines will find yo enjoying the Same. the Boys are all well and are tolerably well satisfide only they want to here from thier famerlys as often as posebl. wee have bin doeing tolerable good bisness only wee are affraid. I know that it is going to be dull. You will Pleas es Mr. Duke harrison and get him write Mr. Jeffrey and get him to bee there protector as my Protectr dont appear as he wants to be botherd with them. I offered to pay him but he wont act. Pleas write me as soon as poseble concerning it and State in your letter when yo will be down. I would like very much for yo to come down if yo dont stay but 3 days.[54]

Despite the urgent nature of the letter Boon did not answer. His silence seemed to annoy Evans, who wrote him again in March:

Dear Bother,
I am very sorry to think that you should loose confidence in me. . . . William Mitchell will be in Louisburge before you come if you do not come soon, as you have lost so much confidence in me that you can not write to me. . . . if you wish William Dunson write to me and i will send him. if you will take $10 more wages in the year than you pay him i will keep him the whole year. the boys all say that you shall come as soon as you can. . . . the espence of bringing your tools will be very little if you come shortly. We have at preasent about $70 worth of work.[55]

Apparently the prospect of work in Wilmington was sufficiently great to attract Boon. Within two weeks after receiving this letter he was in Wilmington. He carried the letter from Duke Harrison to William Jeffreys which Evans had requested in January. He then persuaded

Jeffreys to write him a letter of recommendation, realizing that a word in his behalf from a local man would have greater weight in Wilmington than the word of a resident of Louisburg. Thus, on March 22, 1848, William Jeffreys wrote:

> The bearer of this James Boon (a free man of color from Franklin County, N. C.) comes highly recommended to me by persons whom I know well. . . . I would recommend him to the favorable consideration of the community and he will refer to me in all cases where it may be necessary. This will also be considered as a pass during all lawful hours.[56]

Jeffreys must have been impressed with Boon for he gave a job to him and two of his helpers which lasted for fifty days. Boon was back in Louisburg late in the summer, but his brother, Carter Evans, remained in Wilmington. Two others apparently stopped in Goldsboro en route to Louisburg. In September, 1848, Carter Evans wrote Boon a letter which sheds considerable light on the employment problems of free Negroes at that time:

> Brother—I drop yo few lines to inform you that I am well at presant hoping these few lines may fine you the same. Your man Thomas (Thos) Hall has come from Golds Borough to me for something to doo but I hav notthing for him to Doo and the rest of the hands at Golds Borough are at nothing. TOm says William[57] hav taken his tools and giv them to some other work man to work with. I will keep Tom hear untill I hear from yo so I want you to write fourth with as I hav nothing to doo. . . . Times is verry dull at present.[58]

Wilmington, with its peculiar hostility to free Negroes and its lack of work, was no place for Boon, and he did not return. He worked in Louisburg during the following winter. In the summer of 1849 he went to Raleigh and was joined there by the group he had left in Wilmington. Immediately he secured work in Raleigh on which he was able to employ seven other men.[59] Jobs came rapidly in Raleigh, and for the next few years Boon worked alternately in Raleigh and Louisburg. He took up temporary residence in Raleigh in 1849, and by 1852 he considered it his home.[60] His rovings were over. Even if James Boon was not satisfied with the capital of the North State, he had perhaps tired of moving. At any rate, Raleigh was about as good as any town he had found, and what was more it was not too far from Louisburg, where his property and family were.

Because of Boon's reputation for reliability his credit was good, and he used it extensively. He made heavy purchases regularly at a large number of stores in Louisburg, Wilmington, and Raleigh. In his papers are many statements from Yarbrough and Perry; Gaston Utley; Haywood Little and Company; A. L. Perry; Patterson and Dent; P. I. Brown; Ballard, Harris and Davis; John King; and Richard F. Yarbrough and Company. He also frequented auctions where he purchased goods.

Items purchased by Boon can be classified into three groups: materials used in connection with Boon's work; food and clothing for Boon and his family; and various items for the men who worked for him. The following is a typical account of Boon's purchases of building materials:

JAMES BOON DR. TO A. L. PERRY, NOVEMBER 9, 1845

47	weatherboarding	16½ ft. long		7	inches wide		$4.52
20	"	15½ "	"	7¾	"	"	2.00
29	"	16	" "	8	"	"	3.09
102	Railin	12	" "	3	"	"	3.06
128	"	12	" "	3	"	"	3.71
62	"	16	" "	3	"	"	6.20
91	"	12	" "	3	"	"	2.65
14	Plank	16	" "	12	"	"	2.24
107	Railin	16	" "	3	"	"	4.30
10	"	16	" "	3	"	"	1.00
13	Plank	16	" "	10	"	"	1.69
3	"	16	" "	12	"	"	.48
8	"	10	" "	15½	"	" ⎫	1.35
7	"	14	" "	13½	"	" ⎭	

$36.28

Boon's accounts with Ballard, Harris, and Davis are typical of his purchases of items for himself and his family. Among the purchases are the following commodities: molasses, meat, salt, meal, sugar, coffee, whiskey, calico, muslin, "pant stuff," lining, hooks and eyes, and thread.[61] Among those who made purchases on Boon's account were Hilliard Boon,[62] Hillary Dunce,[63] Lewis Booth,[64] and William Mitchell.[65]

With irregular employment and the responsibility of maintaining a family and the men who worked for him, it is not surprising that he experienced many difficulties in trying to remain solvent. Boon's employers were not always regular in their payments. His frequent absence necessitated by the search for employment doubtless caused him to overlook some matters to which he would have attended had he been in Louisburg. It must be added, moreover, that his accounts reveal here and there a tendency to spend rather recklessly, and this certainly added to his financial worries. From the time he began work as a carpenter and contractor until the end of his career, he was hard pressed to meet his financial obligations. His debts fell into three categories: those to his employees, those to merchants, and those to persons who lent him money. In Boon's papers are several items which indicate that sometimes he owed his employees for long periods of time, and in at least one instance an employee resorted to suit in order to recover his wages.[66]

Boon almost always had outstanding bills with the merchants with whom he did business. At times his accounts would run for a year without any settlement whatever. For example, he began an account with Patterson and Dent of Louisburg in February, 1848. He made purchases almost every month until December. It was not until June of the following year that the account was settled.[67] In August, 1848, he began trading with Ballard, Harris, and Davis. In January of the following year, he had not paid anything, and was carried over into the new year. His purchases continued. In May of 1849, he made a small payment on the account, and in August Boon gave the merchants his note for another part. In January, 1850, almost a year and a half after the account was opened, Boon was still in arrears by more than $40.00.[68]

Boon's credit with merchants, good though it was, could be stretched to the breaking point and on the occasions when the snap seemed imminent he borrowed money. Then, too, there were certain situations when cash, not credit, was what was needed. In those cases, Boon borrowed money. The amounts ranged from $2.00 to more than $100.00. Typical is the occasion when he borrowed $5.00 from R. H. Yarbrough in 1849.[69] Sometimes the need was apparently desperate, as in the case when he borrowed $53.00 from Dr. A. S. Perry of Louisburg for one day.[70]

Boon owned some real property in and near Louisburg which was a source of income, at times; and it doubtless helped him in meeting his obligations. There is no lack of clarity in the records of the manner in which he acquired the property,[71] and there is no question concerning his ownership of both town lots and some land in the country.[72] In 1843 he was described as "the owner of some small property in this neighborhood [Louisburg.]"[73] In the same year he is credited with owning about an acre of land near Louisburg,[74] while in 1855 he owned a lot on Court House Street in Louisburg.[75] In 1847 his house and lot were rented to Joseph I. Harper, and in 1848 he leased them to W. H. Furman for a year at the rate of $5.00 per month.[76] From time to time he sold timber off his land,[77] and on one occasion in 1840 he sold $35.23 worth of "rails."[78]

Boon's income from his labor and his property and the money which he borrowed from time to time were insufficient to satisfy the demands of his creditors, and frequently he was pushed to extreme measures in order to escape serious consequences. The schemes Boon devised to remain solvent were almost ingenious for a man who was illiterate and who doubtless enjoyed only a limited amount of legal counsel. A favorite method of Boon's was to cover his debts with a note to his creditors when a request for extension of time failed. In 1849 when he opened a new account with R. F. Yarbrough and Company, he satisfied an old account of $128.27 by giving the firm a note for the amount.[79] Four days later, he gave the same firm another note for $35.07.[80] Apparently the merchants were satisfied with Boon's house as collateral, for on each of the notes there are indications that during this period the rent from Boon's house was paid directly to R. F. Yarbrough and Company. Boon handled his account with Patterson and Dent in much the same way. In the same year, he gave that firm a note for $125.00 to cover outstanding debts with them.[81] Although these were only temporary measures and merely postponed the day when payment of his debts would finally have to be made, they at least satisfied his creditors, for the moment, and gave him a breathing spell during which he could search into his resources for other techniques of maintaining solvency.

When Boon was especially hard pressed for money with which to pay his debts, he resorted to the method of turning his land over to a person by making out a deed of trust to him. If his debts were not paid within a certain time, the trustee was empowered to sell the property and use the funds to pay Boon's creditors. On three occasions, Boon executed deeds of trust to insure the payment of his debts. The first deed was in 1843 and was made in order to redeem three notes held by Richard F. Noble having a total value of $200.[82] The second was executed in 1851 and was for the purpose of insuring the payment of debts totaling $407.61, which Boon owed to eleven creditors.[83] After Boon took up permanent residence in Raleigh he found it necessary to execute a third deed of trust. Because it is symbolic of the kind of business difficulties which Boon had, it merits quotation:

> This indenture made and entered into this 31st day of August . . . 1852 between James Boon of the first part, and Charles G. Scott of the Second part, and Alfred Williams and Henry Mordecai of the third part, all of the county of Wake and State of North Carolina—witnesseth, that

whereas the said James Boon stands justly indebted to William R. Poole in the sum of six hundred and twenty five dollars ($625) by his promissory note . . . bearing date the 26th day of August 1852, and to which said note so due and payable . . . Alfred Williams and Henry Mordecai are his securities, which said note . . . James Boon honestly desires to pay and to indemnify and save harmless his securities from any loss on account of their Suretyship—Now in consideration of the premises and in further consideration of the sum of five dollars . . . paid by the said Charles G. Scott . . . James Boon hath bargained and sold . . . to the said Charles G. Scott . . . the following property to wit: a certain lot or parcel of land lying and being in the County of Franklin near the town of Franklin [a description of the land follows] . . . containing about one acre . . . also one negro Slave a boy by the name of Lewis about eighteen years of age—To have & to hold the aforesaid lot of land and negro slave Lewis to him the said Charles G. Scott . . . provided nevertheless . . . That the said Charles G. Scott shall and may on the failure of the said James Boon to pay off the said debt of Six hundred and twenty five dollars due . . . as aforesaid . . . whenever he may be so required to do, sell for cash after first giving twenty days notice . . . the aforesaid property and the monies arising from said sale to pay off the . . . debt and interest, and the overplus of any he shall pay to the said James Boon. . . .

his
James   X   Boon
mark

Witness: Joseph Jones   Charles G. Scott[84]

Apparently Boon was always able to pay his debts before his trustee was forced to sell his property, for he used the same lot and slave in all three of the deeds of trust which he executed.[85]

Another method Boon used in trying to remain solvent was to assign the debts owed him to his creditors, when this was agreeable to them. In 1834 Boon asked his employer, Benjamin Avery, to pay his creditor, James Moss, the amount of $25.00 which Avery owed him.[86] In 1848 he asked two employers to pay the amount they owed him to another of his creditors.[87] Boon had the feeling, perhaps, that the additional pressure of his own creditors would force his employers to pay him more quickly. It was a means of impressing his creditors, moreover, with the fact that his negligence of his obligations was due in no small degree to dereliction on the part of those who owed him.

With all of Boon's efforts to pay his debts before his creditors resorted to legal means, there were times when he was unsuccessful, and was forced to answer in court for his failures. On several occasions his creditors turned his accounts over to a justice of the peace for collection. His experience in 1847 is typical:

State of North Carolina   M. F. Sykes
Franklin County   vs
                                                James Boon

To any lawful officer to execute and return within thirty days from the date hereof (Sundays excepted).

You are hereby commanded to take the body of James Boon and him safely keep, so that you have him before me or some other Justice of the Peace for said County to answer the complaint of M. F. SYKES for the non payment of the sum of six dollars due by oath. Herein fail not. . . .

                                       G. Lewis, J. P.

Judgment granted against the defendant for five dollars and 51 cents. A just jury hast ordered him pay the sum and forty cents cost given in Court. March 11, 1841.[88]

The question may well arise as to whether or not Boon's financial straits arose out of an unwillingness to fulfill his obligations. There is nothing in the records which suggest any evasion of responsibility born of faithlessness or the lack of honor. Everything seems to point to the fact that Boon was a serious person with a keen sense of honor. His notes, his overdue accounts, and his other papers that reflect the almost impossible task which confronted him of remaining solvent are balanced by the many indications in his records that even if he was not always prompt, he usually satisfied his creditors by finally paying his bills. Scores of receipts indicate that he purchased items on a cash basis, while many others show that he busied himself in the redemption of notes and the payment of bills which were out against him. These receipts run from 1830, the year after he was released from his apprenticeship, down to 1857, the last year in which there is any extant record of him in any connection. They cover the entire range of his transactions, from the purchase of the most insignificant items to the purchase of large quantities of building materials running into the hundreds of dollars.[89] Each of the deeds of trust which he executed described the transaction as an effort on the part of Boon "to make safe and secure" his outstanding debts or that he was "honestly desirous to secure the payment of the claims." The description of Boon by those who recommended him as a "sober steady man," as "a honable free man of culer," and one whose "conduct has been of the Strictest propriety" would not suggest that he was a man without honor or a sense of responsibility.

Boon lived during a period when the hostility toward free Negroes was mounting steadily. He represented a group whose very presence was not wanted. In dozens of different ways, through the practice of local customs, he was isolated and made to suffer the hardships which were directed to all free Negroes. The success of Boon in maintaining himself as a respectable man in several communities becomes more amazing when his life is set against a background of the increasing antagonism toward the group. It must be remembered, also, that he was completely without training, one who could not even sign his name. How was he able to get along as well as he did? How is the meticulous care with which he attended to his business and entered innumerable transactions to be explained?

Boon was a shrewd and clever businessman. There is not a single record among his papers which does not suggest a rather remarkable aptitude for understanding business and the many transactions in which the businessman engages. One is led to believe that Boon, without any help or advice whatever, could have made a creditable showing as a carpenter and contractor, if he could have led a normal existence as a free, unmolested, and unintimidated human being. In antebellum North Carolina, a free Negro's existence was infinitely easier if he was fortunate enough to have a white friend who could protect him from the attacks of the hostile community and who could give him honest and sound advice when it was needed. James Boon found such a friend in the white man to whom he had been bound as an apprentice in 1827. William Jones may not have taught Boon to read and write, as he should have done, but he proved to be his friend in a number of ways. Since Boon was illiterate, it was necessary to have someone to keep his books and accounts for him. William Jones was doing this in 1840 for $5 per year.[90] Since they were so closely associated for the next ten years Jones, in all probability, continued to perform this service. In view of the fact that Boon's business ran into the hundreds of dollars each year and that there were the tedious tasks of keeping a check on the various men in his employ and on his many purchases, a fee of five dollars per year does not seem exorbitant.

During Boon's long periods of absence from Louisburg, it was William Jones who looked after his interests in his home town. He attended to the matter of renting Boon's house and collecting the rent for him. His general interest in matters affecting Boon can be clearly seen in the letter which Jones wrote to him in 1850 when he was in Raleigh:

Mr. James Boon
Dear Sir
    I received your letter of the 10th Inst. requesting me to attend to some

business you omited to tell me of which I will do with plesure. You stated to me you heard that Mr. Waddell had rented out your stalls to Mr. Stallings which I suppose to be so—I received your letter today and have not had time to see Mr. Stallings to know on wat terms he has rented them out of Mr. Waddell. So as soon as I can have the opportunity of seeing him I will have the matter aranged. You also spoke of my making an inquiry of Mr. Jones to know how much timber Mr. Taylor used of your and I went to see him about the matter and he said none of your timber was used that he knew of. I have not found any person to rent your shop yet. Thing is going about the same, if anything acurs where your are concerned and I can not adjust it I will write to you.

Your Friend
William Jones[91]

Jones demonstrated his friendship for Boon in other ways. He wrote letters for Boon and mailed them. When Boon was away, Jones would advance Mrs. Boon money if she needed it. On several occasions in 1840, she called on Jones for cash, which Boon repaid upon his return.[92] He also advanced Boon money on occasion.[93] When it was necessary, in 1849, for Boon to secure a cosigner on a note to James Dent for $125, it was William Jones who placed his signature on the paper. It was men like William Jones, master carpenter, counsel, and benefactor, who did much toward making life bearable for free Negroes when the laws and the community were equally determined to exterminate them in order to create a social system in which there would be no group whose very existence constituted a threat to the institution of slavery.

Boon's family circle was small. There is no indication of his having more than a brother, a wife, and a son. One may well question the relationship of him to Carter Evans, in view of the fact that they had different surnames. The regularity with which they addressed each other as brother in their correspondence, however, and the fraternal affection which is easily discernible, lead one to believe that they actually were brothers. They may have been the sons of different fathers or they may have been reared in different homes; but they recognized each other as brothers throughout their lives, and worked together harmoniously for more than twenty years.

Boon's wife, Sarah, was the slave of Maria Stallings of Louisburg. She was an intelligent, semiliterate woman whose owner obviously gave her privileges which amounted to virtual freedom. She was extremely interested in his business ventures, and undertook to do what she could in his behalf during his absences from Louisburg. When he was away in 1849, she was attending to at least part of his business. She wrote:

> Your wishes have been attended to, as far as they were in my power. I sent to Mr. Hawkins immediately after the reception of your letter to know if he intended to haul the rails he had promised but he has not done it. I sent also to Mr. Taylor to know if the pen should be put up, but he said it could not be put up now, it would be too much in his way, but that he would leave weak after next and then I would do as I pleased. . . . Jack Thaw said he would buy the rails if Mr. Hawkins did not have them hauled before then. I think it would be better for you to come home if you can stay only one day for your hogs are running wild and I fear they will be destroyed for I can do nothing. . . .
> I remain your devoted wife
>
> Sarah Boon[94]

Sarah Boon not only demonstrated her interest in her husband's business affairs, but she also manifested a deep devotion to him and a real concern for his personal welfare. When he was ill in Raleigh in 1850, she wrote in a tone of genuine alarm: "I was truley sorey to hear that your health was bad. I wish you to let me no if you should get down sick and I have no doubt but what my owners would let me come and stay with you." At the same time, Sarah Boon was also alarmed over what she felt to be her husband's infidelity. She had heard of an alleged connection between him and another woman. She was furious and criticized his conduct severely. Then, in a moment of tenderness, she added:

> My dear Husband I frealy forgive. I have no doubt that you will find it in the end that I was rite. I wish it to be banished from our memorys and it never to be thought of again and let us take a new start and work on together as we have binn doing for many years. Miss Marian has give T me great concorlation but before that I was hardly able to creep. I hope you will concider my feelings and give me the sentiments of your mind in ancer to this letter. I think it would be better for you to wind up your buisness in Raleigh if you could conveantley and come some where clost about me witch would be a great prise to me than all the money you could make. . . . I do not think it is rite to me for such a long absence frome me if I cant come to you. You can come to me. . . . I remain your affectnate wife untill Death
>
> Sarah Boon[95]

Although Boon returned to Louisburg for short periods, he never went back to live. During the following months, his visits became more infrequent. In 1851 he rented a house in Raleigh.[96] In 1855 Boon sold his property in Louisburg to E. L. Stegal for $425.[97] His relationship with his wife after that time is unknown.

The status of Boon's son remains vague. Since his mother was a slave, it is assumed that the boy was also a slave. Yet, he was with Boon in Raleigh in 1849, and one has the impression that he moved about as a free person. In 1849 Sarah Boon wrote her husband, "Give my love to my son and tell him I hope he is doing well and attends preaching regularly."[98] In the following year, he was not with his father, and his mother was worried about him. She wrote "I have not heard from our little son since he left but expect to hear soon and I will let you know as soon as I can."[99] Boon may have purchased his son from the Stallings family. It may be that the Stallings family emancipated him, as an act of benevolence, though the court records do not reveal such a transaction. Finally, he may have been accorded virtual freedom without any legal transaction having ever been made. At any rate, he seemed to have been a substantial bond between his father and mother, and his very existence may well have had the effect of preserving the semblance of a family organization when forces were at work to destroy it.

In observing the habits and tastes of James Boon, one gets the impression that he had a formula for living and that he enjoyed it as much as circumstances would permit. He seemed to be a restless, sensitive soul who was always in search for something—security, happiness, respectability. Those were extremely elusive things for a free Negro in the antebellum South. In the absence of them in tangible form, Boon escaped to a fanciful world which permitted him to revel in make-believe. He seemed especially fond of fine clothes, and the records indicate that he had more than a man of his means would ordinarily have. He purchased suits, hats, and shoes frequently. On one occasion when he bought a complete outfit, he paid $10 for a hat.[100] In 1848 he paid $4 for a beaver hat in Wilmington.[101] In 1850 he purchased two dress coats and one "frock coat" at one place and on the same day purchased a "fine silk hat" and a "fine plush cap" at another.[102] Later in the same year, he placed an order with William Green, shoemaker, for a pair of "furestrate boots."[103] In addition to these examples of superior merchandise, there are many indications that he bought ordinary clothes regularly.

One gets the impression that in his later years Boon drank rather immoderately. In 1848 he purchased a barrel of brandy in Wilmington and had it shipped to Louisburg.[104] While there is some evidence of his having sold a portion of it,[105] there is no reason to believe that a man of Boon's tastes retailed the entire barrel. In 1849 he purchased wine or whiskey monthly, usually in half-gallon measures, during April, May, and June.[106] On each of his statements from Ballard, Harris, and Davis, whiskey is among the items purchased. It was perhaps the tendency toward immoderateness that led Dabney Crosby to state that Boon was a satisfactory worker, except "for liquor."[107]

Boon never enjoyed robust health, it seems. On several occasions after 1843, he was ill enough to require a visit from his physician. Between 1844 and 1849 the physician called on him seven times. There were many other occasions during the same period when Boon went to the physician for medicine. The many prescriptions which Boon received of blue pills, liniment, cough medicine, calomel, and quinine tempt one to speculate concerning his maladies, and the temptation is resisted with considerable difficulty.[108]

The last record of Boon's activities is dated 1857. At that time he was only forty-nine years old. Despite the fact that he was still in the prime of life, it is doubtful that he lived long after that. It is difficult to believe that a man of his vitality and business initiative could have continued to live without intruding his name into the records of the community. For our purposes here, James Boon ceased to exist when his record for posterity came to a close.

That James Boon lived for at least forty-nine years has great significance for the student of antebellum history. To have the opportunity to know rather intimately the life of a person of his capabilities and his adroitness is a privilege which is too frequently denied us by the scarcity or inadequacy of the records. James Boon reminds us once more that the history of a nation is to be found not only in the records of victorious battles or in the lives of the notable personages but also in the lives of the most humbly born, the most consistently despised, and the most miserably improvident. The life of James Boon may not have been typical of the lives of most free Negroes of North Carolina and the South, but one cannot escape the conclusion that it reflects, in a measure, the common experiences, the fortunes, both good and ill, which all free Negroes had. Finally, the disparity between the theory of free Negro-white relations of the antebellum period and the reality of Boon's relatively respectable existence in an ostensibly hostile community serves as a warning against the formulation of conclusions regarding societal relationships based entirely on theoretical formulas.

James T. Ayers, Civil War Recruiter

In the score or more years immediately preceding the Civil War, Illinois was one of the important centers of debate over the question of slavery. Few states had within their borders so complete a cross section of sentiment for and against the "peculiar institution" as did Illinois. The point of view ranged all the way from the strong and dynamic abolitionism of Elijah Lovejoy to the persistent and resourceful support of slavery typified in Dumas J. Van Deren.[1] Perhaps much more characteristic of the state were the views of those many citizens who could be found toward the center, between these two extremists, and who wanted "peace and union." Their antislavery sentiments, which were abundant, arose not so much from an appreciation of the moral issues involved as from a sense or feeling that slavery was a force that was eating the heart out of the body politic and destroying its unity. The ardent love of the citizens for the Union was one of the few things that the heterogeneous mass of the citizens of Illinois—immigrants, adventurers, speculators, missionaries, ne'er-do-wells—had in common. Love for the Union was an infectious sort of thing that spread through Illinois and rendered completely impotent any thought of state sovereignty or sectional selfishness. Both sides of the slave controversy were represented in Illinois, but practically all on both sides were together on the question of the relation of their state to the Union.

This early generation of Illinois' citizens had grown up with the state. They had come into this part of the Northwest Territory from neighboring areas—Ohio, Pennsylvania, Indiana, Kentucky, and Tennessee. They represented in their lives the hopes and aspirations of a land so recently become a state in the Union. They had come to this

Originally published in the *Illinois Historical Journal*, XC (September, 1947).

new land to carve out a way of life for themselves—to make a fortune and to secure the blessings of liberty for themselves and their posterity.

A typical migrant into Illinois was James T. Ayers. Born in Germantown, Bracken County, Kentucky, on November 14, 1805, Ayers moved with his family to Madison County, Ohio, at some undetermined date.[2] He lived there until 1831, having married Rebecca Bloomer of Fayette County, Ohio, in 1825.[3] In that same year Ayers began his ministry in the Methodist Episcopal church as a local preacher; and although he never devoted his time exclusively to the ministry, he maintained a keen interest in the affairs of the church until his death.

In 1831, Ayers joined the veritable horde of people who were moving west at the time and migrated with his young wife to Illinois, settling in Tazewell County. He then began a career of farming that extended down to 1862. Later he lived in McLean and Livingston counties. Little is known of Ayers' education except that a later reference said he possessed "fine talents, was fairly educated and a natural orator."[4] While Ayers was not highly trained in formal subjects, his remarkable discernment and insight into the nation's problems must have been the result of lifelong study and discipline.

The area in which Ayers lived in Illinois, and his religious connections, doubtless affected his attitudes and helped to shape his philosophy of life. In the 1830s and 1840s antislavery sentiment was growing in that part of Illinois, and already antislavery societies were flourishing. For example, in 1841, one such society was organized in Tazewell County.[5] The presence of such positive opposition to slavery must have had something to do with Ayers' growing hostility to the institution. Equally important, perhaps, was the militant stand which his church, dominated by the antislavery leader Peter Cartwright, was taking. "The Methodist Church in Illinois prided itself on its solemn and earnest protest against the evil of slavery and pointed to its vigorous anti-fugitive slave law resolutions."[6]

Ayers' hatred for slavery, which had obviously crystallized before 1860, was part of a reforming zeal that was characteristic of the man. In this he reflected the spirit of America and especially that of his section in the Civil War era. He was the kind of idealist who believed in striving to attain a perfect America. He was, in this respect, a true product of his environment. It was not enough, from Ayers' point of view, to hate the institution of slavery in a passive manner. He felt compelled to translate his feeling into action by joining the growing movement for its abolition. His contempt for slavery was extended to the section and the persons who held slaves. On numerous occasions he spoke out against the South and her cause in bitter language which reflected a zeal for the northern cause surpassed by few who fought on that side. On one occasion during the Civil War, he wrote:

> Oh how nice and Comfortably might this Develish Rebellion and southern Revolt have been setled had men wished to do write had men been Disposed to do as they would be done by, or as the Saviour Cotes it, as ye would that men should do to you, do ye even so to them for this is the Law and the Prophets. Had our Southern Brethren heeded this text of the Saviour thare would have been none of this cursed war and blood shead now going on in our midst as at this day.[7]

As an enthusiastic northerner, he had nothing but utter contempt for the South and its civilization. As he traveled through the South he got the impression that the whites had degenerated to the point where they were no more advanced than the slaves, and concluded that "its all nig down here."[8] He did not even regard the South as a part of America, since, in his opinion, it had drifted so far from American ideals. During the war he longed to return to Illinois where once more he could "imbrace our friends and see oald America having been so long down Amidst those sour faced shea and hea Devils in Shape of Human form."[9]

It was slavery that aroused Ayers' greatest resentment toward the South. He constantly prayed for its abolition. He said: "Surely God is and will continue to Punnish those miserable tirants and Soal killers for there sins. I feel glad in my heart the cursed thing is winking out and soon the idea of master and slave will be numbered Among the things that was same as oald fashioned witchcraft Among the new Englanders in former day."[10] He said that slavery had made the whites so "ignorant and stupid" that they could not live without it, and ventured the opinion that the Negroes could get along without their masters better than the masters could without their slaves.

Ayers cannot be referred to as a lover of Negroes, despite his contempt for the institution of slavery. In one instance, when exasperated with a group of Negroes, he described them as "so trifleing and mean the[y] don't Deserve to be free." He was reasonable enough, however, to understand that slavery was the cause of the Negro's plight, and expressed the conviction that the Negro would prosper like any other free man if given an opportunity. On one occasion he said:

> Those that have got out from under master are According to there Chance making good crops of Corn and Cotton and seem to be striving to do

as best they can. . . . . They are an ignorant people and how Could they be otherwise. We should perhaps be but Little better if plaiced in there Position. Educate them set good Examples before them. Let them know they are men and women and are A part and parcel of Gods Creation and I feel Sambo will do tolerably well.[11]

Ayers was as violently opposed to any kind of intimate association between whites and Negroes as any of his southern adversaries. When it was suggested that Negroes with freedom would mingle freely with whites, Ayers said: "Dam the niggers I would Rather Blow there Brains out than they should do this and so would I. No man would abhor the sight of A big buck nigger leading my daughter or Any white mans Daughter Round than I and yet I think we have ungrounded fears."[12]

Ayers possessed a lively, lyrical spirit that made it possible for him to enjoy nature and the various seasons of the year. He loved to walk through the forests, to observe flowers, birds, and the like, and to write about them in the most romantic manner. The lofty height which his soul could reach inspired him, on occasions, to write verse which described his feelings. These poems justify the observation that this veteran of veterans had a song in his heart. The following stanzas from a song—of dubious literary value—written by him in April, 1863, are typical of his poetry:

> South Tunnel here in Tennessee
> Is as Strang A place as one Might see
> Its up & down and down & up
> From Deep Ravines to Mountain Top.
>
> The Rail Road Tunnel you must know
> It passes throug those Mountains here
> And if in Center you should be
> Its dark as Midnight Certainly
>
> . . . .
>
> If all the people here was Write
> And Rebelism used up quiet
> The Last infernal tory shot
> And all the Torys Brought to naught
>
> This place then would be paradise
> All nature seems in place so nice
> The Country fine as need to be
> The health they say is Tolerably.

When the war came, no one was more determined than Ayers to join in the fight and make a contribution to the victory to which he was certain the Union forces were entitled. One difficulty, his age, stood in the way. He was more than fifty-five when the war came and was, therefore, too old for combat duty. Not even his age, however, could prevent his enlistment. On September 8, 1862, he went to the county adjoining the one in which he lived and was mustered into Company E of the 129th Illinois Infantry Regiment. Although he was approaching his fifty-seventh birthday, he gave his age as fifty. This dishonesty is suggestive of the extent of Ayers' determination to enter the service at any cost.

Ayers was not long with the 129th Infantry. In the summer of 1863, he began enlisting Negro soldiers under the authority of Andrew Johnson, the military governor of Tennessee; and in the late autumn, when the federal machinery for recruiting Negro soldiers was set up, Ayers received an early assignment in Nashville, Tennessee. It was as a recruiter of Negro soldiers from July, 1863, to October, 1864, that James T. Ayers made his most valuable contribution to the Union.

When hostilities broke out in the spring of 1861, Negroes all over the North hoped to enter the war on the side of the Union and help in securing the freedom of their enslaved brothers in the South. Many of them, like Frederick Douglass, "saw in this war the end of slavery" and their "interest in the success of the North was largely due to this belief." Negroes sought to enlist in the Union Army, but all during 1861 their efforts were in vain. Both the president and the secretary of war were opposed to the use of Negro troops, and the War Department instructed the officers in the field even to refrain from taking slaves as contraband of war.[13]

It was not until the spring of 1862 that the Union government gave serious consideration to the matter of arming Negroes and using them in the struggle against the Confederacy. In May, 1862, General David Hunter sent out a call from Port Royal, South Carolina, for Negroes to serve in the Union Army. Negroes responded, and shortly the "First South Carolina Volunteer Regiment" was activated. When criticized for his actions, General Hunter denied that he had acted beyond the authority given him by the secretary of war, and contended that he was acting in the best interest of the Union cause.[14] Lincoln was not ready, however, to place guns in the hands of Negroes, and not until the autumn of 1862 did he relax his policy with regard to arming Negroes.

With the issuance of the first Emancipation Proclamation in September, 1862, Lincoln began to tolerate the enlistment of Negroes in the Union Army. The reorganization of Hunter's regiment was under way in October, and on November 7, 1862, the first company was mustered. Meanwhile, other regiments of Negro soldiers were being organized in the North and in the South. Finally, "in December, 1862, General Augustus L. Chetlain assumed control of Negro volunteering in Tennessee, and thereafter the policy was definitely considered as a successful venture."[15] When the Emancipation Proclamation became effective on January 1, 1863, the federal government adopted a policy not only looking toward receiving slaves within its lines, but also recruiting Negroes to fight in what had become a war of liberation as well as a struggle to save the Union.

In the spring of 1863, the machinery for recruiting Negro soldiers in the South was set up by Adjutant General Lorenzo Thomas, who, on March 25, was sent to the Mississippi River Valley to put it into operation.[16] On May 22, 1863, a special bureau was established in the adjutant general's office for the "conduct of all matters referring to the organization of Negro troops." General Order Number 143 established a detail of clerks and appointed a competent officer at the head of the new bureau. Several field officers were detailed to inspect the work of recruiting at various stations which were to be the headquarters for such work. Boards were to be convened to examine applicants for commissions to command colored troops. The order further stated: "No person shall be allowed to recruit for colored troops except specially authorized by the War Department; and no such authority will be given to persons who have not been examined and passed by a board; nor will such authority be given to any one person to raise more than one regiment."[17] The reports of boards were to specify the grade of commission for which each candidate was fit, and authority to recruit was to be given in accordance. Recruiting stations and depots were to be established by the adjutant general as circumstances required.

Another order, Number 144, issued on the same day, prescribed the rules for the guidance of boards in examining applicants for commissions in regiments of colored troops. Each board was to sit daily except Sunday and was to report to the adjutant general every week. Applicants were required to show that they were physically, mentally, and morally fit to command troops. The decisions and recommendations of the board were to be final and any applicant who was rejected was not to be reexamined.[18]

In October, 1863, the program for recruiting Negro soldiers was further organized by the establishment of recruiting stations in Maryland, Tennessee, and Missouri. Tennessee was already in process of being reconstructed under Andrew Johnson, who had set up a program for recruiting Negro soldiers. By this time, moreover, the government could act with greater decision with regard to the border states, since the danger of their secession was no longer imminent. The order provided that all able-bodied Negroes were eligible for military employment. Where loyal masters consented to the enlistment of their slaves, the masters were to receive $300 for each one. It further provided that if a sufficient number of recruits should not be obtained within thirty days after the opening of the recruiting station, slaves could be taken without obtaining the consent of loyal owners.[19]

In setting up and perfecting the machinery for the recruiting and processing of Negro soldiers, the federal government established a system that was to grow in importance in the maintenance of a citizen army with each passing year. It is interesting to observe that no such system was employed for the recruiting of white soldiers during the Civil War. As Professor Shannon has correctly pointed out, the government showed more wisdom in dealing with Negro soldiers than with the whites. It was possible to engage in considerable experimentation in recruiting Negro soldiers in the South, because state pride did not have to be considered and "national authority could assert itself with but little hindrance."[20]

In pursuance of the order of October 13, 1863, establishing recruiting stations in Tennessee, an office was opened in Nashville with George L. Stearns of Medford, Massachusetts, as commissioner for the organization of United States colored troops. He was given the rank of major with the powers of an assistant adjutant general. Upon finding that Negro troops were being used at the front for fatigue duty, Major Stearns, a former abolitionist who had fought with John Brown in Kansas, protested this action and advised that Negro troops be put in camps of instruction and prepared for the duties of the field. He and Governor Johnson could not agree on the disposition of Negro troops; and when the secretary of war sustained the governor, Major Stearns resigned.[21] Captain R. D. Mussey was placed in temporary command in December, 1863. On February 6, 1864, Brigadier General Augustus L. Chetlain was assigned to command all colored troops in Tennessee, with headquarters at Memphis.[22] Three days later, Captain Mussey was charged with the organization of Negro troops in middle and east Tennessee, with headquarters at Nashville.[23]

By the end of 1863, the recruiting of Negro troops had progressed to the point that on December 24, the adjutant general could make the following report to the secretary of war:

> The majority of the freedmen manifest a partiality for the military service, and are undoubtedly happy and contented in their position in the army. . . . I expect very soon to proceed to Nashville and points covered by Major-General Grant's army and give my personal attention to the organization of colored troops in that section of the country. It is to be presumed that as our armies advance the number of our colored organizations will be largely increased.

Concerning recruiters, the adjutant general had this to say:

> None but intelligent officers and enlisted men from the regular and volunteer service have been detached from their regiments for the purpose of raising colored troops. All have worked faithfully in the cause, and if not quite as successfully as might have been anticipated, it has not been for the want of perseverance.[24]

Just as this machinery for the recruiting of Negro troops was being perfected, James T. Ayers was engaged as one of the recruiters to work out of Captain Mussey's office at Nashville. It will be recalled that he had already worked in the summer of 1863 as a recruiter under Governor Johnson's plan. In Gallatin, Tennessee, in July, 1863, Ayers had enrolled more than two hundred men, and was enthusiastic over the prospects of enlisting more. Doubtless it was this experience and the contacts he made that commended him to the federal authorities late in 1863.

Ayers was most enthusiastic over the decision of the Lincoln administration to use Negroes as soldiers in the Civil War. Doubtless he realized that the Union needed additional fighting men, and perhaps he was also of the opinion that the Negro would make a good soldier. It seems, however, that his greatest satisfaction came from the humiliation which he knew the South would suffer in meeting its former slaves on the field of battle. In writing of the untenable position of the South, he said: "As they waged war on us About the Nigger, why, in Gods name give them [the] nigger; and on this wise you know the oald Adage is that the Hair of the dog is good for the bite."[25] He made his whole position on the use of Negro soldiers clear when he said:

> Niggers to fight such Demons and Devils with, Niggers to Cure the bite, Nigger wool to cure Traitorism, Nigger Powder and Lead seasoned with the Amansipation Proclamation garded and Protected in the hands of A wise and good Administration, handled by Sambo, at the Britch of A good mus-

ket, surely is a plaster good enough for traitors. . . . oh say some you must not arm the Nigger, it will degrade us, Says another, "I would not fight by a nigger." Well I believe that Jake. . . . you did not intend to fight Any how. . . . I would Rather twice toald chance the black than the white nigger [draft dodgers and Copperheads], and of the two the Black is the best. . . . Never Cease giving Pills, no matter who ishues the dose, white or black, of Powder and Lead till traitors are subdued And not only subdued, but Effectually so.[26]

On Christmas Day, 1863, Ayers received his appointment, with the rank of a private, as a recruiter of colored troops, and, fortunately, he began to keep a diary on that day. He was sent to Stevenson, Alabama, to work out of the office there, headed by Captain William F. Wheeler.[27] By the first of the new year, Ayers had presented his credentials and received his authority to recruit Negro soldiers in the Tennessee Valley section of Alabama, in such towns as Bridgeport, Triana, Decatur, Huntsville, and Stevenson. All the zeal that had earlier gone into his work as farmer, local preacher, and antislavery Republican was now directed into the channel of luring freed Negroes into the ranks of the Union Army.

Ayers' methods were presumably typical of those used by other recruiters, and therefore merit some consideration. After a town had been taken by the Union forces, Ayers would move in and proceed to enlist Negro recruits. He would nail up attractive posters provided by the adjutant general's office and then would announce a meeting at which he would speak. If he succeeded in assembling a number of Negroes, he would appeal to them along two lines. In the first place, he would impress on his hearers the importance of getting into the fight in order to extend the blessings of liberty to their more unfortunate brothers who were still enslaved. Then, he would tell them that the ten dollars per month, food, and clothing would give them some semblance of security and independence.

Recruiting in rural areas was somewhat more difficult. Ayers was compelled to go from plantation to plantation, and frequently he bore the first news of emancipation to reach the slaves. For example, when he arrived at the Eldridge plantation near Huntsville, Alabama, in May, 1864, the slaves told him that they had not heard of the Emancipation Proclamation. Almost always he met the stern resistance of white men or women who branded him as an inciter of trouble and one who interfered with the peace and happiness of the slaves. Ayers was not perturbed by the opposition of the white masters, and went about his job, for the most part, as though they did not exist. On one Alabama plantation, where he was searching for a Negro who had promised to join the army but who had apparently lost his enthusiasm for the Union cause, the slave's mistress had hidden him. When Ayers demanded the Negro, a long argument ensued between the recruiter and the woman. She told him that it was wicked for the North to take her slaves, while Ayers countered with the assertion that slavery itself was wicked. Both resorted to the Bible to bolster their arguments, and Ayers confessed to his diary that he was so impressed by her intelligence and her charm that he forgot about his recruiting. The arguments were not always so pleasant. On another occasion, after a heated dispute with a woman concerning slavery, the woman sought to end the discussion by saying, "I want you always to know sir I hait you in my verry Hart." Ayers was tempted to call her by several unfavorable names, but he merely said, "You are a disgrace to the sects [sex]. Shame on you Siss." He then ordered her into the house and signed up four Negroes for the Fifteenth Tennessee Colored Regiment.[28]

Despite Ayers' efforts, he was not altogether satisfied with the results. Not only was there the opposition offered by the white civilians in the areas where he worked, but there also seemed to be a surprising lack of interest on the part of the Negroes with whom he talked. At times Ayers became completely bewildered as to how to entice Negroes into the army. On one such occasion, he penned the following lines:

> The Recruiting business Let me say,
> it keeps me busy every day,
> A man that cannot Learn while he,
> Recruits for Darkies must ignorant be.
> (So think I at least.)[29]

In September, 1864, Ayers said, "I keep geathering the Boys in slowly But I want to get Away from here as soon as I can." Ayers particularly disliked the lack of enthusiasm among the Negroes for entering the army. He complained that they offered all kinds of excuses, physical disability and otherwise. "I am Hartily sick of hearing them any more and hope to get Dismissed from this Recruiting business," he wrote. But he concluded, "perhaps I have in this way been of more service to my Country than in Any other way I could have been imployed, so all write."[30]

Apparently, the secretary of war was not satisfied with the progress of the program of recruiting Negro troops. On February 5, 1864, he wired the adjutant general, then in Nashville, and made inquiries concerning the program. In part, he said: "I wish you would send me by telegraph a statement of the whole number of colored troops organized, so far as you have information. Some clamor is being raised at the lack of energy and industry on that subject." General Thomas dispatched the following reply:

> The whole number of colored troops organized and mustered into service in Middle and East Tennessee will number 7,500. In addition, General Dodge, at Pulaski, has a third regiment nearly full. I now intend to enlist the able-bodied negroes in the employ of loyal citizens. . . . The people of Tennessee appreciate the views of the Administration, and beyond doubt the recruiting of colored troops in this section will prove eminently successful.[31]

The recruiting in the spring of 1864 was slow in Tennessee and Alabama. Some of the obstacles recruiters faced were beyond their power to remove. One, for example, was the opposition of the generals of the Union Army, who feared that the wholesale enlistment of Negroes would take away an important supply of black civilian labor that was being utilized in connection with encampments, the setting up of barracks, and the like. General Sherman was so incensed over the interference with Negro civilian laborers by recruiting officers that he issued an order blocking such activities. In part, the order, dated June 3, 1864, stated:

> I. Recruiting officers will not enlist as soldiers any negroes who are profitably employed by any of the army departments, and any staff officer having a negro employed in useful labor on account of the Government will refuse to release him from his employment by virtue of a supposed enlistment as a soldier.
> II. Commanding officers of the military posts will arrest, and, if need be, imprison any recruiting officer who, to make up companies of negro soldiers, interferes with the necessary gangs of hired negroes in the employment of the quartermaster's or commissary or other department of the Government without the full consent of the officers having them in charge.[32]

This order by General Sherman greatly disturbed Adjutant General Thomas, who expressed his point of view to the secretary of war in the following communication:

> I have just been shown the inclosed order of Major-General Sherman, which . . . I conceive, will stop enlistments from the colored men coming into his army. I consider the threat of imprisonment to recruiting officers

especially harsh. Far better to enlist the negroes, and let them perform their fair share of labor and fatigue duty, than keep them at hard labor—in many instances greater than they were subjected to by their former owners.[33]

After an exchange of letters between Sherman and Thomas, the former rescinded his order against the enlistment of Negro soldiers, offering the suggestion that recruiting should be done in a purposeful and orderly manner, giving full protection to the Negroes who enlisted.[34] Although the matter was apparently cleared up, Sherman's counter order of June 26 did not reach his subordinate officers promptly. In September Ayers recorded in his diary that he was arrested on a charge of kidnapping Negroes and sent under guard to Huntsville by order of General Gordon Granger. Fortunately, however, he was released by showing his own papers and presenting a letter from Colonel R. D. Mussey, out of whose office he was recruiting.[35]

One of the things that irritated the generals in the field was the haphazard enlisting of Negroes for new regiments before old regiments had been completely filled. This procedure taxed the army to supply an unnecessary number of officers for the new contingents. The commanding officers were, therefore, pleased with the proposal to prevent such action. Major General George H. Thomas, commanding officer of the United States Volunteers, wrote to the adjutant general on August 9, 1864, as follows:

> I would respectfully call your attention to the following facts and suggestions relative to the U. S. colored infantry service and the plan adopted and pursued by Col. R. D. Mussey, superintendent for organization of colored troops, *i.e.*, that of the formation of new regiments exclusively, to the neglect and prohibition of securing recruits for regiments already in existence, and which have not reached the maximum of their organization.
>
> By the formation of new regiments the army is called upon to furnish officers necessary to the efficiency of such organizations, and thereby unnecessarily depriving commands already in the field of their officers, or else taking from the ranks men whose services can illy be spared, whereas by the filling up of those regiments already in existence and fully officered this drain upon the army would be removed.[36]

The commanding officer of the volunteers then asked that Colonel Mussey be instructed to fill up existing regiments before starting others, and there are indications that Colonel Mussey proceeded to pursue such a course of action.

On October 10, 1864, Colonel Mussey made an extensive report to Major C. W. Foster, chief of the Colored Bureau in the adjutant general's office. In this communication, Colonel Mussey said that he thought it inadvisable to begin other Negro regiments after those begun had been completed. Although Negroes were still enlisting, they were not doing so "in such numbers as to warrant the formation of new regiments." He then set forth his plan for the reorganization of the recruiting program in the area under his jurisdiction. It called for all colored recruiting to be placed under the control of one person. "As it is," he said, "there are recruiting parties from the old regiments of whose whereabouts, operations, and success I know nothing, unless they stumble into some place where I have parties recruiting for the new regiments." Colonel Mussey then proposed to have all recruits sent to Nashville "for examination, enlistment, and some drill before they are sent to the commands for which they are enlisted."

A significant item in the colonel's proposals was the use of Negroes to assist in recruiting. He said:

> To make recruiting successful here an armed force of one regiment or more is necessary. . . . Where we have been able to send a force of, say, 80 or 100 men for a few days into the country, we have always got men, and the good conduct of the men upon such scouts has left a favorable impression upon the people.

Finally, Colonel Mussey asserted that recruits should be given some assurance that their families would not suffer from the abuse of "disloyal owners whom they have left to enlist."[37]

Although Ayers had by this time been relieved of his duties as a recruiter, he had earlier pursued much of the policy advocated by Colonel Mussey. On July 26, 1864, ten armed Negroes from Nashville arrived at Huntsville to assist Ayers with his recruiting.[38] He frequently spoke of the salutary effect that such a policy had on Negro prospects. Ayers did all he could, moreover, to assure the families of recruits that they would be protected by the Union Army if their men went away to fight.

In reviewing the recruiting of Negro soldiers in northern Alabama, Ayers' area of operation, Colonel Mussey described it as eminently successful. He said that "some 300 were obtained for the Seventeenth U. S. Colored Infantry," and that frequently slaves ran away from their owners to enlist.[39]

Progress in recruiting was not satisfactory to Ayers, however. In the middle of September, 1864, Ayers complained, "I am so tired of nigger Recruiting I am going as soon as A train goes through to Nashville to Resign and Go back to my Reg. or try."[40] Early in October he went to

Nashville and resigned his position. Several things prompted Ayers to take this step. In the first place, his zeal was so great that any failure to secure recruits discouraged him greatly. As a matter of fact, he did encounter many Negroes who were not interested in joining the army and remained unaffected by his various persuasions. Furthermore, Ayers was never in a position to see the results of recruiting as a whole, and therefore concluded that it was a failure and not worth his time. Then, too, by the early autumn of 1864, Ayers was more interested in the presidential campaign than in anything else. He spent his spare moments writing campaign poetry and songs, and recorded in his diary that it would be a national calamity if Lincoln were not reelected. In Ayers' mind, everything was of secondary importance to the reelection of Lincoln. Finally, Ayers' health was not good. He was fifty-nine years old, and frequently complained of a number of ailments. He felt that "ranging around" looking for "nigger recruits" who were disinterested was too strenuous for a man in feeble health. He longed to return to his regiment and carry on his religious meetings around the campfire with the men he knew and loved.

The recruiting of Negro troops in territory lately occupied by the Confederates was unquestionably a success. Of the 186,017 Negroes who served in the Union Army, 104,387 were recruited in Confederate territory. In the area where Ayers worked, Tennessee furnished 20,133 Negro troops, while Alabama provided 4,969.[41] In working as diligently as he did to recruit Negro troops, Ayers made a significant contribution to the success of the northern cause, for the Negroes whom he and others enlisted proved of inestimable value. An authority on the organization of the Union Army has observed that:

> They were more accustomed to obedience to orders than were the white men. What they lacked in individual initiative . . . they made up by the superior training they received from their better selected officers. . . . Courage was of necessity most prominent among negro privates and their officers. Orders such as that of Kirby Smith [a Confederate officer] . . . that armed negroes and their officers should be given no quarter, not only made it an especially courageous thing to enlist in or command a negro regiment but were also conducive to the bravest of fighting when in close quarters.[42]

The program of recruiting Negroes is significant, not only because it provided the North with much-needed manpower, but also because it established for the federal government the machinery of recruitment that was to be used from that day to this. The techniques and approaches which were conceived and developed to entice Negroes into the army from 1863 to 1865 are, with some modifications, the techniques and approaches used today. In carrying forward this program, Ayers and his fellows made important contributions to the organization and administration of the Army of the United States.

After Ayers was relieved of his task as a recruiting agent for Negro soldiers, he proceeded to rejoin his old outfit, the 129th Illinois Volunteer Regiment, to which he remained attached until the end of the war. But it was October, 1864, when he was transferred; and the election of Lincoln was Ayers' greatest immediate concern. Throughout the war years he had held nothing but contempt for the anti-Lincoln forces in the North, and he thought that their advocacy of "appeasement" unduly hampered a vigorous prosecution of the war. He even contended that men like Clement L. Vallandigham, Daniel Voorhees, and Don Carlos Buell had promised help to the South, an act of comfort that caused the South to continue to hope for victory. He wrote:

> But if those Peace Candidates are Defeated this fall, the thing will be settled in my opinion for surely they the south know well as we and even better that they cant hoald out four years more. . . . All in the world that has made this war Linger thus far has been this Howl in the North by this Peace Party. If they are handsomely beaten this fall A settlement will be made.[43]

The possibility of a victory for the Democrats haunted Ayers like a nightmare. He cordially despised General McClellan and all his supporters. On a note of despair he said, "If this Peace party does prevail we are all gon to the Devil head long sure and certain in my mind. God forbid they should prevail."[44]

In a lengthy poem Ayers gave vent to his deepest antipathy for the northern Democrats, whom he and others contemptuously called copperheads. He was certain that they pursued their policy of appeasement because they did not have the courage to fight. In this poem of twelve stanzas he proposed that all copperheads should be brought into the army, placed in the front lines, and given a taste of what the supporters of the Union had gone through every day. After proposing that they be subjected to cold, hunger, filth, injury, and every conceivable inconvenience, he concluded:

> And finally in A Hospital minas A leg or so
> Somewhat ematiated and most dredfully low
> We'll Lay whats Left of Copperhead upon A dirty bunk
> To Regain his waisted energies on weak tea and tough junk.

To the Call of uncle Abraham we Cherfully all flew
Severed the tyes which bound our Harts bade cherished ones adieu
And we will not brook the insults which are heaped upon our heads
By the traitorous northern Cowards the Slimy Copperheads.[45]

Ayers spent the remainder of the month of October arranging for a twenty-day furlough and journey to Illinois where he could cast his vote. On October 28, he left Nashville and proceeded home, where, he said, "My vote will be cast if I live for Father Abraham For President and Andy for vice President and Oglesby[46] for Govenor and in short my vote will be Union all through sure as life."[47] During the time that Ayers was waiting for transportation to Illinois he wrote a campaign song of which two stanzas and chorus follow:

The Rebs have Tramped down our fields
Destroyed our walls and Ditches
But Abe Can build our fence Again
And Andy mend the Breeches

Chorus
Lincoln is the man we need
Johnson two is handy
Yanky doodle Boys hurrah
For Uncle Abe and Andy
. . . .
We'll have a man for President
Whose Courage never fails him
That Common sense which built the fence
Is just the thing that Ails him.[48]

The visit home was not altogether a happy one because of the critical illness of Ayers' daughter, Mrs. John Warick. He secured an extension of his furlough and was still in Illinois when he learned of the reelection of Lincoln. He was overjoyed and showed it clearly in what he recorded in his diary:

We have Just got the Glorious news that Lincoln is Elected President By an overwhelming Majority, Leaving Pore Little Mack far in the Rear and as harmless to us now as he was to the Rebs when he was so snugly stowed Away on the Gunboat. Pore little feller, we'll ask him in when we want him.[49]

At the end of December, Ayers left Fairbury, Illinois, and returned to Nashville, where he was promptly dispatched to his old regiment, which was on the southeastern seaboard. He was routed through New York and by steamer to Savannah, Georgia. Ayers detested the city of New York and referred to it as "A place I never want to see Again while I

Remain in the flesh." Accommodations for the soldiers were especially poor, and Castle William, where Ayers was quartered, was "nee deep or Less in Dirt and filth and Stunk worse than A desent hog pen, beside Graybacks thick as hale and Large Enoughf for oxen had they been yoked up." He viewed the city as containing the worst elements in the nation's population, including "those bounty Jumpers and Conscripts, and Rakings of all Gods creation." He was quick to ascribe the city's degeneracy to the presence of large numbers of copperheads, and blamed them for the draft riots of 1863 and the poor accommodations for soldiers during his stay there. He took one last thrust at the city by summing up his attitude in the following statement:

> Well long have I herd of the great Citty of New York but if what I saw and indured thare is Anything of A fair Specimen of her Common Hospitality and Refinement I hope to be Excused. One would Suppose that so great a Citty as this would and Could have fed Housed and taken better Care of A Small handful of war worn veteran western soaldiers, but Alass for her She is so full of Poison Like Snakes in Dogdays she seems to have Lost all feelings of Decency and Common Humanity, and her Snakeship only thinks of Bountys, Bounty Jumping McClelling Copperheadism, and Valan Digam Thunder Hammer toryism or some kind of Devilism. Well New York Thou great Citty of Harlots, tho thou Exalt thyself up to Heaven thou shalt be thrust down to Hell.[50]

The trip from New York to Savannah was Ayers' first ocean voyage and he was thrilled with the experience, despite the storms that tossed the ship until almost everyone was seasick. The description that he gave was vivid, indeed.

> While on this great Water tossing from side to side, Sea Roaring, winds Howling, wave surging, foam boiling, men heaving and vomiting, Captain giving orders, Sailors flying from post to Post to obey orders, I could but think of Moses Account of the mighty flood, and Says Moses, "the Fountains of the Great Deep ware broken up and the windows of Heaven ware opened."[51]

Ayers' joy upon returning to his regiment was inexpressible, and he immediately resumed his place among his men. He was perfectly contented sitting around the campfire, listening to the experiences of the men during the many months he had been away from them, and "sipping Away at our Hot Coffee mixing up A little Hard tack and sowbelly." He was especially happy to see the men in such excellent spirits, and observed that there was a noticeable decline in profanity and vulgarity among them. He performed many of the functions of a chaplain, although he was not officially designated as one.[52] He had engaged in that type of work before he left his regiment, and while he recruited Negro soldiers he seems to have prayed and preached to soldiers whenever the opportunity presented itself. In January, 1865, he organized a lyceum and encouraged the men to hold debates several evenings each week.

He was more interested, however, in purely religious exercises; and at the first opportunity he began to serve the men by conducting such meetings. As his regiment made its way up to Georgia and the Carolinas as a part of the rear guard of Sherman's army, Ayers conducted religious services regularly. He was especially anxious to prepare the men for their return to civilian life as he saw the war coming to a close. On March 19, 1865, he spoke at a "glorious good meeting" at Charleston, South Carolina, "from thease words: And while he was yet A great way off his Father saw him and Ran and fell on his neck and imbraced and kisst his son." It seems to have been an appropriate text, and, according to Ayers, it had a "powerful offect. God bless the Effort and Convert the Boys is my prayer for Jesus Sake." Ayers was encouraged in his work by the interest which the men displayed. On one evening more than twenty came forward and solicited his prayers. The veteran soldier was again moved to utter a prayer: "Oh how I wish I was more gifted and had more grace so I might be more useful. Lord give me wisdom."[53]

As in most of his undertakings, Ayers expressed his feelings concerning the religious meetings which he was conducting by writing verses. While in Charleston he composed a religious poem of ten stanzas, three of which follow:

> Sinners perhaps this news with you
> May have no weight altho tis true
> The Carnel pleasures of the Earth
> Cast off the thoughts and fears of Death
>
> . . . .
>
> The Blooming youth all in his prime
> Is Counting up his Length of time
> He oft times says tis his intent
> When he gets oald he will Repent.
>
> But oh the sad and awful State
> Of those who Stay and Come two Late
> The foolish Virgins did begin
> To knock but Could not enter in.[54]

All the soldiers were not moved by Ayers' vigorous efforts, however, and he did not fail to register his disgust with them. He said that there were some "Scalawags" in his outfit "as mean and Devilish as Satan wants them to be." There were those who would steal and rob all that they could lay their "unholy hands on and often treat the women Rudely." On one occasion when Ayers and some others were gathering boards with which to make seats for one of the evening meetings, several soldiers stole every piece of timber that had been gathered—"A thing I could not believe men Could be found mean Enoughf to Do." He added that such men were a disgrace to the great Union Army and were "found mostly Among those Substitutes and thousand doler men."[55]

Ayers enjoyed the "mopping up" operations which he witnessed almost as much as he enjoyed the religious services. He liked the way in which the commanding officers seized wagons, mules, or whatever was necessary for a rapid advance. In January, 1865, he and the men had a "gay oald time" setting fire to several large buildings near their camp at Hardeeville, South Carolina. In the following month he said that if he had his way he would take all the troops and government property out of Savannah, where they were, "Set the place all in flames and let it go to the Devil whare it belongs."[56] He was not at all disturbed over the fact that so much of South Carolina was ruined by "fire and sword," for he recalled that this state was the first to secede and that it was at Charleston that "Rebellion was plotted and Hatched" and that the war started there when the "Rebs" fired on Fort Sumter.[57]

Ayers was thrilled to witness the raising of the flag of the United States at Fort Sumter, April 14, 1865. Although he said that the spectacle was "Grand beyond Description" he gave a vivid account of the event. The vessels in battle formation around the fort were as thick as a forest of trees, Ayers said. Flags and colors decorated not only Sumter but the nearby islands as well. He observed the celebration from a large tree. The big guns at Fort Moultrie, Sumter, the Battery, and on the vessels roared in a salute so powerful that "the earth trembled." The day was made perfect with the news that the Confederate forces had surrendered at Appomattox Court House several days earlier.[58]

Ayers left almost immediately with his regiment for Alexandria, Virginia, moving up through North Carolina and then through the great Dismal Swamp to Chesapeake Bay, over which he sailed to Alexandria. He was at New Bern, North Carolina, when he received the news of the death of President Lincoln. It was a terrible blow for this son of Illinois who had admired his fellow-citizen so ardently. He poured out his grief in his diary when he said:

> Never was thare A baser act Commited and never did A purer patriot fall in Defence of his Country. . . . God will Avenge His Blood on the transgressors. . . . In the assassination and Death of Abraham Lincon Illinois has Lost her noblest and brightest son. But believing as I do that he was A Christian . . . we are the Loosers while he is the gainer being far better off than we who remain.[59]

Ayers prayed for the capture of the leading Confederate officials, especially since he was convinced that they were responsible for the death of Lincoln. He was at Alexandria, waiting to be mustered out, when he learned of the capture of Jefferson Davis and his staff. On this occasion he wrote a diatribe against Davis that has few counterparts in Civil War literature. In part, he said:

> I hope he will hang and as he was Caught in womens Close I hope he will be Honored with A womans Suit to hang in—pore Coward puppy, two mean to Live, two mean to Dy—A man Starver, A soal killer, A dastard Rascal, A midnight assassin, A thief, A Rober, A Liar, A forsworn vilian, A Confirmed Traitor, A Slave Driver, A nigger breeder, A negro Equality man mixing his own Blood with niggers. . . . Hang him . . . in a suit of some one of his Negro womens Close and Leave him on the Gallows for Crows and vultures to feed on. Make him an Example so as to deter others.[60]

The end of the Civil War did not close the military career of Ayers. He had caught the spirit of the soldier and he thoroughly enjoyed the life, despite the inconveniences. Furthermore, he had become intensely interested in the Negro and his welfare and apparently felt that he could assist in the difficult task of adjusting this group to its new freedom. On June 5, 1865, he joined the 104th Regiment of United States Colored Troops as chaplain.[61] Shortly thereafter, he proceeded to Fort Duane in Beaufort, South Carolina, where the group was stationed.[62] On July 1, 1865, he received his commission as a first lieutenant in Company G of the 104th United States Colored Troops. Thus he became a member of the select group he had so roundly castigated during the war. He had the typical enlisted man's contempt for officers. On one occasion he insisted that it was the interference of officers that prevented him from being more successful as a recruiter.[63]

A part of Ayers' contempt for officers stemmed from the fact that he was convinced that their diversions and distractions were responsible for many of the reverses of the Union armies. He was especially opposed to their fraternizing with Confederate women. He hoped that

Sherman's order to issue no rations to noncombatants would drive from their midst "A Large Portion of those dirty sluts who are here specially for the Accommodation of shoulder Straps . . . . Lets Clean them out, give them Pills Boys instead of Bread and kicks instead of huggin and kissing that is all the way we can manage them I think."[64] In May, 1864, he welcomed a change of commanding officers at Huntsville, Alabama, because he believed that it would enhance the efficiency of the force stationed there. He feared that the improvement would not last long, however, for soon these "shouldered straped" men would perhaps spend too much time "hunting after Crinoline" as their predecessors had done, and "they two may get so ingaged and interested in that Line as to forget there duty . . . . what A pitty it is so many puffed up shoalders strapped fools Act so. Man is a strange being the more favours he has bestowed on him the biger A fool he is or often so."[65]

At the time that Ayers became a wearer of the shoulder straps he ranked fifth on the roster of officers of the regiment with only a colonel, a lieutenant colonel, a major, and a surgeon outranking him. He was not of much service to his new outfit, however, for his health had so declined that he spent most of his remaining days in the hospital. It is nothing short of amazing that a man of Ayers' advanced age and poor health had been able to withstand the rigors of a soldier's life as well as he had. He constantly complained of his health. While in the "little Stinkhole place Trianna" in Alabama he was seized with "A severe Chill Lasting some three hours and then A Raging fever afterwards. Surely I had Liked to have went to the Boneyard."[66] When he resigned from his position as a recruiter he was placed with a group of convalescents and complained of a "Severe Disinterry."[67] When he was on his furlough in November, 1864, he complained that his health was still "quiet pore," and later he said that he suffered with so many ailments that he was unable to rest at night. When he returned to his outfit early in 1865 and attempted to keep up with the pace set by the younger and more healthy men, he collapsed and had to be sent in an ambulance to an army hospital in Savannah, where he remained for several weeks.[68] Apparently, only his remarkable resiliency and recuperative powers sustained him during the closing weeks of the war. Upon arrival at his new post he was almost immediately committed to the Regimental Hospital in Beaufort, South Carolina, where he died of typhus on September 10, 1865.[69]

Ayers' family was not immediately notified of his passing. As late as November 30, 1865, his son Joseph B. Ayers wrote to officials in Washington inquiring as to the whereabouts of his father.[70] When the adjutant general got around to making a reply, on January 13, 1866, he had the following to say: "I have the honor to inform you [h]is name is not borne on the records of that regiment [104th U.S. Colored Troops] and that his name does not appear on the Record of officers of U.S. Colored Troops on file in this office."[71] It is not known just where and how the news concerning Ayers' death reached his family. In all probability the records of the 104th U.S. Colored Troops were in transit to Washington when Joseph B. Ayers made the inquiry concerning his father. It is presumed that upon receipt of them the adjutant general's office notified the family of his passing.

Ayers' service record was never completely filed, perhaps because of his hasty departure from the 129th Illinois Infantry Regiment and his enlistment with the 104th U.S. Colored Troops. Consequently, the record of his service with the Illinois group is incomplete, while the only record of his death is in a published list of "deaths and interments at Beaufort, South Carolina."[72] This is, perhaps, the principal reason why a request for a pension was denied Ayers' wife in 1868.[73] It is interesting to observe that Ayers, although devoted to his children and to his first wife, never mentioned in his diary his marriage to Mrs. Mary Jane Watson in 1858.

If Illinois had recovered from the staggering blow it suffered in the loss of its greatest son in April, 1865, it could well have mourned in September, 1865, the passing of one who was certainly not the least of its sons. Many may have cheered the state more loudly, but none loved it more dearly. He was happiest when he was at home, and although he did not return to Illinois at the war's end he constantly wrote of the joy he would experience upon returning there to stay. Many may have made more significant contributions to the Union cause, but none was more devoted to it than he. During the early part of his service he wrote: "They say my Country needs me and I am willing to forego all this and even more if need be to save my Country. My life is Ready if need be to Lay on the alter of my Country all, all, Everything I have, my Life with it all, and more had I more, for my Country."[74] He was constantly praying for his country and its leaders. A typical prayer follows: "God bless our Nation, our Armies, the President, the Generals, and all our Union officers and Soaldiers, and save our oald Government is my prayer."[75]

As Ayers moved among his fellows, he made an impressive appearance. He was almost six feet in height and weighed 170 pounds.

When he enlisted in the army in 1862, his hair was already gray, and this must have made him rather unique among the privates of Company E of the 129th Infantry. His cheerful disposition, his boundless optimism, and his great faith in the possibilities of his fellow-men made him extremely popular with all who knew him.

The record that Ayers left of his experiences from December, 1863, to April, 1865, is of exceptional value as a mirror of the man and of the period. Few diaries of the period describe so extensively life among the civilians of the wartorn South. Few soldiers in the Union Army saw so much and with such a keen eye as Ayers. His wartime travels carried him from Illinois to Tennessee and Alabama, to Pennsylvania and New York, by ocean steamer into the southeastern states, and by land from Georgia to Washington. Despite his semiliteracy, Ayers has given to posterity an account of the war which has great social value. For his keenness of insight, his effervescent spirit, and his remarkable zeal, he has few peers among those who chose to record their experiences in our second great war for freedom.

John Roy Lynch: Republican Stalwart
from Mississippi

John Roy Lynch's life encompassed a momentous era, and he was a part of much that occurred. Born on a Louisiana plantation in 1847, he knew slavery from experience and observation. He knew the heartbreak of a slave mother when an Irish father died before completing the planned emancipation of her and her children. He knew her bitter disappointment when the father's friend broke his promise and kept them all in slavery. He experienced the tragic breakup of the family, when he was sent to work on a plantation while the others remained in Natchez. He knew hard work, the rewards for doing the "right thing and staying in his place," and the punishments for precocity and for "conduct unbecoming a slave."

Long before John Roy Lynch became paymaster in the United States Army, he knew what war was like. As a teenager he saw Union forces invade the lower Mississippi River Valley, where he lived. This was, for him, a war of deliverance; and when Union forces approached the area, he joined other slaves in a general strike and in the enjoyment of freedom long before the cessation of hostilities. Perhaps this early contact with soldiers—as a camp employee and a waiter on a naval vessel—had something to do with his seizing the opportunity, some thirty-five years later, to become a major in the United States Army. In 1863 and 1864, however, so lofty a rank in so grand an army was beyond his wildest dreams.

For Lynch the postwar years were years of discovery. He picked up a few of the rudiments of education as he served his owner and the guests at meals. The most valuable lesson he learned was that education was important; his mistress, he observed, became outraged when he dis-

Originally published in Howard Rabinowitz (ed.), *Southern Black Leaders of the Reconstruction Era* (Urbana, 1982). Reprinted with permission of University of Illinois Press.

played any knowledge at all. When the whites of Mississippi began to establish schools in 1865, they made no provisions for educating blacks. Lynch had to wait until a group of northern teachers established an evening school for freedmen in 1866. Lynch attended for the four months that it remained open. After that his education was at best informal—reading books and newspapers and listening to the recitations in the white school across the alley from the photographic studio where he worked. Within a few years he had not only become quite literate but had also developed a capacity for expression that made a favorable impression on his listeners. He was developing talents and acquiring experience that would take him successively into politics, public service, the practice of law, and the pursuit of historical studies.

For Mississippi freedmen—indeed, for freedmen everywhere—the postwar years were exceedingly difficult. For more than two years after the Civil War, they had no economic opportunities that would set them on the road to real freedom and independence. The great fear was that the freedmen might actually become independent or dangerous in some other way, and everything was done to forestall any such grave eventuality. The black codes, especially those enacted by Mississippi in 1865, were in many respects reminiscent of the old slave codes. In the effort to prevent freedmen from becoming independent farmers, Mississippi went so far as to forbid the sale of land to Negroes, except in incorporated towns. Under the pretext of preserving the public peace, the state also restricted the activities of freedmen in a dozen different ways.

Meanwhile, Mississippi and the other states of the old Confederacy were governed at every level by whites, most of them native-born and former Confederates. Political participation of blacks, however well qualified, was beyond the thought of any responsible white leader in the South and, indeed, of most citizens in the country. The suggestion that they should become voters was greeted with the same kind of amused incredulity that greeted the suggestion that schools should be provided for the freedmen.

Most southerners seemed to feel that it was difficult enough to go down to defeat in the Civil War and to lose their slaves as well. It was too much to expect them to go beyond the acceptance of defeat and emancipation to regard the freedmen as political and social equals. They had reached the limit in making concessions. They would stand firm against the Freedmen's Bureau, which proposed not only to educate the freedmen but to encourage them to seek economic independence. They would be even more firm, if that were possible, against such groups as the Union League, which catechized Negroes in politics and held before them the prospect of social equality. Southern whites did their best, through laws, economic sanctions, intimidation, and violence, to hold the line. But their intransigence ignored the implications of the very concrete results of the Civil War. The victors would not, at least in 1866 and 1867, permit the vanquished to turn the clock back. Consequently they insisted on a new dispensation in 1867, in which the freedmen were to enjoy political equality. Surely this was an indication that the old order was changing.

Lynch was scarcely twenty years old when new political opportunities came to him and the other freedmen with their enfranchisement in 1867. He made the most of his opportunities. He became active in one of the local Republican clubs in Natchez and wrote and spoke in support of the new state constitution. Soon he displayed the talents that were to take him far in the political world. One of the first to recognize them was Governor Adelbert Ames, who, in 1869, appointed him to the office of justice of the peace. His own account of his experiences as a neophyte judge is a rare documentation of the efforts of freedmen to understand the intricacies of the law and their obligations and rights under it. The picture Lynch gives of himself is that of a venerable sage, freely sharing his advice with the uninitiated who appeared before him. One almost forgets that at the time Lynch was only twenty-one.

Lynch was destined for higher public office, and before the end of his first year as justice of the peace he was elected to the house of representatives of the Mississippi legislature, where he served until 1873. The journals of the legislature make it clear that he was a most active and even popular member. In his first term he became a member of two important standing committees: the Committee on Military Affairs and the Committee on Elections. Immediately he indicated a lively interest in the deliberations; and if he was not always successful in carrying the day for the measures he advocated, he succeeded in serving notice that he would not be ignored. He offered amendments to pending bills, presented riders to measures before the house, and dropped into the hopper his own bills covering a variety of matters.[1]

He was a much more important member in the next session of the legislature, which met in 1871. He even received one vote for the speakership. The new speaker, H. W. Warren of Leake County, made good use of his erstwhile rival. He appointed him to the special committee on resolutions to express sympathy in the death of members of the house and to the joint special committee on printing rules for the use of the house and the senate. Warren also appointed Lynch to the standing committees on public education and the judiciary and to the chairmanship of the Committee on Elections.

Lynch soon established himself as one of the most important members of the legislature. Frequently he offered resolutions, motions, and bills. Apparently he assumed a responsibility that was tantamount to that of majority leader. Lynch frequently offered the motion to consider the business that lay on the speaker's desk, and invariably his motion carried. He offered amendments to pending legislation, and the amendments were supported by a majority of the house. The member from Adams County had clearly achieved a status that was in marked contrast to his position as neophyte and outsider in the previous session.[2]

When the legislature met on January 2, 1872, few would dispute the claim that John R. Lynch could become the most important member of the house. On the first day he gained a seat on the Committee on Credentials; on the second day he was elected Speaker of the House. It is not difficult to believe that he had much to do with the election of his political ally, James Hill, as sergeant at arms of the house. As speaker, Lynch generally voted with the majority and joined the efforts of the legislature to eliminate most of the laws of the pro-Confederate legislature of 1865–66. When the house was unable to agree on a plan for redistricting the state, the body placed the matter in the hands of the speaker. Lynch then devised a plan that would make five districts safely and reliably Republican and one district Democratic. At the end of the session, in April, 1872, the house considered a resolution to tender thanks to "Hon. J. R. Lynch, for the able, efficient, and impartial manner in which he presided over the deliberations of this body during the present session." John Calhoun of Marshall County moved to strike the word *impartial,* which was lost, and the resolution was adopted.[3]

Thus Lynch was clearly becoming one of the state's outstanding and influential young leaders. Although only twenty-four years of age in 1872, he was ready for bigger things. That year his party sent him as a delegate to the Republican National Convention, where he served on the Committee on Resolutions.[4] Upon his return to the state, he and his friends decided that he should run for the lower house of Congress against the white Republican incumbent, L. W. Perce. Lynch described Perce as a strong and able man who had made a creditable and satisfactory record. As a native New Yorker and a veteran of the Union Army, however, Perce was the object of bitter attacks in the Democratic press. When Lynch defeated him for the Republican nomination, one Mississippi newspaper called it "retributive justice." It gloated over Perce's defeat and said, "There is special satisfaction in the overthrow of Perce, whose malignant and slanderous accusations of the white people of Mississippi are familiar to the public."[5]

Lynch's campaign was conducted by three popular and resourceful Negro Republicans, William McCary, Robert H. Wood, and Robert Fitzhugh. The contest was heated and exciting, but there were no bitterness and, apparently, no strong racial overtones. As far as can be ascertained, Lynch's principal reason for ousting Perce was not that Perce was white but that Lynch wanted the seat himself. In the general election, his white Democratic opponent was Judge Hiram Cassidy. Although the congressional district he sought to represent was safely Republican, Lynch would need the votes of white Republicans to defeat Cassidy. After his nomination, Lynch received the support of all or most of Perce's supporters. On several occasions he and Judge Cassidy engaged in joint debates before enthusiastic crowds. When the returns were in, Lynch, the victor by a majority of more than five thousand votes, became Mississippi's first black member of the U.S. House of Representatives.[6]

As congressman-elect Lynch presided over the 1873 session of the lower house of the Mississippi legislature. It was a busy and productive session, which dealt with matters from the changing of persons' names, to regulating the sale of liquor, and incorporating a large number of banks, industrial firms, and colleges. At the close of the session, the House unanimously adopted a resolution complimenting and thanking the Speaker for the manner in which he had presided, "with becoming dignity, with uniform courtesy and impartiality, and with marked ability."[7] Later J. H. Piles of Panola, the chairman of the Committee on Public Works, took the floor and made a presentation to Lynch. He said, in part:

> The members of the House over whom you have presided so long and so well, with so much impartiality and so much of the *debonair*, irrespective of party, have generously contributed, and complimentarily confided the agreeable task upon me of presenting to you the gold watch and chain,

which I now send to your desk by the son of one of Mississippi's deceased Speakers.

Believe me, sir, it is not for its intrinsic worth, nor for its extrinsic show, but rather as a memento of our high admiration and respect for you as a gentleman, citizen, and Speaker.

Indeed, if it were possible to weld into one sentiment, and to emit by one impulse of the voice the sentiments of all, at this good hour, methinks it would be "God bless Hon. J. R. Lynch; he is an honest and fair man. . . ."

Doubtless we shall not all meet again this side of the All Hail Hereafter. We will miss you, Mr. Speaker. Be it my privilege now, on behalf of the House of Representatives, to bid you a long, lingering and affectionate farewell.

Another member of the House, R. W. Houston of Washington County, spoke of the many questions of parliamentary law that had arisen during the session and observed that the Speaker's decisions on those questions had given "no cause to murmur on account of urbanity or impartiality. And I ask, Mr. Speaker, that you accept my profoundest gratitude for the dignified courtesy and distinguished manliness and marked ability which have characterized your entire conduct as the chief honored officer of this body." Lynch replied that his leaving was "more than an ordinary separation . . . wherein we expect soon to meet again." He remarked that all members had been uniformly courteous. "For your manifestations of confidence and respect, accept my earnest and sincere thanks. In regard to your token of admiration, language is inadequate to express my thanks. I shall ever preserve it in grateful remembrance of the generous hearts of those who contributed to it."[8]

When Lynch took his seat at the opening of the Forty-third Congress in December, 1873, he was, at twenty-six years of age, the youngest member of that body. He drew two committee assignments, the Committee on Mines and Mining and the Committee on Expenditures in the Interior Department.[9] Despite his age, he had poise, self-confidence, and considerable legislative experience. On December 9, eight days after he took his seat, Lynch made his maiden speech. He offered an amendment to the bill to repeal the increase of salaries of members of Congress. He spoke with grace and good humor; and although his amendment did not pass, he made a favorable impression on the members of the House.[10]

During his first term in Congress, Lynch was careful to attend to the needs of his constituents. He introduced bills for the relief of private persons, to donate the marine hospital at Natchez to the state of Mississippi, and to provide for an additional term of the U.S. District Court for the southern district of Mississippi. He also offered a bill to fix the time for the election of representatives to the Forty-fourth Congress from the state of Mississippi.[11] He was successful in securing the passage of most of these bills; and throughout his tenure, his success with similar legislation continued.[12]

When the Civil Rights Bill was before the House in June, 1874, Lynch plunged into the debate. He said that he had not been anxious to get into the fight but felt impelled to do so because of the extent of the discussion concerning the bill both in and out of Congress. He argued for the bill "not only because it is an act of simple justice, but because it will be instrumental in placing the colored people in a more independent position; because it will, in my judgment, be calculated to bring about a friendly feeling between the two races in all sections of the country, and will place the colored people in a position where their identification with any party will be a matter of choice and not of necessity."[13]

In succeeding months Lynch engaged in the debate on the Civil Rights Bill whenever it was before the House. He sought to deal with the canard that civil rights meant social equality. He pleaded for the retention of the provision that would open all public schools to children of all races. He chided all Republicans who had not supported the bill. In February, 1875, less than a month before the bill became law, Lynch made an impassioned plea for its passage. He said:

> I appeal to all members of the House—republicans and democrats, conservatives and liberals—to join with us in the passage of this bill, which has for its object the protection of human rights. And when every man, woman, and child can feel and know that his, her, and their rights are fully protected by the strong arm of a generous and grateful Republic, then can all truthfully say that this beautiful land of ours, over which the Star Spangled Banner so triumphantly waves, is, in truth and in fact, the "land of the free and the home of the brave."[14]

Because of his vigorous support of the Civil Rights Act, many white citizens of Lynch's district were more determined than ever to unseat him. They were encouraged, moreover, by the national Democratic trend that had become clear in the elections of 1874. Their opportunity, they thought, would come in their own congressional elections—to be held in 1875 instead of 1874—and in the regular elections of 1876. While Lynch's renomination was assured, nomination was no longer tantamount to election. Many white Republicans in Mississippi were going into the Democratic camp, either because of intimidation or because they believed the Democratic party served their needs.[15]

Lynch was an active, even aggressive, candidate for reelection. His Democratic opponent was the popular Colonel Roderick Seal. Lynch stood by his record in Congress, pointing out how much he had done for his district and for the state. During September and October, 1875, he campaigned vigorously throughout his district. When he spoke at Biloxi in early October, the local reporter said he had been "agreeably impressed" with him. "His deportment and bearing were respectful and polite. . . . He at some length alluded to his record in Congress and gave his reasons for voting for several obnoxious measures, but felt no regret for what he had done."[16] He may have been a victim of foul play during his appearance in Vicksburg. In the course of his speech the lights went out, and a "pell mell stampede of the audience took place which was frightful to behold."[17]

The race was close, but Lynch was victorious. The Democrats, however, made a clean sweep of the other offices. Each side accused the other of misconduct and even fraud. One Mississippi paper exulted over Lynch's victory. The writer said, "Notwithstanding the fraud and intimidation practiced in Claiborne County to defeat the Republican ticket and the determined opposition made against Mr. Lynch on the Sea Coast, we are happy to chronicle the fact that the Republicans of Mississippi will have at least one representative in the Forty-Fourth Congress in the person of Hon. John R. Lynch."[18]

One of the first items on the agenda of the new Democratic legislature was the redistricting of the state. Five districts were to be safely Democratic, and a sixth—taking in every county on the Mississippi River and dubbed the "shoestring district"—was Lynch's district. Although most of the voters were still Republican, there was little hope, even on Lynch's part, that he could win in 1876. His opponent was General James R. Chalmers of Fort Pillow fame, a likely candidate to keep black Republicans in their place.[19] During the campaign Lynch experienced numerous incidents of hostility, which he relates at length in his *Reminiscences.* When it was over, the Democrats claimed a majority of more than four thousand votes. Charging fraud, Lynch sought to contest the election in the House of Representatives. His attorney, T. Hewett of Natchez, served notice on General Chalmers to that effect. When Chalmers indicated that he had not received the notice, Hewett requested that he waive the "want of notice and let the contest proceed." Chalmers declined, insisting that the contest was "prompted by partisan motives and only intended to stimulate and prolong a political assault on the State of Mississippi through him."[20] In the circumstances, the Democratic-dominated House Committee on Elections, of which John R. Harris of Virginia was chairman, would not even consider the case.

Lynch would have another chance to even the score with General Chalmers. In 1880 he announced that he was again a candidate for Congress. The leading paper in his district greeted the announcement with the following rebuff: "Unless we read the times incorrectly she [Adams County] will not only give a majority to [the Democrats] but will also give John such a 'setting down' that he will abandon politics entirely."[21] But Lynch was not easily rebuffed. For more than two months he traveled throughout his district organizing Garfield-Arthur-Lynch clubs and delivering speeches wherever he could find an audience. One hostile newspaper said his canvass was "tame and spiritless, and his speeches [were] received without applause by his meagre audiences."[22] However, another no-less-hostile paper reported that every meeting of the local Lynch club was "larger than the preceding one."[23] A Jackson paper recognized the formidable campaign by Lynch when it observed that Chalmers was making a "gallant fight against heavy odds."[24]

Lynch was not surprised to discover that the district, with the election machinery in the hands of the Democrats, gave Chalmers a majority of 1,468. In Warren County alone, more than 2,000 Lynch votes were thrown out; and several hundred were thrown out in Adams County. It was estimated that of the 5,358 votes declared illegal, 4,641 were for Lynch and 717 for Chalmers.[25] During the campaign, Lynch had served notice that if he were defeated it would be by fraud and that he would contest the election. On December 21 he served notice that he would contest the election. The notice said:

Gen. James R. Chalmers: Please take notice that I intend to contest your pretended election on the second day of this present month as member from the sixth congressional district of Mississippi to the Forty-Seventh Congress of the United States, and to maintain and prove before that body that I was, and you are not, elected as representative to that Congress from said district; and I hereby specify to you the following named frauds and violations of the law of the land and of the purity of elections which I charge were committed on the day of said election, or with ballots cast on that day in the election for Congressman, by our Democratic friends and supporters with your connivance, and in your interest and behalf as Democratic candidate for Congress in that election.

Lynch made specific charges of fraud in Adams, Issaquena, Bolivar, Jefferson, Claiborne, Washington, Coahoma, and Warren counties.[26]

Then followed the long, dreary contest before the Committee on Elections, about which Lynch tells, in great detail, in his *Reminiscences*. Meanwhile the people of the sixth district, who were without effective representation for a year, followed the developments in Washington with great interest. If Lynch had been pessimistic about the outcome of the election itself, some Mississippi Democrats were pessimistic about the outcome before the Committee on Elections. They were especially critical of the young Republicans in the House who made much of "rifled ballot boxes, stifled justice, the shot gun plan, etc." One paper complained that such comments forced the main points at issue into the background.[27] On April 27, 1882, the House of Representatives, by a vote of 125 to 83, adopted a resolution declaring that Lynch was entitled to the seat. Lynch, escorted by William H. Calkins of Indiana, then went to the bar of the House, where the Speaker administered the oath of office.[28]

If Lynch felt vindicated by the decision of the House to seat him, he also felt obliged to seek reelection to that seat a few months hence. General Chalmers, however, was so disillusioned by what he regarded as the unseemly control of the state Democratic party by U.S. Senator L. Q. C. Lamar that he announced he would withdraw from the party, become an independent, and support the Republican administration of President Chester A. Arthur.[29] In September the Republican convention at Magnolia conferred the congressional nomination on Lynch, . who promised a hard fight to retain his seat.[30] As his opponent, the Democrats nominated Judge Henry S. Van Eaton, "a strong man, an excellent lawyer, [and] a forceful debater."[31]

During the campaign the newspaper attacks on Lynch were especially harsh. When he said he did not favor an early or active campaign, a Natchez editor refused to believe him. "Mr. Lynch," he said, "is a cunning politician, and it will do the Democratic party no harm if a close watch is kept upon him, notwithstanding his quiet professions. He knows very well that still hunting is sometimes better than the most noisy drive."[32] When Lynch visited Ellisville and, instead of speaking, inspected the registration rolls, the same editor pointed to this as an example of "still hunting."[33] The Ellisville *Eagle* said that

Lynch's visit was not very productive, since he "found no material to become as clay in the hand of the potter. He said and did enough to give his little game dead away, and to put us on our guard."[34]

Lynch was not merely "still hunting." He spoke throughout the sixth district during the campaign. At Williamsburg the judge of the Covington County circuit court adjourned the afternoon session of the court, and Lynch spoke for more than two hours.[35] In Natchez he spoke to a "tolerably fair audience" on November 4. He assured his listeners that as a Republican he could do more for them in Washington than a Democrat could.[36] If the Adams County voters believed Lynch, there were others who did not. He carried his home county by a comfortable majority but lost the election by some 800 votes. Complimenting Judge Van Eaton for conducting a fair and honest campaign and thanking him for his courtesies, Lynch announced that he would not contest the election.[37]

The loss of his seat in Congress did not lead to Lynch's retirement from politics. He had been the chairman of the Republican state executive committee since 1881, and he would continue to serve in that capacity until 1892. He had been a delegate to the Republican National Convention in 1872 and would be a delegate to four subsequent conventions—in 1884, 1888, 1892, and 1900. At the 1884 convention he received the highest recognition he would ever receive as a party man, even though the circumstances that brought the honor resulted from a factional dispute.

The two principal contenders for the Republican nomination in 1884 were President Chester A. Arthur and James G. Blaine. The followers of Blaine were supporting Powell Clayton of Arkansas for temporary chairman. The Arthur supporters were willing to concede that choice but were prepared to challenge the Blaine forces at some other point. Then young Henry Cabot Lodge and Theodore Roosevelt, who were supporting Arthur, learned that Clayton hoped to receive a cabinet post in return for delivering the votes of Texas and Arkansas to Blaine. Outraged, they decided to oppose Clayton's becoming temporary chairman.[38]

The two young easterners worked throughout the night to garner support for an opposing candidate. When Clayton's name was presented, Lodge got the floor and said he wanted to make a nomination. He assured the convention that he did not wish to introduce a personal contest or to make a test vote as to strength of candidates. He merely wanted to make a nomination for temporary chairman.

which shall have the best possible effect in strengthening the party throughout the country. . . . I therefore have the honor to move, as it is certainly most desirable that we should recognize, as you have done, Mr. Chairman, the Republicans of the South—I therefore desire to present the name of a gentleman well known throughout the South for his conspicuous parliamentary ability, for his courage and character. I move you, Mr. Chairman, to substitute the name of the Hon. John R. Lynch of Mississippi.

The motion was promptly seconded by C. A. Simpson of Mississippi and Silas P. Dutcher of New York.[39] There ensued a lengthy debate with many speeches from both sides. Then the roll of the states was called, and Lynch was elected by a vote of 414 to 384.[40]

Because Lynch was not aware of the possibility of becoming the temporary chairman until the convention opened, he had not prepared a keynote address. Upon taking the chair, he spoke briefly of the importance of unity in the convention and of supporting the nominees "whoever they may be." In condemning the Democrats for their fraud and intimidation in elections he concluded: "I am satisfied that the people of this country are too loyal ever to allow a man to be inaugurated President of the United States, whose title to the position may be brought forth by fraud, and whose garments may be saturated with the innocent blood of hundreds of his countrymen. I am satisfied that the American people will ratify our action."[41] It was the first time a Negro American had delivered the keynote address before a major national political convention, and there would not be another such occasion until 1968.

As a politician, Lynch had few peers in Mississippi or elsewhere. He was a loyal Republican, but he was also loyal to his own supporters within the party. He was a formidable and resourceful foe both within the Republican party and outside it. Much of the appraisal of him by a Mississippi newspaper in 1881 was accurate: "He made and unmade men, organized and disorganized rings and cliques, and directed and controlled legislatures like a very autocrat. He is yet a man of power and authority—yet a shining light in the Republican camp."[42]

From Lynch's retirement from Congress in 1883 to his death in 1939 he was engaged in a variety of activities of both a public and private nature. His strong partisanship prompted him to decline a position offered him in 1885 by Democratic President Grover Cleveland. He did, however, accept an appointment by President Harrison as fourth auditor of the treasury, a position he held from 1889 to 1893. We know almost nothing of the manner in which Lynch conducted that office or if, indeed, he was happy in his position in the bureaucracy. He continued his political activities, however; and one gets the impression that politics continued to be of greater interest to him than his position in the treasury.

Meanwhile Lynch had become very active in the plantation and city real-estate market in Adams County. He purchased his first parcel of land in Natchez in January, 1869, when he was twenty-one years of age. Before the end of the year he had purchased another parcel of land in Natchez.[43] That was merely the beginning. Between 1870 and 1898 he purchased eleven tracts of land in Natchez, ranging from one to four lots, and four plantations in Adams County.[44] The property in Natchez was clustered in three areas, each on the outskirts of the city. Several of his lots were on Homochitto Street, in the southwestern part of Natchez. He also had several parcels on Saint Catherine Street, in east Natchez, and several along Pine Ridge Road, in the northeastern part of the city.

None of his plantations were actually on the Mississippi River. Ingleside, which he purchased in 1885 and sold in 1893, was the smallest rural tract, with 84 acres.[45] It was located just south of the city. Providence, a few miles south of Ingleside, was purchased in 1875 and sold in 1898. It contained 189 acres at the time of the purchase, but Lynch purchased some adjoining acreage, so that at the time he sold it there were 221 acres in Providence.[46] In 1891 Lynch purchased 90 acres of the Saragossa plantation, presumably with a view to acquiring all of it later. He had not done so by the time he sold it in 1894.[47] His largest plantation was Grove, the farthest from Natchez, six miles from the city on the southwest side. In 1884 Lynch purchased a part of the plantation, amounting to 694 acres. Two years later he purchased the remainder, 840 acres "more or less."[48] He did not part with Grove until 1905, perhaps the last piece of property he had in Mississippi.[49] Lynch's brother William was involved in some of the transactions and perhaps served as his attorney and business manager.[50]

In the early 1890s Lynch began to study law.[51] In 1896 he passed the Mississippi bar on the second attempt. Shortly thereafter, he became a partner in the law firm of Robert H. Terrell in Washington, D.C. Terrell had been a clerk in Lynch's office when Lynch was fourth auditor of the treasury, and Lynch had developed a high regard for the young man. Lynch continued to practice law in Mississippi and the District of Columbia until he went into the army in 1898.

Surely it was not a strong interest in military life or a deep sense of patriotism that lured Lynch into the United States Army during the Spanish-American War. It was, rather, a high regard for President William McKinley, whom he had known during his years in Congress, and a keen sense of party responsibility when the president asked him to serve. To his surprise he was immensely pleased with the life of an army officer; and since he was at loose ends, he also found it a source of fulfillment. His marriage to Ella Somerville in 1884, by whom he had one daughter, had ended with a divorce in 1900. There was at least no family reason why he should not accept the regular-army commission that was offered him in 1901.

As paymaster, Lynch had the opportunity to travel to many parts of the world. He went to Haiti and to other islands in the Caribbean. For a time he was stationed at San Francisco, where he witnessed the earthquake and fire in 1906. He journeyed to the Philippines and visited other faraway places. Everywhere he showed that zest for life and healthy curiosity about people and places that had characterized his early years. During these travels he met Mrs. Cora Williamson, whom he married in 1911, the year he retired from the army.

In the following year Lynch and his wife moved to Chicago, where he entered the practice of law and engaged in real estate business. In 1915 they purchased a home at 4028 Grand Boulevard (later South Parkway and still later Dr. Martin Luther King, Jr., Drive) where they lived for the remainder of their lives. In Chicago Lynch lived a rather quiet life. He was not active in politics, and the records do not reveal a very active law practice or real estate business.[52] He saw clients in the late afternoon and evening. Most of his business dealt with real estate transactions. He took great care in explaining to his clients the meaning of all statements in the legal documents, and he made certain that their income was adequate to make the payments on the property they were purchasing.[53]

When Oscar DePriest was nominated for Congress in 1928, Lynch, who was referred to as a "patent expert," was asked to comment on his years in Congress and on what would be required of a Negro in Congress in the twentieth century. He said: "We need a man who will have the courage to attack not only his political opponents, but those within his own party who fail to fight unfair legislation directed toward people of color who helped to elect them. He should use every effort to force the hand of the man who says he is our friend while seeking support, but maneuvers just the opposite way when vital issues come up."[54]

Doubtless the requirements he set up for DePriest were requirements that Lynch felt he had set up for himself some forty-five years earlier.

While Lynch's principal lifelong interests were centered in politics, business, and military affairs, he participated in the discussion of the general problem of the position of Negro Americans in the life of their country. To be sure, he frequently spoke on the subject during his years in Congress, but he also played a part with his fellow blacks as they searched for solutions to the critical problems they faced. As early as 1879 he participated in the National Conference of Colored Men held in Nashville. It was an important gathering to consider the implications of Negro migration. Among those in attendance were William H. Councill of Alabama, John W. Cromwell of Washington, Norris Wright Cuney of Texas, Richard R. Wright of Georgia, and William Still of Pennsylvania. Lynch presided over the meeting and may have had something to do with writing the address that commended Negroes for leaving their communities, viewing it as "evidence of healthy growth in manly independence."[55]

Several years later Lynch discussed the problem of Negro labor in an article entitled "Should Colored Men Join Labor Organizations?" He enthusiastically endorsed the proposition that Negroes should join a labor organization if it did not seek to accomplish its objectives "through a resort to lawlessness and violence. They should maintain their reputation of being a law-abiding and law-observing people, except so far as may be necessary for the protection of themselves and their families." Lynch believed that organizations were indeed the best way for laborers to secure the rights to which they were entitled without violating the law. He urged Negro parents to educate their sons and daughters who planned to enter the industrial field so that they could not be denied membership in labor organizations—which he did not seem to trust—because they lacked the training. "There ought not to be any discrimination in the interest of, or against, any class of persons on account of race, color or religion," he concluded.[56]

Lynch believed the history of Negroes in American life had a direct and important bearing on their current and future status. He was an avid reader, and although he did not mention specific titles of books, he doubtless read many works that impugned the ability and integrity of Negroes during Reconstruction. He stated in 1913 that "in nearly everything that has been written about Reconstruction during the last quarter of a century," the claim had been set forth that the enfranchisement of black men had been a mistake, that the Reconstruction governments in the South were a failure, and that the Fifteenth Amendment was premature and unwise.

The contemporary interpretations of the Reconstruction era greatly distressed Lynch, and in 1913 he published a book entitled *The Facts of Reconstruction* to "present the other side." His primary objective, he said, was "to bring to public notice those things that were commendable and meritorious, to prevent the publication of which seems to have been the primary purpose of nearly all who have thus far written upon that important subject." He insisted, however, that his work contained no extravagant or exaggerated statements and there had been no effort to "conceal, excuse, or justify any act that was questionable or wrong."[57] Lynch's work is the most extensive account of the post–Civil War years written by a Negro participant.

Lynch's efforts to write Reconstruction history had little or no immediate impact on the historical profession. The view that James W. Garner had set forth in 1901 in his *Reconstruction in Mississippi* and that Lynch was seeking to refute was widely accepted. And although Lynch's volume went through three printings in two years, his *Facts* did not find its way into the histories that were written in the two decades following its appearance.[58] It received none of the attention that was lavished on Thomas Dixon's *Birth of a Nation*, which was filmed two years after *Facts* appeared, or Claude Bowers' *The Tragic Era*, which appeared in 1929. The film and Bowers' popular, journalistic version of Reconstruction merely made even more acceptable the interpretation that Lynch was attacking.

During his last years Lynch spent much time working on an autobiography, *Reminiscences of an Active Life*, in which he sought once more to set the record straight. Shortly after he completed the work, his health began to decline. On November 2, 1939, he died in his Chicago residence at the age of ninety-two. Two days later funeral services were held at Saint Thomas Episcopal Church, and he was buried with military rites at Arlington National Cemetery in Washington, D.C., on November 6.[59] The New York *Times* referred to him as "one of the most fluent and forceful speakers in the seventies and eighties."[60] The Chicago *Tribune* called him "the grand old man of Chicago's Negro citizenry."[61]

The political leadership that Lynch provided is an example of how it was possible for a person of remarkable talents to transcend race. As a member of the state legislature and Speaker of the lower house, he won the respect and even the admiration of members on both sides of the aisle. He was not so deferential to whites that he would not seek an office held by a white member of his own party. In successfully opposing an incumbent congressman Lynch argued the point that blacks had as much right to public office as whites. The vigor with which he contested elections, even when unsuccessful, demonstrated a resourcefulness and political acumen that were uncommon among politicians of any race.

Obviously Lynch was no mere party functionary. Whether in Jackson, Mississippi, or Washington, D.C., or at a national convention of the Republican party, he was more "his own man" than an uncritical servant of the party's biddings. His career as an active politician spanned an entire generation that saw the political fortunes of Negro Americans rise to a level of some respectability in some quarters and then descend to a level where they had virtually no repectability anywhere. Through it all Lynch stood for party allegiance but only if, through justice and fairness, the party deserved it.

Stalking George Washington Williams

It was almost forty years ago that I had the experience, but I remember it as distinctly as if it were yesterday. In the spring of 1945 I was just beginning to work on a book that was to be called *From Slavery to Freedom: A History of Negro Americans.* A good way to begin, I thought, was to read the shelves in the library of North Carolina College at Durham, where I was teaching, to see what, if anything, had been written on the subject, aside from Carter G. Woodson's *The Negro in Our History,* published in 1922. To my astonishment, my eyes fell on a two-volume work, *A History of the Negro Race in America from 1619 to 1880; Negroes as Slaves, as Soldiers, and as Citizens,* by George Washington Williams. I discovered that the work had been published in 1882 by a reputable publisher, G. P. Putnam's Sons, was about one thousand pages long, and, beginning with African civilization, covered virtually every aspect of the Afro-American experience in the New World. I saw that it was carefully researched—with plenty of footnotes—logically organized, and well written. Upon examining the card catalogue I learned that Williams was the author of still another work, *A History of Negro Troops in the War of the Rebellion,* published in 1887 by Harper and Brothers.

Among the many things I later learned was that Williams was destined for a life of adventure and excitement almost from the time of his birth in 1849 in Bedford Springs, Pennsylvania. With virtually no education, he ran away from home in 1864—at fourteen years of age—and joined the Union Army. After the Civil War, during which he saw action in various battles, he went to Mexico and fought with the forces that overthrew Maximilian. Returning to the United States, he enlisted in the Tenth Cavalry, one of the four all-Negro units of the

This essay originally appeared in John Hope Franklin, *George Washington Williams: A Biography* (Chicago, 1985), and is reprinted by permission of University of Chicago Press.

regular United States Army, from which he received a medical discharge in 1868.

Williams received a first-rate education at the Newton Theological Institution; semiliterate as an entrant, he became a polished writer and speaker within five years. At the age of twenty-five, following his graduation and marriage, he was installed as pastor of the Twelfth Baptist Church in Boston. The following year, he went with his wife and young son (born in Boston earlier that year) to Washington, where he edited *The Commoner*. Soon afterward he settled in Cincinnati, pursuing a varied career as pastor; columnist for the Cincinnati *Commercial*; lawyer, after studying with President William Howard Taft's father; first black member of the state legislature; and historian of his race.

In 1890 Williams went to study conditions in the Belgian Congo under the patronage of the railroad magnate Collis P. Huntington. After an extensive tour of the country, he wrote an *Open Letter* to King Leopold II, assailing him for his inhuman policies in the Congo. Although he had written a report to President Benjamin Harrison, at the president's request, there was little reaction in the United States to his attacks on King Leopold. Williams then went to England with his English "fiancée" (he was separated from his wife), intending to write a lengthy work on Africa. Illness overtook him, however, and he died in Blackpool at forty-one years of age.

Williams had a wide acquaintanceship among important personages in various parts of the world. He had at least one lengthy interview in Brussels with King Leopold II. He knew Sir William Mackinnon, a British shipping magnate, and George Grenfell, the British missionary. In the United States he met and talked with Presidents Rutherford B. Hayes, Grover Cleveland, and Benjamin Harrison. Senator George F. Hoar of Massachusetts was one of his staunchest supporters. In Ohio he counted Governor Charles Foster, Senator John Sherman, Judge Alphonso Taft, Murat Halstead (editor of the Cincinnati *Commercial*), and Senator Charles Fleischmann among his friends. He also had contact with such literary figures as Henry Wadsworth Longfellow, George Bancroft, and George Washington Cable.

He knew Frederick Douglass; Congressman John Mercer Langston; T. Thomas Fortune, editor of the New York *Freeman*; Richard T. Greener, an early black graduate of Harvard; Robert Terrell, the first black judge in the District of Columbia; and such leading black Bostonians as Judge George L. Ruffin, the civic leader James M. Trotter, and

Lewis Hayden, abolitionist and legislator. It would be my good fortune to find, from time to time, correspondence between Williams and his many acquaintances that would greatly assist me in putting together the missing pieces of the Williams story.

Although I had never had a course in Afro-American history, I reproached myself for not having heard of this man and learned of the many events in his remarkable life. I wondered then, as I have many times since, why this historian of the Negro race had dropped into complete obscurity. I knew enough about the period in which he lived to realize that his obscurity was the result, at least in part, of social forces at work in this country in the late nineteenth century. Those forces dictated that Afro-Americans were not to be remembered for their constructive contributions to society, for their involvement in the literary history of the country, or for their revelations of the rape of Africa by Europeans and Americans. If Williams was unknown in the two generations that separated me from him since his death in 1891, I was determined that I would do what I could to repair the situation.

Fortunately there was a sketch of Williams in the *Dictionary of American Biography*, and I devoured it immediately, not knowing at the time that it was replete with factual errors. Shortly thereafter, when in Washington, I called on Dr. Carter G. Woodson, the founder and executive director of the Association for the Study of Negro Life and History. I asked Dr. Woodson about George Washington Williams. To my pleasant surprise he said he knew something of Williams although he was too young to have known him personally. He told me a few things about him and said that if I wrote a paper on Williams he would invite me to read it at the annual fall meeting of the association. He then said that he believed Mrs. Williams was still living, and in Washington. I could hardly accept the fact that anyone widowed in 1891 would still be alive in 1945! Shortly after I returned to Durham, however, I received word from Dr. Woodson that it was indeed the case. He gave me Mrs. Williams' address, whereupon I wrote her immediately. Within a few weeks I heard from one Henry P. Slaughter that, alas, Mrs. Williams had died on May 15, at ninety-two years of age, and that he had what letters and materials of George Washington Williams the widow had possessed. He indicated to me that he would be pleased to have me examine the materials.

Since I had accepted Dr. Woodson's invitation to write a paper on Williams, I did not have much time. As soon as I could arrange it, I went to Washington and was received graciously by Henry P. Slaughter, who brought out the small bundle of letters (less than a dozen) and three notebooks containing the diary that Williams kept while in Africa in 1890 and 1891. Slaughter was himself a remarkable man. As a minor civil servant in the federal government, he had spent much of his spare time and most of his resources collecting materials—manuscripts, books, pamphlets, newspapers—by and about Negroes. In 1945 his collection was, perhaps, the finest of its kind in private hands. His three-story townhouse had been converted into a library, with bookshelves running the length of the house on every floor. It was cluttered beyond description. Slaughter permitted me to read the letters from Williams to his wife, from which I took notes. He showed me the diary, suggesting I take it back to North Carolina, but I declined because I did not want the responsibility for its safety. That is something I have regretted to this day. Since the diary dealt with his trip to Africa, I did not need it at the time, I merely wanted to concentrate on his career as a historian.

In the autumn of 1945 I read a paper before the Association for the Study of Negro Life and History entitled "George Washington Williams, Historian." In the following January it was published in the *Journal of Negro History.* Except for the brief sketch in the *Dictionary of American Biography,* it was the first piece on Williams to appear since his death. It added something to what the author of the article in the DAB wrote, but I am now depressed by the number of factual errors I made and by the things I did not then know about Williams. Nevertheless, I had been able to fill in a sufficient number of details to give some idea of what manner of man Williams was.

In order for Williams' life to be reconstructed, almost all the information on his activities had to be dredged up by painstaking efforts. There were no Williams papers except for the few letters and the African diary in the possession of Henry P. Slaughter. And after my initial examination of the letters, I had the misfortune not to be able to look at any of that material again. Each time I visited Washington, I would call on Slaughter and ask to see the Williams diary. Each time he stalled. Finally, he shocked me by declaring that he was planning to do a biography of Williams himself and therefore preferred not to let me see the materials again. I was not worried about competition from Slaughter, for he was already seventy-nine and unlikely to complete the work. But I did wonder why he did not want me to examine the material.

Shortly thereafter, Slaughter sold his entire collection to Atlanta

University. I rushed to Atlanta and requested permission to see the Williams diary but was informed that there was no Williams material at all in the collection. I was crushed, for by this time the desire to see the diary had become almost an obsession. I began to wonder if I, or anyone else, could do a biography of Williams without seeing it. The one consolation I had came from my surmise as to what had happened to the Williams manuscripts. When I visited Slaughter, I saw piles of newspapers from which he planned to take clippings but never did. I suspect that when some of that clutter was hauled away as trash, the Williams material went with it. My conclusion has been tentatively confirmed by more than thirty-five years of fruitless searching for the diaries.

I knew almost nothing of the early life of Williams until one day, at Howard University, I discovered a letter he wrote in March, 1869—when he was nineteen years old—to General Oliver Otis Howard seeking admission to that university. It was a long letter, full of misspellings and other errors to be sure, telling the general about his early life, his drifting from one town to another with his parents, his service in the army during the Civil War, and his burning desire to secure an education and be of service to his people. This letter opened up new leads to his life with his parents and siblings at his birthplace in Bedford Springs, his army career, and his training for the ministry. In 1874, as a fund-raising project during his pastorate in Boston, Williams wrote a history of the Twelfth Baptist Church. I found a printed copy and learned a great deal not only about the history and importance of the church but also about Williams' Boston years as a student and as a pastor.

It was almost impossible to learn anything about the year Williams spent in Washington after he left Boston in 1875. He went to the capital to found a newspaper, *The Commoner*, which would succeed the *New National Era*, a paper published by Frederick Douglass that had folded during the panic of 1873. It was an important time in Washington, for it was in the midst of the Reconstruction era, when the fate of Negro Americans was being decided in the Congress. There was nothing about Williams in the Douglass papers and very little in the daily press. I searched everywhere for the newspaper that Williams allegedly edited, but there were no copies at the Library of Congress and the other likely places. It was not even listed in the *Union List of Newspapers*.

That period in his life remained a blank until my research assistant told me he had seen a reference to a newspaper, *The Commoner*, that was in the library of the American Antiquarian Society in Worcester, Massachusetts. I would not allow myself to believe that this was the *Commoner* edited by Williams. I wrote the society, almost casually, inquiring about the newspaper, its editor, and its contents. I was surprised and delighted to receive a reply saying that the paper in their collection was edited by the Reverend George Washington Williams, that they had what they thought was a full run—about six months— and that they would send it to me on microfilm if I cared to examine it. It turned out to be a treasure trove, for Williams had been the editor, publisher, columnist, reporter, and just about everything else. In it I learned much about his interests, values, views on numerous subjects from religion to Reconstruction, and relations with others.

From the time Williams went to Cincinnati in 1875, he became more and more visible, and material on his Ohio years is relatively abundant. Shortly after his arrival in Cincinnati, Murat Halstead, editor of the Cincinnati *Commercial*, invited him to write a column for the paper. Many of his columns were autobiographical, and are especially informative on his years in the United States Army and his service with the republican forces in Mexico. As an active member of the Republican party in Ohio, he made numerous speeches, some of which were reported in the daily press. Williams himself became a candidate for public office and the center of much attention not only in Cincinnati but across the state as well. As a successful candidate for the legislature in 1879, he was able to place his name and his work in the public record for posterity to examine.

When he left the legislature in 1881, Williams decided to devote full time to his history of the Negro race in America. Indeed, he had already begun while a member of the state legislature. One of the benefits one derives from researching a problem for a long time is that people get to know about it and often share relevant information. At a meeting of the board of the Chicago Public Library, a staff member who had done her doctoral work in Ohio libraries offered me a list of the books Williams borrowed from the Ohio State Library while in the legislature in 1880. The list is filled with works on general history, histories of the United States, military history, and books out of which Williams could have pieced together some information about blacks.

Since Williams indicated in the preface to his *History of the Negro Race* his indebtedness to librarians in many parts of the country, I directed inquiries to those libraries. In each—the American Antiquarian Society, the Boston Athanaeum, the Massachusetts Historical

Society, etc.—there were records of his having done research, of having used manuscripts, of having requested services from time to time. There were also, unfortunately, records of his not having paid for all of the manuscript copying he engaged clerks at the libraries to do for him.

Once Williams had gained considerable attention through the publication of his first major work, he was never altogether invisible again. Newspapers and letters tell of his leaving Ohio and settling in Boston, where he was admitted to the bar on the motion of a resident lawyer. After a few months he returned to Washington, presumably to begin research on a history of Reconstruction. He had not cut his ties with politics, however, and, soon after his arrival, President Chester Arthur appointed him United States minister to Haiti. But although the Senate had confirmed him before the president left office on March 4, 1885, and the outgoing secretary of state had given him his commission, the new secretary of state would not permit him to take up his post.

I knew of the Haitian appointment too but lacked some of the reasons for his not taking office until I discovered a full file on the matter in the papers of the Department of State housed in the National Archives. It was here that I found the details of his appointment and confirmation, the numerous objections to him voiced in the black community, and the department's own findings regarding Williams' conduct the previous summer. When the incoming Cleveland administration refused to permit him to take up his duties in Port-au-Prince, Williams sued the United States for his salary. The details of the case were reported in the decision of the United States Court of Claims, which upheld the position of the Department of State. Having done just about all that he could to advance himself in the United States, he turned his attention to Africa.

The African phase of Williams' career is in many ways the most interesting; it was also by far the most complicated to reconstruct. There was almost nothing to go on. I knew that Williams went to the Congo early in 1890, and in due course I was able to locate the *Open Letter* that he wrote to the king of the Belgians. I found two other important documents, a report to the president of the United States and a report on the problem of building a railroad through the Congo. These three documents told me much, but not nearly enough. How did Williams get to the Congo? He was certainly not a man of wealth despite his predilection for fine hotels and restaurants. Whom did he see in Africa, and what did they think of his venture? Did anyone from

Europe know him and have any connection with his African venture? These and many other questions plagued me for years.

Gradually I acquired information that led me to some of the answers. I worked the libraries of Belgium and secured considerable information about the part played by the king; I also found references to Williams suggesting he was an imposter or a blackmailer. In England I learned much in the Public Record Office and other libraries. For example, the Baptist Missionary Society of Britain maintained missions in the Congo in the early 1890s, and the missionaries sent full reports to the London office about problems they encountered and even about people who visited them. One frequent visitor was Williams. Before he wrote his *Open Letter* to King Leopold, the Baptist Missionary Society in London already knew what Williams thought of the king and his policies. The missionaries' reports are housed in the society's library in London.

Williams' *Open Letter*, the first public criticism of the Belgian monarch, created quite a stir in Brussels. A special session of the parliament was called for the purpose of praising Leopold's policies and, by indirection, criticizing Williams for his temerity in speaking ill of the king. In the course of studying this aspect of Williams' life, I discovered that the best vantage point from which to watch developments in Brussels was not in the Belgian capital or in Washington (for the United States minister to Brussels took almost no notice of the matter), but in London. The British minister to Belgium, Lord Vivian, watched events very closely and sent reports almost daily to the Foreign Office in London. These reports provided much information not only about the proceedings in Brussels but also about Vivian's view of Leopold's Congo policies.

I still did not know how Williams got to the Congo, who financed the trip, what his day-to-day experiences were, and why he wrote a report on the Congo railway. For years I fretted over these questions and reproached myself for not having taken that diary when it was offered to me in 1945. Then, one day I recalled a sentence from the ill-fated diary. It went something like this: "Today, I wrote Mr. Huntington." Perhaps this was Collis P. Huntington, president of the Southern Pacific Railroad, who might have had an interest in a railroad in the Congo. I knew he was a trustee of Hampton Institute and had expressed an interest in Africa. I inquired about the Huntington papers at the Huntington Library, at the Stanford University Library, at the Museum at Norfolk, and at Syracuse University. There was no encouragement from any of these places, but Syracuse's discouragement acted as a spur. The people at Syracuse told me their Huntington collection was so large that they did not know what they had, and it would be years before they could organize and catalog the manuscripts.

A few years later I was in the vicinity of Syracuse and decided to visit the Arents Research Library there. The librarians were cordial, but reminded me of what they had written to me. When I found that the letters were arranged by year, I started going through beginning with January, 1890. There must have been a half-dozen boxes of letters sent to Collis P. Huntington the first three days of the year 1890 from all sorts of people asking for railroad passes or for a renewal of the passes they already had. Then, although these were *incoming* letters, I came across an *outgoing* letter written by Huntington on January 7, 1890, to George W. Williams, who was in Brussels. In two or three sentences the letter told me all that I wanted to know. It read, "I enclose herewith my check on London and Westminster Bank . . . for £100. . . . I hope all will go well with you in your new field of work, and shall await with interest your first letter giving impressions of the Congo Country." Huntington did not have to wait until Williams reached the Congo to receive reports. Williams began writing from the Canary Islands, and from that point on until Williams sailed from Egypt for England almost a year later, his letters to Huntington constitute a veritable diary. He shared with his benefactor all his experiences. It was at this point that I began to feel I no longer needed the diary that Slaughter presumably lost.

Williams' death outside the United States without any relatives at his bedside turned out, ironically, to be a favor to posterity. On instructions from London, the United States consul at Liverpool went to Blackpool and took charge. He made an inventory of Williams' personal effects, arranged for the funeral and the interment, and sent Mrs. Williams in Washington certain personal effects, including three notebooks containing her husband's African diary. The consul also made daily reports to the secretary of state; and it is in these reports that I learned, for example, that Williams was engaged to an Englishwoman. It was rumored that he met Alice Fryer en route from Egypt to England in the spring of 1891. I was unable to confirm this until November, 1983, when I found in the Public Record Office in England the passenger list of SS *Golconda*. It shows that Miss Fryer boarded the ship at Madras, India, and Williams at Ismailia.

In 1975, my wife and I were visiting England and decided to go to

Blackpool to see what we could learn about Williams' last days. On my first morning there I went to the Blackpool Town Hall and encountered Alan Bryant, the director of the Blackpool Tourist Bureau. I told him the story of Williams and how he came to die in Blackpool. Bryant expressed great interest though he regretted that Williams had died in Blackpool, since that town is known as a popular resort. Even so, he volunteered to help in every way that he could. He called the local newspaper, which sent over a reporter who wished to interview me as well as to escort me to the newspaper office where I could read the newspapers for August, 1891.

During our fruitful conversations I wondered aloud if Williams was buried in the vicinity. In less than five minutes, Bryant's secretary produced the following information: The funeral was held in the local Baptist church, just across the square, on August 5, 1891, the services conducted by the Reverend Samuel Pelling. Williams was buried in the Layton Cemetery, a mile from the town square, Section F., Grave 123.

That afternoon at 2:30, on the thirtieth anniversary of my first acquaintance with George W. Williams, two reporters and a photographer, the warden of the cemetery, my wife, and I formed a procession to his grave. I laid a wreath on the unmarked grave of the man whose career I had followed for so long. The grave is no longer unmarked. Now he sleeps beneath a black granite slab on which are engraved the words "George Washington Williams, Afro-American Historian, 1849–1891."

Stalking George Washington Williams has been worth every minute I have spent on it, and not merely for the joy of the sleuthing. It is also because the search brought to light an American of extraordinary achievement.

John Hope Franklin: A Life
of Learning

As I began the task of putting the pieces together that would describe how I moved from one stage of intellectual development to another, I was reminded of a remark that Eubie Blake made as he approached his ninety-ninth birthday. He said, "If I had known that I would live this long I would have taken better care of myself." To paraphrase him, if I had known that I would become a historian I would have kept better records of my own pilgrimage through life. I may be forgiven, therefore, if I report that the beginnings are a bit hazy, not only to me but to my parents as well. For example, they had no clear idea of when I learned to read and write. It was when I was about three or four, I am told.

My mother, an elementary school teacher, introduced me to the world of learning when I was three years old. Since there were no day-care centers in the village where we lived, she had no alternative to taking me to school and seating me in the rear of her classroom where she could keep an eye on me. I remained quiet but presumably I also remained attentive, for when I was about five my mother noticed that on the sheet of paper she gave me each morning, I was no longer making lines and sketching out some notable examples of abstract art. I was writing words, to be sure almost as abstract as my art, and making sentences. My mother later said that she was not surprised much less astonished at what some, not she, would have called my precocity. Her only reproach—to herself, not me—was that my penmanship was hopelessly flawed since she had not monitored my progress as she had done for her enrolled students. From that point on, I would endeavor to write and, through the written word, to communicate my thoughts to others.

This essay was the Charles Homer Haskins Lecture, delivered before the American Council of Learned Societies, New York City, April 14, 1988, and printed in the Council's *Occasional Papers, Number 4* (New York, 1988).

My interest in having some thoughts of my own to express was stimulated by my father who, among other tasks, practiced law by day and read and wrote by night. In the absence of any possible distractions in the tiny village, he would read or write something each evening. This was my earliest memory of him and, indeed, it was my last memory of him. Even after we moved to Tulsa, a real city, and after we entered the world of motion pictures, radio, and television, his study and writing habits remained unaffected. I grew up believing that in the evenings one either read or wrote. It was always easy to read something worthwhile, and if one worked at it hard enough he might even write something worthwhile. I continue to believe that.

Two factors plagued my world of learning for all of my developing years. One was race, the other was financial distress; and each had a profound influence on every stage of my development. I was born in the all-Negro town of Rentiesville to which my parents went after my father had been expelled from court by a white judge who told him that no black person could ever represent anyone in his court. My father resolved that he would resign from the world dominated by white people and try to make it among his own people. But Rentiesville's population of less than two hundred people could not provide a poverty-free living even for one who was a lawyer, justice of the peace, postmaster, farmer, and president of the Rentiesville Trading Company which, incidentally, was not even a member of the New York Stock Exchange.

The quality of life in Rentiesville was as low as one can imagine. There was no electricity, running water, or inside plumbing. There was no entertainment or diversion of any kind—no parks, playgrounds, libraries, or newspapers. We subscribed to the Muskogee *Daily Phoenix*, which was delivered by the Missouri, Kansas, and Texas Railroad as it made its way southward through the state each morning. The days and nights were lonely and monotonous, and for a young lad with boundless energy there was nothing to do but read. My older sister and brother were away in private school in Tennessee, and one did not even have the pleasure of the company of older siblings. Now and then one went to Checotah, six miles away, to shop. That was not always pleasant, such as the time when my mother, sister, and I were ejected from the train because my mother refused to move from the coach designated for whites. It was the only coach we could reach before the train moved again, so my mother argued that she would not move because she was not to blame if the train's white coach was the only one available when the train came to a halt. Her argument was unsuccessful, and we had to trudge back to Rentiesville through the woods.

There were the rare occasions when we journeyed to Eufala, the county seat, where I won the spelling bee for three consecutive years. There was Muskogee to the north, where I went at the age of five for my first pair of eye glasses—the malady brought on, I was told, by reading by the dim light of a kerosene lamp. It was a combination of these personal and family experiences that forced my parents to the conclusion that Rentiesville was not a viable community. They resolved to move to Tulsa. First, my father would go, find a place, set himself up in the practice of law, and we would follow six months later, in June, 1921, when my mother's school closed for the summer recess.

That June, however, we received word that in Tulsa there was a race riot, whatever that was, and that the Negro section of that highly segregated community was in flames. At the age of six I sensed from my mother's reaction that my father was in danger. We were all relieved several days later, therefore, when a message arrived that he had suffered no bodily harm, but that the property he had contracted to purchase was destroyed by fire. He practiced law in a tent for several months, and our move to Tulsa was delayed by four years.

In the month before I reached my eleventh birthday, we arrived in Tulsa. It was quite a new world, and although a city of less than moderate size at the time, it was to my inexperienced eyes perhaps the largest city in the country. I did not see much of it, however, for racial segregation was virtually complete. I thought that Booker T. Washington, the school where I enrolled in grade seven, was the biggest and best school until one day I saw Central High for whites. It was a massive, imposing structure covering a city block. I was later to learn that it had every conceivable facility such as a pipe organ and a theater-size stage, which we did not have. I also learned that it offered modern foreign languages, and calculus, while our school offered automobile mechanics, home economics, typing, and shorthand. Our principal and our teachers constantly assured us that we need not apologize for our training and they worked diligently to give us much of what was not even in the curriculum.

Now that the family was together again I had the example and the encouragement of both of my parents. My mother no longer taught but she saw to it that my sister and I completed all of our home assignments promptly. Quite often, moreover, she introduced us to some of the great writers, especially Negro authors, such as Paul Laurence Dunbar and James Weldon Johnson, who were not a part of our studies at school. She also told us about some of the world's great music such as Handel's Oratorio "Esther," in which she had sung in college. While the music at school was interesting and lively, especially after I achieved the position of first trumpet in the band and orchestra, there was no Handel or Mozart, or Beethoven. We had a full fare of Victor Herbert and John Philip Sousa, and operettas, in more than one of which I sang the leading role.

Often after school I would go to my father's office. By the time I was in high school, the Depression had yielded few clients but ample time, which he spent with me. It was he who introduced me to ancient Greece and Rome, and he delighted in quoting Plato, Socrates, and Pericles. We would then walk home together, and after dinner he went to his books and I went to mine. Under the circumstances, there could hardly have been a better way of life, since I had every intention after completing law school of some day becoming his partner.

It was in secondary school that I had a new and wonderful experience which my parents did not share. It was the series of concerts and recitals at Convention Hall, perhaps even larger than the theater at Central High School which I never saw. As in the other few instances where whites and blacks were under the same roof, segregation was strict, but I very much wanted to go with some of my teachers who always held season tickets. My parents would *never* voluntarily accept segregation; consequently, the concerts were something they chose to forego. Even at court my father refused to accept segregation. Whenever I accompanied him, which was as often as I could, he would send me to the jury box when it was empty or, when there was a jury trial, have me sit at the bench with him. They took the position, however, that if I could bear the humiliation of segregation, I could go to the concerts.

Thus, I could purchase my own tickets with the money I earned as a paper boy. To be more accurate, I was not the paper boy, but the assistant to a white man who had the paper route in the black neighborhood. It was at one of these concerts that I heard Paul Whiteman present Gershwin's "Rhapsody in Blue" while on a nationwide tour in 1927. I also attended the annual performances of the Chicago Civic Opera Company, which brought to Tulsa such stellar singers as Rosa Raisa, Tito Schipa, and Richard Bonelli. I am not altogether proud of going to Convention Hall; there are times, even now, while enjoying a symphony or an opera, when I reproach myself for having yielded to the indignity of racial segregation. I can only say that in the long run it was my parents who knew best, though later I made a conscious effort to regain my self-respect.

There were many sobering experiences at Fisk, which I entered on a tuition scholarship in 1931. The first was my encounter with at least two dozen valedictorians and salutatorians from some of the best high schools in the United States. The fact that I had finished first in my high school class did not seem nearly as important in Nashville as it had in Tulsa. Imagine my chagrin when a whiz kid from Dayton made all A's in the first quarter while I made two B's and a C+. My rather poor grades were somewhat mitigated by my having to hold three jobs in order to pay my living expenses. I was also absolutely certain that the C+ resulted from whimsical grading by the teaching assistants in a course called "Contemporary Civilization." As I think of it now I still become infuriated, and if there was anyone to listen to my case today I would insist that my examinations be reevaluated and my grade raised accordingly! I *was* consoled by my salutatorian girl friend, now my wife of forty-seven years, who over the years has lent a sympathetic ear to my rantings about the injustices in that course. She can afford to be charitable; she received a grade of B+.

Another sobering experience was my first racial encounter in Nashville. At a downtown streetcar ticket window, I gave the man the only money I possessed, which was a $20 bill. I apologized and explained that it was all I had and he could give me my change using any kind of bills he wished. In an outburst of abusive language and using vile racial epithets, he told me that no nigger could tell him how to make change. After a few more similar statements he proceeded to give me $19.75 in dimes and quarters. From that day until I graduated, I very seldom went to Nashville, and when I did I never went alone. It was about as much as a sixteen-year-old could stand. I thought of that encounter some three years later, and felt almost as helpless, when a gang of white hoodlums took a young black man from a Fisk-owned house on the edge of the campus and lynched him. As president of student government I made loud noises and protests to the mayor, the governor, and even President Franklin D. Roosevelt, but nothing could relieve our pain and anguish or bring Cordie Cheek back. Incidentally, the heinous crime he had committed was that, while riding his bicycle, he struck a white child who was only slightly injured.

Still another sobering, even shattering, experience was my discovery at the end of my freshman year that my parents had lost our home and had moved into a four-family apartment building which they had built. I knew that the country was experiencing an economic depression of gigantic proportions, that unemployment had reached staggering figures, and that my father's law practice had declined significantly. I was not prepared for the personal embarrassment that the Depression created for me and my family, and frankly I never fully recovered from it. The liquidation of all debts became an obsession with me, and because of that experience my determination to live on a pay-as-you-go basis is as great today as it was when it was not at all possible to live that way.

Despite these experiences my years in college were pleasant if hectic, rewarding if tedious, happy if austere. Most classes were rigorous, and everyone was proud of the fact that the institution enjoyed an A rating by the Southern Association of Colleges and Secondary Schools. The faculty was, on the whole, first-rate, and they took pride in their scholarly output as well as in their teaching. Although the student body was all black, with the exception of an occasional white exchange student or special student, the faculty was fairly evenly divided between white and black. It was an indication of the lack of interest in the subject that we never thought in terms of what proportion of the faculty was white and what proportion was black.

Since I was merely passing through college en route to law school, I had little interest in an undergraduate concentration. I thought of English, but the chairman of that department, from whom I took freshman English, discouraged me on the ground that I would never be able to command the English language. (Incidentally, he was a distinguished authority in American literature and specialized in the traditions of the Gullah-speaking people of the Sea Islands. I was vindicated some years later when he chaired the committee that awarded me the Bancroft Prize for the best article in the *Journal of Negro History*.) My decision to major in history was almost accidental. The chairman of that department, Theodore S. Currier, who was white, had come into that ill-fated course in contemporary civilization and had delivered the most exciting lectures I had ever heard. I decided to see and hear more of him.

During my sophomore year I took two courses with Professor Currier, and my deep interest in historical problems and the historical process and what he had to say was apparently noted by him. Soon we developed a close personal relationship that developed into a deep friendship. Soon, moreover, I made the fateful decision to give up my plan to study and practice law and to replace it with a plan to study, write, and teach history. My desire to learn more about the field resulted in his offering new courses, including seminars, largely for my benefit. He already entertained the hope that I would go to Harvard, where he had done his own graduate work. I had similar hopes, but in the mid-1930s with the Depression wreaking its havoc, it was unrealistic to entertain such hopes. With a respectable grade point average (that C+ prevented my graduating *summa cum laude*), and strong supporting letters from my professors, I applied for admission to the Harvard Graduate School of Arts and Sciences.

Harvard required that I take an aptitude test that must have been the forerunner to the Graduate Records Examination. It was administered at Vanderbilt University, just across town but on whose grounds I had never been. When I arrived at the appointed place and took my seat, the person in charge, presumably a professor, threw the examination at me, a gesture hardly calculated to give me a feeling of welcome or confidence. I took the examination but cannot imagine that my score was high. As I left the room a Negro custodian walked up to me and told me that in his many years of working there I was the only black person he had ever seen sitting in a room with white people. The record that Fisk made that year was more important. The Association of American Universities placed Fisk University on its approved list. On the basis of this new recognition of my alma mater, Harvard admitted me unconditionally. Apparently this was the first time it had given a student from a historically black institution an opportunity to pursue graduate studies without doing some undergraduate work at Harvard. The university declined, however, to risk a scholarship on me.

Admission to Harvard was one thing; getting there was quite another. My parents were unable to give me more than a very small amount of money and their good wishes. I was able to make it back to Nashville, where Ted Currier told me that money alone would not keep me out of Harvard. He went to a Nashville bank, borrowed $500, and sent me on my way.

Shortly after my arrival in Cambridge in September, 1935, I felt secure academically, financially, and socially. At Fisk I had even taken two modern foreign languages in order to meet Harvard's requirement, and in Currier's seminars I had learned how to write a research paper. Since I was secretary to the librarian at Fisk for four years, I had learned how to make the best use of reference materials, bibliographical aids, and manuscripts. Even when I met my advisor, Professor A. M. Schlesinger, Sr., I did not feel intimidated, and I was very much at ease with him while discussing my schedule and my plans. After I got a job washing dishes for my evening meal and another typing dissertations and lectures, a feeling of long-range solvency settled over me. Although I had a room with a Negro family that had taken in black students since the time of Charles Houston and Robert Weaver, I had extensive contact with white students who never showed the slightest condescension toward me. I set my own priorities, however, realizing that I had the burden of academic deficiencies dating back to secondary school. I had to prove to myself and to my professors that the Association of American Universities was justified in placing Fisk University on its approved list. I received the M.A. degree in nine months and won fellowships with which I completed the Ph.D. requirements.

There were few blacks at Harvard in those days. One was completing his work in French history as I entered. As in Noah's Ark, there were two in the law school, two in zoology, and two in the college. There was one in English and one in comparative literature; there were none in the Medical School and none in the Business School.

The most traumatic social experience I had there was not racist but antisemitic. I was quite active in the Henry Adams Club, made up of graduate students in United States history. I was appointed to serve on the committee to nominate officers for the coming year which, if one wanted to be hypersensitive, was a way of making certain that I would not be an officer. When I suggested the most active, brightest graduate student for president, the objection to him was that although he did not have some of the more reprehensible Jewish traits, he was still a Jew. I had never heard any person speak of another in such terms, and I lost respect not only for the person who made the statement but for the entire group that even tolerated such views. Most of the members of the club never received their degrees. The Jewish member became one of the most distinguished persons to get a degree in United States history from Harvard in the last half-century.

The course of study was satisfactory but far from extraordinary. Mark Hopkins was seldom on the other end of the log, and one had to fend for himself as best he could. I had no difficulty with such a regimen, although I felt that some of my fellow students needed more guidance than the university provided. In my presence, at the beginning of my second year, one of the department's outstanding professors verbally abused a student visiting from another institution and dismissed him from his office because the student's question was awkwardly phrased the first time around. Another professor confessed to me that a doctoral committee had failed a candidate because he did not *look* like a Harvard Ph.D. When the committee told him that he would have to study four more years before applying for reconsideration, the student was in the library the following morning to begin his four-year sentence. At that point, the chairman of the committee was compelled to inform the student that under no circumstances would he be permitted to continue his graduate studies there.

When I left Harvard in the spring of 1939 I knew that I did not wish to be in Cambridge another day. I had no desire to offend my advisor or the other members of my doctoral committee. I therefore respectfully declined suggestions that I seek further financial aid. It was time, I thought, to seek a teaching position and complete my dissertation *in absentia*. I had taught one year at Fisk following my first year at Harvard. With five preparations in widely disparate fields and with more than two hundred students, I learned more history than I had learned at Fisk *and* Harvard. I early discovered that teaching had its own very satisfying rewards. For some fifty-two years, there have been many reasons to confirm the conclusions I reached at Fisk, St. Augustine's, North Carolina College at Durham, Howard, Brooklyn, Chicago, Duke, and short stints in many institutions here and abroad.

After I committed myself to the study, teaching, and writing of history, I was so preoccupied with my craft that I gave no attention to possible career alternatives. Less than two years into my career, however, when I was working on my second book, the president of a small but quite respectable historically black liberal arts college invited me to become dean of his institution. It was at that point that I made a response that was doubtless already in my mind but which I had not yet articulated. I thanked him and respectfully declined the invitation on the grounds that my work in the field of history precluded my moving into college administration. When the president received my letter, he sent me a telegram informing me that he was arriving the following day to explain his offer. During the three hours of conversation with him I had ample opportunity to state and restate my determination to remain a teacher and writer of history. Each time I did so I became more unequivocal in my resistance to any change in my career objectives. I believe that he finally became convinced that he was indeed wrong in offering me the deanship in the first place. From that day onward, I had no difficulty in saying to anyone who raised the matter that I was not interested in deanships, university presidencies, or ambassadorships. And I never regretted the decision to remain a student and teacher of history.

There is nothing more stimulating or satisfying than teaching bright, inquisitive undergraduates. It was puzzling, if dismaying, when a student complained, as one did at Howard, that my lengthy assignments did not take into account the fact that his people were only eighty-five years removed from slavery. It was sobering, but challenging, when an undergraduate asked, as one did at Brooklyn, if I would suggest additional readings since he had already read everything in the syllabus that I distributed on the first day of class. It was reassuring to find that some students, such as those at Chicago, came to class on a legal holiday because I neglected to take note of the holiday in my class assignments. It was refreshing, even amusing, when students requested, as some did at Duke, that the date for the working dinner at my home be changed because it conflicted with a Duke-Virginia basketball game. As Harry Golden would say, only in America could one find undergraduates with so much *chutzpah*.

There came a time in my own teaching career when I realized that with all my frantic efforts at research and writing I would never be able to write on all the subjects in which I was deeply interested. If I only had graduate students who would take up some of the problems regarding slavery, free blacks, the Reconstruction era and its overthrow, it would extend my own sense of accomplishment immeasurably. That was a major consideration in my move in 1964 from Brooklyn College to the University of Chicago where for the next eighteen years I supervised some thirty dissertations of students who subsequently have published more than a dozen books. In view of Chicago's free-wheeling attitude toward the time for fulfilling degree requirements, there is a possibility that eight years after retirement, I might have more doctoral students to complete their work and write more books. Meanwhile, I continue to revel in the excitement of teaching in still another type of institution, the law school at Duke University.

I could not have avoided being a social activist even if I had wanted to. I had been barred from entering the University of Oklahoma to pursue graduate studies, and when the National Association for the Advancement of Colored People asked me to be the expert witness for Lyman

Johnson, who sought admission to the graduate program in history at the University of Kentucky, I was honored to do so. After all, it was easy to establish the fact that Johnson could not get the same training at the inferior Kentucky State College for Negroes that he could get at the University of Kentucky. Johnson was admitted forthwith. To me it was one more blow against segregation in Oklahoma as well as Kentucky. The defense argument collapsed when the University of Kentucky placed one of its history professors on the stand and asked him about teaching Negroes. He replied soberly that he did not teach Negroes, he taught history, which he was pleased to do!

Then, Thurgood Marshall asked me to serve on his nonlegal research staff when the NAACP Legal Defense Fund sought to eliminate segregation in the public schools. Each week in the late summer and fall of 1953 I journeyed from Washington to New York, where I worked from Thursday afternoon to Sunday afternoon. I wrote historical essays, coordinated the work of some other researchers, and participated in the seminars that the lawyers held regularly, and provided the historical setting for the questions with which they were wrestling. I had little time for relaxing at my home away from home, the Algonquin Hotel, but each time I entered this establishment, I made eye contact with an imaginary Tallulah Bankhead, Agnes DeMille, or Noel Coward, who were among the more famous habitues of its lobby.

The historian, of all people, must not make more of his own role in events, however significant, even if it is tempting to do so. It would be easy to claim that I was one of the 250,000 people at the March on Washington in 1963. I was not there and perhaps the truth is even more appealing. Since I was serving as Pitt Professor at the University of Cambridge that year, I was something of a resource person for the BBC-TV. On Richard Dimbleby's popular television program, *Panorama*, I tried to explain to the British viewers what had transpired when James Meredith sought to enter the University of Mississippi. I suspect there was a bit of advocacy even in the tone of my voice. In the summer of 1963 I took British viewers through what the BBC called "A Guide to the March on Washington." Here again, with film clips on Malcolm X, James Baldwin, A. Philip Randolph, and others, I explained why the march was a very positive development in the history of American race relations. Finally, in 1965, I was actually on the Selma march. No, I did not march *with* Martin, as some imaginative writers have claimed. I doubt that Martin ever knew that I was there, far back in the ranks as I was. I was *not* at Pettus Bridge in Dallas County, but joined the march at the city of St. Jude on the outskirts of Montgomery. I took pride in marching with more than thirty historians who came from all parts of the country to register their objection to racial bigotry in the United States. And I want to make it clear that I was afraid, yes, frightened out of my wits by the hate-filled eyes that stared at us from the sidewalks, windows, businesses, and the like. It was much more than I had bargained for.

One must be prepared for any eventuality when he makes any effort to promote legislation or to shape the direction of public policy or to affect the choice of those in the public service. This came to me quite forcefully in 1987 when I joined with others from many areas of activity in opposing the Senate confirmation of Robert H. Bork as associate justice of the Supreme Court of the United States. In what I thought was a sober and reasoned statement, I told the Judiciary Committee of the United States Senate that there was "no indication—in his writings, his teachings, or his rulings—that this nominee has any deeply held commitment to the eradication of the problem of race or even of its mitigation." It came as a shock, therefore, to hear the president of the United States declare that the opponents of the confirmation of Judge Bork constituted a "lynch mob." This was a wholly unanticipated tirade against those activists who had merely expressed views on a subject in which all citizens had an interest.

It was necessary, as a black historian, to have a personal agenda, as well as one dealing with more general matters, that involved a type of activism. I discovered this in the spring of 1939 when I arrived in Raleigh, North Carolina, to do research in the state archives, only to be informed by the director that in planning the building the architects did not anticipate that any Afro-Americans would be doing research there. Perhaps it was the astonishment that the director, a Yale Ph.D. in history, saw in my face that prompted him to make a proposition. If I would wait a week he would make some arrangements. When I remained silent, registering a profound disbelief, he cut the time in half. I waited from Monday to Thursday, and upon my return to the archives I was escorted to a small room outfitted with a table and chair which was to be my private office for the next four years. (I hasten to explain that it did not take four years to complete my dissertation. I completed it the following year, but continued to do research there as long as I was teaching at St. Augustine's College.) The director also presented me with keys to the manuscript collection in order to avoid requiring the white assistants to deliver manuscripts to me. That arrangement lasted only two weeks, when the white researchers, protesting discrimination, demanded keys to the manuscript collection for themselves. Rather than comply with their demands, the director relieved me of my keys and ordered the assistants to serve me.

Nothing illustrated the vagaries of policies and practices of racial segregation better than libraries and archives. In Raleigh alone, there were three different policies: the state library had two tables in the stacks set aside for the regular use of Negro readers. The state supreme court library had no segregation while, as we have seen, the archives faced the matter as it arose. In Alabama and Tennessee, the state archives did not segregate readers, while Louisiana had a strict policy of excluding Negro would-be readers altogether. In the summer of 1945 I was permitted by the Louisiana director of archives to use the manuscript collection since the library was closed in observance of the victory of the United States over governmental tyranny and racial bigotry in Germany and Japan. As I have said elsewhere, pursuing southern history has been for me a strange career.

While World War II interrupted the careers of many young scholars, I experienced no such delay. At the same time, it raised in my mind the most profound questions about the sincerity of my country in fighting bigotry and tyranny abroad. And the answers to my questions shook my faith in the integrity of our country and its leaders. Being loath to fight with guns and grenades, in any case, I sought opportunities to serve in places where my training and skills could be utilized. When the United States entered the war in 1941 I had already received my doctorate. Since I knew that several men who had not been able to obtain their advanced degrees had signed on as historians in the War Department, I made application there. I was literally rebuffed without the department giving me any serious consideration. In Raleigh, where I was living at the time, the Navy sent out a desperate appeal for men to do office work, and the successful ones would be given the rank of petty officer. When I answered the appeal, the recruiter told me that I had all of the qualifications except color. I concluded that there was *no* emergency and told the recruiter how I felt. When my draft board ordered me to go to its staff physician for a blood test, I was not permitted to enter his office and was told to wait on a bench in the hall. When I refused and insisted to the draft board clerk that I receive decent treatment, she in turn insisted that the doctor see me forthwith, which he did. By this time, I had concluded that the United States did not need

me and did not deserve me. I spent the remainder of the war successfully outwitting my draft board, including taking a position at North
Carolina College for Negroes whose president was on the draft appeal
board. Each time I think of these incidents, even now, I feel nothing but
shame for my country—not merely for what it did to me, but for what
it did to the million black men and women who served in the armed
forces under conditions of segregation and discrimination.

One had always to be mindful, moreover, that being a black scholar
did not exempt one from the humiliations and indignities that a society with more than its share of bigots can heap upon a black person,
regardless of education or even station in life. This became painfully
clear when I went to Brooklyn College in 1956 as chairman of a department of fifty-two white historians. There was much fanfare accompanying my appointment, including a front-page story with picture in
the New York *Times.* When I sought to purchase a home, however, not
one of the thirty-odd realtors offering homes in the vicinity of Brooklyn
College would show their properties. Consequently, I had to seek
showings by owners who themselves offered their homes for sale. I got
a few showings including one that we very much liked, but I did not
have sufficient funds to make the purchase. My insurance company
had proudly advertised that it had $50 million to lend to its policy
holders who aspired to home ownership. My broker told me that the
company would not make a loan to me because the house I wanted was
several blocks beyond where blacks should live. I cancelled my insurance and, with the help of my white lawyer, tried to obtain a bank loan.
I was turned down by every New York bank except the one in Brooklyn
where my attorney's father had connections. As we finally moved in
after the hassles of more than a year, I estimated that I could have
written a long article, perhaps even a small book, in the time expended
on the search for housing. The high cost of racial discrimination is not
merely a claim of the so-called radical left. It is as real as the rebuffs, the
indignities, or the discriminations that many black people suffer.

Many years ago, when I was a fledgling historian, I decided that one
way to make certain that the learning process would continue was to
write different kinds of history, even as one remained in the same field.
It was my opinion that one should write a monograph, a general work,
a biography, a period piece, and edit some primary source and some
work or works, perhaps by other authors, to promote an understanding
of the field. I made no systematic effort to touch all the bases, as it

were, but with the recent publication of my biography of George Washington Williams, I believe that I have touched them all. More recently, I have started the process all over again by doing research for a monograph on runaway slaves.

Another decision I made quite early was to explore new areas or fields, whenever possible, in order to maintain a lively, fresh approach to the teaching and writing of history. That is how I happened to get into Afro-American history, in which I never had a formal course, but which attracted a growing number of students of my generation and many more in later generations. It is remarkable how moving or even drifting into a field can affect one's entire life. More recently, I have become interested in women's history, and during the past winter I prepared and delivered three lectures under the general title of "Women, Blacks, and Equality, 1820–1988." I need not dwell on the fact that for me it was a very significant learning experience. Nor should it be necessary for me to assure you that despite the fact that I have learned much, I do not seek immortality by writing landmark essays and books in the field of women's history.

I have learned much from my colleagues both at home and abroad. The historical associations and other learned societies have instructed me at great length at their annual meetings, and five of them have given me an opportunity to teach and to lead by electing me as their president. Their journals have provided me with the most recent findings of scholars and they have graciously published some pieces of my own. Very early I learned that scholarship knows no national boundaries, and I have sought the friendship and collaboration of historians and scholars in many parts of the world. From the time that I taught at the Salzburg Seminar in American Studies in 1951, I have been a student and an advocate of the view that the exchange of ideas is more healthy and constructive than the exchange of bullets. This was especially true during my tenure on the Fulbright Board, as a member for seven years and as the chairman for three years. In such experiences one learns much about the common ground that the peoples of the world share. When we also learn that this country and the western world have no monopoly of goodness and truth or of skills and scholarship, we begin to appreciate the ingredients that are indispensable to making a better world. In a life of learning that is, perhaps, the greatest lesson of all.

PART IV

In the Public Interest

As I indicated in the introduction to this volume, the Negro scholar is seldom content merely to ply his trade when the great social issues of the day roil all about him. The problem seems never ending, and in the first essay of this section I discuss the issues and suggest ways of dealing with them. If "The Dilemma of the American Negro Scholar" did not represent the collective sentiments of the group, it at least introduced the subject and, by implication, invited other reactions to it.

In the second essay of this section, "The Historian and Public Policy," I argue that historians can and do play important roles in affecting, even helping to shape, public policy. Because of their training and the special perspective it has provided them, they are in an excellent position to set forth a rational basis for public policy. On numerous occasions they have done precisely that.

It is difficult to escape the human relations problems that abound in our society. Surely, one of the reasons for this is its very make-up, composed as it is of so many racial, religious, and ethnic groups. Few newcomers have escaped the scorn and obloquy of the older settlers. Some have borne a greater burden than others. Like racism, ethnic rivalry and hostility are almost as old as the country itself and were present almost at the creation. The essay on ethnicity seeks to provide some historical perspective for the problem.

With the increase in immigration restrictions, aimed particularly at Hispanics south of the border and in the Caribbean, and with no really constructive, humane policy for native Americans, it has been suggested by some that there is not enough room for all who wish to settle here. Perhaps that cannot be refuted, but what can be challenged is the basis for the policies that have been put in place and the manner in which the priorities among the competing peoples are set. The final essay deals with some of the issues involved.

The Dilemma of the American
Negro Scholar

The problems of the scholar who belongs to a particular group, ethnic or otherwise, must be considered in the context of the general problem of the scholar in the United States. In America the scholar's role in the community and the nation has always been limited. Indeed, his role has been rather carefully defined by the history of the country. Questions have often been raised about the effective use of the scholar in a society whose fundamental preoccupation has been with problems that have had little or nothing to do with the life of the mind. Intellectual prowess and mental acumen, it was argued almost from the beginning, could make no substantial contribution to the tasks of clearing the forests, cutting pathways to the frontier, and making a living in the wilderness. The intellectual life was reserved for those whose task it was to preserve and promote the moral and religious life of the community. In the early days of the nation there was a widespread feeling, moreover, that these aspects of life could be kept separate from the other aspects. Meanwhile, the rest of the community could live in blissful ignorance, with little or no concern for the great world of scholarship and learning that might be flourishing as far away as London and Paris or as close as the nearest county seat.

This was a mere fiction, but Americans liked to believe in it. In the final analysis, however, those who devoted themselves to intellectual pursuits became forces in the community in spite of the community itself. The lack of respect for learning or the lack of concern for it melted before the exigencies of conflict, when ideological justifications and rationalizations were needed for actions that had already been taken. Thus, when the patriots were fighting for independence,

Originally published in Herbert Hill (ed.), *Soon One Morning: New Writing by American Negroes, 1940–1962* (New York, 1963).

the scholars came to the rescue of the polemicists and agitators, and Locke and Hume and Dickinson and Jefferson became household words among groups considerably larger than those who could be described as learned. It was at this juncture that the peculiar ambivalence that was to characterize American attitudes became evident. On the one hand, there was little regard, if not downright contempt, for the scholar and the serious thinker. On the other hand, there was the acknowledged need for the talents and resources of the man who was devoted to the intellectual life; and there was a willingness to call upon him to strengthen the hand of those who had decided upon a particular course of action.

There has always been some acknowledgment, from that day to this, of the importance of the role of the scholar and intellectual in American life. Too often it has been begrudgingly conceded and too often the pervasive influence of scholarship in policy making and decision making is wholly unrecognized. We have been inclined to discount this influence and to insist that theorizing is the pastime of less practical-minded people. As for ourselves, we move, we act, we get things done, we have no time for indulging in the fantasies that emanate from the ivory tower. We do not seem to care that for this attitude we may be branded unintellectual or even anti-intellectual. We prefer to be known and recognized as practical-minded, down-to-earth. After all, our constitution is a practical, workable document. Our economy reflects our hard-headed approach to exploiting our resources and developing effective and efficient means of production. Even our social order and our institutions are evidence of our pragmatic orientation. I would suspect, however, that the more generous and broad-minded among us would recognize the fact that an untold amount of scholarship went into the writing of our constitution; that theoretical scientists as well as technicians and businessmen helped to make our economy what it has become; and that many scholarly hands contributed to the formulation of our social order and the institutions of which we boast.

The point is that, whether he wanted to or not, the American scholar has been drawn irresistibly into the mainstream of American life, and has contributed his knowledge and his ingenuity to the solution of the major problems that the country has faced. Jonathan Edwards' *Freedom of the Will*, with all its scholarship, good and bad, was primarily an effort to preserve the unity of the older religious institutions in the face of powerful currents of change. Thomas Jefferson was a close student of eighteenth-century political theory, but the most significant manifestation of his scholarship in this area is to be found in the Declaration of Independence, whose practical-mindedness can hardly be surpassed. Even Ralph Waldo Emerson's *American Scholar*, while embodying some remarkable generalizations about the intellectual resources and powers of mankind, was in truth a declaration of American intellectual independence, calling the American scholar to arms in the war against ignorance and in behalf of the integrity of American intellectual life.

In recent years the story has been essentially the same. It was Woodrow Wilson, the former professor at Princeton, testing his theories of congressional government while president of the United States. It was James MacGregor Burns, of Williams College, adding scholarship and a new dimension to the traditional campaign biography with his life of John F. Kennedy. It was John Kenneth Galbraith descending from the insulation of a Harvard economics chair to make searching and stimulating observations on the industrial and business community of the nation. If these and scores of other scholars were faced with dilemmas—of whether to satisfy themselves in attacking the theoretical problems of their fields or to grapple with the fundamental problems of mankind—they resolved them fearlessly and unequivocally by applying their disciplines to the tasks from which they felt that they could not escape. In that way they gave meaning, substance, and significance to American scholarship.

It is in such a setting and context that we must examine the position of the American Negro scholar. The dilemmas and problems of the Negro scholar are numerous and complex. He has been forced, first of all, to establish his claim to being a scholar, and he has had somehow to seek recognition in the general world of scholarship. This has not been an easy or simple task, for, at the very time when American scholarship in general was making its claim to recognition, it was denying that Negroes were capable of being scholars. Few Americans, even those who advocated a measure of political equality, subscribed to the view that Negroes—any Negroes—had the ability to think either abstractly or concretely or to assimilate ideas that had been formulated by others. As late as the closing years of the nineteenth century it was difficult to find any white persons in the labor or business community, in the pulpit or on the platform, in the field of letters or in the field of scholarship, who thought it possible that a Negro could join the select company of scholars in America.

The Negro, then, first of all had to struggle against the forces and personalities in American life that insisted he could never rise in the intellectual sphere. Thomas Nelson Page, the champion of the plantation tradition and the defender of the superiority of the white race, insisted that "the Negro has not progressed, not because he was a slave, but because he does not possess the faculties to raise himself above slavery. He has not yet exhibited the qualities of any race which has advanced civilization or shown capacity to be greatly advanced." In 1895, a future president of the United States, Theodore Roosevelt, argued that "a perfectly stupid race can never rise to a very high plane; the Negro, for instance, has been kept down as much by lack of intellectual development as anything else." If one were to thumb through the pages of the most respectable journals of the early years of this century—*Atlantic, Harper's, Scribner's, Century, North American Review*—he would find the same spirit pervading the articles published there. Industrial and vocational education, they contended, was peculiarly suitable for the Negro. Negroes, they argued, were childish, simple, irresponsible, and mentally inferior. It was the same wherever one looked.

The Negro who aspired to be a scholar in the closing years of the nineteenth century and the opening years of this century must have experienced the most shattering and disturbing sensations as he looked about him in an attempt to discover one indication of confidence, one expression of faith in him and his abilities. If he doubted himself, it would be understandable, for he had been brainwashed, completely and almost irrevocably, by assertions of Caucasian superiority, endorsements of social Darwinism, with its justifications for the degradation of the Negro, and political and legal maneuverings that lowered the Negro still further on the social and intellectual scale. But the aspiring Negro scholar did not doubt himself, and he turned on his detractors with all the resources he could summon in the effort to refute those who claimed he was inferior. In 1888, a Negro, William T. Alexander, published a whole volume to support the claim that the Negro was the intellectual equal of others. "By the closest analysis of the blood of each race," he argued with eloquence, and futility, considering the times, "the slightest difference cannot be detected; and so, in the aspirations of the mind, or the impulses of the heart, we are all one common family, with nothing but the development of the mind through the channel of education to raise one man, or one people above another. . . . So far as noble characteristics are concerned, the colored race possess those traits to fully as great a degree as do the white."

Alexander and numerous contemporaries of his had faced their dilemma, and they had made their choice. They *had* to combat the contentions of Negro inferiority. They *had* to demonstrate that Negroes were capable of assimilating ideas and of contributing to mankind's store of knowledge. They made their argument simply and directly. It was as though whites had said they could not count, and Negroes then counted from one to ten to prove that they could. There were subtle, more sophisticated ways of proving their mental acumen, but if Negroes thought of them, they must have been convinced that such methods would have no effect on those whose arguments were not based on fact or reason in the first place.

It must have been a most unrewarding experience for the Negro scholar to answer those who said that he was inferior by declaring: "I am indeed *not inferior.*" For such a dialogue left little or no time for the pursuit of knowledge as one really desired to pursue it. Imagine, if you can, what it meant to a competent Negro student of Greek literature, W. H. Crogman, to desert his chosen field and write a book entitled *The Progress of a Race.* Think of the frustration of the distinguished Negro physician C. V. Roman, who abandoned his medical research and practice, temporarily at least, to write *The Negro in American Civilization.* What must have been the feeling of the Negro student of English literature Benjamin Brawley, who forsook his field to write *The Negro Genius* and other works that underscored the intellectual powers of the Negro? How much poorer is the field of the biological sciences because an extremely able and well-trained Negro scientist, Julian Lewis, felt compelled to spend years of his productive life writing a book entitled *The Biology of the Negro?*

Many Negro scholars, moreover, never entered any of the standard branches of learning. Perhaps they would have been chemists, geologists, essayists, critics, musicologists, sociologists, historians. But they never were. From the moment of their intellectual awakening they were drawn inexorably, irresistibly into the field that became known as Negro studies. Here they were insulated from the assaults of the white scholars, who could be as vicious and as intolerant in their attacks and in their attitudes as the out-and-out racists were. Here, too, they would work relatively unmolested in a field where they could meet, head on, the assaults of those who would malign them and their race. In a sense, they could establish not only a professional standing by dealing objectively and in a scholarly fashion with the problems related to them and their race, but also the value and integrity of the field of Negro studies itself, which they had brought into being.

The careers of three Negro scholars—W. E. B. Du Bois, Carter G. Woodson, and Alain L. Locke—epitomize the history of Negro scholarship in the first half of the twentieth century. All three were carefully trained and held degrees of doctor of philosophy from Harvard University. After writing a doctoral dissertation that became Volume I in the Harvard Historical Studies, Du Bois moved on from his path-breaking work on the suppression of the African slave trade to a series of studies that not only treated many aspects of the Negro problem but also covered a number of areas in the social sciences and the humanities. He produced *The Philadelphia Negro*, a modern sociological study; he was the editor of the Atlanta University *Studies of the Negro Problem*, called a pioneering work in the field of the social sciences; he wrote *The Souls of Black Folk*, a critique of approaches to the solution of the race problem, *Black Folk Then and Now*, a history of the Negro in Africa and the New World, *Black Reconstruction*, a study of the Negro's part in the years following the Civil War, and literally dozens of other works. In his ninety-fourth year, he completed an epic three-volume novel about the Negro experience, *The Ordeal of Mansard*.

Woodson's first scholarly work, *The Disruption of Virginia*, was a rather general study. He soon settled down to a systematic study of the Negro, however. Successively, he produced his *Education of the Negro Prior to 1860*, his studies of the free Negro, his *Century of Negro Migration*, *The History of the Negro Church*, *The Negro in Our History*, *African Background Outlined*, and many others. In 1915 he organized the Association for the Study of Negro Life and History, and shortly thereafter became editor of the *Journal of Negro History*, which became one of the major historical publications in the United States.

Alain Locke's career was, in several important respects, different from that of Du Bois and Woodson. He was an honor graduate of Harvard College, where he was elected to Phi Beta Kappa. He was a Rhodes Scholar at Oxford and later studied at the University of Berlin. Trained in philosophy, he soon became involved in the literary activity that was later called the "Negro Renaissance." Although he maintained his interest in the theory of value and cultural pluralism, he became a powerful force in articulating the position and aspirations of the new Negro. Thus, his *The New Negro: An Interpretation, The Negro in Art*, and *Plays of Negro Life* eclipsed his "Values and Imperatives," "Ethics and Culture," and "Three Corollaries of Cultural Relativism." After 1925 he never gave very much attention to purely philosophical problems.

Under the shadow and influence of these three figures and others, there emerged a large number of Negro scholars who devoted themselves almost exclusively to the study of some aspect of the Negro. Soon recognized fields emerged: the history of the Negro, the anthropology of the Negro, the sociology of the Negro, the poetry of the Negro, the Negro novel, the Negro short story, and so on.

In moving forthrightly in this direction, what had the Negro scholar done? He had, alas, made an institution of the field of Negro studies. He had become the victim of segregation in the field of scholarship in the same way that Negroes in other fields had become victims of segregation. There were the Negro press, the Negro church, Negro business, Negro education, and now Negro scholarship. Unhappily, Negro scholars had to face a situation, not entirely their own creation, in the perpetuation of which their stake was very real indeed. In the field of American scholarship, it was all they had. It grew in respectability not only because the impeccable scholarship of many of the Negroes commanded it, but also because many of the whites conceded that Negroes had peculiar talents that fitted them to study themselves and their problems. To the extent that this concession was made, it defeated a basic principle of scholarship—namely, that given the materials and techniques of scholarship and given the mental capacity, any person could engage in the study of any particular field.

This was a tragedy. Negro scholarship had foundered on the rocks of racism. It had been devoured by principles of separatism, of segregation. It had become the victim of the view that there was some "mystique" about Negro studies, similar to the view that there was some "mystique" about Negro spirituals which required that a person possess a black skin in order to sing them. This was not scholarship; it was folklore, it was voodoo.

The Negro scholar can hardly be held responsible for this sad turn of events. He had acted in good faith, and had proceeded in the best traditions of American scholarship. American scholarship had always been pragmatic, always firmly based on need. Du Bois and Woodson and Locke were in the same tradition as Jonathan Edwards and Thomas Jefferson. Here was a vast field that was unexplored. Here was an urgent need to explore it in order to complete the picture of American life and institutions. Here was an opportunity to bring to bear on a problem the best and most competent resources that could be commandeered. That the field was the Negro and that the resources were also Negroes are typical irrelevancies of which objective scholarship can take no cognizance. One wonders what would have happened had there been no Du Bois, no Woodson, no Locke, just as one wonders what would have happened had there been no Jonathan Edwards, no Thomas Jefferson. Du Bois could have moved toward imperial or colonial history or toward literary criticism; and Woodson could have moved toward political history or economic geography. Locke could have become a leading authority on values and aesthetics. Perhaps they would have been accepted in the mainstream of American scholarship; perhaps not. Their dilemma lay before them, and their choice is evident. It is not for us to say that American scholarship suffered as a result of the choice they made. We *can* say, however, that it is tragic indeed, and a commentary on the condition of American society, that these Negro scholars felt *compelled* to make the choice they did make. Had conditions been different, had they been free Americans functioning in a free intellectual and social climate, they might well have made other choices. Nothing, however, can degrade or successfully detract from the contributions they made, once they had chosen.

There were other Negro scholars, however, who did not take the road to Negro studies, who preferred to make their mark, if they were to make one at all, in what may be termed the mainstream of American scholarship. When W. S. Scarborough graduated from Oberlin in 1875 with a degree in Greek and Latin, it was widely thought that the only suitable pursuit for Negroes was in the area of vocational studies. Scarborough neither followed such a course nor yielded to the temptation to become a student of Negro life. In 1881 he published his *First Lessons in Greek*, and several years later he brought out his *Birds of Aristophanes: A Theory of Interpretation*. Then he translated the twenty-first and twenty-second books of Livy, published other works in Latin and Greek, and became a competent student of Sanskrit, Gothic, Lithuanian, and Old Slavonic. But there was no place for him in American scholarly circles, not even at the predominantly Negro Howard University, where the white members of the Board of Trustees took the position that the chair in classical languages could be filled only by a Caucasian. Three generations later, the fate of William A. Hinton, one of America's most distinguished syphilologists, whose discoveries revolutionized the techniques for the detection and cure of dread social diseases, was almost the same. Despite his signal accomplishments, Harvard University Medical School kept him on for many years as a nonteaching clinical instructor. Not until he neared retirement and not until the position of the Negro in American society had significantly changed after World War II was Hinton elevated to a professorial rank. Scarborough and Hinton wore down their knuckles rapping at the door of American scholarship. Whenever the door was opened, it was done grudgingly and the opening was so slight that it was still almost impossible to enter.

The wide gap that separates the white world from the Negro world in this country has not been bridged by the work of scholarship, black or white. Indeed, the world of scholarship has, for the most part, remained almost as partitioned as other worlds. The Negro scholars that have become a part of the general world of American scholarship can still be counted on the fingers of a few hands. The number of Negro scholars on the faculties of non-Negro American colleges and universities is still pitifully small. The lines of communication between the two worlds are few and are sparingly used. Thus, the world of scholarship in America is a mirror of the state of race relations generally. Perhaps the world of scholarship is a step or two ahead of the general community; but the vigor and the pragmatism that characterize the American approach to other problems are missing in this all-important area. The Negro scholar is in a position not unlike that of Ralph Ellison's Invisible Man; he is a "fantasy," as James Baldwin puts it, "in the mind of the republic." When he is remembered at all he is all too often an afterthought. When his work is recognized it is usually pointed to as the work of a Negro. He is a competent *Negro* sociologist, an able *Negro* economist, an outstanding *Negro* historian. Such recognition is as much the product of the racist mentality as the Negro restrooms in the Montgomery airport were. It was this knowledge of racism in American scholarship, this feeling of isolation, that drew from Du Bois this comment: "I sit with Shakespeare and he winces not. Across the color line I move arm in arm with Balzac and Dumas, where smiling men and welcoming women glide in gilded halls. From out the caves of evening that swing between the strong-limbed earth and the tracery of stars, I summon Aristotle and Aurelius and what soul I will, and they come all graciously with no scorn nor condescension. So, wed with Truth, I dwell above the Veil. Is this the life you grudge us, O knightly America? Is this the life you long to change into the dull red hideousness of Georgia? Are you so afraid lest peering from this high Pisgah, between Philistine and Amalekite, we sight the Promised Land?"

The path of the scholar is at best a lonely one. In his search for truth he must be the judge of his findings and he must live with his conclusions. The world of the Negro scholar is indescribably lonely; and he must, somehow, pursue truth down that lonely path while, at the same time, making certain that his conclusions are sanctioned by universal standards developed and maintained by those who frequently do not even recognize him. Imagine the plight of a Negro historian trying to do research in archives in the South operated by people who cannot conceive that a Negro has the capacity to use the materials there. I well recall my first visit to the State Department of Archives and History in North Carolina, which was presided over by a man with a Ph.D. in history from Yale. My arrival created a panic and an emergency among the administrators that was, itself, an incident of historic proportions. The archivist frankly informed me that I was the first Negro who had sought to use the facilities there; and as the architect who designed the building had not anticipated such a situation, my use of the manuscripts and other materials would have to be postponed for several days, during which time one of the exhibition rooms would be converted to a reading room for me. This was shocking enough, but not as crudely amusing as the time when the woman head of the archives in Alabama told me that *she* was shocked to discover that despite the fact that I was a "Harvard nigger" (those are her words) I had somehow retained the capacity to be courteous to a southern lady. She ascribed it all to my Tennessee "seasoning" before going into the land of the Yankee!

Many years later, in 1951, while working at the Library of Congress, one of my closest friends, a white historian, came by my study room one Friday afternoon and asked me to lunch with him the following day. I reminded him that since the following day would be a Saturday, the Supreme Court restaurant would be closed, and there was no other place in the vicinity where we could eat together. (This was before the decision in the Thompson restaurant case in April, 1953, which opened Washington restaurants to all well-behaved persons.) My friend pointed out that he knew I spent Saturdays at the Library, and he wondered what I did for food on those days. I told him that I seldom missed a Saturday of research and writing at the Library of Congress, but that my program for that day was a bit different from other days. On Saturdays, I told him, I ate a huge late breakfast at home and then brought a piece of fruit or candy to the Library, which I would eat at the lunch hour. Then, when I could bear the hunger no longer during the afternoon, I would leave and go home to an early dinner. His only remark was that he doubted very much whether, if he were a Negro, he would be a scholar, if it required sacrifices such as this and if life was as inconvenient as it appeared. I assured him that for a Negro scholar searching for truth, the search for food in the city of Washington was one of the *minor* inconveniences.

These incidents point up not only the distress caused by physical inconveniences but also the dilemma of the scholar who, first of all, would persevere in remaining some kind of a scholar and, secondly, would remain true to the rigid requirements of equanimity, dispassion, and objectivity. To the first dilemma, the true scholar who is a Negro has no more choice than the Negro who is a true painter, musician, novelist. If he is committed to the world of scholarship, as a critic, sociologist, economist, historian, he *must* pursue truth in his field; he *must*, as it were, ply his trade. For scholarship involves a dedication and a commitment as truly as does any other pursuit in the life of the mind. If one tried to escape, as my white historian friend declares that he would, he would be haunted by the urge to fulfill his aspirations in the field of his choice; and he would be satisfied in no other pursuit. If he could indeed become satisfied by running away from his field, it is certain that there was no commitment and dedication in the first place. Thus, the true scholar who is a Negro has no real choice but to remain in his field, to "stick to his knitting," to persevere.

But in the face of forces that deny him membership in the mainstream of American scholarship and that suggest that he is unable to perform creditably, the task of remaining calm and objective is indeed a formidable one. There is always the temptation to pollute his scholarship with polemics, diatribes, arguments. This is especially true if the area of his interests touches on the great questions in which he is personally involved as a Negro. If he yields to this attractive temptation, he can by one act destroy his effectiveness and disqualify himself as a true and worthy scholar. He should know that by maintaining the highest standards of scholarship he not only becomes worthy but also sets an example that many of his contemporaries who claim to be the arbiters in the field do not themselves follow.

It is, of course, asking too much of the Negro scholar to demand that he remain impervious and insensitive to the forces that seek to destroy his dignity and self-respect. He must, therefore, be permitted to function as vigorously as his energies and resources allow, in order to elevate himself and those of his group to a position where they will be accepted and respected in the American social order. This involves a recognition of the difference between scholarship and advocacy. On the one hand, the Negro scholar must use his scholarship to correct the findings of pseudo-psychologists and sociologists regarding Negro intelligence, Negro traits, and the alleged Negro propensity for crime. He must rewrite the history of this country and correct the misrepresentations and falsifications in connection with the Negro's role in our history. He must provide the social engineers with the facts of the Negro ghetto, the overt and the subtle discriminations inflicted on the Negro in almost every aspect of his existence, the uses and misuses of political and economic power to keep the Negro in a subordinate position in American life. There is also a place for advocacy, so long as the Negro scholar understands the difference. Recognizing the importance of the use of objective data in the passionate advocacy of the rectification of injustice, the Negro can assume this additional role for his own sake and for the sake of the community. When I wrote the first working paper to be used in the briefs of the National Association for the Advancement of Colored People in their school desegregation arguments, I was flattered when the chief counsel, Thurgood Marshall, told me that the paper sounded very much like a lawyer's brief. I had deliberately transformed the objective data provided by historical research into an urgent plea for justice; and I hoped that my scholarship did not suffer.

When such an opportunity does not present itself, there is still another way to keep one's scholarly work from being polluted by passion—namely, by blowing off steam in literary efforts. A few examples will suffice: Several years ago, while waiting in the segregated Atlanta railway station, I was so mortified and touched by the barbaric treatment of Negro passengers by railway officials and city policemen that I immediately sat down and wrote a piece called "DP's in Atlanta," in which I drew some comparisons between the treatment of these Negroes and the treatment of displaced refugees in Nazi-occupied countries during World War II. After that, I was able to go out to Atlanta University and give the series of lectures that I had been invited to deliver.

On another occasion I had a further opportunity to engage in some writing that was not particularly a scholarly effort; at the same time, it did not seem necessary to deny its authorship. In 1959, I was invited to give the Lincoln sesquicentennial lecture for the Chicago Historical

Society. En route I went into the diner for my evening meal just before the crowd arrived. I thus had a choice seat, at a table for four. Soon the diner was filled and a long line of people was waiting at the entrance—singly and in groups of twos and fours. They all declined to join me, and I sat in splendid isolation for the better part of an hour. As places became vacant near me they took their seats, and I was able to hear their orders to the waiters as well as their conversations with their new companions. When I returned to my compartment, I wrote a short piece called "They All Ordered Fish." You see, it was Ash Wednesday, and these Christian ladies and gentlemen were beginning their forty days of commemoration of the agony of their Lord, Jesus Christ. Neither "DP's in Atlanta" nor "They All Ordered Fish" has ever been published. They remain in the uncollected papers of a Negro scholar who has faced his share of dilemmas.

I suspect that such a repression of one's true feelings would not be satisfying to some, and it may even be lacking in courage. I do not commend it; I merely confess it. It is doubtless a temporary escape from the painful experience of facing the dilemma and making the choice that every Negro scholar must sooner or later make. For the major choice for the Negro scholar is whether he should turn his back on the world, concede that he is the Invisible Man, and lick the wounds that come from cruel isolation, or whether he should use his training, talents, and resources to beat down the barriers that keep him out of the mainstream of American life and scholarship. The posing of the question, it seems, provides the setting for the answer. I have said that the American scholar has been drawn irresistibly into the mainstream of American life, and has contributed his knowledge and ingenuity to the solution of the major problems his country has faced. I now assert that the proper choice for the American Negro scholar is to use his knowledge and ingenuity, his resources and talents, to combat the forces that isolate him and his people and, like the true patriot that he is, to contribute to the solution of the problems that all Americans face in common.

This is not a new and awesome prospect for the Negro. He has had to fight for the right to assist in the defense of his country when his country was locked in mortal struggle with its enemies. He has had to fight for the right to discharge his obligations as a voting citizen. He has had to fight for the right to live in a community in order to help improve that community. It is the same wherever one looks—in education, employment, recreation, scholarship. It is, therefore, a goodly company the American Negro scholar joins as he chooses to make of the course he pursues a battleground for truth *and* justice. On the one hand, he joins those of his own color who seek to make democracy work. On the other hand, he joins his intellectual kinsmen of whatever race in the worthy task of utilizing the intellectual resources of the country for its own improvement. A happier choice could hardly be made. A happier prospect for success, even in the face of untold difficulties, could hardly be contemplated.

The Historian and the
Public Policy

Many years ago the distinguished American historian Carl Becker wrote an essay entitled "Everyman His Own Historian." From the title one might get the impression that Professor Becker was offering to surrender the field that he had mined so well and so successfully to anyone who might come along and claim it. That was not the case! What Professor Becker was actually conceding was that every person had some notion—indeed, to that person a rather clear notion—of what history actually is. I tend to agree with him, for the historian's experience is a confirmation of his assertion. Let a person move into a group of people and be introduced as an historian; and someone will raise a question that he knows is at least as profound as any that Socrates ever raised. To the historian it will sound like "Please, Sir, say something historical!" The actual words, carefully articulated, will be, "Please, Sir, tell me what the next four years will provide in the way of history." It is no use to reply, "I am not a soothsayer; I am an historian." For the reply is likely to be, "That is precisely why I put the question to you and not to someone else."

The general public is not altogether responsible for developing some rather strange and quite unlikely notions of the role of the historian in society. Indeed, some of the ablest and most successful members of the craft have contributed significantly to the development of such notions. In seeking to serve a worthy public purpose, they have used their historical materials to serve a special interest or point of view when it seemed desirable to do so. When the United States was young and needed a sense of unity and national destiny, it was the historian who stepped forward to serve that need. Thus, George Bancroft, one of the

This essay was originally the 1974 Nora and Edward Ryerson Lecture at the University of Chicago and is published here with the permission of the University of Chicago.

earliest historians of the new nation described the founding of the American colonies in a special way when he said, "Tyranny and injustice peopled America with men nurtured in suffering and adversity. The history of our colonization is the history of the crimes of Europe." Just to make certain that he would be successful in rallying the people around the new republic's standard, he declared that the American Revolution was for "the advancement of the principles of everlasting peace and universal brotherhood. A new plebeian democracy took its place by the side of the proudest empires. Religion was disenthralled from civil institutions. . . . Industry was commissioned to follow the bent of its own genius."

Likewise, when there was a need to promote the interests of a particular political party, the historian was available to promulgate the virtues of one party and to impugn the integrity of the other. In his book *Jefferson and Hamilton: The Struggle for Democracy in America*, Claude Bowers was not so much interested in democratic institutions as he was in the immaculate conception and virtuous history of the Democratic party. In portraying Alexander Hamilton, the first secretary of the treasury, as a greater beast than Hamilton ever said the people were, and in describing Jefferson, the first secretary of state, as the able and selfless architect of a democratic coalition to save the nation from the treacherous federalists, Bowers served the Democratic party well. When one recalls that Franklin D. Roosevelt appointed Bowers United States Ambassador to Chile, it can hardly be said that partisan history does not have its own rewards!

In virtually every area where evidence from the past is needed to support the validity of a given proposition, an historian can be found who will provide the evidence that is needed. This is as true in a discussion of whether democratic institutions had their origins in the German forests or on the American frontier as it is in the search for a valid historical explanation for the foibles and idiosyncrasies that characterize race relations in the United States. One final example will suffice. Historians have usually been prepared to provide facile and quick explanations for the subordinate place of Negroes in American life. Some have assumed the role of physical anthropologists or biologists and have argued that blacks occupy a lowly place because of their tragically innate inferiority. Others have become, for the moment, sociologists and have argued that the structure of American society calls for homogeneity or complete assimilation, or at least a move in that direction, for which blacks could not in any case qualify. Still others have been content with the explanation advanced by a noted historian of the southern United States, Ulrich B. Phillips, regarded by some as the greatest historian the South has produced. In his "The Central Theme of Southern History," Phillips declared that the unifying principle of southern history has been "the common resolve indomitably maintained" by the white man that the South "shall be and remain a white man's country. . . . The consciousness of a function in these premises, whether expressed with the frenzy of a demagogue or maintained with a patrician's quietude, is the cardinal test of a Southerner and the central theme of southern history." He of course meant a white southerner, ignoring the fact that there were almost as many black southerners.

But one must attempt to distinguish between the historian's role, on the one hand, in supporting causes or offering explanations *after the fact* and, on the other, of trying to assist in the search for solutions to difficult problems in the area of public policy. It seems to me that one role is essentially partisan and defensive, while the other is more interested in *how* historical events can provide some basis for desirable change. It is a distinction that may not always seem clear to some or, indeed, may not even be regarded as defensible. It is one, however, that can provide a basis for a discussion of the historian and public policy issues.

The role of the historian in public policy issues in the United States was suggested as early as 1908 in an important case that Louis D. Brandeis argued before the United States Supreme Court. In claiming that states had the power to prescribe maximum hours of employment for women in laundries, Brandeis, who would later sit on the United States Supreme Court, presented an enormous brief that not only pointed to the unique characteristics of the woman's physique, but the historic role of women in society. Even if the Brandeis brief would not impress the leaders of the women's liberation movement in the 1970s or 1980s, it had a profound effect on the justices of the Supreme Court in 1908. From that point on, as the Court decided for the women in this case, historical as well as sociological evidence was regarded as admissible in crucial legal and constitutional questions having to do with the human condition.

Almost fifty years after Brandeis made his presentation to the United States Supreme Court, that high judicial body had a profound influence on the emergence of the historian as an important participant in the determination of public policy issues. In seeking a basis for

311

deciding the grave constitutional questions raised in the school desegregation cases in 1953 the Court asked several questions of counsel
that historians were better prepared to answer than any other social
scientists. The crucial argument by counsel for the children who
sought to break down segregation in the public schools was that racial
segregation was a violation of the Fourteenth Amendment to the Constitution that provided equal protection of the laws for all persons,
regardless of race. The crucial question raised by the Court in attempting to render a decision was, "What evidence is there that the Congress
which submitted and the State legislatures and conventions which
ratified the Fourteenth Amendment [in 1868] contemplated or did not
contemplate, understood or did not understand, that it would abolish
[racial] segregation in public schools?" The Court also wanted to know
from counsel whether if neither the Congress nor the states understood that the Fourteenth Amendment required the immediate abolition of segregation in public schools, it was the understanding of the
framers of the amendment that future Congresses might have the
power to abolish such segregation or whether the Court could construe
the amendment as abolishing such segregation of its own force?

These searching and quite difficult questions sent legal counsel
scurrying not to the history books but to the historians! The NAACP
Legal Defense Fund provided the principal counsel for the plaintiffs. It
recognized the crucial importance of the questions raised by the Court
and consequently the defense fund assembled a half-dozen or so specialists in the period to come up with the answers. It was the historians
who went scurrying to the sources, to read the minutes of the 1865–
1866 Joint Committee on Reconstruction, the debates in Congress and
in the legislatures that ratified the Fourteenth Amendment, the private correspondence of key figures of the Reconstruction period after
the Civil War, and to survey public reaction and response to the events
in Washington and the several states. The historians wrote at least a
score of working papers for legal counsel, had innumerable con-
ferences and seminars for the legal staff, and made themselves available for questions as well as additional assignments coming out of the
discussions.

The historians and the lawyers were an unusually effective team.
The historians provided data that traced the evolution of the concept of
equality, with its culmination in the writing and ratification of the
Fourteenth Amendment. They showed how the pre–Civil War views of
the radical abolitionists dominated the egalitarian thinking of the

framers of the Fourteenth Amendment. They were able to show, more-over, how the intent of the framers of the amendment had been frus-trated and vitiated by the separate-but-equal doctrine which, the law-yers contended, was conceived in error. (This doctrine had been set forth by the Supreme Court in 1896 when the justices said that there was no violation in segregating people by race as long as facilities were equal.) The lawyers were then able to take the materials provided by the historians, place them in their legal setting, and by tracing legal precedents as well as changes in the political and social climate, argue quite convincingly that the *original intent* of the Fourteenth Amend-ment had indeed been nullified by the actions of its enemies, who were racial segregationists.

Using the findings of the historians, the lawyers argued that the "history of segregation laws reveals that their main purpose was to organize the community upon the basis of a superior white and an inferior Negro caste." Then, using the Court's own position in the case involving the enforceability of restrictive covenants that sought to achieve racial segregation in housing, the lawyers themselves sounded very much like historians when they said, "History buttresses and gives particular content to the recent admonition of this Court that 'whatever else the framers [of the Fourteenth Amendment] sought to achieve, it is clear that the matter of primary concern was the estab-lishment of equality in the enjoyment of basic civil and political rights and the preservation of those rights from discriminatory action on the part of the States based on considerations of race and color.'" The historians had found the lawyers to be apt, even adroit students of history!

It is not possible, of course, to assess the influence of the historians' findings on the Court's decision to outlaw segregation in the public schools. Perhaps its influence was great, perhaps not. In accepting the arguments of other social scientists that segregation did permanent psychological damage to the pupils, the Court—or more properly, the public reaction to the Court's decision—obscured the other influences that may have been present. But the Court had asked questions that only historians could answer; and deciding in favor of the plaintiffs, the Court also decided in favor of the historians. Under the circumstances the temptation is great indeed to argue that the historians played an important part in deciding the issue of segregation in the public schools. In any event, they had answered the call to participate in an important public policy issue; and it would seem that their participa-

tion had been effective. The more aggressive historians who participated in the case were not at all modest in the claims they made that
they contributed substantially to the decision that ended legal segregation by race in the nation's public schools.

The dispute over segregation in the late 1940s and early 1950s
brought forth another quite unique use of historical evidence in the
effort to break both the law and the custom of segregation. As some
Americans began to inveigh against racial segregation and to fight it in
public discussion as well as in the courts, other Americans contended
that racial segregation was *so deeply imbedded* in American ethos and
practice that it was virtually ineradicable. They assumed that things
had always been that way. "Or if not always, then 'since slavery times,'
or 'since The War,' or 'since Reconstruction.'" Some even thought of
the system of racial segregation as existing along with African slavery.
It was the distinguished historian of the southern United States,
C. Vann Woodward, who, recognizing the distortions and inaccuracies
that arose from such assumptions, decided to try to set the record
straight. If he could show that much of the legal segregation of the
races was of relatively recent origin, then those who defended it could
not fall back on the specious argument that things had always been
that way.

Woodward decided to do what no proponents of segregation had ever
bothered to do, or, for that matter, what no opponents of segregation
had done. He went back to the historical record and examined the
origins of some of the segregationist laws and practices. He did not
attempt to show that there had been *no* legal segregation until late in
the nineteenth century. The time-honored practice of racial segregation in schools, churches, and the army clearly indicated that *some*
segregation had existed much earlier. Nor was he interested, in this
instance, in writing a definitive history of racial segregation. Much
more research than he had done would be required for such an undertaking. He was content to make a modest contribution to the current
debate by suggesting that segregation was neither as universal in origin
nor as venerable in age as many on both sides of the argument assumed
that it was. Because of the lack of basic research in the field, he believed
that he would make mistakes; and he welcomed corrections on the
part of his readers.

Woodward's book, *The Strange Career of Jim Crow,* is a notable
example of the historian's participation in public policy issues. As brief
as it is, it has much to say about the uneven hand with which the South

meted out its laws to disfranchise, segregate, and create a permanently subordinate Negro caste. Those who argued that blacks had not voted in any elections since Reconstruction ended in 1877 seemed quite unaware of the fact that several blacks were elected to the United States Congress in the 1890s and that literally hundreds of blacks held local elective offices in many parts of the southern United States as late as 1900. Those who claimed that the Democratic party had always been the white man's party exclusively did not know that some blacks, at the urging of whites, voted the Democratic ticket until the end of the century or that the Democratic white primary is a twentieth-century phenomenon, or aberration or, if you will, monstrosity. Those who said that the races had always been separated did not understand that some states did not adopt laws to segregate the races on railroad trains and in waiting rooms until the end of the century and that the bulk of the segregation statutes date from the 1890s or later.

Woodward did not deny the existence of widespread anti-Negro feeling, better known as Negrophobia, or long-held views of Negro inferiority. These were indisputable facts which no amount of research or arguing could eradicate; and he did not desire to do so. As a matter of fact, he *did* see an increase in Negrophobia, brought on by uncertainties and anxieties in the political and economic spheres. He *did* see that the belief in Negro inferiority had been bolstered by those who subscribed to social Darwinism as well as social and political demagoguery. But what he saw most clearly and what he wanted his contemporaries to see was that the arguments favoring the sanctity and veneration of segregation could not prevail because they were not grounded in fact and that segregation was merely another gambit in the South's determination to have its own way in the crucial matter of race relations. The South, moreover, was ambivalent, uncertain, shifty, and unclear. Today, there was no segregation; tomorrow there would be. What was true in one county was not necessarily true in another. The laws in one state were quite different from the laws in another state. In the face of all this, it was difficult to argue that segregation had always been and always would be. Racists would have to find some other argument, one that had some shred of validity and credibility in their desperate attempt to hold onto segregation. Woodward believed that they would not be able to find it.

Indeed, as Woodward expected, there were those who criticized him, primarily for not doing what he did not undertake to do—namely, to prove that there had been no segregation until the 1890s. Others

315

gleefully called attention to some early segregation statute that he had overlooked or that he did not know existed. I recall one of my own students who, with great delight, informed me that he had just discovered that Raleigh, North Carolina, had racially segregated cemeteries in 1865 and that "poor" Professor Woodward apparently knew nothing about them. I said that in all probability he did not know about Raleigh cemeteries; then I asked my student to go and reread Woodward's preface to *The Strange Career of Jim Crow.* Such findings detracted little from Woodward's argument that segregation statutes and practices were uneven and that most of the laws came much later.

There is no way of knowing what effect Woodward's book had on the dispute that was raging when he wrote it. One doubts that it converted many segregationists or that it persuaded many legislators to believe that they could safely vote to repeal laws that separated the races. It was, nevertheless, a significant contribution to the discussion and, perhaps, helped to prepare the ground when the segregation statutes slipped largely into disuse after the passage of the Civil Rights Act of 1964. Whenever a Negro American traveled in the South after 1964 and noticed the range of services available to him in hotels, restaurants, and other places of public accommodation, he would perhaps be inclined to challenge William Graham Sumner's 1907 dictum that "stateways cannot change folkways." He might also be inclined to agree with C. Vann Woodward who had argued a decade earlier that since segregation statutes were neither very old nor very sacred, it made no sense to argue that they could never be changed.

The area in which the historian participates in public policy issues has grown enormously in recent years, thanks to the increasing use made of historians by the several levels of government. Today virtually every department in the executive branch of the United States government has its staff of historians, ranging from the highly esteemed branch of historical policy research in the department of state to the rather modest historical section in the National Park Service in the department of the interior. These persons, many of whom are very talented and highly trained, perform yeoman service in their roles as participants in policy formulation and decision-making in their respective departments. It is, of course, important that the department of state have experts who can provide the historical background of United States foreign policy in, say, Southeast Asia or western Europe or South America. It is likewise important that the National Park Service know something of, say, the land conservation policies and the way they were administered before the park service came into formal existence in 1916. These, however, are essentially service functions; and the historians who perform them have a relationship to their departments that is understandably supportive of the team to which they belong. It is no reflection on the ability or integrity of official historians if one should assert that their independence in speaking out on controversial public policy issues is quite limited, especially if their views do not coincide with those of their departments.

It would seem highly important, therefore, that historians with *no* governmental connections should participate in the discussion of public policy issues, using that independence of mind and spirit that their private position affords. Indeed, from their relatively detached position, they could engage, challenge, and debate their governmental colleagues who are a part of the apparatus where public policy is determined. The outsiders could raise questions about the operation of a given policy that is defended on the ground that it is in line with historic public policy in that area. Indeed, and by the same token, the outsiders could challenge the traditional public policy if on the basis of their examination of the record they find it to be out of line with current interests and needs. They, most of all, could challenge the sanctity and validity of a traditional policy that is followed for the sake of tradition and not necessarily for the sake of the public interest.

I do not know how many historians there are today in the Bureau of Indian Affairs, which is a part of the department of the interior. A decade ago, when several Indian tribes were suing the United States government to recover many millions of dollars from proceeds of oil lands that the Indians claimed as theirs, the bureau became suddenly conscious of the value of historians in supporting or challenging the claims of the Indians. The government had its historians, and the Indians had theirs. The result was a very lively debate, not altogether uncongenial but terribly expensive, over the relative merits of the Indian claims. The tribes recovered enormous sums through the courts, on the basis of the evidence that historians provided regarding treaty claims.

One wonders if the Bureau of Indian Affairs continues to have an appreciation of how historians can assist in the formulation of public policy regarding these first Americans. The history of American Indian policy is itself not only sordid but enormously complicated in every possible way. The government has vacillated between a policy of intransigent hostility and one of fawning paternalism and back again.

Indians have been "Uncle Sam's Step-children," "The noble Savages," and the enemies of progress who in the eyes of some would better be dead because they are red. Somewhere, there needs to be a recognition and understanding of the extent of and the reasons for vacillation in public policy in this area. Encroachments on Indian lands, the unilateral abrogation of treaties with the Indians, and barbaric massacres of thousands of Indians by white men are factors that must be considered. The recent confrontation between Indians in South Dakota and the United States government is a clear example of the need to examine past relations and problems as a first step toward resolving the impasse. If the historians in the bureau cannot or will not indicate how and why these shifts in policy add up to a monumentally immoral public posture, then historians outside the bureau should have the temerity and the courage to do so. This is not to suggest that there is justification and defense for the actions of American Indians in seizing the rock of Alcatraz in San Francisco harbor or in seizing the office of the bureau itself or in taking over the South Dakota reservation. It is to suggest that the historic shifts, uncertainties, and vacillations have served to exacerbate the situation unduly and have driven reasonable men to violence. It is the role of the detached, independent historian to point out the historic fallacies in American public policy in this crucially important area.

Few areas, if any, are more important than foreign policy in the requirement that public policy issues reflect the highest integrity in their resolution and formulation. Likewise, few areas, if any, are more in need of the perspective and critical evaluation that historians can provide. Not that the United States needs to be saved from isolationism, for it has really never been isolationist. Not that it needs to be reminded of its role as keepers of the peace, for it has never been successfully cast in such a role. Not that it needs to be kept mindful of its duty as protector of the national rights and territorial integrity of the smaller nations, for it has never consistently functioned in that role. Most of all, the issues of foreign policy of the United States or, indeed, of any nation, need to be regularly reexamined in order to define, more precisely, what its posture should be toward other nations. What is the historian's role in such an examination?

In foreign policy, perhaps more than in any other area, the world's leaders tend to speak of their own nation's historical role in encouraging peoples of the world to become self-governing and to seek the paths of peace. Quite frequently, they summon the events of the past to support their current posture. Almost invariably, it is a misleading posture. Britain was not seeking to encourage self-government in India during her several centuries of control of the subcontinent. The Soviet Union can hardly be accused of protecting the right of self-government in its move into Hungary in 1956. The United States had no deep interest in the self-government of Haiti when the Marines moved into that country in 1916 and remained there for eighteen years. Without emphasizing unnecessarily the moral dimensions of the foreign policy of nations, it is reasonable to assert that the historians ought at least to keep the record straight and make an attempt to keep their nations honest by calling attention to the disparity between historical assertions on the one hand and the facts of history on the other.

One supposes that every nation in the world wants to be regarded as peace-loving and pursues a foreign policy well calculated to preserve the peace. It is so easy for a nation to slip into a warlike posture with the claim that it has to do so in order to maintain the peace. The United States has done it many times, both in the past century and in the present one. So have many other nations. It is comfortable for a nation to assume such a high-minded posture. But there is no guarantee that the claim of being a lover of the peace and a keeper of the peace is, in fact, an accurate statement of a nation's foreign policy position. Thus, the United States has been involved in no less than seven major foreign wars since the beginning of the nineteenth century. This is not to argue that such a record qualifies the United States as a warmonger, but the record of having to resort to war so often in order to keep the peace does not qualify it as a peacemonger, either. In going to war so often in the name of peace, freedom, and democratic institutions, the record is a most difficult one to defend. The historian cannot and should not have any interest in defending such a role if, indeed, the facts suggest that innumerable considerations entered into the decision to fight not only peoples in distant lands but nearby neighbors as well.

As a nation views its history and the various positions that it has taken, it is not difficult to conclude that its postures have been mixed and exist on several levels of morality. At times, in the case of the United States, at least, its public policy has been humane, healthy, and worthy; at other times, it has been bereft of many or any praiseworthy objectives. It is the function of the historian to keep before the people, with as much clarity as possible, the different lines of action that have been taken, the several, often complicated reasons for such action, and to point to the conflicts and inconsistencies, the contradictions and illogicalities, and to the defects and deficiencies when they exist. One might argue that the historian is the conscience of his nation, if honesty and consistency are factors that nurture the conscience. Perhaps that is too much to claim for the historian who, after all, is not in the business of protecting the morals of a people. But the historian, as the servant of the past, is in the best position to provide a rational basis for present actions.

The people, yes the people, shall judge; but they require a sound basis for making judgments. They will have that basis if and when they know what has happened, why it has happened, and, consequently, how the public policies growing out of historical events or shaping those events can serve the common good. If, then, they prefer to ignore their past mistakes and prefer to live in a world of fantasy and make-believe, they will deserve to suffer the fate of repeating the grave errors that they could easily have avoided.

Ethnicity in American Life:
The Historical Perspective

The United States is unique in the ethnic composition of its population. No other country in the world can point to such a variety of cultural, racial, religious, and national backgrounds in its population. It was one of the salient features in the early history of this country; and it would continue to be so down into the twentieth century. From virtually every corner of the globe they came—some enthusiastically and some quite reluctantly. Britain and every part of the continent of Europe provided prospective Americans by the millions. Africa and Asia gave up great throngs. Other areas of the New World saw inhabitants desert their own lands to seek their fortunes in the colossus to the North. Those who came voluntarily were attracted by the prospect of freedom of religion, freedom from want, and freedom from various forms of oppression. Those who were forced to come were offered the consolation that if they were white they would some day inherit the earth, and if they were black they would some day gather their reward in the Christian heaven.

One of the interesting and significant features of this coming together of peoples of many tongues and races and cultures was that the backgrounds out of which they came would soon be minimized and that the process by which they evolved into Americans would be of paramount importance. Hector St. Jean de Crevecoeur sought to describe this process in 1782 when he answered his own question, "What, then, is the American, this new man?" He said, "He is either an European, or the descendant of an European, hence that strange mixture of blood, which you will find in no other country. . . . He is an American, who, leaving behind him all his ancient prejudices and manners, receives new ones from the new mode of the life he has

Originally published in Anti-Defamation League, *Ethnicity in American Life* (New York, 1971).

embraced, the new government he obeys, and the new rank he holds. He becomes an American by being received in the broad lap of our great *Alma Mater.* Here individuals of all nations are melted into a new race of men, whose labours and posterity will one day cause great changes in the world."

This was one of the earliest expressions of the notion that the process of Americanization involved the creation of an entirely new mode of life that would replace the ethnic backgrounds of those who were a part of the process. It contained some imprecisions and inaccuracies that would, in time, became a part of the lore or myth of the vaunted melting pot and would grossly misrepresent the crucial factor of ethnicity in American life. It ignored the tenacity with which the Pennsylvania Dutch held onto their language, religion, and way of life. It overlooked the way in which the Swedes of New Jersey remained Swedes and the manner in which the French Huguenots of New York and Charleston held onto their own past as though it was the source of all light and life. It described a process that in a distant day would gag at the notion that Irish Catholics could be assimilated on the broad lap of Alma Mater or that Asians could be seated on the basis of equality at the table of the Great American Feast.

By suggesting that only Europeans were involved in the process of becoming Americans, Crevecoeur pointedly ruled out three quarters of a million blacks already in the country who, along with their progeny, would be regarded as ineligible to become Americans for at least another two centuries. To be sure, the number of persons of African descent would increase enormously, but the view of their ineligibility for Americanization would be very slow to change. And when such a change occurred, even if it merely granted freedom from bondage, the change would be made most reluctantly and without any suggestion that freedom qualified one for equality on the broad lap of Alma Mater. It was beyond the conception of Crevecoeur, as it was indeed beyond the conception of the founding fathers, that Negroes, slave or free, could become true Americans, enjoying that fellowship in a common enterprise about which Crevecoeur spoke so warmly. It was as though Crevecoeur was arguing that ethnicity, where persons of African descent were concerned, was either so powerful or so unattractive as to make their assimilation entirely impossible or so insignificant as to make it entirely undesirable. In any case Americanization in the late eighteenth century was a precious commodity to be cherished and enjoyed only by a select group of persons of European descent.

One must admit, therefore, that at the time of the birth of the new nation there was no clear-cut disposition to welcome into the American family persons of any and all ethnic backgrounds. Only Europeans were invited to fight for independence. And when the patriots at long last relented and gave persons of African descent a chance to fight, the concession was made with great reluctance and after much equivocation and soul-searching. Only Europeans were regarded as full citizens in the new states and in the new nation. And when the founding fathers wrote the Constitution of the United States, they did not seem troubled by the distinctions on the basis of ethnic differences that the Constitution implied.

If the principle of ethnic exclusiveness was propounded so early and so successfully in the history of the United States, it is not surprising that it would, in time, become the basis for questioning the ethnic backgrounds of large numbers of prospective Americans, even Europeans. Thus, in 1819, a Jewish immigrant was chilled to hear a bystander refer to him and his companion as "more damned emigrants." A decade later there began a most scathing and multifaceted attack on the Catholic church. On two counts the church was a bad influence. First, its principal recruits were the Irish, the "very dregs" of the Old World social order; and secondly, its doctrine of papal supremacy ran counter to the idea of the political and religious independence of the United States. Roman Catholics, Protestant Americans warned, were engaged in a widespread conspiracy to subvert American institutions, through parochial schools, the Catholic press, immoral convents, and a sinister design to control the West by flooding it with Catholic settlers. The burning of convents and churches and the killing of Catholics themselves were indications of how deeply many Americans felt about religious and cultural differences for which they had a distaste and suspicion that bordered on paranoia.

Soon the distaste for the foreign-born became almost universal, with Roman Catholics themselves sharing in the hostility to those who followed them to the new Republic. Some expressed fear of the poverty and criminality that accompanied each wave of immigrants. Some felt that those newly arrived from abroad were a threat to republican freedom. Some saw in the ethnic differences of the newcomers an immediate danger to the moral standards of Puritan America. Some feared the competition that newcomers posed in the labor market. Some became convinced that the ideal of a national homogeneity would disappear with the influx of so many unassimilable elements. Soon, nativist societies sprang up all across the land, and they found national expression in 1850 in a new organization called the Order of the Star Spangled Banner. With its slogan, "America for Americans," the order, which became the organizational basis for the Know-Nothing party, engendered a fear through its preachments that caused many an American to conclude that his country was being hopelessly subverted by the radical un-Americanism of the great variety of ethnic strains that were present in the United States.

If there was some ambivalence regarding the ethnic diversity of white immigrants before the Civil War, it was dispelled by the view that prevailed regarding immigrants in the post–Civil War years. The "old" immigrants, so the argument went, were at least assimilable and had "entered practically every line of activity in nearly every part of the country." Even those who had been non-English speaking had mingled freely with native Americans and had therefore been quickly assimilated. Not so with the "new" immigrants who came after 1880. They "congregated together in sections apart from native Americans and the older immigrants to such an extent that assimilation had been slow." Small wonder that they were different. Small wonder that they were barely assimilable. They came from Austro-Hungary, Italy, Russia, Greece, Rumania, and Turkey. They dressed differently, spoke in unfamiliar tongues, and clung to strange, if not exotic customs. It did not matter that Bohemians, Moravians, and Finns had lower percentages of illiteracy than had the Irish and Germans or that Jews had a higher percentage of skilled laborers than any group except the Scots. Nor did it matter that, in fact, the process of assimilation for the so-called "new" group was about as rapid as that of the so-called "old" group.

What did matter was that the new nativism was stronger and more virulent than any anti-immigration forces or groups of the early nineteenth century and that these groups were determined either to drive from the shores those who were different or to isolate them so that they could not contaminate American society. Old-stock Americans began to organize to preserve American institutions and the American way of life. Those who had been here for five years or a decade designated themselves as old-stock Americans and joined in the attack on those recently arrived. If the cult of Anglo-Saxon superiority was all but pervasive, those who were not born into the cult regarded themselves as honorary members. Thus, they could celebrate with as much feeling as any the virtues of Anglo-Saxon institutions and could condemn as vehemently as any those ideas and practices that were not strictly

Anglo-Saxon. Whenever possible they joined the American Protective Association and the Immigrant Restriction League; and in so doing they sold their own ethnicity for the obscurity that a pseudo-assimilation brought. But in the end, they would be less than successful. The arrogance and presumption of the Anglo-Saxon complex was not broad enough to embrace the Jews of eastern Europe or the Bohemians of central Europe or the Turks of the Middle East. The power and drive of the Anglo-Saxon forces would prevail; and those who did not belong would be compelled to console themselves by extolling the virtues of cultural pluralism.

By that time—near the end of the nineteenth century—the United States had articulated quite clearly its exalted standards of ethnicity. They were standards that accepted Anglo-Saxons as the norm, placed other whites on what may be called "ethnic probation," and excluded from serious consideration the Japanese, Chinese, and Negroes. It was not difficult to deal harshly with the Chinese and Japanese when they began to enter the United States in considerable numbers in the post–Civil War years. They simply did not meet the standards that the arbiters of American ethnicity had promulgated. They were different in race, religion, language, and public and private morality. They had to be excluded; and eventually they were.

The presence of persons of African descent, almost from the beginning, had helped whites to define ethnicity and to establish and maintain the conditions by which it could be controlled. If their color and race, their condition of servitude, and their generally degraded position did not set them apart, the laws and customs surrounding them more than accomplished that feat. Whether in Puritan Massachusetts or cosmopolitan New York or Anglican South Carolina, the colonists declared that Negroes, slave or free, did not and could not belong to the society of equal human beings. Thus, the newly arrived Crevecoeur could be as blind to the essential humanity of Negroes as the patriots who tried to keep them out of the Continental Army. They were not a part of America, these new men. And in succeeding years their presence would do more to define ethnicity than the advent of several scores of millions of Europeans.

It was not enough for Americans, already somewhat guilt-ridden for maintaining slavery in a free society, to exclude blacks from American society on the basis of race and condition of servitude. They proceeded from that point to argue that Negroes were inferior morally, intellectually, and physically. Even as he reviewed the remarkable accomplishments of Benjamin Banneker, surveyor, almanacker, mathematician, and clockmaker, Thomas Jefferson had serious doubts about the mental capabilities of Africans, and he expressed these doubts to his European friends. What Jefferson speculated about at the end of the eighteenth century became indisputable dogma within a decade after his death.

In the South every intellectual, legal, and religious resource was employed in the task of describing the condition of Negroes in such a way as to make them the least attractive human beings on the face of the earth. Slavery was not only the natural lot of blacks, the slaveowners argued, but it was in accordance with God's will that they should be kept in slavery. As one sanctimonious divine put it, "We feel that the souls of our slaves are a solemn trust and we shall strive to present them faultless and complete before the presence of God. . . . However the world may judge us in connection with our institution of slavery, we conscientiously believe it to be a great missionary institution—one arranged by God, as He arranges all moral and religious influences of the world so that the good may be brought out of seeming evil, and a blessing wrung out of every form of the curse." It was a difficult task that the owners of slaves set for themselves. Slaves had brought with them only heathenism, immorality, profligacy, and irresponsibility. They possessed neither the mental capacity nor the moral impulse to improve themselves. Only if their sponsors—those to whom were entrusted not only their souls but their bodies—were fully committed to their improvement could they take even the slightest, halting steps toward civilization.

What began as a relatively moderate justification for slavery soon became a vigorous, aggressive defense of the institution. Slavery, to the latter-day defenders, was the cornerstone of the republican edifice. To a governor of South Carolina, it was the greatest of all the great blessings which a kind Providence had bestowed upon the glorious region of the South. It was, indeed, one of the remarkable coincidences of history that such a favored institution had found such a favored creature as the African to give slavery the high value that was placed on it. A childlike race, prone to docility and manageable in every respect, the African was the ideal subject for the slave role. Slaveholders had to work hard to be worthy of this great Providential blessing.

Nothing that Negroes could do or say could change or seriously affect this view. They might graduate from college as John Russwurm did in 1826, or they might write a most scathing attack against slavery, as David Walker did in 1829. It made no difference. They might teach in an all-white college, as Charles B. Reason did in New York in the 1850s, or publish a newspaper, as Frederick Douglass did during that same decade. Their racial and cultural backgrounds disqualified them from becoming American citizens. They could even argue in favor of their capacities and potentialities as Henry Highland Garnet did, or they might argue their right to fight for union and freedom, as 186,000 did in the Civil War. Still, it made no sense for white Americans to give serious consideration to their arguments and their actions. They were beyond the veil, as the Jews had been beyond the veil in the barbaric and bigoted communities of eastern Europe.

The views regarding Negroes that had been so carefully developed to justify and defend slavery would not disappear with emancipation. To those who had developed such views and to the vast numbers who subscribed to them, they were much too valid to be discarded simply because the institution of slavery had collapsed. In fact, if Negroes were heathens and barbarians and intellectual imbeciles in slavery, they were hardly qualified to function as equals in a free society. And any effort to impose them on a free society should be vigorously and relentlessly resisted, even if it meant that a new and subordinate place for them had to be created.

When Americans set out to create such a place for the four million freedmen after the Civil War, they found that it was convenient to put their formulation in the context of the ethnic factors that militated against complete assimilation. To do it this way seemed more fitting, perhaps even more palatable, for the white members of a so-called free society. And they had some experience on which to rely. In an earlier day it had been the Irish or the Germans or the free Negroes who presented problems of assimilation. They were different in various ways and did not seem to make desirable citizens. In time the Irish, Germans, and other Europeans made it and were accepted on the broad lap of Alma Mater. But not the free Negroes, who continued to suffer disabilities even in the North in the years just before the Civil War. Was this the key to the solution of the postwar problems? Perhaps it was. After all, Negroes had always been a group apart in Boston, New York, Philadelphia, and other northern cities. They all lived together in one part of the city—especially if they could find no other place to live. They had their own churches—after the whites drove them out of theirs. They had their own schools—after they were excluded from the schools attended by whites. They had their own social organizations—after the whites barred them from theirs.

If Negroes possessed so many ethnic characteristics such as living in the same community, having their own churches, schools, and social clubs, and perhaps other agencies of cohesion, that was all very well. They even seemed "happier with their own kind," some patronizing observers remarked. They were like the Germans or the Irish or the Italians or the Jews. They had so much in common and so much to preserve. There was one significant difference, however. For Europeans, the ethnic factors that brought a particular group together actually eased the task of assimilation and, in many ways, facilitated the process of assimilation, particularly as hostile elements sought to disorient them in their drive toward full citizenship. And, in time, they achieved it.

For Negroes, however, such was not the case. They had been huddled together in northern ghettoes since the eighteenth century. They had had their own churches since 1792 and their own schools since 1800. And this separateness, this ostracism, was supported and enforced by the full majesty of the law, state and federal, just to make certain that Negroes did, indeed, preserve their ethnicity! And as they preserved their ethnicity—all too frequently as they looked down the barrel of a policeman's pistol or a militiaman's shotgun—full citizenship seemed many light years away. They saw other ethnic groups pass them by, one by one, and take their places in the sacred Order of the Star Spangled Banner, the American Protective Association, the Knights of the Ku Klux Klan—not always fully assimilated but vehemently opposed to the assimilation of Negroes. The ethnic grouping that was a way station, a temporary resting place for Europeans as they became Americans proved to be a terminal point for blacks who found it virtually impossible to become Americans in any real sense.

There was an explanation or at least a justification for this. The federal government and the state governments had tried to force Negroes into full citizenship and had tried to legislate them into equality with the whites. This was not natural and could not possibly succeed. Negroes had not made it because they were not fit, the social Darwinists said. Negroes were beasts, Charles Carroll declared somewhat inelegantly. "Stateways cannot change folkways," William Graham Sumner, the distinguished scholar, philosophized. The first forty years of Negro freedom had been a failure, said John R. Commons, one of the nation's leading economists. This so-called failure was widely acknowledged in the country as northerners of every rank and description acquiesced, virtually without a murmur of objection, to the southern settlement of the race problem characterized by disfranchisement, segregation, and discrimination.

Here was a new and exotic form of ethnicity. It was to be seen in the badges of inferiority and the symbols of racial degradation that sprang up in every sector of American life—in the exclusion from the polling places with its specious justification that Negroes were unfit to participate in the sacred rite of voting; the back stairway or the freight elevator to public places; the separate, miserable railway car, the separate and hopelessly inferior school; and even the Jim Crow cemetery. Ethnic considerations had never been so important in the shaping of public policy. They had never before been used by the American government to define the role and place of other groups in American society. The United States had labored hard to create order out of its chaotic and diverse ethnic backgrounds. Having begun by meekly suggesting the difficulty in assimilating all groups into one great society, it had acknowledged failure by ruling out one group altogether, quite categorically, and frequently by law, solely on the basis of race.

It could not achieve this without doing irreparable harm to the early notions of the essential unity of America and Americans. The sentiments that promoted the disfranchisement and segregation of Negroes also encouraged the infinite varieties of discrimination against Jews, Armenians, Turks, Japanese, and Chinese. The conscious effort to degrade a particular ethnic group reflects a corrosive quality that dulls the sensitivities of both the perpetrators and the victims. It calls forth venomous hatreds and crude distinctions in high places as well as low places. It can affect the quality of mind of even the most cultivated scholar and place him in a position scarcely distinguishable from the Klansman or worse. It was nothing out of the ordinary, therefore, that at a dinner in honor of the winner of one of Harvard's most coveted prizes, Professor Barrett Wendell warned that if a Negro or a Jew ever won the prize the dinner would have to be canceled.

By the time that the Statue of Liberty was dedicated in 1886 the words of Emma Lazarus on the base of it had a somewhat hollow ring. Could anyone seriously believe that the poor, tired, huddled masses, "yearning to breathe free," were really welcome here? This was a land where millions of black human beings whose ancestors had been here for centuries were consistently treated as pariahs and untouchables!

What interpretation could anyone place on the sentiments expressed on the statue except that the country had no real interest in or sympathy for the downtrodden unless they were white and preferably Anglo-Saxon? It was a disillusioning experience for some newcomers to discover that their own ethnic background was a barrier to success in their adopted land. It was a searing and shattering experience for Negroes to discover over and over again that three centuries of toil and loyalty were nullified by the misfortune of their own degraded ethnic background.

In the fullness of time—in the twentieth century—the nation would confront the moment of truth regarding ethnicity as a factor in its own historical development. Crevecoeur's words would have no real significance. The words of the Declaration of Independence would have no real meaning. The words of Emma Lazarus would not ring true. All such sentiments would be put to the severe test of public policy and private deeds and would be found wanting. The Ku Klux Klan would challenge the moral and human dignity of Jews, Catholics, and Negroes. The quotas of the new immigration laws would define ethnic values in terms of race and national origin. The restrictive covenants would arrogate to a select group of bigots the power of determining what races or ethnic groups should live in certain houses or whether, indeed, they should have any houses at all in which to live. If some groups finally made it through the escape hatch and arrived at the point of acceptance, it was on the basis of race, now defined with sufficient breadth to include all or most peoples who were not of African descent.

By that time ethnicity in American life would come to have a special, clearly definable meaning. Its meaning would be descriptive of that group of people vaguely defined in the federal census returns as "others" or "non-whites." It would have something in common with that magnificent term "cultural pluralism," the consolation prize for those who were not and could not be assimilated. It would signify the same groping for respectability that describes that group of people who live in what is euphemistically called "the inner city." It would represent a rather earnest search for a hidden meaning that would make it seem a bit more palatable and surely more sophisticated than something merely racial. But in 1969 even a little child would know what ethnicity had come to mean.

In its history, ethnicity, in its true sense, has extended and continues to extend beyond race. At times it has meant language, customs, religion, national origin. It has also meant race; and, to some, it has always meant only race. It had already begun to have a racial connotation in the eighteenth century. In the nineteenth century, it had a larger racial component, even as other factors continued to loom large. In the present century, as these other factors have receded in importance, racial considerations have come to have even greater significance. If the history of ethnicity has meant anything at all during the last three centuries, it has meant the gradual but steady retreat from the broad and healthy regard for cultural and racial differences to a narrow, counter-productive concept of differences in terms of whim, intolerance, and racial prejudice. We have come full circle. The really acceptable American is still that person whom Crevecoeur described almost two hundred years ago. But the true American, acceptable or not, is that person who seeks to act out his role in terms of his regard for human qualities irrespective of race. One of the great tragedies of American life at the beginning was that ethnicity was defined too narrowly. One of the great tragedies of today is that this continues to be the case. One can only hope that the nation and its people will all some day soon come to reassess ethnicity in terms of the integrity of the man rather than in terms of the integrity of the race.

The Land of Room Enough

One of the truly great moments in modern history is the peopling of the New World by inhabitants of the Old. And one of the more magnificent themes in that moment is the recurring promise that in the United States there was room enough for all who sought to escape the burdens of class, religious, racial, and other discriminations. At first they came in small numbers, as if to test the viability of a New World civilization. Then, they came in larger numbers, then in droves as they gained faith in the possibility of building a social order to fit their fondest dreams.

It did not matter to the Europeans that this New World was already inhabited and that the inhabitants were faring quite well without any assistance or intervention on the part of the white man. The Powhatans in Virginia, the Pequots in Massachusetts, and the Tuscaroras in the Carolinas were "civilized"—some by a future "official" designation, others by virtue of the state of their development. They had their own way of life, a religion, family life, an economy, and varying stages of political organization. They were more than prepared to pursue their own destiny and to view with some disdain the various Europeans who began to come to the New World in the seventeenth century.

There is no need to quibble over who came first. It could have been an intrepid Genoese sailor, a stout-hearted Scandinavian, or a bold and daring African. They were one in their search for a better life and in their courage to pursue it relentlessly. What is important is the success of Europeans in building a New World civilization that they perceived to be a distinct improvement over what they had left behind, and their

Originally published in *Daedalus*, Vol. CX, No. 2 (Spring, 1981), pp. 1–12. Reprinted by permission of *Daedalus: Journal of the American Academy of Arts and Sciences.*

growing sense of confidence that theirs was superior to anything they found here or anything that was likely to make it to these shores. Consequently they simply appropriated the land with impunity, even if the Pequots or the Tuscaroras or whoever were peacefully settled and cultivating it. Worse still, they sought strenuously to enslave those people, as if it was their sacred duty to bring them under their control to use them for their own purposes. It was best not only for themselves, they reasoned, but for the Indians as well.

What they found here, the Europeans claimed, was a state of heathenism that could not possibly claim respect or even tolerance. The condition of those native to the New World was so abjectly uncivilized as to invite the scorn of its observers, the spread of Christianity, the accumulation of public and private wealth through trade and exploitation, and the "enhancement of national and personal prestige and glory through colonization."[1] Consequently, no serious thought was given to the possibility that native Americans might share equally or even substantially in the social order that grew out of the dreams of Europeans. They would have to wait for centuries before they could even get a hearing before those who presided over the courts that dispensed human justice and equality in the New World.

Europeans were persuaded not only that they were capable of building a civilization that was superior in every respect, but also that they themselves were superior to any of their contemporaries. New England settlers dismissed the hospitality and friendliness of the native Americans as the "Lord's mercy to His Chosen People," rather than native good nature. In general, the New Englanders thought, their genial hosts were trapped in the snare of the Devil, which would explain their unregenerate state.[2] In turn, it would explain the European sense of superiority over the indigenous peoples of the New World and the justification for their taking whatever lands they desired, in the name of Christian civilization.

The protracted contact of Europeans with Africans, beginning in the middle of the sixteenth century, led to generally unfavorable impressions that were to affect black-white relations profoundly from that day to the present. The firmest fact about an African was that he was black. Soon, black became "an emotionally partisan color, the handmaid and symbol of baseness and evil, a sign of danger and repulsion."[3] It was not long before a whole group of unattractive and undesirable qualities were ascribed to Africans, qualities which seemed, for the most part, to be permanent. They were ugly, by reason of color, physiognomy, and hair texture. They were heathens, almost hopelessly so, since their heathenism was tied to their other base qualities. They were savages, and regardless of how different certain groups of them might be from each other, all of them seemed light years behind the English in their stage of civilization. They were lustful and lecherous, and their sexuality was virtually beyond control. Finally, they represented the evil, a spectacle of disobedience for all the world to see, which resulted from the disobedience of Ham, the son of Noah, in begetting a child while in the Ark. This earned his son Canaan and all his descendants the eternal curse of God.[4]

Such were the attitudes of Europeans, especially Englishmen, toward Africans when they came to mainland English America early in the seventeenth century. These attitudes help to explain how Africans slipped almost unnoticed from a status of indentured servitude to one of permanent slavery before the middle of the century. A Virginia magistrate took the fateful step in 1642 when he sentenced two white indentured servants to an additional year of service for running away and a black indentured servant to labor for the remainder of his life for precisely the same offense. In that single decision the judge not only consigned a black man to perpetual slavery but, in the process, began the tradition of the crudest form of racial discrimination that would form so large a part of race relations over the ensuing three centuries. In short order, slavery would be legalized, and slavery would be the lot for most blacks. In due course the body of law imposing distinctions based on African slavery and inevitably on race would grow to the point that it commanded the attention of a large and important section of American jurisprudence.

It is not surprising that the slave code rested securely on the presumption that slavery was the best if not the only condition for Africans. It placed them under the constant supervision of their white masters; and if there was any conceivable good in them, this was easily the very best way of bringing it out. Their every waking hour was spent under the surveillance of the owner or his agent, while their hours of repose were carefully regulated by legislation as well as plantation rules. Meanwhile, the most learned and influential men of the South built up, through their writings and speeches, a most elaborate justification for and defense of Negro slavery. There were, of course, the scriptural defenses based on the curse of Canaan as well as the apparent acceptance of the institution during the pre-Christian *and* Christian eras. These were sufficient to win the support of at least the average God-fearing southerner with or without slaves.[5]

If any doubters remained, they could consult the scientists who argued in their lengthy treatises that certain anatomical attributes of Africans made them suitable for slavery in the South. Dr. Samuel A. Cartwright of New Orleans claimed that blacks could withstand the heat of the sun better than whites because of a peculiarity in the structure of the eye.[6] Dr. Samuel G. Morton of Philadelphia, a noted craniologist, asserted that slavery was an acceptable status for the "pliant Negro, [who] yielding to his fate, and accommodating himself to his condition, bore his heavy burthen with comparative ease."[7] This was because the mean internal capacity of the Negro cranium was less, by twelve cubic inches, than that of the Anglo Saxon. Louis Agassiz, Harvard's eminent naturalist, confirmed Morton's general claim by declaring that development of the brain of an adult Negro "never gets beyond that observable in the Caucasian in boyhood."[8]

Negro slavery, many claimed, was good for all concerned. It provided the slave with the only possible opportunity to become civilized and Christianized, thus bringing under control his lower, savage instincts. Meanwhile, since any society needed workers in order to provide the leisure necessary for the more gifted to elevate the social order, African workers were ideally suited for such function. The now-classic statement made in 1854 by South Carolina's James H. Hammond set forth that position clearly.

> In all social systems, there must be a class to do the menial duties, to perform the drudgery of life. That is, a class requiring but a low order of intellect and but little skill. . . . It constitutes the very mud-sill of society, and of political government, and you might as well attempt to build a house in the air, as to build one or the other, except on this mud-sill. Fortunately for the South, she found a race adapted to that purpose to her hand. . . . We use them for our purpose and call them slaves.[9]

In 1858 few persons in the United States and no one in the South would argue that Africans, as slaves, should not occupy an inferior legal and social position in American society. Even the abolitionists gave their attention not to the task of ameliorating conditions among slaves but to transforming slaves into free people. The ideology of white supremacy had become so deeply ingrained, however, that whites treated blacks as inferiors regardless of their status. It is instructive to recall that whites made virtually no distinction among those blacks who were free and those who were slaves, particularly when one searches for bases for the racial distinctions and discriminations directed against other nonwhites in the United States.

Almost from the beginning American whites rejected the proposition that free blacks were entitled to the same treatment as other free persons. The pronouncement of the Virginia magistrate in 1642 in sentencing a free black indentured servant to a life of slavery for running away was a precedent that subsequent authorities seemed all too eager to follow. In 1790, Congress enacted a law limiting naturalization to white aliens. Two years later it restricted enlistment in the militia to able-bodied white men, thus declaring to the 5,000 Negroes who had fought in the War for Independence that their services were no longer required. And when Congress passed laws for the operation of the government when it moved to the new capitol at Washington in 1801, it excluded free blacks from participating in the affairs of that government. Only free white males could be mayor or sit on the Board of Aldermen or the Board of the Common Council. In the following year Congress passed a law, signed by President Thomas Jefferson, specifically excluding blacks from carrying the United States mail, a gratuitous expression of distrust of free Negroes who had done nothing to merit it.[10]

In the early nineteenth century white Americans faced two issues that were related to the future of Negroes in the United States. The first was whether slaves should be treated as property or men. If they were men, Gouverneur Morris had said to the Constitutional Convention in 1787, then make them citizens and let them vote. But the view of Virginia's George Mason and his supporters prevailed, and the Constitution did nothing to indicate that slaves were equal to others in the enjoyment of their rights. The second issue was whether free blacks should be treated as other free persons. In the first fifty years of the nation's history, the dominant view was that they should not be. Even if men did not violate the Constitution in maintaining slavery, they clearly violated it in denying full citizenship rights to free blacks.

If such rights could be denied to free blacks during slavery, it made it much easier to deny those rights to blacks in general once all of them were free. Indeed, the precedent of racial inequality had been so well established during slavery that it became the universal model in the years following the Civil War. Instead of emancipated blacks moving into a status of full equality at the close of the Civil War, they were consigned to a status where their color and previous condition of servitude were more important than their freedom in determining what they could and could not do. In other words, they were like free Negroes before the Civil War—pariahs, outcasts, and still unequal even before the law.

Thus, by the last quarter of the nineteenth century, the United States had established a policy that denied to persons of African descent the opportunity of becoming assimilated. This was so contrary to the general spirit and attitude toward others, especially those whose native homes were in western Europe. It was made clear to those people that the process of complete Americanization was merely a matter of time, and their models were those sturdy colonists who had settled on one frontier or another at any time between the seventeenth and nineteenth centuries. But here were those other early settlers, Africans, who served as models for none of the peoples who were assimilable, but who provided an example when white Americans wanted to qualify the assimilability of other nonwhites who were becoming a problem.

Blacks could hardly have been used as an exact model for the development of a policy toward native Americans, since the white man's experiences with the two groups were so different. Nevertheless, blacks were seldom regarded as equal citizens, even after the ratification of the Fourteenth Amendment, and one suspects that this general attitude toward blacks helped white Americans view native Americans as deserving something less than equal treatment. After all, how could one respect a group that had the very first opportunity and had not developed the continent. Furthermore, they proved to be obstructionists—sometimes mild, but sometimes fierce—to the white man's advancement across the country. They were "failures" as slaves, and their independence was mistaken for indolence. When they pursued their own type of subsistence farming or hunting in the Gulf plains, they were driven out to make way for the cotton kingdom. And when they saw American "civilization" closing in on them and surrounding them, they fought their "last stand" without success but with independence and pride.

These responses proved, if anything, that the native Americans could not become an integral part of the white man's America. But something special had to be done for them, and that was the allotment of reservation lands combined with American citizenship. The effort to provide economic support and political enfranchisement for the freedmen had been a failure (W. E. B. Du Bois called it a "splendid failure") because the government never provided an adequate economic base and because white southerners and their northern allies willed it to fail. Except in a negative way, the experience with the freedmen was of little help in the development of a government policy for native Americans.

However strong were the beliefs that native Americans were inferior to whites, few if any whites placed them on the same degraded level with blacks. There was no elaborate ideology of white supremacy over native Americans as there was over black Americans. Perhaps the relatively small numbers of native Americans and their dispersal over a large area did not require whites to devote an excessive amount of time and thought to the inferiority of native Americans. However bitter was the fight over every inch of land that native Americans were forced to yield, it did not leave any legacy of hate and degradation comparable to that left to blacks after the Civil War and Reconstruction.

Even if white Americans viewed native Americans as inferior—and they did—and even if white Americans despised the native Americans for resisting their incursions—and they did—that did not preclude an effort toward a generous solution of the "Indian problem" in both the public and private sectors. Churches and philanthropic organizations wanted to do something for the "savage Indian," and they established schools that would have a civilizing effect in the hope of awakening in him "broader desires and ampler wants." Meanwhile, the United States Congress in 1887 passed the General Allotment Act that assigned 160 acres of land to each head of a family, with lesser amounts to bachelors, women, and minors, and conferred citizenship on those Indians who resided separate and apart from their tribe and "adopted the habits of civilized life."[11]

American citizenship and a sedentary existence on a land allotment were insufficient to lure native Americans into adopting the "habits of civilized life" of the white Americans. Since the allotment act provided that reservation lands remaining after allotment were to be purchased by the federal government and the sale price held in trust for the "education and civilization" of native Americans, reformers and policy makers alike felt certain that the new dispensation was headed for success. Some observers compared the act in historical importance to the Magna Carta or the Declaration of Independence for whites or the Emancipation Proclamation for blacks. In actual practice much of the unallotted land fell into the hands of whites, since the secretary of the interior tended to force allotment upon the tribes faster than they were ready to accept it. Soon, Congress provided that even the allotted lands could be leased to others—namely, whites—for agriculture, grazing, mining, and lumbering. By the end of the century it was clear that whites were benefiting from the allotment act more than native Americans.

Any observer of the 1890s looking at the policy of the United States toward black Americans and native Americans must have been puzzled at what had been done in the name of reform. For persons of African descent, emancipation did not relieve them of their degraded position. Meanwhile, the judicial interpretation of the Fourteenth Amendment, the centerpiece of the Reconstruction program, benefited railroads and other corporations much more than it benefited the freedmen for whom it was ostensibly intended. After *A Century of Dishonor*, the title of Helen Hunt Jackson's book detailing Indian policy, Americans could not be certain that the new day for native Americans was better than the old. Indeed, the old assumptions regarding Indian inferiority and unassimilability persisted; and no amount of so-called reform legislation could change the attitudes of white Americans toward those who were already here when they arrived. For black men and red men, the American creed of equality was scarcely more than a mirage in the early years of the twentieth century.

Perhaps it was the new social Darwinism of the late nineteenth century that counseled a rejection of Negroes' claim for equality, for they had been tested and found wanting; and that permitted a kind of condescending benevolence toward the native American, for even as the white man took his lands he was still the noble savage. But a new vantage point, that of the white man's burden, began to influence America's policies and attitudes toward darker peoples generally. In extending its influence abroad, the most dramatic example of which resulted from its acquisitions in the Spanish-American War, the United States confronted the problem of dealing with Cubans, Filipinos, Puerto Ricans, and other similar groups outside the continental United States. Her experience in such matters had been brief, up to this time, limited as it was to the Eskimos of Alaska, acquired in 1867, and the Polynesian peoples of Hawaii, finally annexed in 1898, after several earlier efforts.

It was not possible to anticipate either the pleasures or the pain that Puerto Rico would bring to the United States when it was acquired in 1898. What could have been anticipated, it seems, was that in dealing with a territory not contiguous to the United States, the inevitable question of its future status would arise. But since there were as yet no clear precedents, the United States was not ready to answer the question. And in dealing with a territory, many of whose people were of African descent or had some admixture of African, Indian, and Spanish ancestry, it was dealing with a race problem not unlike the one in the United States. This one would be almost hopelessly complicated, however, by the difference in perceptions between the people of the United States and those of Puerto Rico of the importance of race. While white Americans, by tradition and legislation, regarded all such persons as Negroes, subject to the degraded opinion held of them, Puerto Ricans, with all the rich and subtle color distinctions they made among themselves, could not possibly have understood clearly the implications of the white Americans' classification of them.

Once they began to migrate to the United States, especially after this country conferred citizenship on them in 1917, they discovered what it meant to be a pariah in the country that had adopted them. They were trying to get away from the sugar plantations which had come to be known as "Uncle Sam's sweatshop," but on the mainland they could not be certain that they would obtain any kind of work. Their initial optimism was not fulfilled, and soon some began to return to the island. It was obvious, however, that the return was not a solution, and more and more of them became permanent residents of the mainland. By 1930 there were 45,000 Puerto Ricans in New York City alone, with a steady increase that had reached about a million by 1970. By the latter year they were in other American cities, most notably Boston, Philadelphia, Miami, and Chicago.

In one sense Puerto Ricans presented a picture of the classic immigrant leaving home to better his condition and bringing with him such ethnic identifications as history, culture, religion, and language. In due course they could be assimilated and completely Americanized. In another sense, however, they did not fall into the category of the classic immigrant, and that was because a substantial number of them possessed sufficient African features to be noticeable. The result was as confusing to them as it was to whites who were quick to reject the darker ones as unassimilable and consign them to a permanent low status in the social and economic order. The tragedy of the resulting segregation and discrimination was even greater when it cut across family lines where a portion of a family was regarded as black and treated as such, while another was accepted as white and accorded privileges denied their darker sons and daughters or brothers and sisters.

The implications of this for Negro-Puerto Rican relations were as unfortunate as they were inevitable. On the lower rungs of the economic ladder, they competed, sometimes quite bitterly, for the community's most unattractive, lowest-paying jobs. And in the early years of Puerto Rican migration, the greater experience and better language facility frequently gave blacks the edge, thus deepening the antagonisms between the two groups. At the same time, many Puerto Ricans were mistaken for Negro Americans and treated as such, causing them to go to great lengths to renounce any affiliation or identification with their African cousins. On occasion they expressed a preference for the terms *Latino* or *Hispanic* if that would assist them in escaping from the term *Puerto Rican*, which became, at times, almost pejorative. The white community was not above pitting the two wretched minorities against each other where competition for jobs or housing was concerned and where it was to the whites' advantage to do so.

After thirty years of large-scale migration the 1.7 million Puerto Ricans on the mainland in 1977 were no better off and possibly even worse off than those who had come a generation earlier.[12] They remained at the bottom of the economic ladder, lower than other Hispanics as well as black Americans. Continuing to live in squalor in some of the nation's worst slums, falling victim to some of the nation's worst racism, and failing, except in a very few cases, to rise significantly on the political or economic ladder, their situation remained desperate. The time came when their lowly status on the mainland prompted them to join those forces back home who contended that complete independence from American domination, rather than commonwealth status or statehood, was the only solution worth seeking. Neither native Americans nor Negro Americans provided any meaningful experience that seemed applicable in dealing with the problem of Puerto Ricans in the United States.

Like the Puerto Ricans and the native Americans, Mexican-Americans in the United States were essentially people of the New World, an admixture of Indian, Spanish, and African among some of them. When they began to migrate to the United States after 1900, they had behind them a long history of conflict with the people of the United States. They were opposed to the incursions of people from the United States during the early days of Mexico's independence, in the 1820s and 1830s, especially those who insisted on bringing their slaves. Shortly after independence Mexico had outlawed slavery, as had all other Latin American countries, except Cuba and Brazil. They resisted America's encroachments that developed into a full-scale independence movement when American settlers in Texas refused to accept Mexican law. Annexation of Texas in 1845 and the enormous cession of lands to the United States after the Mexican War in 1848 left Mexico bereft of its richest and most desirable lands. With Texas, New Mexico, Arizona, Colorado, Nevada, Utah, and California in the hands of the United States, the beaten fledgling republic to the south had few resources with which to repair her losses.

Mexico's disadvantages were numerous. Her people were dark-skinned; and Americans were developing increasing variations on the theme of white supremacy. In religion they were Roman Catholic, at a time when the Protestant crusade was reaching its peak in the United States. Mexican culture was regarded by Americans as decadent and inferior, when their own was reaching perfection, if one listened to southerners, or was in a progressive, experimental stage according to liberal northerners. Consequently, it was assumed that Mexicans living in their own ceded territories were unable to contribute much, if anything, to the march of civilization. And contact with them merely confirmed the lowest opinions that white Americans had of them. White squatters regularly appropriated land held by Mexicans in California and other areas in the Southwest, calling their victims lazy, indolent, unambitious, and undeserving of the lands they occupied.

Under the circumstances it would not be surprising if the Mexicans had preferred to maintain some distance between themselves and the white Americans. But with hard times and few opportunities at home, the United States was one of the few promising places within their reach, if only they could overcome the obvious prejudices against them. They began to migrate to the United States in substantial numbers in the early years of the century. Unlike the Puerto Ricans who flocked to the city, the Mexicans initially went into the rural areas to become farm laborers. Indeed, they were often recruited and brought into the country to take up the slack during periods of labor shortages. Some came on their own, with neither visas nor passports, thus becoming particularly vulnerable as "undocumented aliens." As fruit and vegetable pickers in California, Arizona, Idaho, Washington, and Colorado, they were exploited mercilessly by the large farmers; and when their own leaders began to organize them into unions, the stage was set for reprisals, deportations, and other actions to blunt the effects of unionization.

Those who went to the cities faced discrimination in housing and jobs, as well as competition with blacks and Puerto Ricans. Everywhere, even in the Southwest, where many had always lived and to which large numbers came annually from across the border, Mexican-Americans received the distinct impression that aside from their seasonal or periodic labor, they were not to enjoy the advantages and blessings of American civilization. In due course, however, leaders would rise among them who could speak out in their behalf and demand equality of treatment as workers and as human beings. If their demands were not always heeded, no one could any longer ignore them. They added significantly to the racial and ethnic quandary which all Americans faced in the closing decades of the twentieth century.

While many Mexican-Americans were citizens of the United States, there were many others, resident in the United States, who were citizens of Mexico. Their treatment, therefore, was of interest not only to their union leaders or American public officials of different levels of jurisdiction, but to the government of Mexico as well. And their flagrant mistreatment—as fruit pickers or as seekers of housing or as victims of brutality at the hands of the local police—merely added to the litany of grievances that the Mexican government had composed through the years. More than once, particularly in recent years, their treatment was the subject of delicate discussions between the heads of state or other high officials on both sides of the border. Even if such discussions did not result in a dramatic improvement of their lot, Mexican-Americans could get some satisfaction from the knowledge that a sovereign state, with increasing leverage, could espouse their cause if it was inclined to do so. Neither native Americans, black Americans, nor Puerto Ricans enjoyed such an enviable position.

As one views these four groups of Americans, one is impressed with the bonds of disadvantage and even degradation that tie them together. In varying degrees they were victims of American racism, developed initially out of the American experience with persons of African descent but extended to others of darker hue—native Americans, Puerto Ricans, and Mexican-Americans—as they sought equal treatment at the hands of white Americans. Their struggle for full equality has been an ongoing one, and they would have much to tell each other both about their limited successes and numerous failures. They are, in general, clustered at the lower end of the occupational and economic scale, victims of discrimination in employment and in compensation for work done. They are, for the most part, confined to certain sections of the city where housing, although expensive, is limited and frequently substandard. All too often the several groups are in fierce competition with each other for jobs, housing, and other favors of society. Such competition leads to invidious comparisons, jealousy, and envy, making them easy prey to further victimization as those of racial and ethnic advantage use them as pawns in the game of pitting one wretched group jockeying for position against the others.

Despite the fact that black Americans were clearly the greatest victims of a well-defined racism that dated at least from the seventeenth century, the other groups tended to feel that blacks had been the most successful in combatting racism. The examples of their civil rights organizations, their activities in the field of litigation, and their political influence are a source of envy as well as admiration, but more important and to the point is the fact that they have provided inspiration for the others. The Civil Rights Act of 1964, the Voting Rights Act the following year, and a host of presidential orders, commissions, and agencies are seen as coming primarily from the efforts of Negro Americans. Blacks are seen, moreover, as making rapid strides up the economic ladder. No other group can boast of gains such as those of blacks which are heralded in each issue of *Black Enterprise* and *Ebony*. As one reads in these magazines the glowing accounts of success and achievement by blacks, he has to remind himself that these are exceptions, that the percentage of unemployed blacks in the work force is twice that of whites and that in many cities across the country as many as 40 percent of black teenagers are unemployed. In such dismal statistics they are closer to the other groups than one might think.

There is little doubt that the vigorous drive by blacks for equality during the past two decades has encouraged other groups to make similar moves. This is not to suggest that the movement in other groups was wholly derivative, but that the climate of the 1960s in which blacks had an important role stimulated a widespread movement for equality among numerous groups. Thus, *La Causa* of the mid-1960s became a crusade to assert the dignity of Mexican-Americans, and the Mexican-American Legal Defense and Education Fund undertook to protect the rights of its people as its counterpart, the NAACP Legal

Defense Fund, had been doing for blacks since the 1930s. Likewise, the American Indian Movement (AIM) that began in the 1960s was notably successful in publicizing the plight of native Americans and winning support from a wide variety of sources. Puerto Ricans did not need the climate of the 1960s to spawn movements for dignity, self-respect, and even independence. Almost from the time that they began to come to the mainland in significant numbers, they founded organizations to improve their condition. Today they range from the quite proper Puerto Rican Association for Community Affairs in New York City to the radical, terrorist FALN (Armed Forces of National Liberation).

Despite the common bond of discrimination that all four groups share, there are significant differences. One of these has to do with language and culture. Puerto Ricans and Mexican-Americans are proud of their distinct cultures and especially of their language. One Puerto Rican recently said that the Spanish language was for his people a unifying factor and a guardian of their identity.[13] Both groups tend to hold fast to it, the Puerto Ricans apparently with greater tenacity than the Mexican-Americans. Blacks and native Americans, on the other hand, have only English as a common language and a culture that has been almost completely diluted and eclipsed by the culture of the dominant racial and ethnic groups.

Another difference is that Puerto Ricans on the mainland have a homeland to which they are deeply and permanently attached. Frequent visits, where possible, reinforce the attachment and cause many to regard themselves as Puerto Ricans first and Americans second. The attachment of Mexican-Americans to Mexico does not seem to be nearly as deep. Many of them are not immigrants but have always lived on the lands ceded by Mexico to the United States. Others were recruited from Mexico as laborers and, under the circumstances, would just as soon forget the wretched conditions from which they came. Still others came without permission and return the same way if and when they care to. On the other hand, the connections of Afro-Americans with their ancestral lands lie deep in the past. They came to the New World involuntarily and, for centuries, had no opportunity to return. In recent years with the independence of African states and with the example of blacks serving as political and economic leaders in numerous countries, Afro-Americans have experienced a renewed interest in the land of their fathers.

Native Americans had no such experiences. Their attachment to their own land was attested to by their resentment of the way in which

Europeans dispossessed them. But nothing could dispossess them of the notion that America was *their* homeland. As the first settlers they never conceded that others, in the name of a superior civilization, had a right to push them aside. Without the power or the weapons to turn back the Europeans, they finally made their peace with them on the theory that the New World was indeed the land of room enough. Only through the kind of litigation that black Americans had pushed were native Americans able to hold onto the theory and then recover and save some of the land as well as some of the rights for themselves.

If being an American is to share in the history and culture of the country, to contribute to its well-being, and to be a part of its future, the Americanism of these four groups cannot be successfully challenged by anyone. The Indians were here before any other known group, and their imprint has had a profound impact on virtually every aspect of American life and history. Afro-Americans, for three centuries, have been a central feature of America's history, and no amount of gainsaying can eradicate their importance. Mexican-Americans are native to much of this country's Southwest; there as well as elsewhere, their culture is as American as that claimed by any former European. Likewise, Puerto Ricans, in their Caribbean location as well as their mainland situation, have added both substance and flavor to American culture. Thus, these groups need not yield to any group in their claim to be integral parts of American life, even as they remain conscious of their own distinctiveness.

One of the tragedies of the present situation is that the sense of sharing common problems and seeking common goals is minimal. It is true that under the circumstances the four groups are almost natural competitors, since they must scratch around at the bottom of the economic ladder for whatever falls from above. But it is also true that with increased education and greater technical skills and with a better understanding of the benefits of cooperation, they could effect the kind of intergroup arrangements that would transcend and neutralize many of the divisive forces that exist. In an age of shrinking economic opportunities, it is "more tempting for one group to see the other as a potential rival than as an ally," as Joel Dreyfuss has observed.[14] Even so, the alternative to cooperation is a continuation of the crudest forms of bitter group rivalries, energetically promoted by the groups that have always benefited from such rivalries. The most compelling argument clearly favors an elimination of suspicions, jealousies, and rivalries, and the adoption of all feasible methods of peaceful cooperation. This is not to suggest that their ultimate goals are or should be identical.

Within the past three or four decades it has become fashionable for various hyphenated Americans to emphasize the distinctive aspects of their respective cultures. It was as though the process of Americanization had reached the point of success where they could afford to look back to their origins and pay homage to their languages, history, and the special features of their culture. The whole process was a sign of complete or extensive assimilation, and the new way of looking at themselves and their past became a luxury no less important than their expensive homes and automobiles. These same decades witnessed an important rise in the decibels of protest and in the crusade for equality on the part of native Americans, black Americans, Puerto Ricans, and Mexican-Americans. It was as though this was *not* the land of room enough and as though the assimilation of the others had been accomplished at their expense. These cries of anguish and these demands for attention to their problems serve as a reminder that the very term assimilability is one that suggests there are problems that lie outside its scope. These are the problems of those who have not been assimilated. And as a Puerto Rican woman recently said, "There is never a lack of problems. The poor live off hope."[15]

.

PART V

Leadership Roles

These are not, as the title of this section might imply, exhortations about the leadership roles that historians should play in our society. They are, instead, presidential addresses that I have delivered before learned societies since my first election to national office by the American Studies Association in 1968. For the most part, they deal with historical problems in which I undertook to offer some reflections based on my own research, writing, and teaching. My address before the Southern Historical Association in 1971 examined the problem of change and the quite well-defined and, one might add, sparse terms on which the South was willing to undergo change. The address before the Organization of American Historians in 1975 grew out of my examination of southern militancy and the discovery that in the 1850s the South claimed that its armed forces were *the* major factor in winning the War for Independence. This is a claim the North disputed with such vehemence that for a time it was a major feature of the sectional crisis.

My address before the American Historical Association in 1979 relied heavily on my many years of study of the era of Reconstruction and my view that it remains one of the most hotly disputed, as well as one of the most misunderstood, periods in the history of the United States. Consequently, Reconstruction history *and* lore have had a significant effect on current opinions and policies. It is remarkable how many contemporary politicians and would-be policy makers summon inaccurate accounts and interpretations of the Reconstruction to support the positions they take on some contemporary political, social, or economic problem.

In my address before the American Studies Association—the first one delivered but the final one presented here—I dealt with a problem common to scholars in general. This had to do with the role of the American scholar in the international scholarly community. As a Fulbright professor in Australia and the United Kingdom and later as member and chairman of the Board of Foreign Scholarships—the Fulbright Board—I traveled to many parts of the world. I talked with numerous scholars, American and foreign, as well as public officials in numerous countries. These experiences helped me develop the views and notions about the proper posture of the American scholar abroad that I set forth in this address.

The Great Confrontation: The South
and the Problem of Change

The vision of the New World as the utopia of their dreams—or as the challenge to create one—seized all Europeans who decided to cast their lot with what was, perhaps, the most remarkable overseas venture in the history of mankind.[1] Not every New World settler came of his own volition, of course. There were the kidnapped orphans and derelicts from Britain's streets and tippling houses, the debtors from scores of Europe's jails, and the hapless Africans whose "most sacred rights of life & liberty" were violated by a "cruel war against human nature itself."[2] Regardless of their background or antecedents, all who came were soon caught up, in one way or another, in the relentless drive to find or create an Eden that would completely satisfy the aspirations of its people. Indeed, many would project "visions of liberation and perfection in the vacant spaces of the New World."[3]

The search for the perfect society was everywhere. New Englanders believed that they were approaching utopia as they developed a set of religious and economic institutions whose centralized control tolerated neither variations nor aberrations. Those in the Middle Atlantic area saw in their very diversity the key to a prosperous and peaceful future. In the South the remarkable success of a staple economy built on a reliable and durable labor system gave white settlers the opportunity to establish and maintain a social order free of the anxieties that plagued some of their neighbors to the North. It appeared to most of those in authority and leadership that only the refinements were necessary to forge a state of existence that would be lasting and satisfying.

But utopia was not quickly or easily attained—not for everybody or,

This essay was delivered as the presidential address at the annual meeting of the Southern Historical Association in Houston, Texas, on November 18, 1971. It was originally published in the *Journal of Southern History*, Vol. XXXVIII (February, 1972), Copyright 1972 by *Journal of Southern History*; reprinted by permission of the Managing Editor.

indeed, for anybody. Soon, religious misfits were challenging authority in New England, stimulating in due course a whole body of restless souls who would expand into new areas to attempt what they had failed to accomplish in their first New World homes. Pennsylvanians and New Yorkers soon discovered that their vaunted pluralism was not entirely satisfactory; and they also began the westward trek. Even residents in the South, unhappy with limited profits or unable to compete in a slave economy, looked beyond the mountains to the new Southwest for new worlds to conquer. Those remaining behind seemed no happier after the dissidents departed than before. They continued to seek some new arrangement in their economy, some modification in their religious practices or in their relationships with their fellows that would be more satisfying. In some areas they began to industrialize, to embrace or at least witness the emergence of new religions, and even to free their slaves.

These new arrangements created as many problems as they solved. Industrialization required capital that was not always available. The former slaves of the "free" states, although not overwhelming in numbers, were new competitors in the free labor markets and their troublesome presence raised questions about their place in the social order. The new religions and the modernization of the old religions caused anxious moments of soul-searching and raised doubts regarding the stability of human and even divine institutions. The quest for the perfect society seemed never ending.

There was, however, one region—the South—where, thirty years before the Civil War, the search for utopia came to a grinding halt. If the quest of southerners for perfection had been less vigorous, it was nevertheless more fortuitous; for they had discovered what they regarded as the components of a perfect civilization. In due course they became the zealous guardians of what they had discovered.

It was in the context of the sectional controversy that white southerners sharpened their conception of the perfect society; and by the time they defined it they discovered that they had achieved it. In the North the Transcendentalists advanced the idea of the perfectibility of man, but the emphasis was on how imperfect the social order was. In the South there was rather general agreement on the depravity of man, but the real emphasis was on how perfect the social order was. In a dozen areas the northern reformers sought to bring about change. They called for equal rights for women, the recognition of labor as an equal partner with management or capital in the economy, democratization of the schools, and above all, the abolition of slavery. Some were quite specific about such things as prison reform, pacifism, and religious pluralism, while others registered no confidence in the social order by retreating into communitarian settlements such as Icaria in Iowa or Zoar in Ohio.

In the South things could hardly have been better. The economic system was, for all practical purposes, perfect. As one writer claimed, slavery was the force that "beautifully blends, harmonizes, and makes them [capital and labor] as one. . . . This union of labour and capital in the same hands, counteracts . . . all those social, moral, material, and political evils which afflict the North and Western Europe."[4] Observed from any angle—whether it be the perfect distribution of labor by means of the slave system or the inevitable cooperation of the indolent with the industrious or the most effective utilization of the soil and other resources—the South's economic system was as close to perfection as one could hope for or even want.

The South's political system was, in the eyes of white southerners, a remarkable achievement. White men, relieved of the cares and the drudgery of manual toil, were free to give their attention to the problem of governance. It was, as James Henry Hammond put it, a harmony of the South's political and social institutions. "This harmony gives her a frame of society, the best in the world, and an extent of political freedom, combined with entire security, such as no other people ever enjoyed upon the face of the earth."[5] It was sheer folly, the slavocracy insisted, to argue that the essential element of a republic was the perfect political equality of all persons. On the contrary, Representative Thomas L. Clingman insisted, inequality was a significant element of the constitutional republican form.[6] As far as slavery was concerned, the Constitution itself recognized slavery and the inequality of persons. That fact was extremely important to the southern position. As William Pinkney pointedly asked in 1820, "If it be true that all the men in a republican Government must help to wield its power, and be equal in rights . . . why not all the *women?*"[7] No, the South's political system was the ideal system, even if it did not, and perhaps *because* it did not, extend equality to blacks or to women!

The role of the white woman in southern life was defined with a precision that made it almost legal. There were, of course, some legal restrictions on women, such as their inability to sue or be sued alone or to own property separate from their husbands or to dispose of property they owned before marriage without the permission of their husbands.[8] But the southern woman's role as defined by custom and tradition was one infinitely more exacting than the requirements of the law. For she had to fulfill the queenly role in what Anne Firor Scott has called "The Image," while having to perform the dozens of tasks in the rather unattractive everyday life that was "The Reality." Thus, "She was timid and modest, beautiful and graceful," she was "'the most fascinating being in creation . . . the delight and charm of every circle she moves in.'" But she was also a submissive creature "whose reason for being was to love, honor, obey, and occasionally amuse her husband, to bring up his children and manage his household."[9] It could be a grim and drab business, especially when isolation from friends and insulation from many of her husband's activities doomed her to an accommodation that made the image supremely difficult to live up to.

One facet of the insulation must have been extremely painful; and that was the manner in which her lord and master, by his own conduct, defined the role of the black woman. The nocturnal visit—or, for that matter, the emboldened daytime visit—to the slave cabin, the regular trips to Charleston or Mobile or New Orleans when it was "not convenient" to have other members of the family accompany him, and the regular appearance of mulatto babies on the plantation took their toll in the capacity of the mistress to live up to expectations. But the other woman's lot must have been at least as difficult. "When she is fourteen or fifteen," one of them said, "her owner, or his sons, or the overseer, or perhaps all of them, begin to bribe her with presents. If these fail to accomplish their purpose, she is whipped or starved into submission to their will."[10]

When Frederick Law Olmsted visited Richmond in the autumn of 1855 he was "surprised at the number of fine-looking mulattoes, or nearly white colored persons" that he saw. "Many of the colored ladies were dressed not only expensively, but with good taste and effect, after the latest Parisian mode." About a fourth of those whom Olmsted observed "seemed . . . to have lost all distinguishingly African peculiarity of feature, and to have acquired, in place of it, a good deal of that voluptuousness of expression which characterizes many of the women of the south of Europe."[11] The wife of one planter "found it impossible to long keep a maid . . . for none could escape the licentious passions of her husband, who was the father of about one-fourth of the slaves on his plantation, by his slave women."[12] Another "watched her husband with unceasing vigilance; but he was well practised in means to evade it."[13] Small wonder one mistress was beside herself with rage, when a visitor mistook one of the girl servants for a member of the slaveholder's family and addressed her with appropriate familiarity.[14] But the half-million mulattoes in the United States by 1860 were an integral part of the perfect society to which the white southerner had become so attached and committed.[15]

The white southerner's social order was one in which his own sense of superiority was constantly nurtured by the subordination to which he subjected all blacks. It mattered not whether the blacks were slave or free—although their natural lot was, of course, as slaves—they existed for the sole purpose of gratifying the needs, desires, even the ego, of the whites. It was so important to the white elite to maintain the southern social order that they enlisted every white, regardless of economic or social status, in its support.[16] Color became the badge of distinction, and every white man could be proud of his own racial distinction. "We have among us," Judge Abel P. Upshur declared, "but one great class, and all who belong to it have a necessary sympathy with one another; we have but one great interest, and all who possess it are equally ready to maintain and protect it."[17]

A sense of racial superiority became at once a principal defense of slavery and an obsession with it as the "cornerstone" of southern civilization. "[P]ublic liberty and domestic slavery were cradled together," Robert Toombs declared.[18] This view complemented James Henry Hammond's argument that Africans had the requisite vigor, docility, and fidelity to perform the "drudgery of life" while the whites preoccupied themselves with "progress, civilization, and refinement."[19] Others, in large numbers, lent their philosophical speculations and their scientific "findings" to further justification for the inevitable lot of Negroes as slaves. Physiologically they were inferior, emotionally they were juvenile, and intellectually they were hopelessly retarded. Fortunately for them, the argument went, they were the chattel of an aristocracy characterized by talent, virtue, generosity, and courage.[20]

The fact that more than one-tenth of all Negroes in the United States were free and that some of them were most accomplished in the economic and intellectual spheres did not shake the confidence of white southerners in their perfect society that refused to recognize blacks as persons worthy of any respectable social status. Free Negroes were pariahs, and the whites enacted laws to confirm it. The fact that the annual crop of runaways was regularly increasing created an apprehension that whites successfully concealed. A slave who ran away was afflicted with a disease called "drapetomania," which could be cured by flogging, or he was the victim of the evil designs of abolitionists, which could be dispelled by more stringent laws and direct action.[21] The fact that there were slave revolts and rumors of them merely confirmed the demented and immoral character of some of the slaves which could best be dealt with by constant surveillance. In any case, slavery was a great missionary institution, "one arranged by God." As Bishop Stephen Elliott of Georgia put it, "we are working out God's purposes, whose consummation we are quite willing to leave in his hands."[22]

White southerners did not leave such matters altogether in God's hands. If their religious institutions were ordained by God, they were, in turn, built and managed by man and with a view toward refining and sustaining the perfect society. In forging what one observer has called "a southern religion" the whites made certain that the orthodoxy of their churches, regardless of denomination, was in perfect harmony with the southern social order.[23] The churches condemned all signs of social instability such as intemperance, gambling, divorce, and dancing. Indeed, some religious groups objected to any and all programs of reform, holding to the view that their mission was to save souls rather than rehabilitate society.

Under the circumstances this was a better stance, even if some idealists preferred to advocate social change. As the leading politicians and planters would look with suspicion if not scorn on those who criticized things as they were, it was scarcely prudent to challenge them. Better still, it proved to be the better part of wisdom to speak out for the status quo. Thus, the leading clergymen not only rationalized slavery as an institution whose severity was mitigated by the influence of Christianity, but some of them defended it with incomparable zeal. Slavery was not a sin, they told its critics, for it conformed to the highest code known to man and was based on divine revelation.[24] Indeed, it was the abolitionists who were sinful, for they refused to recognize the explicit sanctions of slavery in the Scriptures.[25] In the course of the slave controversy the southern clergy did not fail to provide their political leaders with every conceivable moral and religious defense of the institution that they could possibly use.

Thus, southerners, believing that their social system was the best that had evolved, must have been immensely pleased by the actions of their religious leaders in breaking off from their northern brethren. By 1845, when southern Baptists followed the example of the Pres-

byterians and Methodists in setting up their own sectional denomina-
tions, slavery had become as much a part of the religious orthodoxy of
the South as the Creation in the Book of Genesis or Armageddon in the
Book of Revelations. The work of promoting and defending slavery,
when entrusted to the southern clergy, could not have been in safer
hands. It was left for James Henley Thornwell, the brilliant Presbyterian minister and philosopher, to put the matter succinctly when
he said that slavery was "one of the conditions in which God is conducting the moral probation of man—a condition not incompatible
with the highest moral freedom, the true glory of the race, and, therefore, not unfit for the moral and spiritual discipline which Christianity
has instituted."[26]

By 1860 it was sheer folly to criticize the social order that the white
southerners had developed. They had succeeded where others had
failed; and they were unwilling to countenance any suggestion for
change. They insisted that it was the North that needed to change. Yet,
it was the North that was pressing for change in the South. With his
characteristic sneer, George Fitzhugh observed that the "invention and
use of the word Sociology in free society, and of the science of which it
treats, and the absence of such word and science in slave society, shows
that the former is afflicted with disease, the latter healthy."[27] The
North's radical movements, such as communism, socialism, and anar-
chism, were a clear indication of its failure. If slavery was more widely
accepted, man would not need to resort "to the unnatural remedies of
woman's rights, limited marriages, voluntary divorces, and free love, as
proposed by the abolitionists."[28]

If the South was unwilling to make any significant concessions
toward change during the antebellum years, it saw no reason why
defeat at the hands of the North during a bloody Civil War should
justify or provide any reason for change. To be sure, the slaves had been
set free, the Confederacy had collapsed, and southern agrarianism had
proved no match for the northern industrial juggernaut. But that was
sheer might, which was not necessarily right. "They say *right* always
triumphs," Emma LeConte wailed in 1865, "but what cause could have
been more just than ours?"[29] Such southerners were not prepared to
accept the changes that came in the wake of the Civil War.

Emma LeConte apparently spoke for many. While white southerners were compelled to recognize the most obvious results of the war,
such as the end of the legalized institution of slavery, they were willing
to make few concessions regarding the place of blacks in the social

order or, indeed, the existence of a new social and political order. The attempts to nullify the effects of the Reconstruction amendments and the moves at the first opportunity—in 1865 and again at the time of the overthrow—are clear indications that they would resist change with all the resources at their command. The hue and cry over the importance of preserving the integrity of the South's political institutions was never so loud as when whites were vowing to keep blacks from holding office, regardless of ability, training, or experience. By the end of the century the virtually total disfranchisement of blacks indicated how successfully southern whites had resisted change.

That the postwar readjustments were essentially a realignment to prevent revolutionary or even significant change can be seen in the superficial adjustments that white southerners made to the "new order." They would accept the former slaves as free agricultural workers, but only on terms that made a mockery of freedom. Sharecropping and peonage made it possible for the leaders of the old order to subject masses of poor whites to a new form of degradation and to keep most Negroes in a state of involuntary servitude.[30] They would accept industrialization, but only on their own terms. This would assure them that the new industry would operate along lines that were strikingly similar to the plantation system. The new factories were largely if not exclusively for whites; and when blacks were employed, they would have their "place" on the lowest rung on the employment ladder, with no hope of climbing up. The Negro factory worker, who could not even approach the pay window to receive his inferior wage until all whites had been paid, knew that whites would stop at nothing in their determination to degrade him.[31]

We now know that the romantic picture of woman's role in the antebellum South was more imaginary than real. In the years following the war more southern white women everywhere openly played the role that many had covertly played before the war.[32] The census continued to describe them as "keeping home" while, in fact, they were managing farms and plantations, teaching in the local schools, working in factories, and entering numerous service occupations.[33] Meanwhile, their black counterparts shared the lot consigned to all former slaves, happily with some lessening in the exploitation of them as mistresses or concubines.

Regardless of race or color, the gallant men of the South did not greet the changing role of women with enthusiasm. Some regarded it as an affront to their own masculinity, while others were certain that it was an advance herald of the doom of their way of life. If women persisted in their quest for equality, they would undermine some of the most important foundations of civilization. Only men, said Georgia's Senator Joseph E. Brown, could deal with "the active and sterner duties of life," such as farming, road building, attending public assemblages, and voting.[34] Leave such matters as voting to men, and the future of society would be in safe hands. Furthermore, if white women gained the franchise, black women voters would follow in their wake, and such a calamity was too terrible to contemplate. Surely, this must have been in the minds of some of the women who themselves opposed their own enfranchisement.[35]

And during the antebellum years the southern churches had learned their role well, so well in fact that they continued to function as principal bulwarks against change in the postwar years. Southern clergymen remained vigorous and vocal proponents of the Confederate cause, while their "churches became centers of conservative political sentiment and of resistance both to the invasion of northern culture and to the doctrine of the New South."[36] They did much to insulate the South from social as well as religious change by opposing church unity, a liberal theology, and a new role for religious institutions in the social order.

Southern churches could differ, almost violently, over such matters as immersion as opposed to other forms of religious induction, but they were not in conflict over the prime role of the church in preparing its children of God for the next world. Not only should its members be content with the world as it was, but they should be aggressive defenders of the social order as God ordained it. "Organized religion in the South became," as Hodding Carter put it, "the mighty fortress of the *status quo*."[37] It seems fruitless to argue that the churches merely reflected the views of their communicants or even that they shaped the views of their communicants. What is important is that the conflict between the position of the church on religious and social questions was indistinguishable from the position of other southern institutions. It stood against change as firmly as any other.

It was in the area of race relations that the South of the postwar years was more committed to stability—a euphemism for the status quo—than in any other area. And since the threat of change appeared to be greater, what with Radicals enfranchising the freedmen and enacting civil rights laws, the active, vehement resistance to change was greater. That is why southern whites became active in 1865 in defining the place of Negroes in southern life and continued to do so until the definition had extended to every conceivable aspect of life. The way to make absolutely certain that the status of blacks would not change was to institutionalize and legalize their subordinate and degraded place in southern life.

If the place of blacks was to be subordinate, whites argued, they must not be permitted to participate in the affairs of government. The move that began in 1865, only to be rather mildly interrupted for a few years during Reconstruction, was resumed in the 1870s and virtually completed by the end of the century.[38] If their place was to be degraded, whites reasoned, they must be separated on all means of transportation, in all places of public accommodation, in schools, churches, hospitals, orphanages, poorhouses, jails, penitentiaries, and cemeteries.[39] They were to receive no address of courtesy but were always to extend it to whites of any age or status. Their oath in the court was to be taken on a separate Bible, and they were never to challenge the claims or assertions of whites.[40] The enforcement of these laws and customs was the responsibility of all whites, who could resort to violence with impunity to prevent any breach whatsoever.

As the South entered the twentieth century it was as deeply committed to its social order as it had ever been; and it was as determined to resist change as it had been a half-century earlier. But the resistance would be more difficult, for the forces of change were everywhere, and they seemed to be sweeping everything before them. If the forces were all powerful and all pervasive, then the South would perhaps be forced to adopt what Wilbur J. Cash called a "revolution in tactics," without yielding significant ground on important matters.[41] It would thus be in a position to force the new dispensation to accommodate itself to the South's social order, rather than the other way around.

When progressivism called for a greater role for government in the regulation of many aspects of life, the South's leaders responded with their own special brand of progressivism. Indeed they took the initiative in the promotion of direct primary elections, but they made certain that the increased democracy would be for whites only.[42] The great movement to extend education swept over most of the South, but the widespread practice of discriminating against Negroes in the expenditure of public funds detracted from the movement as a truly progressive one.[43] In more than one state the reform movement was carried forward on a wave of race-baiting and race-hating, with the clear understanding that the benefits of reform, whether they were political or economic, would not breach the line that separated the races.

One of the most effective obstacles to the success of women's suffrage was the specter of race. There were, of course, the expected arguments in 1917 and 1918 that the proposed constitutional amendment permitting women to vote was "against the civilization of the South."[44] And there were some courageous southern suffragettes who *demanded* the vote. But by 1917 no leading southern member of the House of Representatives and no southern member of the Senate had declared for women's suffrage.

There persisted the argument, developed in the previous century, that the suffrage amendment would open the door to voting by Negro women and, perhaps, even Negro men. "REMEMBER THAT *woman suffrage*," one southerner cried, "means a reopening of the entire *negro suffrage* question, loss of State rights, and another period of reconstruction horrors, which will introduce a set of female carpetbaggers as bad as their male prototypes of the sixties."[45] Indeed, the connection in the minds of many southerners between race and women's suffrage was so strong that the suffragists themselves devoted much attention to the task of dispelling the connection. They did so by assuring southern whites that if they enfranchised women they could continue to disfranchise blacks![46]

Despite fierce opposition by many southerners, including some women, to the changing role of women, the march toward freeing southern women from some of the trammels of the nineteenth century seemed inexorable. In time they would sit in a few seats of power such as the governor's chair in Texas, in one Arkansas seat in the United States Senate, and on the North Carolina supreme court. Some of them would reject the tired and largely false claim that blacks had been lynched to protect their virtue and would call for civilized conduct to replace the barbarism of the rope and faggot.[47] But as the status of southern women improved, there remained the lag between blacks and whites of the so-called weaker sex; and few raised their voices in the effort to close the gap in wages, in educational opportunities, and in the general esteem of southern chivalry.

The secularization of life in general tended to undermine the effectiveness of southern organized religion and to challenge age-old orthodoxies and fundamentalist doctrines. It would be incorrect, however, to assume that the conservative character of southern religion disappeared altogether or that southern churches were easily adjusting to social and economic change. All too often Protestant churches in the South became centers of refuge for the most conservative social and political forces and, as in earlier years, led the resistance to change.[48]

Nowhere was the resistance to change more pronounced than in the opposition of southern religious groups to theories that challenged the literal interpretation of the Holy Scriptures. They vigorously opposed the teaching of what they called atheism, agnosticism, and Darwinism.[49] In Texas Governor Miriam A. Ferguson, in denouncing Darwinism, said that she would not let "that kind of rot go into Texas textbooks."[50] In Tennessee a young high school teacher was found guilty of teaching evolution and was saved from punishment only by a technicality. In several states in the 1920s the Bible crusaders put up a vigorous, if unsuccessful, fight to eliminate Darwinism from the public schools.[51] In all these efforts southern religious groups manifested a fierce and fearsome hostility to change.

In the antebellum years the fight for the freedom of the slaves was spearheaded by northern white abolitionists, although both slaves and free Negroes did much more for freedom than has generally been conceded.[52] In the post-Reconstruction years the fight for racial equality and human dignity was waged largely by blacks, with only an infrequent assist by whites. In the twentieth century the struggle to destroy every vestige of racial distinction passed through several stages, with whites—largely in the North—giving greater assistance on some occasions than on others.

In their struggle for complete equality blacks, whether in the South or in the North, could be fairly certain to receive northern white assistance in matters of transportation, voting, education in general, and in the enjoyment of places of public accommodation. They could not be nearly as certain of such support in matters of employment, housing, security in their persons, and equal education in the urban ghetto. In that sense the resistance to significant change in race relations could be as vigorous in the North as in the South.[53]

But if northern whites could react crudely and even violently to the pressures of the new masses of blacks in the urban ghettoes, they were merely catching up with a problem that southerners had faced for centuries. They were less prepared to meet it, for although they had always consigned Negroes to an inferior place in their society, they had been smug in their satisfaction that the numbers were insignificant and the "problem" correspondingly minor.[54] They had much to learn, and they became apt, even eager, students of the southern method of dealing with the problem of race.

Even as Negroes left the South in increasing numbers between 1910 and 1950 white southerners discovered that the nationalizing of the race problem did not relieve them of having to confront the significantly changing status of those blacks who remained. Negroes wanted better jobs and equal pay. They wanted to vote and hold office. They wanted to desegregate public transportation and the schools. They wanted to eradicate every vestige of second-class citizenship, and they insisted that there could be no compromise with the high principles that were the birthright of *all* Americans.[55]

For white southerners this was the most serious challenge to their social order since the Civil War. They had always conceived of their "perfect society" in terms of the subordination of Negroes. Now that it was once again challenged, they would respond characteristically by that remarkable combination of praising things as they were and resisting the change that they abhorred. The South had devoted centuries to building its civilization, they insisted. Except for a few malcontents and those exposed to outside subversive influences, Negroes in the South were not only better off than elsewhere but were happy with their condition. "Go down South where I live," John E. Rankin told the House of Representatives in 1948. That is "where more Negroes are employed than anywhere else in the country, where they enjoy more happiness, more peace, more prosperity, more security and protection than they ever enjoyed in all history."[56]

But change was taking place so rapidly that there was scarcely time to celebrate the old order. Two world wars and a New Deal had facilitated the South's industrial revolution. Government, federal and state, had introduced social controls and social programs that poverty and privation forced the South to accept. The successful drive of southern women to liberate themselves from their long entrapment was greatly accelerated by changes and reforms in the political and economic spheres. Even religious institutions felt the winds of change and responded with various forms of accommodation. And in all these changes white southerners asked the age-old question, "How will it affect the blacks?" It was an affirmation of V. O. Key's assertion that "Whatever phase of the southern . . . process one seeks to understand, sooner or later the trail of inquiry leads to the Negro."[57]

Not only were these numerous developments affecting the blacks in a dozen different ways, but specific developments in the area of race relations overshadowed other disquieting events. Some southern white leaders observed what was happening on the racial front in utter disbelief, while others regarded it as their greatest challenge that must be confronted and combated. In the process some of their responses were as graceless as they were reprehensible.

When President Harry S. Truman issued executive orders and recommended legislation to protect Negroes in their enjoyment of civil rights, Senator Richard B. Russell, Jr., of Georgia condemned the moves as steering this country toward a "police state" and threatened to introduce legislation looking toward the removal of blacks from the South.[58] In 1947 a federal district court judge, J. Waties Waring, ruled that the Democratic primary of South Carolina could not exclude Negroes from participating in its elections. Immediately, a South Carolina member of the House of Representatives, W. J. Bryan Dorn, wailed that it opened the way for communists to vote in the Democratic primary.[59] Another representative from South Carolina, L. Mendel Rivers, predicted that the decision would cause bloodshed, and he seriously considered the possibility of instituting impeachment proceedings against Judge Waring.[60] The return of Harry Truman to the White House in 1948 and the refusal of the United States Supreme Court to review the Waring decision effectively subdued the confrontation that Russell and Rivers and company sought to bring about.

White southerners all across the region attempted to meet the changes that blacks sought in the field of education by launching a massive program to equalize the facilities and programs in white and Negro schools. If they approached success in this ploy, it was effectively undermined by the Supreme Court decision in 1954 that declared legally segregated schools unconstitutional. The South's response was varied, but the major response was rejection of the law of the land. Its leading members of the United States Congress—more than one hundred of them—signed a manifesto that praised the "separate but equal" decision of 1896 as "founded on elemental humanity and commonsense" and condemned the 1954 decision as an "unwarranted exercise of power by the Court" that "planted hatred and suspicion where there has been heretofore friendship and understanding."[61]

The signatories of this "Declaration of Constitutional Principles" were among the South's most respected and influential leaders. In declaring that they would "use all lawful means to bring about a reversal" of the decision, they vowed to "refrain from disorders and lawless acts." But Senator Harry F. Byrd, Sr., was already developing a plan of "massive resistance" that in due course would compromise the principles of law and order to which he and his colleagues claimed to be committed.[62]

While it is not possible to assess the impact of the southern manifesto on subsequent developments, there can be no gainsaying that it set the stage and tone for the resistance that followed during the next decade or so. The search for alternatives to desegregated schools led to a veritable spate of maneuvers ranging from pupil placement to the closing of some public schools and the establishment of private all-white schools. The path of massive resistance led to the establishment of white citizens' councils and violent confrontations with blacks who had resorted to various forms of protest and demonstration against noncompliance with the decisions in their communities.

It is not the interracial confrontations, important and tragic as they were, that are of prime significance in this discussion. It is the South's confrontation with change, its response in defending what it regarded as a perfect society, that is instructive. The massive resistance, the fire hoses, police dogs, and the electronic cattle prods were, in a real sense, a desperate but futile confrontation with the inexorable forces of change. It all added up to the hopeless defense of a position that, in terms of the nation's laws and its expressed social philosophy, was illogical and indefensible.

The futility of this defense lay in the failure to take into account the myths and fallacies that were the basis of the white South's conception of its perfect society. It failed to recognize the inherent inconsistencies and contradictions in its argument that it could enjoy a social order that was founded on the exploitation of a group that was an integral part of that social order. It failed to see that in arrogating to a few the privileges and rights that belonged to the many, it was depriving itself of the resources that could do so much to create the social order that had, for so long, proved elusive. Its inflexibility had resulted in driving out much of its best talent, white as well as black, that could not flourish or even survive where confrontation with change meant unreasoned and unreasonable resistance to free expression and experimentation. It had also resulted in the development of techniques to defy and circumvent both law and custom. Its obsession was to maintain a government, an economy, and arrangement of the sexes, a relationship of the races, and a social system that had never existed, as Paul M. Gaston has suggested, except in the fertile imagination of those

365

who would not confront either the reality that existed or the change that would bring them closer to reality.[63]

One would hope that a region whose experience and talents had proved to be so ample in so many ways—in the creative arts, in certain aspects of the science of government, and in the capacity to transform so many phases of its economic order—might yet be able to confront fundamental changes in its social order. For only by such confrontation, tempered by a healthy recognition of the importance of change, can the South expect to survive as a viable and effective unit in the body politic and to point the way toward the ordering of a truly vital social organism where men and women, black and white, can live together in their common search for a better society.

The North, the South, and the
American Revolution

The historiography of the War for Independence during the half-century following the close of the struggle can hardly be regarded as notable. The onerous task of gathering and publishing the official documents was pursued with commendable industry. Soldiers of every rank dutifully undertook to record their recollections of the conflict. Before the end of the century at least one enterprising historian had attempted to write the history of his own colony's role in the war.[1] A few had even essayed a comprehensive history of the war, but not even the contemporary critics viewed these accomplishments with pride.[2] Neither the highly colored and blissfully inaccurate lives of the founding fathers nor the new nationalistic writings following the War of 1812 succeeded in inspiring any of the nation's writers to focus their attention on the days of glory when the nation won its independence. As late as 1826, fifty years after the Declaration of Independence, Jared Sparks could assert with accuracy that no complete history of the Revolution had yet appeared.[3]

The observation by Sparks was a call for increased study of the Revolutionary years as well as a recognition of what had not yet been accomplished. He would set the example by publishing *The Diplomatic Correspondence of the American Revolution, The Life and Writings of George Washington*, and numerous other works bearing on the Revolutionary era. Others would follow. In 1822 the indefatigable Hezekiah Niles began to publish the sources of the Revolution, while William Tudor was publishing incidents of the war and biographies of the heroes. With Jonathan Elliott, Peter Force, and Timothy Pitkin

This essay was delivered as the presidential address of the Organization of American Historians at Boston, Massachusetts, April 17, 1975, and was published in the *Journal of American History*, LXII (June, 1975), 5–23. Reprinted with the permission of the *Journal of American History*.

joining the ranks, the Revolutionary era by 1840 had become one of the principal fields of study for American historians, publicists, poets, and novelists.[4]

These early histories of the American Revolution escaped almost entirely the influences of the new scientific methods that were just beginning to gain respectability in the continental universities. Displaying little imagination and written in the labored style so typical of the early nineteenth century, they showed little originality except in the liberties which the authors took with the manuscripts and other sources they used. They emphasized the unifying forces at work in the colonies, and they expatiated on the heroic sacrifices of the patriots. Some present-day anticolonialists might well envy their powerful descriptions of the struggle for freedom against tyranny and the determination of the people to rid themselves of the control of a lecherous colonial power![5] At times these historians of the New Republic reflected the ancient prejudices of Whigs against Tories. At other times, their works showed the pervasive influences of the Federalist-Republican struggle. On the whole, however, they tended to be nationalist in scope as in their prejudices.

Although a few southern historians had given attention to the War for Independence, there was no sustained interest in the subject before 1840. In 1785 David Ramsay published his two-volume *History of the Revolution in South Carolina, from a British Province to an Independent State*, which was described by one recent admirer as "the first substantial account of any phase of the Revolution and a foundation stone for all subsequent study of the Revolution in the South." Ramsay was not satisfied with this work that had been conceived during the period of his imprisonment by the British at St. Augustine. After four additional years of research and writing he published his *History of the American Revolution*, which would stand "unrivaled in American historiography until George Bancroft's great multivolume history reached the Revolutionary period in the 1850's."[6] This tells us more about the status of scholarship on the American Revolution than it tells us about the quality of Ramsay's works.[7] But there were even few Ramsays in the South, and in the early part of the century southerners seemed content with the desultory pursuit of Revolutionary history largely by northern writers. Even in the years following the War of 1812 there is no discernible increase of southern interest in the Revolution.

Exceptions to this general inactivity were the biographies and personal memoirs that served to build up the reputations of the heroes and near-heroes of the Revolution. In 1802 Colonel William Moultrie published his memoirs, an apologia for his role in certain military operations.[8] A decade later General Henry Lee, the hero of several Revolutionary campaigns in different parts of the country, spent a portion of his time in a debtor's prison planning and executing the work that was one of the best personal accounts of the war ever written.[9] Biography soon became a principal vehicle for writing about the Revolution. Within a decade after his death the father of our country received the attention of no less than three biographers. And if Ramsay's work of 1807 was the soundest brief account and John Marshall's five volumes the most exhaustive, Parson Mason L. Weems's fanciful idealization was easily the most successful, especially after he added the cherry tree story in the fifth edition.[10] Weems, the Maryland book peddler, bestowed his ample talents on others such as General Francis Marion and Benjamin Franklin, but none was as successful as his life of George Washington.

Where pride in community, state, and section began to flourish, as it did when the South became more conscious of its position as a section, the people would not continue to remain indifferent to their past. As southerners began to see how northern writers tended to glorify the deeds of the heroes of their section, they began to realize that even under the most favorable circumstances, southerners could not entrust to northerners the responsibility of recording something so important as the South's role in the American Revolution. And these were no favorable or even ordinary circumstances. Northerners were openly attacking southern institutions, and their writers were beginning to make distinctions between the North and South that showed no favorable disposition to the South. When Bancroft's first volume appeared in 1835, the reviewer in the *Southern Literary Messenger* was concerned that Bancroft claimed that the people of the colonies "formed one body politic before the Revolution." Against the proposition that Virginia and the South had no distinct and unique character and mission the reviewer felt "bound to protest. We hold ourselves prepared to maintain the negative against all comers and goers, with tongue and pen; and to resist the practical results, if need be, with stronger weapons."[11] Whatever Bancroft's intentions it is doubtful that he expected to provoke such a response. When the fourth volume of Richard Hildreth's *History of the United States* appeared in 1851, it drew the fire of *De Bow's Review.* It was a clear example, the editor said, of sectional bias. So "keen and bitter are the prejudices and antipathies of the author towards the South, and everything Southern; towards Mr. Jefferson, and the whole republican party afterwards, and so delighted is he to dwell upon any points which may be tortured to their disadvantage, that we can place but little confidence in his integrity as a historian, and none whatever in his feelings as a man."[12]

Thus, as the South prepared to defend itself from northern attacks on its institutions, it discovered almost simultaneously that it needed to give more attention to its past. By that time northern writers were attacking on a wide front, bringing into question the South's past performance—even during the Revolution—as well as its present conduct.

In 1847 Lorenzo Sabine, the Massachusetts historian, published *The American Loyalist or Biographical Sketches of Adherents to the British Crown in the War of the Revolution.* In earlier studies of the Revolution there had been some reference to colonists who would not join the patriots and to some who even supported the crown. The work by Sabine, however, was the first ambitious and comprehensive study of the subject. By the time it appeared, many Americans were interested to learn who among the colonists were subversive and treacherous enough to support the British. In one place in his book Sabine observed, quite incidentally, that the loyalist sentiment in the South was so strong that the section's contribution to the winning of independence was extremely limited and, on the whole, without effect. In singling out South Carolina the author conceded that there was some patriotic zeal in that colony, but then cautioned that " 'One swallow does not make a summer,' nor 'One feather make a bed;' and so, a Laurens, father and son, a Middleton, a Rutledge, Marion, Sumter, and Pickens, do not prove that the Whig leaven was diffused throughout the mass of her people." He added that one of the reasons for the southerner's inability to commit himself more fully to the Revolutionary cause was the presence of large numbers of slaves who might become troublesome during the time of upheaval.[13]

If Sabine had deliberately planned it, he could not have wounded the pride of southerners more deeply or evoked a more spirited retaliation. The provocation came at a time, moreover, when southerners were insisting that their position more nearly reflected a spirit of national unity and well-being than the disruptive activities of northern abolitionists. Southerners had also been pressing their argument that slavery, the cornerstone of their civilization, greatly contributed to the stability and prosperity of the entire country. The Sabine attack appeared to southerners to be part of a grand northern design to impugn their loyalty and challenge their institutions. They could not ignore it any more than they could ignore the frontal assaults of the abolitionists. They would refute Sabine and his kind in the press, on the platform, in the pulpit, on the floor of Congress, and even in the North.

Literally scores of southerners insisted that their ancestors were the leaders in the War for Independence. Virginians were responsible for securing Illinois from Britain, Elwood Fisher told his Cincinnati audience; and then they magnanimously ceded it to the Confederation. Another argued that the number of southern enlistments and the length of service by southerners clearly proved that they "suffered more of the privations of war than their Northern co-patriots."[14] One proud southerner said that the Revolution in South Carolina had been "conceived and organized by the native population" and that from the first the people "neither wavered nor faltered throughout its progress." Southern troops, another argued, were more loyal than New England troops, who would not march into Virginia with Cornwallis "until they had received in hard money, one month's pay in advance."[15]

As for the slaves, southerners insisted that they were an asset during the Revolution. Even when whole districts of the country were left entirely to women, children, and slaves, the bondsmen, "far from proving treacherous, or deserting their masters, continued their labours upon the plantation, and no faithful watch-dog was ever more true in giving the alarm, on the approach of an enemy."[16] They vehemently denied that their slaves deserted them and went over to the British. They claimed that the only slaves that the British obtained from the southern colonists were obtained by seizure.[17] Judge Augustus Baldwin Longstreet said that he had never heard of such a thing as slaves taking sides against their masters. "But I heard of thousands of instances, wherein they served them in battle, took care of the wives and children, [and] bore them away from peril."[18]

The argument over the South's valor and the role of her slaves in the War for Independence finally found its way to the floor of the United States Senate. Among the ardent defenders of the South's contribution to the War for Independence was South Carolina's Senator Andrew P. Butler. As early as 1850 he had declared that the "quarrel of Boston was espoused without calculation by the people of Charleston"; and he expressed the view that it would now be strange indeed "if those who had a common history should be the parties to destroy the bonds of a union formed in a spirit of cordial confidence."[19] During the debates on Kansas, when Butler spoke against the move to make Kansas a free state, it was Charles Sumner who answered him:

> But it is against the people of Kansas, that the sensibilities of the Senator are particular aroused. Coming, as he announces, "from a State"—ay, sir, from South Carolina—he turns with lordly disgust from this newly-formed community, which he will not recognize even as "a body-politic." Pray, sir, by what title does he indulge in this egotism? Has he read the history of "the State" which he represents? He cannot surely have forgotten its shameful imbecility from Slavery, confessed throughout the Revolution, followed by its more shameful assumptions for Slavery since.[20]

Sumner had already overreached himself, but he went on to make remarks against Senator Butler that offended most southerners. This led to the well-known episode, the caning of Sumner on the Senate floor by Butler's cousin, Representative Preston Books. Butler, however, made his own reply by suggesting that "ingratitude is the monster of vices, and when it is associated with injustice, it ought to be condemned by the consuming indignation of even those who may tomorrow be our adversaries. . . . The man who now reproaches South Carolina . . . is a degenerate son reproaching the dearest and nearest comrade with his mother. You cannot get over the errors he has committed in history; you cannot obviate the malignity with which the arrow has been shot. . . . I challenge him to the truth of history. There was not a battle fought south of the Potomac which was not fought by southern troops and southern slave holders."[21] There was no rebuttal, for Sumner lay critically ill from the thrashing that Brooks had given him.

William Gilmore Simms, South Carolina's leading novelist and man of letters, had watched this tragic dispute for years, and his temper rose with every exchange between the North and South. He had been among the first writers to praise the South's role in the War for Independence, and as early as 1843 he delivered a lengthy oration on the subject. On that occasion he said that the history of South Carolina did not need to be written. "It is deeply engraven upon the everlasting monuments of the nation. It is around us, a living trophy upon all our hills. It is within us, an undying memory in all our hearts. It is a record which no fortune can obliterate—inseparable from all that is great and glorious in the work of the Revolution."[22] Simms, the Unionist of the 1830s, had by 1843 become one of the South's most ardent champions.[23] When Sabine's book appeared Simms was no longer certain that South Carolina's role in the Revolution did not need to be written. He had published a history of his state in 1840, and he had given much attention to the Revolutionary era.[24] Apparently that was not enough. He would set the record straight, once and for all.

First, Simms made a blistering attack on Sabine in his review of *The American Loyalists*, which appeared in two issues of the *Southern Quarterly Review* in 1848. He asserted that the present generation of public men of South Carolina had no doubt that the colony's "patriotic devotion in the revolution was inferior to none and was superior to most of the states of the Confederacy." Sabine had found this not to be so, but he did not prove his claim because he could not do so. "The claims of Carolina to the distinction which her public men assert," said Simms, "may be slurred over by ingenuous misrepresentation, but she cannot be defrauded of them. They are to be estimated relatively with the difficulties with which she had to contend, the deficiencies of her numbers, the purity of her purpose, the rancor of her enemies, the spirit and wisdom of the favorite sons who swayed her councils and fought her battles, and the severity and frequency of her fields of fight." Simms then proceeded to argue that the southern army was composed largely of men from the five colonies of Virginia, Maryland, South Carolina, North Carolina, and Georgia. Not a dozen patriots from New England fought in the South; and the generals from the North who led southern armies, Lincoln and Greene, were surely not extraordinary.[25]

Next, Simms contributed an essay, "The Morals of Slavery," to the *Pro-Slavery Argument*, which appeared in 1852. This was a revision of an article that had first appeared in the *Southern Literary Messenger* in 1837. In the revised version Simms gave special attention to the role of slaves during the Revolution. Despite the efforts of the British to lure the slaves away, they were unsuccessful, Simms contended. "The entire mass of the slave population adhered, with unshaken fidelity, to their masters—numbers followed or accompanied them to the field, and fought at their sides, while the greater body faithfully pursued their labors on the plantation, never deserting them in trial, danger, or privation, and exhibiting, amidst every reverse of fortune, that respect, that propriety of moral, which did not presume in adversity, and took no license from the disorder of the times."[26]

Then, in 1853 Simms brought out, in revised and extended form, his article on Sabine's book, which was itself a book. The intervening years had not cooled Simms's ardor or quieted his temper, and he launched into a bitter personal attack on Sabine. He was not prepared, he said, to quarrel with the "taste, or passion for novelty, which of late, seems disposed to busy itself in rescuing the memories of the American loyalists from the appropriate obscurity." Perhaps it was natural or even necessary for the person to engage in such work. He admitted, moreover, that such researches were essential to the "unity and completeness of our records, if not to their authority and value. . . . But to employ history, as Mr. Lorenzo Sabine seems to have done, as a sort of universal dragnet; and to arrest, and to preserve together in the reservoir, without discrimination, the fish, flesh and fowl, of this mixed multitude, is to make a 'hell-broth' of it, indeed, such as the witches of Shakespeare and Middleton might be led to admire and to envy for the various loathesomeness of the ingredients." Simms, tempted to dismiss the whole Sabine undertaking, said that the entire exercise was a waste of type and paper and declared, "That Mr. Sabine's book will be found readable in the proportion of one page to fifty, is quite beyond the range of literary probability."[27] Small wonder that some years later a biographer of Simms concluded that his "petulance and want of courtesy" led him to "gross indiscretions and injured his own cause."[28]

Finally, Simms decided to take the fight into the North. In his younger years he had lived there for an extended period. As he gained prominence in literary circles, he cultivated a large group of New York friends, including William Cullen Bryant, Bancroft, and James Lawson of Scribner's. He eagerly accepted the invitation that was extended by his friends to give three lectures in New York City in November, 1856. He was frank to say that he hoped to "disabuse the public of the North of many mistaken impressions which do us wrong."[29] En route to the great city Simms agreed to speak in Buffalo, Rochester, and Syracuse.

On November 11, 1856, Simms addressed a Buffalo audience of more than twelve hundred on "South Carolina in the Revolution." The material for the lecture, which he would repeat in Rochester and New York City, was drawn from his several works on the subject. One reporter said that the lecture was interesting and instructive, and the only portion giving dissatisfaction "was his severe animadversions on a portion of the North." Another called it "an ill-digested, bitter and to at least nine-tenths of the audience, offensive defence of South Carolinian politicians of the Brooks school." A third reporter was even less restrained: "With an impudence unsurpassed, he comes into our midst and makes an harangue abusive of a Northern State and running over with fulsome and false praise of the least deserving State of the Union." Simms fared no better in Rochester, where an editor said that as a literary production the lecture was "destitute of merit," and as a lecture before a literary association it was "an imposition."[30]

It was in New York that Simms hoped to make his greatest impression. There, he would be among friends; he had a distinguished list of patrons; and his lectures were to be delivered in Dr. E. H. Chapin's Universalist Church of the Divine Unity. The first lecture, on November 18, would be on "The South in the Revolution," while on November 21 and 25 he would lecture on southern scenery, life, and manners. On the first evening an audience of more than one hundred was "scattered through Mr. Chapin's Church." Simms spoke for an hour and a half, at the end of which he received "a round of applause."[31]

It is reasonable to assume that Simms alienated a considerable portion of his audience at the beginning of his talk when he mounted an attack on Sumner, still recovering from the assault by Brooks. For some eighty years, Simms began, the people of South Carolina had reposed securely in the faith that the fame of their ancestors was beyond reproach. It was not to be so, for there had been allegations made "by a Senator in the Senate House," and he had regaled his listeners of the unmanly deeds of South Carolinians who were "false to their duties & their country;—recreant to their trusts . . . traitors in the cabinet and cowards in the field!" And this cruel history "poured forth with a malignant satisfaction, seemingly with no other purpose than to goad and mortify the natural pride and sensibility of a hated party!"[32]

The remainder of the lecture sought to correct the notion that South Carolina had not contributed its full share to the winning of independence. Simms provided statistics to show how extensive South Carolina's commitment was to the War for Independence; and he recounted events to show the valor of the men of the South in their drive to defeat the enemy. In passing, he observed that his state had done nothing to cause anyone from Massachusetts to claim that South Carolina had not done its share.

Simms must have been stunned by the merciless attacks on him by the New York press. The New York *Tribune* took him to task for making no mention of South Carolina's Negroes, "who, after all, were her greatest drawback, and, since they served as plunder, the chief instigation to the ferocious civil war, by which she was ravaged and disgraced."[33] The New York *Herald* asserted that the Simms lectures, a "quixotical undertaking," were "professedly to bolster up the much injured chivalry of South Carolina, and to palliate some of their recent exploits."[34] Although edited by Bryant, long-time friend of Simms, the

375

most that the New York *Post* could say was that it was dismayed by the several instances of lack of courtesy shown Simms.[35] When less than twenty people came out for his second New York lecture, Simms not only cancelled any further New York appearances but all other engagements in the North as well. He told his hosts at Troy that he was compelled to forgo his engagements "in consequence of the singular odium which attends my progress as a South Carolinian, and the gross abuse which has already assailed myself personally, and my performances."[36] Shortly thereafter, Simms wrote a friend, he hastened home to his "forest cover, with the feeling of the wounded hare flying to the thicket."[37]

Simms was merely the best known and perhaps the most eloquent among those who debated the comparative valor of the North and South during the Revolution. And the debate made up in intensity and fervor what it lacked in numbers. Sabine had spoken categorically and uncompromisingly for the North or, more properly, against the South. Sumner had done the same and his words had brought down on himself the wrath of Brooks and the vilification of other southerners. But Sumner was not without his supporters in the Congress. Benjamin Wade of Ohio raised the question in 1856 of whether the country could indeed have secured its independence had the slave power been in control. John Letcher of Virginia disposed of Wade by reminding him that at the time of the Revolution all the states were slaveholding. "Now sir," he continued, "according to the gentleman's theory, is it not remarkable that, with all our colonies slaveholding, our arms should have been favored by Divine Providence, and our cause so eminently successful? How does he reconcile this glorious result with his theory of sin, guilt, and shame of slavery?"[38]

Sumner had another supporter in Anson Burlingame, a Massachusetts member of the Thirty-fourth Congress who did not hesitate to make statements that were as unequivocal as any that Sabine or Sumner had made. In June, 1856, he told his colleagues in the House of Representatives that "Massachusetts furnished more men in the Revolution than the whole South . . . and more by ten-fold than South Carolina." Then, relying on data provided by Sabine, Burlingame argued that "more New England men now lie buried in the soil of South Carolina than there were of South Carolinians, who left their State to fight the battles of the country." Perhaps the greatest insult he heaped upon the South was his assertion that General Benjamin Lincoln was compelled to give up the defense of Charleston because the people of the city would not fight.[39]

For every Wade or Burlingame who spoke for the North there seemed to be a dozen loyal sons of the South anxious to speak out in her defense. And after the attack by Sabine, their retaliatory efforts seem to have been well coordinated. William Porcher Miles of Charleston struck a keynote when he called on all brave southerners to stand together in their hour of peril. "Let us cherish . . . the recollection of our revolutionary glory as the highest and purest in all our past record. There we see no timidity or time serving—no want of faith or manly self-confidence—no superstitious attachment to old and revered sentiments on the one hand, nor the pursuit of wild and impracticable dreams on the other. There we see bold wisdom and wise bravery—prudence warmed by valor, and courage tempered and informed by reason."[40]

In the climate of the 1850s there was nothing more serious than the question of slave fidelity. They must be made to appear loyal both in 1776 and in 1850 if the North was not to have the upper hand in this all-important argument. In fact, Edward Bryan of Charleston argued that the South's history, "like that of the ancient republics, shows that in war our slaves have been found faithful allies." This was certainly the case during the Revolution, he asserted, despite "British promises of the most enticing nature, and with the most sedulous instigations to revolt."[41]

On the general question of the South's contribution to the winning of the War for Independence, southern speakers and writers were of one voice that was loud and clear. William Trescot declared that the Revolution merely showed how proficient the South was, and it proved that "southern armies subsist on their own soil, with half the trouble and expense that foreign foes must employ. The military experience of the country points to the South as emphatically the region of soldiers."[42] In an address before the Fair of the American Institute in New York in 1851 James De Bow said that the southern states supplied about one-third of the yearly enlistments in the War for Independence, and as the war moved South, the region sent twice as many.[43] Meanwhile, Colonel Lawrence M. Keitt declared that "in the darkest hours of the Revolution, when the cloud of defeat hung from all the arches of our sky" it was the southern fighters who "kept the fires of independence brightly burning."[44]

It was a strange spectacle indeed. Here were two sections that were virtually at war with each other in the 1850s, not merely over the current problems that beset them but also over their comparative strengths and weaknesses during the War for Independence. And the arguments advanced by northerners and southerners were eloquent and moving, even if they did not win any new supporters from the other side. They seemed content to assert and reassert their firmly held positions, apparently believing that the very exercise itself would strengthen the validity of their arguments.

One wonders just how comfortable and smug it made Sabine and his colleagues feel to assert categorically that the South's contribution to the Revolution was less than one might have expected. In the 1840s and 1850s an increasing number of northerners were convinced that in the dispute then raging they had by far the more defensible position and that it had its foundation in the superior stance that the North enjoyed during the Revolution. To them the "shameful imbecility from slavery" during the Revolution led directly to the "horrors of human bondage" in the 1850s. But one must also wonder just how completely satisfied Simms and his colleagues felt in arguing that the South's contribution to the Revolution was greater than that of the North. In the decades preceding the Civil War many southern leaders were advancing the notion that the South's way of life was superior to that of the North and that the greater courage and heroism of southerners who fought for the cause of freedom during the War for Independence led directly to the undisputed advantage in culture and civilization that the South enjoyed in subsequent years.

As one reviews the charges and countercharges of dereliction during the Revolution advanced by both North and South seventy-five years after the Revolution, one gets the impression that the spokesmen for each section were engaged in a debate that was as pointless as it was fatuous. Neither side seemed concerned about the intervention of France or, indeed, the ineffectual stand of the British as factors contributing to the victory of the colonists. It is difficult to believe, moreover, that sectionalism had reached the point in 1776 where anyone was conscious of fighting as a northerner or as a southerner. Perhaps the Sons of Liberty in Massachusetts thought of themselves as sons of Massachusetts, but hardly as northerners. Perhaps the South Carolina patriots fought and acted as South Carolinians, but hardly as southerners. When Sabine and Sumner and Wade and Burlingame spoke with scorn of the role that the South played in the Revolution, they spoke as sectionalists of the 1840s and 1850s whose position scarcely represented those of the 1770s for whom they presumed to speak. Likewise, when Butler and Keitt and Letcher and Simms rushed to the defense of their section, they spoke in language that their forebears would scarcely have recognized at the time of the Revolution. Advocates on both sides were attempting to be relevant, but a better description of them is that their respective positions reflected an artless anachronism.

The one thing about which the sectional adversaries of the 1850s fretted most was the question of slavery. In their frenzy to establish the legitimacy of their current positions they summoned the Revolutionary experience to their support. But it would not work. Sumner could be outraged by the "shameful imbecility" from slavery in the southern colonies, but surely there was no clear distinction between the moral and ideological positions of New England and the South. It should not have been necessary for Letcher to remind Sumner that at the time of the Revolution "all the states of this Union were slaveholding states."[45] Sumner and his associates should have known something of the bitter struggle of New England slaves to secure their freedom during the era of the Revolution. There were numerous cases in the courts in which slaves were suing for their freedom; and it is of more than passing interest that John Adams, who represented the British soldiers after the Boston massacre, was legal counsel for slave owners in four cases but never represented a slave petitioner.[46] Into the general court of Massachusetts there was, moreover, a steady flow of petitions of slaves praying for emancipation; and Paul Cuffe and his brother went to jail because they refused to pay their taxes, arguing that since they were denied the franchise in Massachusetts they were being taxed without representation.[47] Sumner should also have known that down to the Revolution, New Englanders were deeply involved in the African slave trade. The rum they exported to Africa, representing three-fourths of the total colonial export in 1770, greatly facilitated the slave trade in which more than a few New Englanders were engaged.[48]

The southern position was no better. Bryan could argue that South Carolina's slaves were an asset; and Longstreet could claim that slaves never took sides against their masters, but surely they had heard of Lord Dunmore's offer in 1775 of freedom to all slaves who joined "His Majesty's Troops . . . for the more speedily reducing this Colony to a proper sense of their duty to His Majesty's crown and dignity."[49] Washington did not share Longstreet's later views that slaves during the Revolution would remain loyal and faithful to their masters under any and all circumstances. He told General Richard Henry Lee that if Dunmore were not crushed immediately, his strength would increase "as a snow ball by rolling; and faster, if some expedient cannot be hit upon to convince the slaves and servants of the impotency of his design."[50] If his lordship's proclamation did not bring more than one thousand into the British fold, it was clearly because the stiffened hands of the Virginia patriots made any wholesale flight of slaves impossible. Even so, wherever the British armies went they attracted many blacks, and Maryland, Virginia, and South Carolina were especially alarmed over the future of slavery regardless of the outcome of the war. Thomas Jefferson estimated that in 1778 alone more than thirty thousand Virginia slaves ran away. Ramsay asserted that between 1775 and 1783 South Carolina lost at least twenty thousand blacks. It was estimated that during the war Georgia lost about 75 percent of its fifteen thousand slaves.[51] As late as 1781 Richard Henry Lee wrote his brother that two neighbors had lost "every slave they had in the world. . . . This has been the general case of all those who were near the enemy."[52] It is strange indeed that the southerners of the antebellum years appeared to have no knowledge of this side of the Revolution.

If the adversaries of the two sections failed to grasp clearly what had transpired during the Revolution, they did not do any better in coping with the issues of their own time. Regarding northern attacks on southern institutions, Simms warned in 1844 that the South could not always be patient. "The cup of wrath will one day fill to overflowing, and run over, it may be, in measureless retribution."[53] But neither Simms nor any of his colleagues was willing to concede that the rights for which the colonists, including some five thousand blacks, fought in the Revolution should be extended to blacks. Virginia's George Fitzhugh put the matter quite bluntly in 1854 when he declared that "the Athenian democracy would not suit a negro nation, nor will the government of mere law suffice for the individual negro. He is but a grown up child, and must be governed as a child, not as a lunatic or criminal. The master occupies towards him the place of parent or guardian."[54] The black abolitionists, traveling in Canada and Europe in their campaign against slavery, and the well-to-do free Negroes of Richmond, Charleston, and New Orleans needed parents and guardians or, indeed, from Fitzhugh's point of view, should not have been free. One can only wonder what Fitzhugh needed and how really free he was.

Meanwhile, the spokesmen for New England enlightenment had much about which to be embarrassed. Even as they taunted southerners for their inferior role in the Revolution and for their deep commitment to slavery, their own inconsistencies were showing. An example was the show of force and violence by Connecticut residents toward Prudence Crandall whose serious crime in 1833 was that she proposed to have one black student in her school. There were, moreover, the numerous northern merchants who were determined to do business with the South and get as much profit out of slave labor as possible. Nathan Appleton of Boston went so far as to invite Senator Robert Toombs of Georgia to speak in Tremont Temple to explain to New Englanders what southern civilization was all about.[55]

An even greater source of embarrassment was the long, dreary effort of blacks and their white friends to end segregation in the schools of Boston and in other northern communities. Negroes of Boston had long struggled against segregation in public education of that city. In 1844, when the school committee reaffirmed its policy of maintaining racially segregated schools, a group of blacks protested the action. In chiding the committee for its stand, they said that the maintenance of such schools was contrary to the laws of the commonwealth, and they would withdraw their children from the racially segregated school that had been "established in contravention of that equality of privileges which is the vital principle of the school system of Massachusetts."[56]

In 1849 Sumner joined the black parents in their effort to break down school segregation. In the celebrated case brought by a black pupil, Sumner, as counsel for the plaintiff, reminded the court that the equality he was demanding was the equality before the law that was "declared by our fathers in 1776, and made the fundamental law of Massachusetts in 1780. . . . The fact that a child is black, or that he is white, cannot of itself be a qualification or a disqualification. Not to the skin can we look for the criterion of fitness."[57] The supreme court of Massachusetts disagreed. Speaking for the court Chief Justice Lemuel Shaw said:

> Conceding . . . that colored persons . . . are entitled by law . . . to equal rights . . . the question then arises, whether the regulation in question, which provides separate schools for colored children is a violation of any of these rights. . . .

> In the absence of special legislation on this subject, the law has vested the power in the committee to regulate the system of distribution and classification. . . . The committee, apparently upon great deliberation, have come to the conclusion, that the good of both classes of schools will be best promoted, by maintaining the separate primary schools for colored and for white children.[58]

It was not until 1855, after more agitation and protestation, that the legislature enacted a law providing that in determining the qualifications of students to be admitted to the public schools, no distinction was to be made on account of "race, color, or religious opinions."[59]

When the country fell apart in 1861, it was not because the North and South were at such great odds over their respective roles in the Revolution. They could have continued their arguments on the subject, however pointless and fruitless, almost indefinitely; and some would have continued to enjoy the forensics immensely. But those arguments, in both form and substance, betrayed a certain uneasiness on both sides regarding the soundness of their position in the antebellum years, as well as in 1776. Southerners protested too much their own patriotism, which they were beginning to redefine in terms of their adherence to principles instead of their loyalty to political or even legal institutions.[60] They also protested too much the fidelity of their own slaves who were to be trusted no more in 1856 than in 1776.[61] Northerners, apparently secure in the view that their own patriotism was beyond question, protested too much their adherence to the principle of equality for all peoples. The northerners of 1856 were not much more certain that they wanted to practice the principle of equality than were the northern slavers and slaveholders of 1776.

In a real sense these forebears of Revolutionary and antebellum times have provided a mirror in which, in 1975, we can see ourselves clearly. It was they who marked out the route by which we have traveled to this time and place. In doing this they were no more prepared or inclined to solve the difficult problems that they faced than we are. And as we look upon them, we see them preferring to argue about peripheral matters and passing on to us the stubborn, pervasive, and persistent problems that are central to our well-being as a nation and as a people. As we look upon them, we see ourselves mired in the same questions of justice and equality that our forebears evaded and, in doing so, transmitted to us a similar will to evade them. How long we can do so and survive as a viable and plausible democracy is a question that is as urgent as it is venerable. Perhaps we have said enough about the valor and heroism of the North and the South in the Revolution. The time has come for us to do something about living up to the principles for which both sides claimed to have fought.

Mirror for Americans:
A Century of Reconstruction History

Perhaps no human experience is more searing or more likely to have a long-range adverse effect on the participants than violent conflict among peoples of the same national, racial, or ethnic group. During the conflict itself the stresses and strains brought on by confrontations ranging from name-calling to pitched battles move people to the brink of mutual destruction. The resulting human casualties as well as the physical destruction serve to exacerbate the situation to such a degree that reconciliation becomes virtually impossible. The warring participants, meanwhile, have done irreparable damage to their common heritage and to their shared government and territory through excessive claims and counterclaims designed to make their opponents' position appear both untenable and ludicrous.

Situations such as these have occurred throughout history; they are merely the most extreme and most tragic of numerous kinds of conflicts that beset mankind. As civil conflicts—among brothers, compatriots, coreligionists, and the like—they present a special problem not only in the prosecution of the conflict itself but in the peculiar problems related to reconciliation once the conflict has been resolved. One can well imagine, for example, the utter bitterness and sense of alienation that both sides felt in the conflict that marked the struggle for power between the death in 1493 of Sonni Ali, the ruler of the Songhay empire, and the succession of Askia Muhammad some months later. The struggle was not only between the legitimate heir and an army commander but also between the traditional religion and

This presidential address was delivered at the ninety-fourth annual meeting of the American Historical Association in New York, December 28, 1979. It was originally published in the *American Historical Review*, LXXXV (February, 1980), and is reprinted by permission.

the relatively new, aggressive religion of Islam, a struggle in which the military man and his new religion emerged victorious.[1]

Historians have learned a great deal about these events, although they are wrapped in the obscurity and, indeed, the evasive strategies of the late Middle Ages. Despite the bitterness of the participants in the struggle and the dissipating competition of scholars in the field, we have learned much more about the internal conflicts of the Songhay empire of West Africa and about the details of Askia Muhammad's program of reconstruction than we could possibly have anticipated— either because the keepers of the records were under his influence or because any uncomplimentary accounts simply did not survive. Interestingly enough, however, the accounts by travelers of the energetic and long-range programs of reconstruction coincide with those that the royal scribes provided.[2]

Another example of tragic internal conflict is the English Civil War of the seventeenth century. The struggle between Charles I and those who supported a radical Puritan oligarchy led not only to a bloody conflict that culminated in the execution of the king but also to bizarre manifestations of acrimony that ranged from denouncing royalism in principle to defacing icons in the churches. Not until the death of Oliver Cromwell and the collapse of the Protectorate were peace and order finally achieved under Charles II, whose principal policies were doubtless motivated by his desire to survive. The king's role in the reconstruction of England was limited; indeed, the philosophical debates concerning, as well as the programs for, the new society projected by the Protectorate had a more significant impact on England's future than the restoration of the Stuarts had.

Thanks to every generation of scholars that has worked on the English Civil War and its aftermath, we have had a succession of illuminations without an inordinate amount of heat. Granted, efforts to understand the conflict have not always been characterized by cool objectivity and generous concessions. But, because historians have been more concerned with understanding the sources than with prejudging the events with or without sources, we are in their debt for a closer approximation to the truth than would otherwise have been the case.[3]

I daresay that both the Africanists concerned with Songhay and the students of the English Civil War will scoff at these general statements, which they may regard as a simplistic view of the struggles that they have studied so intensely. I am in no position to argue with them. The point remains that, whether one views the internal conflicts of the people of Songhay in the fifteenth century, the English in the seventeenth century, or the Americans in the nineteenth century, each conflict was itself marked by incomparable bitterness and extensive bloodshed. The aftermath, moreover, was marked by continuous disputation over the merits of the respective cases initially as well as over the conduct of the two sides in the ensuing years. These continuing disputations, it should be added, tell as much about the times in which they occurred as about the period with which they are concerned. And, before I do violence either to the facts themselves or to the views of those who have studied these events, I shall seek to establish my claim in the more familiar environment of the aftermath of the Civil War in the United States.

In terms of the trauma and the sheer chaos of the time, the aftermath of the American Civil War has few equals in history. After four years of conflict the burden of attempting to achieve a semblance of calm and equanimity was almost unbearable. The revolution in the status of four million slaves involved an incredible readjustment not only for them *and* their former owners but also for all others who had some understanding of the far-reaching implications of emancipation. The crisis in leadership occasioned by the assassination of the president added nothing but more confusion to a political situation that was already thoroughly confused. And, as in all similar conflicts, the end of hostilities did not confer a monopoly of moral rectitude on one side or the other. The ensuing years were characterized by a continuing dispute over whose side was right as well as over how the victors should treat the vanquished. In the post-Reconstruction years a continuing argument raged, not merely over how the victors did treat the vanquished but over what actually happened during that tragic era.

If every generation rewrites its history, as various observers have often claimed, then it may be said that every generation since 1870 has written the history of the Reconstruction era. And what historians have written tells as much about their own generation as about the Reconstruction period itself. Even before the era was over, would-be historians, taking advantage of their own observations or those of their contemporaries, began to speak with authority about the period.

James S. Pike, the Maine journalist, wrote an account of misrule in South Carolina, appropriately called *The Prostrate State,* and painted a lurid picture of the conduct of Negro legislators and the general lack of decorum in the management of public affairs.[4] Written so close to the period and first published as a series of newspaper pieces, *The Prostrate State* should perhaps not be classified as history at all. But for many years the book was regarded as authoritative—contemporary history at its best.[5] Thanks to Robert Franklin Durden, we now know that Pike did not really attempt to tell what he saw or even what happened in South Carolina during Reconstruction. By picking and choosing from his notes those events and incidents that supported his argument, he sought to place responsibility for the failure of Reconstruction on the Grant administration and on the freedmen, whom he despised with equal passion.[6]

A generation later historians such as William Archibald Dunning and those who studied with him began to dominate the field. Dunning was faithfully described by one of his students as "the first to make scientific and scholarly investigation of the period of Reconstruction."[7] Despite this evaluation, he was as unequivocal as the most rabid opponent of Reconstruction in placing upon Scalawags, Negroes, and northern radicals the responsibility for making the unworthy and unsuccessful attempt to reorder society and politics in the South.[8] His "scientific and scholarly" investigations led him to conclude that at the close of Reconstruction the planters were ruined and the freedmen were living from hand to mouth—whites on the poor lands and "thriftless blacks on the fertile lands."[9] No economic, geographic, or demographic data were offered to support this sweeping generalization.

Dunning's students were more ardent than he, if such were possible, in pressing their case against Radical Republicans and their black and white colleagues. Negroes and Scalawags, they claimed, had set the South on a course of social degradation, misgovernment, and corruption. This tragic state of affairs could be changed only by the intervention of gallant men who would put principle above everything else and who, by economic pressure, social intimidation, and downright violence, would deliver the South from Negro rule. Between 1900 and 1914 these students produced state studies and institutional monographs that gave more information than one would want about the complexion, appearance, and wearing apparel of the participants and much less than one would need about problems of postwar adjustment, social legislation, or institutional development.[10]

Perhaps the most important impact of such writings was the influence they wielded on authors of textbooks, popular histories, and fiction. James Ford Rhodes, whose general history of the United States was widely read by contemporaries, was as pointed as any of Dunning's students in his strictures on Reconstruction: "The scheme of Reconstruction," he said, "pandered to ignorant negroes, the knavish white natives, and the vulturous adventurers who flocked from the North."[11] Thomas Dixon, a contemporary writer of fiction, took the findings of Rhodes's and Dunning's students and made the most of them in his trilogy on Civil War and Reconstruction. In *The Clansman*, published in 1905, he sensationalized and vulgarized the worst aspects of the Reconstruction story, thus beginning a lore about the period that was dramatized in *Birth of a Nation*, the 1915 film based on the trilogy, and popularized in 1929 by Claude Bowers in *The Tragic Era*.[12]

Toward the end of its most productive period the Dunning school no longer held a monopoly on the treatment of the Reconstruction era. In 1910 W. E. B. Du Bois published an essay in the *American Historical Review* entitled, significantly, "Reconstruction and Its Benefits." Du Bois dissented from the prevailing view by suggesting that something good came out of Reconstruction, such as educational opportunities for freedmen, the constitutional protection of the rights of all citizens, and the beginning of political activity on the part of the freedmen. In an article published at the turn of the century, he had already hinted that "Reconstruction had a beneficial side," but the later article was a clear and unequivocal presentation of his case.[13]

Du Bois was not the only dissenter to what had already become the traditional view of Reconstruction. In 1913 a Mississippi Negro, John R. Lynch, former speaker of the Mississippi House of Representatives and former member of Congress, published a work on Reconstruction that differed significantly from the version that Mississippi whites had accepted. Some years later he argued that a great deal of what Rhodes had written about Reconstruction was "absolutely groundless." He further insisted that Rhodes's account of Reconstruction was not only inaccurate and unreliable but was "the most one-sided, biased, partisan, and prejudiced historical work" that he had ever read.[14] A few years later Alrutheus A. Taylor published studies of the Negro in South Carolina, Virginia, and Tennessee, setting forth the general position that blacks during Reconstruction were not the ignorant dupes of unprincipled white men, that they were certainly not the corrupt crowd they had been made out to be, and that their political influence was quite limited.[15]

The most extensive and, indeed, the most angry expression of dissent from the well-established view of Reconstruction was made in

1935 by W. E. B. Du Bois in his *Black Reconstruction*. "The treatment of the period of Reconstruction reflects," he noted, "small credit upon American historians as scientists." Then he recalled for his readers the statement on Reconstruction that he wrote in an article that the *Encyclopaedia Britannica* had refused to print. In that article he had said, "White historians have ascribed the faults and failures of Reconstruction to Negro ignorance and corruption. But the Negro insists that it was Negro loyalty and the Negro vote alone that restored the South to the Union, established the new democracy, both for white and black, and instituted the public schools."[16] The *American Historical Review* did no better than the *Encyclopaedia Britannica*, since no review of *Black Reconstruction*, the first major scholarly work on Reconstruction since World War I, appeared in the pages of the *Review*. The work was based largely on printed public documents and secondary literature because, the author admitted, he lacked the resources to engage in a full-scale examination of the primary materials[17] and because Du Bois thought of his task as the exposure of the logic, argument, and conclusions of those whose histories of Reconstruction had become a part of the period's orthodoxy. For this task he did not need to delve deeply into the original sources.

From that point on, works on Reconstruction represented a wide spectrum of interpretation. Paul Herman Buck's *Road to Reunion* shifted the emphasis to reconciliation, while works by Horace Mann Bond and Vernon L. Wharton began the program of fundamental and drastic revision.[18] No sooner was revisionism launched, however, than E. Merton Coulter insisted that "no amount of revision can write away the grievous mistakes made in this abnormal period of American history." He then declared that he had not attempted to do so, and with that he subscribed to virtually all of the views that had been set forth by the students of Dunning. And he added a few observations of his own, such as "education soon lost its novelty for most of the Negroes"; they would "spend their last piece of money for a drink of whiskey"; and, being "by nature highly emotional and excitable . . . they carried their religious exercises to extreme lengths."[19]

By mid-century, then, there was a remarkable mixture of views of Reconstruction by historians of similar training but of differing backgrounds, interests, and commitments. Some were unwilling to challenge the traditional views of Reconstruction. And, although their language was generally polite and professional, their assumptions regarding the roles of blacks, the nature of the Reconstruction governments in the South, and the need for quick—even violent—counteraction were fairly transparent. The remarkable influence of the traditional view of Reconstruction is nowhere more evident than in a work published in 1962 under the title *Texas under the Carpetbaggers.* The author did not identify the carpetbaggers, except to point out that the governor during the period was born in Florida and migrated to Texas in 1848 and that the person elected to the United States Senate had been born in Alabama and had been in Texas since 1830.[20] If Texas was ever under the carpetbaggers, the reader is left to speculate about who the carpetbaggers were! Meanwhile, in the 1960s one of the most widely used college textbooks regaled its readers about the "simple-minded" freedmen who "insolently jostled the whites off the sidewalks into the gutter"; the enfranchisement of the former slaves set the stage for "stark tragedy," the historian continued, and this was soon followed by "enthroned ignorance," which led inevitably to "a carnival of corruption and misrule."[21] Such descriptions reveal more about the author's talent for colorful writing than about his commitment to sobriety and accuracy.

Yet an increasing number of historians began to reject the traditional view and to argue the other side or, at least, to insist that there was another side. Some took another look at the states and rewrote their Reconstruction history. In the new version of Reconstruction in Louisiana the author pointed out that "the extravagance and corruption for which Louisiana Reconstruction is noted did not begin in 1868," for the convention of 1864 "was not too different from conventions and legislatures which came later."[22] Others looked at the condition of the former slaves during the early days of emancipation and discovered that blacks faced freedom much more responsibly and successfully than had hitherto been described. Indeed, one student of the problem asserted that "Reconstruction was for the Negroes of South Carolina a period of unequaled progress."[23] Still others examined institutions ranging from the family to the Freedmen's Savings Bank and reached conclusions that were new or partly new to our understanding of Reconstruction history.[24] Finally, there were the syntheses that undertook, unfortunately all too briefly, to make some overall revisionist generalizations about Reconstruction.[25]

Up to this point my observations have served merely as a reminder of what has been happening to Reconstruction history over the last century. I have not intended to provide an exhaustive review of the literature. There have already been extensive treatments of the subject, and there will doubtless be more.[26] Reconstruction history has been argued over and fought over since the period itself ended. Historians have constantly disagreed not only about what significance to attach to certain events and how to interpret them, but also (and almost as much) about the actual events themselves. Some events are as obscure and some facts are apparently as unverifiable as if they dated from several millennia ago. Several factors have contributed to this state of affairs. One factor, of course, is the legacy of bitterness left behind by the internal conflict. This has caused the adversaries—and their descendants—to attempt to place the blame on each other (an understandable consequence of a struggle of this nature). Another factor is that the issues have been delineated in such a way that the merits in the case have tended to be all on one side. A final factor has been the natural inclination of historians to pay attention only to those phases or aspects of the period that give weight to the argument presented. This inclination may involve the omission of any consideration of the first two years of Reconstruction in order to make a strong case against, for example, the Radicals. Perhaps such an approach has merit in a court of law or in some other forum, but as an approach to historical study its validity is open to the most serious question.

Perhaps an even more important explanation for the difficulty in getting a true picture of Reconstruction is that those who have worked in the field have been greatly influenced by the events and problems of the period in which they were writing. That first generation of students to study the postbellum years "scientifically" conducted its research and did its writing in an atmosphere that made the conclusions regarding Reconstruction foregone. Different conclusions were inconceivable.[27] Writing in 1905 Walter L. Fleming referred to James T. Rapier, a Negro member of the Alabama constitutional convention of 1867, as "Rapier of Canada." He then quoted Rapier as saying that the manner in which "colored gentlemen and ladies were treated in America was beyond his comprehension."[28]

Born in Alabama in 1837, Rapier, like many of his white contemporaries, went North for an education. The difference was that instead of stopping in the northern part of the United States, as, for example, William L. Yancey did, Rapier went on to Canada. Rapier's contemporaries did not regard him as a Canadian; and, if some were not precisely clear about where he was born (as was the *Alabama State Journal*, which referred to his birthplace as Montgomery rather than Florence), they did not misplace him altogether.[29] In 1905 Fleming made Rapier a Canadian because it suited his purposes to have a bold, aggressive, "impertinent" Negro in Alabama Reconstruction come from some nonsouthern, contaminating environment like Canada. But it did not suit his purposes to call Yancey, who was a graduate of Williams College, a "Massachusetts Man." Fleming described Yancey as, simply, the "leader of the States Rights men."[30]

Aside from his Columbia professors, Fleming's assistance came largely from Alabamians: Thomas M. Owen of the Department of Archives and History, G. W. Duncan of Auburn, W. W. Screws of the Montgomery *Advertiser,* and John W. Du Bose, Yancey's biographer and author of *Alabama's Tragic Decade.*[31] At the time that Fleming sought their advice regarding his Reconstruction story, these men were reaping the first fruits of disfranchisement, which had occurred in Alabama in 1901. Screws's *Advertiser* had been a vigorous advocate of disfranchisement, while Du Bose's *Yancey,* published a decade earlier, could well have been a campaign document to make permanent the redemption of Alabama from "Negro-carpetbagger-Scalawag rule."[32] It is inconceivable that such men would have assisted a young scholar who had any plans except to write an account of the Reconstruction era that would support their views. In any case they could not have been more pleased had they written Fleming's work for him.

But the "scientific" historians might well have been less pleased if they had not been caught up in the same pressures of the contemporary scene that beset Fleming. They, like Fleming, should have been able to see that some of the people that Fleming called "carpetbaggers" had lived in Alabama for years and were, therefore, entitled to at least as much presumption of assimilation in moving from some other state to Alabama decades before the war as the Irish were in moving from their native land to some community in the United States. Gustavus Horton, a Massachusetts "carpetbagger" and chairman of the constitutional convention's Committee on Education in 1867, was a cotton broker in Mobile and had lived there since 1835. Elisha Wolsey Peck, the convention's candidate for chief justice in 1867, moved to Alabama from New York in 1825. A few months' sojourn in Illinois in 1867 convinced Peck that the only real home he could ever want was Alabama. Charles Mayes Cabot, a member of the constitutional convention of 1865 as well as of the one of 1867, had come to Alabama from his native Vermont as a young man. He prospected in the West in 1849 but was back in Wetumka in the merchandising business by 1852.[33]

Whether they had lived in Alabama for decades before the Civil War or had settled there after the war, these "carpetbaggers" were apparently not to be regarded as models for northern investors or settlers in the early years of the twentieth century. Twentieth-century investors from the North were welcome provided they accepted the established arrangements in race relations and the like. Fleming served his Alabama friends well by ridiculing carpetbaggers, even if in the process he had to distort and misrepresent.

In his study of North Carolina Reconstruction published in 1914, Joseph G. de Roulhac Hamilton came as close as any of his fellow historians to reflecting the interests and concerns of his own time. After openly bewailing the enfranchisement of the freedmen, the sinister work of the "mongrel" convention and legislatures, and the abundance of corruption, Hamilton concluded that Reconstruction was a crime that is "to-day generally recognized by all who care to look the facts squarely in the face." But for Reconstruction, he insisted, "the State would to-day, so far as one can estimate human probabilities, be solidly Republican. This was clearly evident in 1865, when the attempted restoration of President Johnson put public affairs in the hands of former Whigs who then had no thought of joining in politics their old opponents, the Democrats." Hamilton argued that in his own time some men who regularly voted the Democratic ticket would not call themselves "Democrats." In an effort to appeal to a solid Negro vote, the Republicans had lost the opportunity to bring into their fold large numbers of former Whigs and some disaffected Democrats. In the long run the Republicans gained little, for the Negroes, who largely proved to be "lacking in political capacity and knowledge, were driven, intimidated, bought, and sold, the playthings of politicians, until finally their so-called right to vote became the sore spot of the body politic."[34] In his account of Reconstruction, which placed the blame on the Republican-Negro coalition for destroying the two-party system in North Carolina, Hamilton gave a warning to his white contemporaries to steer clear of any connection with blacks whose votes could be bought and sold if the franchise were again extended to them.

And the matter was not only theoretical. In 1914, while Hamilton was writing about North Carolina Reconstruction, Negro Americans were challenging the several methods by which whites had disfranchised them, and Hamilton was sensitive to the implications of the challenge. He reminded his readers that, after the constitutional amendment of 1900 restricting the suffrage by an educational qualification and a "grandfather clause," the Democrats elected their state ticket. His eye was focused to a remarkable degree on the current political and social scene. "The negro has largely ceased to be a political question," he commented, "and there is in the State to-day as a consequence more political freedom than at any time since Reconstruction."[35] The lesson was painfully clear to him, as he hoped it would be to his readers: the successful resistance to the challenges that Negroes were making to undo the arrangements by which they had been disfranchised would remove any fears that whites might have of a repetition of the "crime" of Reconstruction. Segregation statutes, the white Democratic primary, discrimination in educational opportunities, and, if necessary, violence were additional assurances that there would be no return to Reconstruction.

Unfortunately, the persistence of the dispute over what actually happened during Reconstruction and the use of Reconstruction fact and fiction to serve the needs of writers and their contemporaries have made getting at the truth about the so-called Tragic Era virtually impossible. Not only has this situation deprived the last three generations of an accurate assessment of the period but it has also unhappily strengthened the hand of those who argue that scientific history can be as subjective, as partisan, and as lacking in discrimination as any other kind of history. A century after the close of Reconstruction, we are utterly uninformed about numerous aspects of the period. Almost forty years ago Howard K. Beale, writing in the *American Historical Review,* called for a treatment of the Reconstruction era that would not be marred by bitter sectional feelings, personal vendettas, or racial animosities.[36] In the four decades since that piece was written, there have been some historians who have heeded Beale's call. It would, indeed, be quite remarkable if historians of today were not sensitive to some of the strictures Beale made against those who kept alive the hoary myths about Reconstruction and if scholars of today's generation did not attempt to look at the period without the restricting influences of sectional or racial bias. And yet, since the publication of Beale's piece, several major works have appeared that are aggressively hostile to any new view of Reconstruction.[37] Nor has Beale's call been heeded to the extent that it should have been.

If histories do indeed reflect the problems and concerns of their authors' own times, numerous major works on Reconstruction should have appeared in recent years. After all, since the close of World War II this nation has been caught up in a reassessment of the place of Negroes in American society, and some have even called this period the "Second Reconstruction."[38] Central to the reassessment has been a continuing discussion of the right of blacks to participate in the political process, to enjoy equal protection of the laws, and to be free of discrimination in education, employment, housing, and the like. Yet among the recent writing on Reconstruction few major works seek to synthesize and to generalize over the whole range of the freedmen's experience, to say nothing of the problem of Reconstruction as a whole. Only a limited number of monographic works deal with, for example, Reconstruction in the states, the regional experiences of freedmen, the freedmen confronting their new status, aspects of educational, religious, or institutional development, or phases of economic adjustment.

In recent years historians have focused much more on the period of slavery than on the period of freedom. Some historians have been most enthusiastic about the capacity of slaves to establish and maintain institutions while in bondage, to function effectively in an economic system as a kind of upwardly mobile group of junior partners, and to make the transition to freedom with a minimum of trauma.[39] One may wonder why, at this particular juncture in the nation's history, slavery has attracted so much interest and why, in all of the recent and current discussions of racial equality, Reconstruction has attracted so little. Not even the litigation of *Brown* v. *The Board of Education*, which touched off a full-dress discussion of one of the three Reconstruction amendments a full year before the decision was handed down in 1954, stimulated any considerable production of Reconstruction scholarship.[40] Does this pattern suggest that historians have thought that the key to understanding the place of Afro-Americans in American life is to be found in the slave experience and not in the struggles for adjustment in the early years of freedom? Or does it merely mean that historians find the study of slavery more exotic or more tragic and therefore more attractive than the later period of freedom? Whatever the reason, the result has been to leave the major thrust of the Reconstruction story not nearly far enough from where it was in 1929, when Claude Bowers published *The Tragic Era*.

That result is all the more unfortunate in view of what we already know and what is gradually and painfully becoming known about the period following the Civil War. With all of the exhortations by Howard Beale, Bernard Weisberger, and others about the need for more Reconstruction studies, the major works with a grand sweep and a bold interpretation have yet to be written. Recent works by Michael Perman and Leon F. Litwack, which provide a fresh view respectively of political problems in the entire South and of the emergence of the freedman throughout the South, are indications of what can and should be done in the field.[41] And, even if the battle for revision is being won among the professionals writing the monographs (if not among the professionals writing the textbooks), it is important to make certain that the zeal for revision does not become a substitute for truth and accuracy and does not result in the production of works that are closer to political tracts than to histories.

Although it is not possible to speak with certainty about the extent to which the Reconstruction history written in our time reveals the urgent matters with which we are regularly concerned, we must take care not to permit those matters to influence or shape our view of an earlier period. That is what entrapped earlier generations of Reconstruction historians who used the period they studied to shape attitudes toward problems they confronted. As we look at the opportunities for new syntheses and new interpretations, we would do well to follow Thomas J. Pressly's admonition not to seek confirmation of our views of Reconstruction in the events of our own day.[42] This caveat is not to deny the possibility of a usable past, for to do so would go against our heritage and cut ourselves off from human experience.[43] At the same time it proscribes the validity of reading into the past the experiences of the historian in order to shape the past as he or she wishes it to be shaped.

The desire of some historians to use the Reconstruction era to bolster their case in their own political arena or on some other ground important to their own well-being is a major reason for our not having a better general account of what actually occurred during Reconstruction. To illustrate this point, we are still without a satisfactory history of the role of the Republican party in the South during Reconstruction. If we had such a history, we would, perhaps, modify our view of that party's role in the postbellum South. We already know, for example, that the factional fights within the party were quite divisive. The bitter fight between two factions of Republicans in South Carolina in 1872 is merely one case in point. On that occasion the nominating convention split in two and each faction proceeded to nominate its own slate of officers. Only the absence of any opposition party assured a Republican victory in the autumn elections.[44] In some instances blacks and whites competed for the party's nomination to public office, thus indicating quite clearly the task facing a Negro Republican who aspired to public office.[45] That is the task that John R. Lynch faced when he ran for Congress in 1872 and defeated the white incumbent, L. W. Pearce, who was regarded even by Lynch as "a creditable and satisfactory representative."[46] And it was not out of the question for white Republicans to work for and vote for white Democrats in order to make certain that Negro Republican candidates for office would be defeated.[47] So little is known of the history of the Republican party in the South because the presumption has generally been that Lincoln's party was, on its very face, hostile to southern mores generally and anxious to have Negroes embarrass white southerners. Indeed, had historians been inclined to examine with greater care the history of the Republican party in the South, they would have discovered even more grist for the Democratic party mill.

Thus, studying works on Reconstruction that have been written over the last century can provide a fairly clear notion of the problems confronting the periods in which the historians lived but not always as clear a picture of Reconstruction itself. The state of historical studies and the level of sophistication in the methods of research are much too advanced for us to be content with anything less than the high level of performance found in works on other periods of United States history. There is no reason why the facts of Reconstruction should be the subject of greater dispute than those arising out of Askia Muhammad's rule in Songhay or Cromwell's rule in Britain. But we are still doing the spadework; we are still writing narrowly focused monographs on the history of Reconstruction. We need to know more about education than Henry L. Swint, Horace Mann Bond, and Robert Morris have told us.[48] Surely there is more to economic development than we can learn from the works by Irwin Unger, George R. Woolfolk, Robert P. Sharkey, and Carl Osthaus.[49] And race, looming large in the Reconstruction era, as is usually the case in other periods of American history, is so pervasive and so critical that the matter should not be left to Herbert G. Gutman, Howard Rabinowitz, John H. and La Wanda Cox, Thomas Holt, and a few others.[50]

Recent scholarship on the Reconstruction era leaves the impression that we may be reaching the point, after a century of effort, where we can handle the problems inherent in writing about an internal struggle without losing ourselves in the fire and brimstone of the Civil War and its aftermath. Perhaps we have reached the point in coping with the problems about us when we no longer need to shape Reconstruction history to suit our current needs. If either or both of these considerations is true, we are fortunate, for each augurs well for the future of Reconstruction history. It would indeed be a happy day if we could view the era of Reconstruction without either attempting to use the events of that era to support some current policy or seeking analogies that are at best strained and provide little in the way of an understanding of that era or our own.

"Not since Reconstruction" is a phrase that is frequently seen and heard. Its principal purpose is to draw an analogy or a contrast. Since it usually neither defines Reconstruction nor makes clear whether it is a signpost of progress or retrogression, searching for some other way of relating that period to our own may be wise, if not necessary. In the search for the real meaning of Reconstruction, phrases like "not since Reconstruction" provide no clue to understanding the period. Worse still, they becloud the relationship between that day and this. To guard against the alluring pitfalls of such phrases and to assure ourselves and others that we are serious about the postbellum South, we would do well to cease using Reconstruction as a mirror of ourselves and begin studying it because it very much needs studying. In such a process Reconstruction will doubtless have much to teach all of us.

The American Scholar and
American Foreign Policy

There can hardly be a quarrel with the view that those of us who regard ourselves as scholars also view ourselves as central figures in all efforts to strengthen the intellectual life of the country. We are together in our deep commitment to the pursuit of truth and the illumination of the dark corners of ignorance. We are together, I believe, in our view that knowledge is power and that it has an effective role to play in the improvement of society. To be sure, we may have different views regarding the uses of knowledge or the manner in which it should be applied. Some of us are more action-oriented than others. Some of us are more content than others to let knowledge speak for itself or to let it be used as they see fit by those who had no hand in discovering it. These differences are not irreconcilable, nor do they create an impasse that produces a fruitless stalemate. They merely represent differences in temperament, philosophy, and approach. They can be debated and they are debated in the calm of the seminar room, the library, or the laboratory.

The differences concerning the role of the American scholar in the affairs of the world and particularly as a representative of American learning abroad are somewhat more substantial and more difficult of resolution. Representation of American scholarship abroad is no new or recent phenomenon. Jefferson and Franklin are merely the two best-known eighteenth-century Americans who shared the fruits of their scholarship with the learned men of Europe. In the nineteenth century Americans went abroad not only to study but to inform. Men like George Sylvester Morris and George Herbert Palmer were primarily students of European thought; but in the years that followed their

This essay is an adaptation of the address John Hope Franklin presented as president of the American Studies Association in Kansas City, Missouri, in 1968, and which appeared in *The American Scholar*, Vol. XXXVII, Number 4.

periods of study they assumed the role of teachers in Europe through their writings and their lectures before European audiences. When Emerson lectured in England in 1847, he was already famous there, and his success is attested to by a return engagement the following year. At the end of the nineteenth century Josiah Royce delivered the Gifford Lectures at Aberdeen. If Emerson's 1837 Phi Beta Kappa address on the American scholar was the declaration of American intellectual independence, Royce's lectures at Aberdeen in 1899 were a clear indication of American intellectual maturity.

The present century has witnessed a noticeable quickening of American cultural and intellectual involvement with the rest of the world. In 1899 Charles Beard, who later would have most serious doubts about many aspects of American involvement abroad, helped to found Ruskin Hall at Oxford; and when the century opened he was teaching in England and Wales. During these years the popularity of William James soared, and hundreds sat at his feet when he lectured at Edinburgh and Oxford in 1902 and 1908, respectively. Meanwhile, Americans by the hundreds began to go to China and other faraway places to promote learning at every level. And, as Merle Curti has pointed out in his *Prelude to Point Four,* long before the Truman program was launched, many highly trained Americans were sharing their scientific knowledge and technical skills with those in other parts of the world.

There can be no doubt that those Americans who became a part of the international intellectual community had widely differing views about their country and its foreign policy. Beard was seldom, if ever, in agreement with American foreign policy, but that did not prevent his teaching in England in 1900 and, from time to time in later years, his traveling to places as far apart as Japan and Yugoslavia to consult and advise on municipal reform. Some of the early Harmsworth Professors of American History at Oxford in the 1920s did not share the isolationist stance of the United States government, but they plied their trade, secure in the belief that their role in the world of learning could be one thing while the role of their government among governments of other nations could be quite another.

One of the assets that the early American intellectual ambassadors enjoyed was that their missions abroad were entirely independent of government sponsorship, or even interest. This is not to say that the American government had no interest in using American scholars abroad. Competent manpower was too short in the post-Jackson years to overlook historians like George Bancroft, who became United States Minister to Great Britain, and John L. Motley, who served as Secretary of the U.S. Legation at St. Petersburg. From time to time in subsequent years American men of letters would officially represent their country abroad. But those who studied or taught in various parts of the world had no involvement with their government or its policy in the country in which they happened to be. There was no sense of pressure, real or otherwise, to conform to or defend their country's policies.

During the late New Deal days the United States government itself at last became interested in American scholarly representation abroad. Already it was lagging behind the French government, which for many decades had been in the business of promoting educational and cultural activities abroad, and, among others, the British, which had established its educational and cultural arm, the British Council, in 1934. When the Interdepartmental Committee on Cooperation with the American Republics was established in 1938 it looked toward the exchange of persons for education and training in numerous fields. Soon the Division of Cultural Relations, which was established in the Department of State, assumed general responsibility for promoting educational and cultural exchange with other nations. After World War II Senator J. W. Fulbright promoted the extensive enlargement of this area of activity by securing the passage of a bill that underwrote a worldwide program for the exchange of teachers, students, lecturers and researchers. From that day forward the government of the United States was committed to the most ambitious program of international educational and cultural relations that the world has ever known. The dramatic story of the enlargement of the world of scholarly endeavor for thousands of American professors and students during the last twenty years is too well known to recount here. It is enough to say that it has brought to the world a new appreciation for the importance of American scholarship and a new sense of involvement on the part of American scholars in the world community.

But this enlarged interest on the part of the United States government and the use of public funds to finance teaching and study abroad have raised among many scholars some serious questions and doubts regarding their role. From the beginning some have been wary of government support, even when they had no serious question to raise regarding the government's foreign policy. They feared the heavy hand of the government and, consequently, declined to seek its support lest some unarticulated *quid pro quo* was involved. In recent years, as the national debate over the nation's foreign policy has become more intense, some who heretofore had no objection to receiving support for foreign study and teaching have had second thoughts and entertained grave doubts about the entire operation. They have contended that American scholars abroad who held grants from the United States government are, in fact, representatives of the United States and, as such, should not participate in the program, including service on screening committees to nominate grantees, if they cannot support current American foreign policy.

It would, of course, be a most happy situation if the United States government pursued a foreign policy with which all American scholars could agree. That, most of us will agree, is highly unlikely. And even if that were the case, it would not follow that American scholars with government grants for research and lecturing abroad should rush out and promulgate that foreign policy. This government has its own machinery for the promulgation and implementation of its foreign policy and, happily, American scholars abroad are not, and should not be, a part of it. Most government-sponsored programs abroad are binational in character and operation. Indeed, many of them are even binational in support. And the grants to Americans are actually made not by the United States but by the host country. It would, therefore, be a bit unseemly if, say, an American Fulbright professor in Germany regarded himself as an agent of United States foreign policy in a program in which the government of Germany pays 80 percent of the cost!

Not all American scholars who criticize American foreign policy express their feelings by declining to participate. A few have accepted government grants and then have declined to pay that portion of their taxes that, by their estimate, is used in the military operation in Southeast Asia. The theory of taxation, even when subjected to analysis by the most erudite American scholars, surely does not concede such divisibility of taxes. If it did, a citizen could refuse to pay that portion of his taxes that was to be used to build a park that he did not care to use or to collect garbage when he had his own electric disposal. I suspect that such a stance places the American scholar in a position unworthy of him.

There are others, moreover, who have been the recipients of foreign scholarships and who, while abroad, have proceeded to express their disagreement with American foreign policy in a variety of ways. Some have committed obscenities against the American flag, thereby defaming not merely the symbol of their country but the intellectual community of which they are a part. Still others have counseled their host country to denounce the United States, thereby boldly presuming that the statesmen of their host country were not wise enough to formulate their *own* foreign policy.

This is not to say that American scholars abroad should not express their personal views, however critical, of American foreign policy. The very essence of the life of the mind is the freedom to inquire, to examine, and to criticize. But that freedom has the same restraints abroad that it has at home: to state one's position, if impelled by personal conviction, with clarity, reason, and sobriety, always mindful of the point that the scholar recognizes and tolerates different views that others may hold and that his view is independent, not official.

It is, indeed, difficult to visualize the circumstances in which American scholars could not or should not make an independent judgment of policy. And if that judgment is adversely critical, it does not follow that American scholars should withdraw from the international intellectual community because they do not agree with it. To do so would confirm the suspicion that American scholarship has no real independence and would, indeed, encourage the government to assume that it can have some influence in an area where it has no right to make such an assumption.

It seems to me that one must reject the notion, from whatever line of reasoning it stems, that American public support of academic pursuits is an arm of American foreign policy that can compromise the independence of American scholarship. For followed to its logical conclusion, it could destroy all American participation in the international intellectual community. It would, of course, mean that American scholars should go abroad with government or binational support only when they feel that they can support American foreign policy. It could mean that American scholars who happen to be Republicans should not accept grants from a Democratic administration; for whoever heard of a Republican, except for a misguided "hawk" here and there, who could approve of a Democratic foreign policy. It could mean that since the United States government is always interested in showing its most favorable side, American studies professors who are critical of America's past and present should remain at home. It could even mean that if one disapproves of some domestic policy of the government, such as the persistence of racial discrimination in federal employment, he should take no government grants for foreign research or teaching lest it be interpreted as approbation.

I would be surprised, even alarmed, if American scholars were pleased with all aspects of American foreign and domestic policy. If that were so, our government would have lost one of its most important means for continued improvement, namely, the searching and constructive criticism of the American academic community. I would be appalled if that academic community, critical and even unhappy over American foreign policy in Southeast Asia or in South Africa or the Middle East or Europe, reached the conclusion that it should have no contact with its counterpart in other lands. This would result in the elimination of an important link among the men and women of the world, a link that has been, through the ages, more durable than foreign offices or even than governments themselves. We know that the academic communities of some countries do not enjoy full intellectual independence. When they do not, it should not be the occasion for us to withdraw merely because they are not as free as we would want them to be.

A few years ago, when I was attending the International Congress of Historical Sciences at Stockholm, the chairman of the delegation of Soviet historians approached an American historian and asked for the name of the chairman of the United States delegation. There was no chairman and no U.S. delegation, as such. There were, of course, many Americans in attendance. Some were on vacation in Europe and just dropped by to see what was going on. Some were Fulbright professors or researchers, and enjoyed the opportunity to attend since they were already abroad. Others went directly from the United States to read papers or to represent their own learned societies. They were wholly unorganized, and no American could possibly know what other Americans were in attendance. It was difficult, if not impossible, for the Soviet delegation to understand the reply that there was no American delegation and surely no chairman. It was nevertheless a rewarding encounter that hopefully brought the historians of the two countries a bit closer together. There were no miracles; and no one expected any. The Americans present—even those on government-sponsored grants—represented their professions, *not* their country. And happily they were wise enough to see their roles clearly.

Last year it was my privilege to visit several countries of the Near East and South Asia. In some of these countries the feeling against the

United States ran high. In some cases it appeared to me that no great premium was placed on maintaining full diplomatic relations with the United States. Even where the antipathy against the United States was unmistakable, the warm and friendly attitude toward the scholarly community of the United States was clear. It would be naïve to suggest that the American scholar can be an effective substitute for the regular channels of diplomatic relations; but it would be equally unrealistic not to recognize the effective role that the American scholar can play in maintaining in his own area of interest a sane dialogue between the scholars of his country and those of other countries of the world.

This points up, it seems to me, the desirability of the American scholar's being quite certain that his role in the international intellectual community is different from the foreign policy that his country might pursue. Without becoming alienated from his country's interests, he must recognize that his intellectual interests and commitments are, in the long run, a complement to peace and, consequently, to the well-being of his country. For the international intellectual community, of which he must be a part, is just as viable and, indeed, more real than it was in the days of Thomas Jefferson or George Bancroft or William James. It transcends national boundaries, and it rises above the foreign policy of nations. It can be as closely knit as the interests and problems of its members permit it to be; and it can survive international political tensions, cold wars, and even military operations. It can keep the hope of peace alive in a world where political crises and international competition cast a pall; and it can overcome the narrow, myopic view with which the so-called politician-statesmen pursue their goals.

It would be a tragic misunderstanding of their role if the scholar-statesmen of our several disciplines mistook their own function as, somehow, tied to the role of the politician-statesmen. If they were to do so, they could unwittingly lend their talents, even in a negative way, to the furtherance of objectives with which they may not agree. For in refusing to pursue their own goals, maintain their own commitments, and continue the dialogue with their fellows in other parts of the world, they help to dim the light of reason in a world desperately in need of that light.

We need to maintain the world of the *scholar*-statesman, only the faint outlines of which are as yet known to the politician-statesman. It is a world in which the nematologists of Iraq and Texas work together on a common problem. It is a world in which the professor of American literature from Pennsylvania works with his students in Sweden and in which a specialist in American history from Delhi lectures on his subject in Chicago. It is a world in which the scholars of the United States give all that they have to make certain that their scholar-statesmen are in constant *and* fruitful contact with their counterparts elsewhere. If the politician-statesmen have all but destroyed their world by their intransigent, doctrinaire, and intolerant positions and policies, they may well be looking for more worlds to conquer. And if they look toward the world of the scholar-statesman, someone must tell them that this world is not open to conquest. For under such circumstances it may well be that the world of the scholar-statesman is the last best hope on earth and, thus, may save us all from what otherwise could be certain destruction.

Notes

Notes to *"The Birth of a Nation*: Propaganda as History"

1. The salient facts in Thomas Dixon's life are in Raymond Allen Cook, *Fire from the Flint: The Amazing Careers of Thomas Dixon* (Winston-Salem, N.C., 1968). Dixon's autobiography, "Southern Horizons," has never been published. I am grateful to Professor Arthur S. Link for sharing with me his notes from the manuscript.
2. Cook, *Fire from the Flint*, 71.
3. *Ibid.*, 115.
4. *Ibid.*, 166.
5. New York *Times*, March 4, 1915.
6. This account of Dixon's first viewing of the film has appeared in many places. For a relatively recent account, see Bosley Crowther, "'Birth of a Nation,' Fifty Years After," New York *Times Magazine*, February 7, 1965, pp. 25 ff.
7. Kelly Miller, *As to the Leopard's Spots: An Open Letter to Thomas Dixon, Jr.* (Washington, D.C., 1905), 20.
8. Sutton E. Griggs, *The Hindered Hand; or, The Reign of the Repressionist* (Nashville, Tenn., 1905), 332–33.
9. Thomas Dixon, Jr., "Booker T. Washington and the Negro," *Saturday Evening Post*, CLXXVIII (August 19, 1905), 1.
10. New York *Times*, March 31, 1915.
11. Arthur S. Link, *Wilson: The New Freedom* (Princeton, N.J., 1956), 252–53; Cook, *Fire from the Flint*, 169–70; and Thomas Dixon, "Southern Horizons: An Autobiography," in manuscript, 424–26.
12. Later, Wilson vigorously denied that he had ever expressed an opinion about the film. He asked his secretary to convey this fact to Mrs. Walter Damrosch who had inquired of the president's views (Wilson to Joseph Tumulty, March 29, 1915). Still later, he said to Tumulty, "I have always felt that this was a very unfortunate production" (Wilson Papers, Vol. VI, p. 485, courtesy of Arthur S. Link, editor of the Woodrow Wilson Papers).
13. Cook, *Fire from the Flint*, 171–72, and Dixon, "Southern Horizons," 430–35.
14. New York *Times*, March 31, 1915.
15. *Ibid.*, April 18, 1915, and *The Survey*, XXXIV (June 5, 1915), 209–210.
16. Jane Addams, in *Crisis: A Record of Darker Races*, X (May, 1915), 19, 41, and (June, 1915), 88.
17. Cook, *Fire from the Flint*, 176.
18. See the roundup of reviews in the New York *Times*, March 7, 1915.
19. *New Republic*, II (March 20, 1915), 185.
20. See, *e.g.*, *Crisis*, X (May, 1915), 40–42.

21. Francis B. Simkins, "New Viewpoints of Southern Reconstruction," *Journal of Southern History*, V (February, 1939), 49–61.
22. John Hope Franklin, *Reconstruction After the Civil War* (Chicago, 1961), 5–7.
23. For a corrective of Dixon's misrepresentations of South Carolina during Reconstruction, see Joel Williamson, *After Slavery: The Negro in South Carolina During Reconstruction* (Chapel Hill, 1965).
24. Of the several biographies of Stevens, the following two carefully treat Stevens' racial views and especially his relations with his housekeeper: Ralph Korngold, *Thaddeus Stevens, A Being Darkly Wise and Rudely Great* (New York, 1955), 72–76, and Fawn M. Brodie, *Thaddeus Stevens, Scourge of the South* (New York, 1959), 86–93.
25. Quoted in Cook, *Fire from the Flint*, 127.
26. New York *Times*, March 4, 7, 1915.
27. Thomas Dixon to Tumulty, May 1, 1915, and Thomas Dixon to Woodrow Wilson, September 5, 1915, both in Wilson Papers, VI, 485.
28. David M. Chalmers, *Hooded Americanism: The History of the Ku Klux Klan* (New York, 1965), 30.
29. Bosley Crowther, "Birth of a Nation," New York *Times Magazine*, 35.

Notes to "Whither Reconstruction Historiography?"

1. E. Merton Coulter, *The South During Reconstruction, 1865–1877* (Baton Rouge, 1947).
2. Julian A. C. Chandler *et al.* (eds.), *The South in the Building of the Nation* (13 vols.; Richmond, 1909–13).
3. E. Merton Coulter, *Civil War and Readjustment in Kentucky* (Chapel Hill, 1926).
4. E. Merton Coulter, *College Life in the Old South* (New York, 1928).
5. *New York Times Book Review*, December 21, 1947, p. 1.
6. *Christian Century*, January 28, 1948, p. 110.
7. *American Historical Review*, LIII (April, 1948), 565–67.
8. *Journal of Southern History*, XIV (February, 1948), 134–36.
9. *Annals of the American Academy of Political and Social Science*, CCLVIII (July, 1948), 153–54.
10. *Saturday Review of Literature*, Vol. XXXI, No. 19 (February 14, 1948), 26–28.
11. Howard K. Beale, "On Rewriting Reconstruction History," *American Historical Review*, XLV (July, 1941), 807–827; Francis B. Simkins and Robert H. Woody, *South Carolina During Reconstruction* (Chapel Hill, 1932); Francis B. Simkins, "New Viewpoints of Southern Reconstruction," *Journal of Southern History*, V (February, 1939), 49–61; Horace M. Bond, "Social and Economic Forces in Alabama Reconstruction," *Journal of Negro History*, XXIII (July, 1938), 290–348; Horace M. Bond, *Negro Education in Alabama: A Study in Cotton and Steel* (Washington, D.C., 1939); Vernon Wharton, *The Negro in Mississippi, 1865–1890* (Chapel Hill, 1947); W. E. B. Du Bois, "Reconstruction and Its Benefits," *American Historical Review*, XV (July, 1910), 781–99; W. E. B. Du Bois, *Black Reconstruction* (New York, 1935); and Robert W. Shugg, *Origins of Class Struggle in Louisiana* (Baton Rouge, 1939).
12. William Archibald Dunning, *Reconstruction: Political and Economic* (New York, 1907), 212.
13. Simkins, "New Viewpoints of Southern Reconstruction," 51.
14. As a matter of fact the statement, almost exactly as it appears in Coulter, is in J. S. Pike, *The Prostrate State* (New York, 1874), 15, and Coulter cites Pike as a reference. But he does not quote from the work nor does he make it clear whose views are being expressed.
15. Regarding the convention of freedmen held at Raleigh in September, 1865, Coulter says, "This convention, like most Negro gatherings, partook of a politico-religious nature with shouts and sobs and at times with fights waxing hot over such triv-

ialities as who should be the seventh vice-president" (Coulter, *The South During Reconstruction*, 60). This description follows very closely the account given by Sidney Andrews, who attended the convention. But Andrews adds, "Yet, when all these things are admitted, there is to be commended the sincere earnestness of the delegates as a body, the liberal spirit of their debates, the catholicity of their views of duty in the present emergency, the patient and cheerful tone of heart and head which prevailed, and the unfailing good-humor which bridged all passions and overcame all difficulties . . . on the whole the Convention did its work with commendable directness; and there were a number of speeches, and one or two lengthy debates, that would have been creditable to any white man's convention with even picked delegates." Sidney Andrews, *The South Since the War* (Boston, 1866), 124, 126.

16. Professor Coulter rarely cites the only general work on the Bureau: Paul S. Peirce, *The Freedmen's Bureau* (Iowa City, 1904). Although he could have secured statistics on the activities of the Bureau from this work, if he found it impossible to use either the published reports or the great mass of unpublished material in the National Archives, he nowhere gives a full picture of the expenditures of the Bureau or of its varied services to destitute whites as well as to Negroes.

17. Simkins and Woody, *South Carolina During Reconstruction*, 131.

18. Quoted *ibid.*, 92.

19. Edward King, *The Great South* (Hartford, 1875), 460.

20. My italics.

21. King, *The Great South*, 97. My italics.

22. Regarding marriage Professor Coulter, at page 53, says, "Negroes found it difficult to treat marriage as a permanent arrangement, and for some years after the war there were few marriages. In thirty-one Mississippi counties there were in 1866 only 564 marriages; in 1870, the habit of marrying having taken on a stronger hold, there were 3,427." The information was secured from Robert Somers, *The Southern States Since the War* (London, 1871), 251. But Somers was misquoted. Somers gave the figure of 564 as the number of marriages in *1865*, the year of emancipation, not *1866*. Somers added that the number "rose the following year [1866] to 3,679, and with the exception of 1868, when it fell to 2,802, has kept very near that mark ever since. The number of marriage licenses to negroes in 1870 was 3,427." The following remark by Somers is significantly different from the point of view of Professor Coulter: "It is not the less gratifying that negroes, when freed from all control, should have entered into the marriage state of their own accord at this ample rate, more especially as the cost of a marriage licence had been increased from *one* dollar under the old system to *three* dollars under the new." See, also, the discussion of Negro marriages in Whitelaw Reid, *After the War: A Southern Tour* (New York, 1866), 126–27.

23. King, *The Great South*, 273. Coulter's reference is to page 272. There was no pertinent discussion on that page, and it may be assumed that the correct reference was to page 273.

24. Andrews, *The South Since the War*, 350.

25. *Ibid.*

26. *Ibid.*, 222.

27. Professor Coulter also makes reference to the festive spirit of the Negro and describes it as being "native" with him. On page 54, he says that in freedom this spirit found expression "not only in his religion but also in many societies and lodges, mostly secret, and in holidays which he found and which he made. He loved gala and regalia." This manifestation was hardly a racial trait. Rather it was a national trait that was noticed by many travelers as well as others. See the article by Arthur M. Schlesinger, "Biography of a Nation of Joiners," *American Historical Review*, L (October, 1944), 1–25.

28. Frederick M. Davenport, *Primitive Traits in Religious Revivals* (New York, 1917).

29. Simkins and Woody, *South Carolina During Reconstruction,* 409.

30. *Ibid.,* 25, 322, 362. One shrewd observer said, "The blacks were unquestionably less addicted to ardent spirits than the Southern whites; but I suspect that it was mainly because, up to the emancipation, they were kept from it in a measure by police regulations, and because they were as yet too poor to purchase much of it." John William DeForest, *A Union Officer in the Reconstruction,* ed. J. H. Croushare and D. M. Potter (New Haven, 1948), 103. This observation was originally published in *Atlantic Monthly,* XXII (September, 1868).

31. See the account of a drunken brawl by whites in Somers, *The Southern States Since the War,* 127.

32. For accounts of the later careers of some of the Negro leaders of South Carolina see Simkins and Woody, *South Carolina During Reconstruction,* 545–47; A. A. Taylor, *The Negro in South Carolina During the Reconstruction* (Washington, D.C., 1924), 290–307; *Biographical Dictionary of the American Congress* (Washington, D.C., 1928), 774–75, 941, 1440, 1444, 1532; and *Dictionary of American Biography* (New York, 1928–1937), III, 403–404; XV, 327; XVII, 224.

33. Former Lieutenant Governor A. J. Ransier, for example, did become a laborer on the streets of Charleston. The report that Lieutenant Governor Richard Gleaves became a hotel waiter in New York appears to be unconfirmed. Simkins and Woody, *South Carolina During Reconstruction,* 545–46.

34. See Bond, *Negro Education in Alabama,* 24–25.

35. See the criticism of the codes in Shugg, *Origins of Class Struggle,* 214.

36. See Wharton, *The Negro in Mississippi,* 89–90, for local contemporary criticism of the Mississippi black code. The editor of the Columbus *Sentinel,* for example, called the framers of the code "as complete a set of Political Goths as were ever turned loose to work destruction upon a State." Another said that they were "a set of men who seem bent on following the dictates of every blind prejudice, let the consequences be ever so ruinous to the State and the people."

37. Wharton, *The Negro in Mississippi,* 91.

38. See Wharton's discussion, in which he tells how officials in Mississippi ignored an army order to forbid the prosecution of Negroes where the law discriminated against them. *Ibid.,* 91.

39. *Ibid.,* 60. See also the discussion of hostility to Negroes owning land in Reid, *After the War,* 564–65.

40. Andrews, *The South Since the War,* 206.

41. See the discussion in connection with this point in Bond, *Negro Education in Alabama,* 47–62.

Notes to "As for Our History"

1. William P. Trent *et al., The Cambridge History of American Literature* (3 vols.; New York, 1917–21), II, 288; John W. DuBose, *The Life and Times of William Lowndes Yancey* (2 vols.; Birmingham, 1892), I, 376.

2. Avery O. Craven, *The Growth of Southern Nationalism, 1848–1861* (Baton Rouge, 1953), 8.

3. See especially David Ramsay, *History of the Revolution of South Carolina from a British Colony to an Independent State* (2 vols.; Charleston, 1785); John Daly Burk, *The History of Virginia from Its First Settlement to the Present Day* (3 vols.; Petersburg, 1804–1805); J. G. M. Ramsey, *The Annals of Tennessee to the End of the Eighteenth Century* (Charleston, 1853); John H. Wheeler, *Historical Sketches of North Carolina, from 1584 to 1851* (2 vols.; New York, 1851).

4. Wesley Frank Craven, *The Legend of the Founding Fathers* (New York, 1956), 93.

5. John W. Higham, "The Changing Loyalties of William Gilmore Simms," *Journal of Southern History,* IX (May, 1943), 211; Craven, *Legend of the Founding Fathers,* 112.

6. Craven, *Legend of the Founding Fathers*, 109–13.
7. For a discussion of the role of the historian in the growth of nationalism, see Louis L. Snyder, *The Meaning of Nationalism* (New Brunswick, 1954), 27 ff.
8. Lorenzo Sabine, *The American Loyalists* (Boston, 1847), 42.
9. For examples of refutations, see "Southron" [William Gilmore Simms], *South Carolina in the Revolutionary War: Being A Reply to Certain Misrepresentations and Mistakes of Recent Writers in Relation to the Course and Conduct of this State* (Charleston, 1853); Lawrence M. Keitt, "Patriotic Services of the North and South," *DeBow's Review,* XXI (November, 1856), 491–508; and Joseph Johnson, *Traditions and Reminiscences Chiefly of the American Revolution in the South* (Charleston, 1851).
10. W. Gilmore Simms, *The Sources of American Independence: An Oration, on the Sixty-Ninth Anniversary of American Independence; Delivered at Aiken, South Carolina, Before the Town Council and Citizens Thereof* (Aiken, 1844), 22.
11. "Southron," *South Carolina in the Revolutionary War,* 62.
12. Lawrence M. Keitt, *Address of Lawrence M. Keitt, Esq. on the Laying the Corner-Stone of the Fire-Proof Building, at Columbia, December 15, 1851* (Columbia, 1851), 8.
13. *Proceedings at the Inauguration of the Monument Erected by the Washington Light Infantry, to the Memory of Col. William Washington, at Magnolia Cemetery, May 5, 1858* (Charleston, 1858), 13.
14. See, for example, Thomas L. Jones, *An Oration Delivered on the Fourth Day of July, 1847, At the County Seat of Polk County, North Carolina* (Greenville, 1847); and William E. Martin, *The South, Its Dangers and Its Resources. An Address Delivered at the Celebration of the Battle of Moultrie, June 28, 1850* (Charleston, 1850).
15. Rollin G. Osterweis, *Romanticism and Nationalism in the Old South* (New Haven, 1949), 138.
16. "The Difference of Race Between the Northern and Southern People," *Southern Literary Messenger,* XXX (June, 1860), 407.
17. A notable exception is R. R. Howison, whose *History of Virginia* was published in 1848. For a discussion of his views see Clement Eaton, *Freedom of Thought in the Old South* (Durham, 1940), 270–71.
18. *Southern Review,* I (April, 1867), 285.
19. Benjamin H. Hill, Jr., *Senator Benjamin H. Hill of Georgia: His Life Speeches and Writings* (Atlanta, 1893), 405. See also E. Merton Coulter, *The South During Reconstruction, 1865–1877* (Baton Rouge, 1947), 181–83.
20. "The Want of a History of the Southern People" in Thomas Nelson Page, *The Old South, Essays Social and Political* (New York, 1892), 253, 257.
21. Wendell Holmes Stephenson, "John Spencer Bassett as a Historian of the South," *North Carolina Historical Review,* XXV (July, 1948), 299, 300.
22. W. Stull Holt (ed.), *Historical Scholarship in the United States* (Baltimore, 1938), 245–47; and Michael Kraus, *A History of American History* (New York, 1937), 533–45. See also Alcée Fortier, "The Teaching of History in the South," *Iowa Journal of History and Politics,* XXX (January, 1905), 92–93, and William P. Trent, "Historical Studies in the South," *American Historical Association Papers* (Washington, 1890), 57–65.
23. Ulrich Bonnell Phillips, *Life and Labor in the Old South* (Boston, 1929), 201, 203.
24. Walter Lynwood Fleming, *Documentary History of the Reconstruction* (Cleveland, 1907), II, 328.
25. Julian A. C. Chandler *et al.* (eds.), *The South in the Building of the Nation* (13 vols.; Richmond, 1909–13).
26. Phillip M. Hamer, "The Records of Southern History," *Journal of Southern History,* V (February, 1939), 3–17.
27. Wendell H. Stephenson, "The South Lives in History," *Historical Outlook,* XXIII

(April, 1932), 153–63; Clement Eaton, "Recent Trends in the Writing of Southern History," *Louisiana Historical Quarterly,* XXXVIII (April, 1955), 26–42. For a recent report to a committee of the Southern Historical Association calling attention to many still neglected areas of southern history, see "Research Possibilities in Southern History," *Journal of Southern History,* XVI (February, 1950), 52–63.

28. Eaton, "Recent Trends." See also American Historical Association, *List of Doctoral Dissertations in History Now in Progress at Universities in the United States* (Washington, 1952).

29. Francis B. Simkins, "Tolerating the South's Past," *Journal of Southern History,* XXI (February, 1955), 3–16.

30. The most exhaustive studies of the nonslaveholding element of the South have been made by Frank L. Owsley and his students. The findings are conveniently summarized in his *Plain Folk of the Old South* (Baton Rouge, 1949). See also Kenneth M. Stampp, "The Historian and Southern Negro Slavery," *American Historical Review,* LVII (April, 1952), 613–24, and his *The Peculiar Institution* (New York, 1956).

31. Bell Irvin Wiley, *Southern Negroes, 1861–1865* (New Haven, 1938).

32. Benjamin Quarles, *The Negro in the Civil War* (Boston, 1953).

33. Howard K. Beale, "On Rewriting Reconstruction History," *American Historical Review,* XLV (July, 1940), 807–27; and Vernon L. Wharton, *The Negro in Mississippi, 1865–1890* (Chapel Hill, 1947).

34. C. Vann Woodward, *Origins of the New South, 1877–1913* (Baton Rouge, 1951).

Notes to "Slaves Virtually Free in Antebellum North Carolina"

1. The literature on both sides is abundant. U. B. Phillips, *American Negro Slavery* (New York, 1918), is one of the ablest and best-known works which sets forth the point of view that, on the whole, Negro slaves were treated very well in the antebellum South. Concerning the treatment of slaves, Phillips said, "In the actual regime severity was clearly the exception, and kindliness the rule," p. 306. One of the most recent and best discussions of the absence of humanity on the southern plantation is Frederic Bancroft's *Slave Trading in the Old South* (Baltimore, 1931). One of Bancroft's conclusions was that "slavery maintained as a profitable and convenient institution was essentially ruthless in general and inhumane in some of its main features," p. 197. The bibliographies in these and other works of similar nature will furnish additional sources, primary and secondary, concerning the treatment of slaves in the antebellum South.

2. Professor Sydnor says that the master's treatment of his slaves depended chiefly on his character, but goes on to say that the "white man's attitude toward slavery was determined largely by the economic interests of his class." See C. S. Sydnor, *Slavery in Mississippi* (New York, 1933), 249. Coleman also suggests the importance of social and economic factors in the treatment of slaves when he observes, somewhat subjectively, "Slavery in the Bluegrass State . . . was much more a domestic than a commercial institution. And it was in this environment of lavish nature, prodigal outlay . . . and benevolent bondage that the folks in the big house . . . enjoyed life in those colorful and romantic days of ante-bellum Kentucky." J. W. Coleman, *Slavery Times in Kentucky* (Chapel Hill, 1940), 47.

3. Guion G. Johnson, *Ante-Bellum North Carolina* (Chapel Hill, 1937), 469 ff. See also, Rosser H. Taylor, *Slaveholding in North Carolina* (Chapel Hill, 1926), 30–47.

4. Walter Clark (ed.), *The State Records of North Carolina* (Goldsboro, 1906) XXIII, 63.

5. *Ibid.,* 65.

6. *Ibid.,* 197.

7. *Ibid.,* 201.

8. *Ibid.,* 202.

9. See John C. Hurd, *Law of Freedom and Bondage in the United States* (Boston, 1858), II, 95 ff.
10. This accounts, in part at least, for the concentration of free Negroes, some of whom were runaway slaves from other states, in the counties bordering on Virginia and South Carolina.
11. Alice D. Adams, *The Neglected Period of Anti-Slavery in America (1808–1831)* (Boston, 1908), 34.
12. A printed copy of the resolution is in the Legislature Papers of North Carolina for 1826–27.
13. *Laws Passed by the General Assembly of North Carolina, 1826–27* (Raleigh, 1827), 15.
14. For a complete discussion of Walker's *Appeal* see Clement Eaton, "A Dangerous Pamphlet in the Old South," *Journal of Southern History*, II (August, 1936). See also, Joseph C. Carroll, *Slave Insurrections in the U.S., 1800–65* (Boston, 1938), 120–27.
15. *Laws of North Carolina, 1830–1831*, 10.
16. *Ibid.*, 11.
17. *Laws of North Carolina, 1790–1804*, 3. See, for example, the records of the Court of Pleas and Quarter Sessions of Craven County, 1804.
18. In the decade ending in 1830, the free Negro population had increased from 14,712 to 15,793. U.S. Census Office, *The Fifth Census* (Washington, 1832), 91–93.
19. *Laws of North Carolina, 1823–1831*, 12.
20. John Cummings, *Negro Population in the United States* (Washington, 1915), 57.
21. *Creswell et al. v. Emberson*, XLI, *North Carolina*, 103.
22. Myers and wife, and the same administrator as *John A. Lillington* v. *Williams et al.*, LVIII, *North Carolina*, 286. As early as 1816, when the assembly passed an act against the desire of the administrator of the deceased's estate, the court held that the act was void. *Allen's Administrator* v. *Peden*, IV, *North Carolina*, 332.
23. After 1826, it was not lawful for county courts to manumit slaves. The power of manumission had been transferred to the superior courts.
24. Petition in the Legislative Papers for 1838–1839.
25. See the endorsement of the bill. MS. in the Legislative Papers for 1838–1839.
26. *Wm. T. Lemmond et al.* v. *Richard Peoples et al.*, XLI, *North Carolina*, 93. See, also, the will of a testator which provided that his slaves be turned over to a friend and that $3,000 and 200 acres of land be conveyed to provide for the slaves' care. The court said that the provision had no support by policy or law. "The result will be to establish in our midst a set of privileged negroes, causing the others to be dissatisfied and restless, and affording a harbor for the lazy and evildisposed." *J. G. Lea et al.* v. *Thos. J. Brown et al.*, LVI, *North Carolina*, 141.
27. *Lucy Thomas et al.* v. *Nathaniel J. Palmer*, LIV, *North Carolina*, 173.
28. *Dunlap* v. *Ingram et al.*, IV, Jones Equity, 183.
29. D. L. Corbitt, "Slave Selling Himself," *North Carolina Historical Review* (October, 1924), 451–52.
30. *John C. Washington, Executor, et al.* v. *Elizabeth Blount et al.*, XLIII, *North Carolina*, 165.
31. P. M. Sherrill, *The Quakers and the North Carolina Manumission Society* (Durham, 1914), 32.
32. *Ibid.*, 38. The society was strongest in those counties where the Quakers were most numerous, namely, Guilford, Randolph, Chatham, Orange, Davidson, and Forsyth counties.
33. See the opinion of William Gaston in this matter, quoted extensively in Sherrill, *Quakers*, 33 ff.
34. D. L. Corbitt, "Freeing Slaves," *North Carolina Historical Review* (October, 1924), 449.

35. *Trustees of the Quaker Society of Contentnea* v. *Wm. Dickinson*, XII, *North Carolina*, 120 ff. In a strong dissent, Mr. Justice Hall said that there was nothing in the law of 1796 or in Quaker creed that forbade them to hold *title* to slaves. He said, "The Court ought not to take a step into the moral world and anticipate preventive remedies for possible infractions of the law." It is interesting to observe that the attorney for the Quaker Society was the same William Gaston who, in 1809, had advised the Society of Friends that the law of 1796 did not prohibit their acquisition of Negro slaves. The point of view of the chief justice was upheld in 1833. *Elizabeth Redmond* v. *Bethuel Coffin, Executor of Thomas Wright et al.*, XVII, *North Carolina*, 351.
36. *Joshua White* v. *John C. White*, XVIII, *North Carolina*, 264 ff.
37. *John Newlin* v. *Richard Freeman*, XXIII, *North Carolina*, 386 ff.
38. Stephen B. Weeks, *Southern Quakers and Slavery* (Baltimore, 1896), 227.
39. In 1826 alone, nearly $5,000 was collected by the North Carolina Yearly Meeting for the purpose of colonizing Negroes. Weeks, *Southern Quakers*, 230, and *ibid.*, 238 ff. See also, Early Lee Fox, *The American Colonization Society.*
40. For example, Thomas Day, a wealthy cabinetmaker of Milton, who had three slaves and a white journeyman to work in his business, could hardly be called a benevolent free Negro slaveholder. See the unpublished population schedules of the Census of 1860 in the Bureau of the Census, Washington, D.C.
41. See the minutes of the Court of Pleas and Quarter Sessions of Craven County, March, 1811, which shows that Thomas Newton, a free Negro, liberated his slave wife, ms. in the Archives of the North Carolina Historical Commission, Raleigh, North Carolina.
42. Ms. in the Legislative Papers for 1856, in the Archives of the North Carolina Historical Commission, Raleigh, North Carolina.
43. Mss. in the Legislative Papers for 1840, in the Archives of the North Carolina Historical Commission, Raleigh, North Carolina.
44. *Journal of the House of Commons, 1827* (Raleigh, 1828), 180.
45. Mss. in the Legislative Papers for 1856, in the Archives of the North Carolina Historical Commission, Raleigh, North Carolina.
46. Greensborough *Patriot*, December 23, 1854.
47. *Western Democrat*, December 15, 1854.
48. Minutes of the Court of Pleas and Quarter Sessions of Craven County, March, 1808. See also the minutes for the September term, 1808, when a similar permit was granted to March, the slave of John Tillman.
49. Minutes of the Court of Pleas and Quarter Sessions of Craven County, September, 1809, in the Archives of the North Carolina Historical Commission, Raleigh, North Carolina.
50. Carter G. Woodson, *Education of the Negro Prior to 1860* (Washington, D.C., 1919), 46.
51. Weeks, *Southern Quakers*, 231.
52. *Memoirs of Wm. Forster* (London, 1865), II, 31.
53. Woodson, *Education of the Negro*, 182.
54. Presbyterian Synod of North Carolina, *Minutes of the 38th Session* (Raleigh, 1851), 21. Some Episcopalians were also engaged in the task of teaching slaves to read and write. See the account of the activities of the Reverend Alexander Stewart in Joseph B. Cheshire, *Sketches of Church History in North Carolina* (Wilmington, 1892), 73.
55. Woodson, *Education of the Negro*, 394.
56. Henry P. Battle, "George Horton, Slave Poet," *North Carolina University Magazine*, VII (May, 1888), 229 ff., and Sterling Brown and others, *The Negro Caravan*, 287 ff.
57. Ms. in the Pettigrew Family Papers, in the Library of the University of North

Carolina. Unfortunately, it is not possible to date the poem since the manuscript contains no indication of when it was written.

58. Julius Melbourn, *Life and Opinions of Julius Melbourn, passim.*
59. For a recent discussion of the life of Melbourn after he obtained his freedom see John Hope Franklin, "The Free Negro in the Economic Life of Ante-Bellum North Carolina," Part II, *North Carolina Historical Review,* XX (October, 1942), 369.
60. Walter Clark, *State Records of North Carolina* (Goldsboro, 1896), XXIV, 727.
61. Ms. in the Legislative Papers for 1830–31.
62. *Laws of North Carolina, 1830–1831,* p. 7.
63. Michael Collins to the Editor at Warrenton, n.d., ms. in the Michael Collins Papers, in the library of Duke University.

Notes to "Slavery and the Martial South"

1. Paul Leicester Ford (ed.), *The Writings of Thomas Jefferson* (New York, 1894), III, 266–267.
2. Basil Hall, *Travels in North America in the Years 1827–1828* (Edinburgh, 1830), III, 230.
3. Alexis de Tocqueville, *Democracy in America* (New York, 1893), 507–508.
4. James S. Buckingham, *The Slave States of America* (London, 1842), II, 28.
5. Frances Kemble, *Journal of a Residence on a Georgia Plantation* (New York, 1864), 57–58, 305.
6. Max Farrand (ed.), *Records of the Federal Convention* (New Haven, 1927), II, 370.
7. Ulrich B. Phillips, *Race Problems, Adjustments and Disturbances in the Ante-Bellum South* (Richmond, 1909), 200.
8. Richard Hildreth, *Despotism in America* (Boston, 1840), 37.
9. Charles Sumner, "The Barbarism of Slavery," speech delivered in the U.S. Senate, June 4, 1860 (Washington, 1860), p. 13.
10. H. S. Fulkerson, *Random Recollections of Early Days in Mississippi* (Vicksburg, 1885), 143.
11. Frederick L. Olmsted, *Journey in the Back Country* (London, 1860), 30.
12. Fulkerson, *Random Recollections,* 129.
13. Helen T. Catterall, *Judicial Cases Concerning American Slavery and the Negro* (Washington, 1929), II, 57.
14. Olmsted, *Journey in the Back Country,* 82–83.
15. Howell M. Henry, *The Police Control of the Slave in South Carolina* (Emory, Virginia, 1914), 31 ff.
16. *The Code of Alabama* (Montgomery, 1852), 235.
17. *Ibid.;* and John B. Miller, *A Collection of the Militia Laws of the United States and South Carolina* (Columbia, 1817), 71 ff.
18. Henry, *Police Control of the Slave,* 32.
19. Charles S. Sydnor, *Slavery in Mississippi* (New York, 1933), 78.
20. Hall, *Travels in North America,* III, 74–75.
21. William Chambers, *Things as They Are in America* (New York, 1854), 272.
22. Buckingham, *The Slave States of America,* I, 568.
23. J. Benwell, *An Englishman's Travels in America* (London, 1857), 178, 184–85.
24. Adelaide Wilson, *Historic and Picturesque Savannah* (Boston, 1889), 81.
25. New Orleans *Daily Picayune,* January 2, 1857.
26. Edwin Clifford Holland, *A Refutation of the Calumnies Circulated Against the Southern and Western States* (Charleston, 1822), 61, 62.
27. Olmsted, *Journey in the Back Country,* 203.
28. William Asbury Christian, *Richmond, Her Past and Present* (Richmond, 1912), 53; and Herbert Aptheker, *American Negro Slave Revolts* (New York, 1943), 218 ff.

29. Theodore D. Jervey, *Robert Y. Hayne and His Times* (New York, 1909), 131–32; and Henry, *Police Control of the Slave*, 152–53.
30. Nashville *Republican*, September 10, 1831.
31. Norfolk *Herald*, August 21, 1831, reprinted in Nashville *Republican*, September 10, 1831.
32. Frederick T. Wilson, *Federal Aid in Domestic Disturbances, 1787–1903* (Washington, 1903), 56, 261–63.
33. Charles Gayarré, *History of Louisiana* (New Orleans, 1903), IV, 267–68.
34. Aptheker, *American Negro Slave Revolts*, 255.
35. Harvey T. Cook, *The Life and Legacy of David Rogerson Williams* (New York, 1916), 130.
36. Guion G. Johnson, *Ante-Bellum North Carolina* (Chapel Hill, 1937), 514–15.
37. Aptheker, *American Negro Slave Revolts*, 335.
38. *Journal of the Legislature of South Carolina for the Year 1833*, p. 6.
39. New Orleans *Daily Picayune*, December 24, 1856.
40. William S. Jenkins, *Pro-Slavery Thought in the Old South* (Chapel Hill, 1935), 125.
41. Quoted in Edward Ingle, *Southern Sidelights* (New York, 1896), 31.
42. *Selections from the Letters and Speeches of the Hon. James H. Hammond of South Carolina* (New York, 1866), 34.
43. Thomas R. Dew, *Review of the Debate in the Virginia Legislature of 1831 and 1832* (Richmond, 1832), 112–13.

Notes to "The Southern Expansionists of 1846"

1. Albert K. Weinberg, *Manifest Destiny: A Study of Nationalist Expansionism in American History* (Baltimore, 1935), 100 ff.
2. This point was frequently made in the debates on the Oregon question in 1846. See *Congressional Globe*, 29th Cong., 1st Sess., Appendix, 72 ff.
3. John D. P. Fuller, *The Movement for the Acquisition of All Mexico, 1846–1848* (Baltimore, 1936), 15 ff.
4. Chauncey S. Boucher and Robert P. Brooks (eds.), *Correspondence Addressed to John C. Calhoun*, American Historical Association, *Annual Report, 1929* (Washington, 1930), 217.
5. *Congressional Globe*, 28th Cong., 2nd Sess., 88, 321, 324.
6. Stephen Smith to John C. Calhoun, December 30, 1845, in J. Franklin Jameson (ed.), *Correspondence of John C. Calhoun*, American Historical Association, *Annual Report, 1899* (2 vols.; Washington, 1900), II, 1068–69.
7. Richmond *Enquirer*, January 26, 1846. In the same issue, see also the prediction of the Mobile *Register* that California would soon be a part of the United States.
8. *Congressional Globe*, 29th Cong., 1st Sess., 92. See also Fuller, *The Movement for the Acquisition of All Mexico*, 28 ff.
9. Jameson (ed.), *Correspondence of John C. Calhoun*, 1083–84.
10. For the expansionist views of Adams and Johnson, see *Congressional Globe*, 29th Cong., 1st Sess., 143, 288, 324.
11. *Ibid.*, Appendix, 184.
12. See Jameson (ed.), *Correspondence of John C. Calhoun*, 691; *Congressional Globe*, 29th Cong., 1st Sess., 504 ff, 795; and Ulrich B. Phillips (ed.), *The Correspondence of Robert Toombs, Alexander H. Stephens, and Howell Cobb*, American Historical Association, *Annual Report, 1911* (2 vols.; Washington, 1913), II, 71–72.
13. A valuable corrective regarding the lack of emphasis on the drive for Oregon up to 54° 40′ in the campaign of 1844 has been made by Edwin A. Miles in "'Fifty-four Forty or Fight'—An American Political Legend," *Mississippi Valley Historical Review*, XLIV (September, 1957), 291–309, and by Hans Sperber, "'Fifty-four Forty or Fight': Facts and Fictions," *American Speech*, XXXII (February, 1957), 5–11.
14. *Congressional Globe*, 29th Cong., 1st Sess., 319.

15. Fuller, *The Movement for the Acquisition of All Mexico*, 58, and Weinberg, *Manifest Destiny*, 117 ff.

16. See Arthur Cole, *The Whig Party in the South* (Washington, 1913). For an illuminating and significant discussion of the interests and sources of strength of the Whig party in the South, see Charles Grier Sellers, Jr., "Who Were the Southern Whigs?" *American Historical Review,* LIX (January, 1954), 335–46.

17. [Richard K. Crallé (ed.)], *The Works of John C. Calhoun* (6 vols.; New York, 1851–1856), IV, 258 ff. See also Charles M. Wiltse, *John C. Calhoun* (3 vols.; Indianapolis, 1944–1951), III, 260 ff.

18. *Congressional Globe*, 29th Cong., 1st Sess., 570 ff.

19. *Ibid.,* 514, 540, 604.

20. Memphis *Enquirer,* February 24, 1846.

21. Nashville *Republican Banner,* January 16, April 22, 1846.

22. Charleston *Mercury,* April 9, 1846.

23. Thomas P. Martin, "Free Trade and the Oregon Question, 1842–1846," in *Facts and Factors in Economic History* (Cambridge, 1932), 470–91.

24. Reported in Richmond *Enquirer,* February 7, 1846. For Chalmers' views, see *Congressional Globe*, 29th Cong., 1st Sess., 540.

25. George D. Phillips to Howell Cobb, December 30, 1845, in Phillips (ed.), *The Correspondence of Robert Toombs*, 70. For examples of enthusiastic southern endorsement of Senator Allen's resolution to give notice, see letters to him from Lloyd Selby, Warrenton, Mississippi, February 6, 1846; William Mims, Americus, Georgia, May 9, 1846; and Old Dominion, New Orleans, Louisiana, May 19, 1846, in William Allen Papers (Manuscripts Division, Library of Congress).

26. Howell Cobb to Mrs. Howell Cobb, June 14, 1846, in Phillips (ed.), *The Correspondence of Robert Toombs*, 81–82.

27. *Congressional Globe*, 29th Cong., 1st Sess., Appendix, 118.

28. *Ibid.,* 29th Cong., 1st Sess., 307. Chase said, too, that "surrender, on the part of any nation, was the signal for its downfall, and an invitation to all the nations of the earth to commence their aggressions upon her." For another discussion of southern expansionists in the Twenty-ninth Congress, see Norman A. Graebner, *Empire on the Pacific* (New York, 1955), 125 ff.

29. *Congressional Globe*, 29th Cong., 1st Sess., 288.

30. *Ibid.,* 315, 317, 548, 294–96.

31. *Ibid.,* Appendix 89. In the end, however, Hunter did not stand with the ardent expansionists.

32. *Ibid.,* 29th Cong., 1st Sess., 150. See also Henry W. Hilliard, *Politics and Pen Pictures at Home and Abroad* (New York, 1892), 136 ff.

33. *Congressional Globe*, 29th Cong., 1st Sess., 308; *ibid.,* Appendix, 120, 243, 247.

34. *Ibid.,* 29th Cong., 1st Sess., 296–97.

35. *Ibid.,* Appendix, 120; *ibid.,* 29th Cong., 1st Sess., 165, 167.

36. *Ibid.,* Appendix, 107, 109.

37. *Ibid.,* 29th Cong., 1st Sess., 289. The Nashville *Republican Banner,* February 13, 1846, called the Johnson speech "intemperate, unkind, and inconsiderate." At the end of a long critique the editor said that the Johnson "rantings" were like those of Giddings and other abolitionists.

38. See Henry Hilliard's speech in which he emphasized this point, *Congressional Globe*, 29th Cong., 1st Sess., 148.

39. *Ibid.,* 308; *ibid.,* Appendix, 267; *ibid.,* 29th Cong., 1st Sess., 548–49.

40. *Ibid.,* 672–73. See also Marquis James, *The Raven, A Biography of Sam Houston* (New York, 1929), 361.

41. Justin Smith, *The War with Mexico* (2 vols.; New York, 1919), I, 82 ff.

42. See Wiltse, *John C. Calhoun*, III, 252, 278, for an account of the pressures Calhoun put on Polk to proceed cautiously in the Oregon negotiations.

43. Frederick Merk, "The Oregon Pioneers and the Boundary," *American Historical Review*, XXIX (July, 1924), 681–99.
44. Robert Toombs to George W. Crawford, February 6, 1846, in Phillips (ed.), *The Correspondence of Robert Toombs*, 74.
45. Calhoun and Berrien abstained from voting on the war resolution when it was passed by the Senate. *Congressional Globe*, 29th Cong., 1st Sess., 804. See also Jameson (ed.), *Correspondence of John C. Calhoun*, 689–91. For Howell Cobb's attitude, see the letter to his wife, May 10, 1846, in Phillips (ed.), *The Correspondence of Robert Toombs*, 76.

Notes to "The Enforcement of the Civil Rights Act of 1875"

1. The bill's history has been discussed by several historians. See David Donald, *Charles Sumner and the Rights of Man* (New York, 1970); L. E. Murphy, "The Civil Rights Law of 1875," *Journal of Negro History*, XII (1927), 110–27; Alfred H. Kelly, "The Congressional Controversy Over School Segregation," *American Historical Review*, LXIV (1959), 537–63; and James McPherson, "Abolitionists and the Civil Rights Act of 1875," *Journal of American History* LII (1965), 493–510. For a sample of debate on the bill, see *Congressional Record*, 43rd Cong., 2nd Sess., No. 3, Pt. 2, pp. 939–1005, 1791–1870.
2. 18 *Statutes at Large* 335.
3. Benjamin Butler to Robert Harlan in *Harper's Weekly*, April 24, 1875.
4. New York *Times*, March 2, 6, 1875.
5. *Ibid.*, March 3, 14, 20, April 22, 1875.
6. *Ibid.*, March 6, 1875.
7. *Ibid.*, June 8, 1875.
8. *Ibid.*, June 9, 1875.
9. U.S. Attorney Walter Van Dyke to Attorney General George H. Williams, March 24, 1875, Records of the Department of Justice, Record Group 60, National Archives; *New York Times*, September 29, December 30, 1875, March 7, 1876. Unless otherwise indicated correspondence of the attorneys general and other Justice Department manuscripts are in Record Group 60.
10. New York *Times*, March 3, 1875.
11. *Ibid.*, March 3, 7, 1875.
12. *Ibid.*, September 6, 1875.
13. *Ibid.*, June 12, 1875.
14. 6 *Federal Cases* 946; *New York Times*, March 23, 1877.
15. In Little Rock a Negro woman was refused a seat in the ladies' car, *ibid.*, December 14, 1875. For a similar incident, see 25 *Federal Cases* 882.
16. 27 *Federal Cases* 127.
17. Charge by Judge Halmor H. Emmons to the grand jury of the Circuit Court for the Western District of Tennessee, March, 1875, 30 *Federal Cases* 1005.
18. Justice Department, Instruction Book E, pp. 333, 338, 359.
19. U.S. Attorney W. W. Murray to Williams, Memphis, Tenn., March 4, 1875.
20. Telegram of U.S. Attorney Warner H. Bateman to Williams, Cincinnati, March 8, 1875.
21. U.S. Attorney H. P. Farrow to Williams, Atlanta, March 9, 1875.
22. U.S. Attorney J. O. Glover to Williams, Chicago, March 13, 1875; U.S. Commissioner A. N. Wilson to Williams, Savannah, March 15, 1875; U.S. Commissioner R. W. Best to Williams, Raleigh, March 15, 1875; U.S. Attorney J. R. Beckwith to Williams, New Orleans, March 16, 1875; Van Dyke to Williams, San Francisco, March 24, 1875.
23. See Justice Department, Instruction Book E for letters to U.S. attorneys in Memphis and Cincinnati, March 9, 1875, and San Francisco, April 5, 1875.
24. Farrow to Williams, Atlanta, March 9, 1875.
25. William Travis to Williams, Cincinnati, March 22, 1875.

26. Williams to Travis, March 26, 1875, Justice Department, Letter Book K.
27. Collector E. J. Castellor to Attorney General Charles Devens, Natchez, Miss., May 14, 1879; and Devens to Castellor, May 20, 1879, Justice Department, Letter Book M.
28. The attorneys general who served between March 1, 1875, when the act was passed, and October 15, 1883, when it was declared unconstitutional by the Supreme Court, are as follows: George H. Williams until May 5, 1875, Edwards Pierrepont, 1875–76, Alphonso Taft, 1876–77, Charles Devens, 1877–81, Wayne McVeigh, 1881, and Benjamin Brewster, 1881–85.
29. *New York Times*, April 22, 1875.
30. *Ibid.*, April 27, June 15, 1875.
31. *U.S.* v. *Newcomer*, 27 *Federal Cases* 127.
32. *Cully* v. *Baltimore & Ohio R.R. Co.*, 6 *Federal Cases* 946, and New York *Times*, March 23, 1877.
33. *U.S.* v. *Buntin*, 10 *Federal Reporter* 730.
34. U.S. Attorney J. R. Hallowell to Smith L. Rogers, Topeka, Kans., September 2, 1879; Rogers to Devens, Ottawa, Kans., September 5, 1879; and Rogers to Devens, Ottawa, Kans., September 22, 1879.
35. New York *Times*, March 14, 1875.
36. *U.S.* v. *Samuel D. Singleton*, File No. 9358, Supreme Court transcript, Justice Department; New York *Times*, November 25, December 10, 1879, January 15, 1880.
37. No. 18258, cases not cited, 30 *Federal Cases* 999. For a similar view, see the charge to the jury by Judge Morrill of the U.S. District Court for the Eastern District of Texas, New York *Times*, May 5, 1875.
38. New York *Times*, June 9, 1875.
39. U.S. Attorney Warren S. Lurty to Pierrepont, Harrisonburg, October 21, 1875.
40. New York *Times*, May 5, June 8, 1875.
41. *Gray* v. *Cincinnati Southern R.R. Co.*, 11 *Federal Reporter* 683.
42. New York *Times*, March 6, 1875.
43. *Ibid.*, June 12, 1875.
44. 30 *Federal Cases* 1005; New York *Times*, March 23, 1875.
45. New York *Times*, May 1, 2, 1875, and *Harper's Weekly*, May 15, 1875, p. 395. See also the ruling in a California case, New York *Times*, June 7, 1876.
46. *U.S.* v. *Dodge*, 25 *Federal Cases* 882. Indeed in its October, 1877 term the Supreme Court ruled that a Louisiana law requiring white and Negro passengers to be accommodated in the same cabin was unconstitutional. Hall *v.* DeCuir, 95 *U.S.* 485.
47. *Green* v. *City of Bridgeton*, 10 *Federal Cases* 1090. See also *Smoot* v. *Central Railway Co.*, 13 *Federal Reporter* 337, in which the judge denied that he had jurisdiction to rule on separate accommodations.
48. U.S. Attorney J. H. Standish to Pierrepont, Grand Rapids, July 7, 1875; S. F. Phillips, solicitor general and acting attorney general, to Standish, July 12, 1875, Justice Department, Instruction Book F. Standish had written at the suggestion of Judge Emmons.
49. *U.S.* v. *Murray Stanley*, File No. 7826, Supreme Court transcript, Justice Department. The case was filed with the Court October 6, 1876.
50. *U.S.* v. *Michael Ryan*, File No. 7914, Supreme Court transcript, Justice Department.
51. *Ibid.*, U.S. Attorney J. M. Coghlan to Attorney General Taft, San Francisco, October 3, 1876.
52. *U.S.* v. *Samuel Nichols*, File No. 8060, February 5, 1877; *Richard A. Robinson and Sallie J. his wife* v. *Memphis & Charleston R.R. Co.*, File No. 9402, February 7, 1880; and *U.S.* v. *Samuel D. Singleton*, File No. 9358, March 10, 1880, Supreme Court transcripts, Justice Department.

53. U.S. Attorney Nelson Trusler to Devens, Indianapolis, January 14, 1879; Devens to Trusler, January 17, 1879, Justice Department, Instruction Book H.
54. Devens to S. L. Woodford, March 4, 1880, Justice Department, Instruction Book I.
55. Devens to Charles L. Holston, April 30, 1880, Justice Department, Instruction Book K.
56. Devens to U.S. Attorney James A. Wardner, November 30, 1880, *ibid.*
57. See Minutes of the Supreme Court of the United States, Record Group 267, National Archives Microfilm Publication M215, Role 14.
58. Phillips to George B. Sawyer, November 17, 1881, Justice Department, Instruction Book L.
59. 109 *U.S.* 3.
60. *Proceedings of the Civil Rights Mass Meeting, Lincoln Hall, October 22, 1883* (Washington, 1883), 6.
61. *Daily Arkansas Gazette*, October 19, 1883.
62. *Mississippi Weekly Pilot*, April 10, 1875, quoting the Handsboro *Democrat*, in Vernon L. Wharton, *The Negro in Mississippi, 1865–1890* (Chapel Hill, 1947), 184.
63. *The Nation*, XXIV (April 5, 1877), 202. See also Rayford W. Logan, *The Negro in American Life and Thought: The Nadir, 1877–1901* (New York, 1954), 159–69.

Notes to "The Two Worlds of Race"

1. Benjamin Quarles, *The Negro in the American Revolution* (Chapel Hill, 1961), 15–18.
2. John Hope Franklin, *From Slavery to Freedom: A History of American Negroes* (New York, 1956), 156–57.
3. Carter G. Woodson, *The Education of the Negro Prior to 1861* (Washington, D.C., 1919), 93–97.
4. P. J. Staudenraus, *The African Colonization Movement, 1816–1865* (New York, 1961), 22–32.
5. John Hope Franklin, *The Militant South, 1800–1861* (Cambridge, Mass., 1956), 83–86.
6. Louis Filler, *The Crusade Against Slavery, 1830–1860* (New York, 1960), 142–45.
7. Leon F. Litwack, *North of Slavery: The Negro in the Free States, 1790–1860* (Chicago, 1961), 216–17.
8. Benjamin Quarles, *The Negro in the Civil War* (Boston, 1953), 200.
9. John Hope Franklin, *Reconstruction After the Civil War* (Chicago, 1961), 154–58.
10. Rayford W. Logan, *The Negro in American Life and Thought: The Nadir, 1877–1901* (New York, 1954), 239–74.
11. John Hope Franklin, "History of Racial Segregation in the United States," *Annals of the Academy of Political and Social Science*, CCCIV (March, 1956), 1–9.
12. George W. Williams, *History of the Negro Race in America from 1619 to 1880* (New York, 1882), x.
13. Franklin, *From Slavery to Freedom*, 437–43.
14. Edmund David Cronon, *Black Moses: The Story of Marcus Garvey and the Universal Negro Improvement Association* (Madison, Wisc., 1955), 202–206.
15. Lee Nichols, *Breakthrough on the Color Front* (New York, 1954), 221–26.
16. *To Secure These Rights: The Report of the President's Committee on Civil Rights* (New York, 1947), 166.
17. John Hope Franklin, "As for Our History," herein, pp. 59–70.

Notes to "Edward Bellamy and the Nationalist Movement"

1. Morris Hillquit, *History of Socialism in the United States* (New York, 1910), 17; Allyn B. Forbes, "The Literary Quest for Utopia, 1880–1900," *Social Forces*, VI (December, 1927), 180 ff.

2. While the Knights of Labor were pledged to a policy of arbitration, they neverthe-less became "embroiled in a number of strikes, boycotts, and other disturbances," Arthur M. Schlesinger, *Political and Social Growth of the United States* (New York, 1933), 204. The arbitrary tax proposed by Henry George aroused the indigna-tion of a great portion of the large landowners in all sections of the country.

3. One writer suggests that his keen sense of justice may be attributable to the clerical environment. Forbes, "Literary Quest for Utopia," 83.

4. Edward Bellamy, "How I Wrote 'Looking Backward,'" *Ladies' Home Journal* (April, 1894), reprinted in *Edward Bellamy Speaks Again* (Kansas City, 1937), 217.

5. *Edward Bellamy Speaks Again*, 218.

6. "Excerpts from the Journal of Edward Bellamy" (unpublished), 5.

7. Frances Willard, "An Interview with Edward Bellamy," *Our Day*, V (April, 1890), 539.

8. Nor was he without slight eccentricities. Mrs. Bellamy told me that in the pres-ence of guests he would rise from the dinner table and begin pacing the floor. Soon he would exclaim, "I have a thought!" whereupon he was off to his study, where no one ever dared to enter.

9. "The Religion of Solidarity," unpublished manuscript in the possession of Mrs. Edward Bellamy, p. 5.

10. *Ibid.*, 16.

11. Bellamy makes these comments on the first page of the manuscript of "The Religion of Solidarity" and on the last page observes that part of the original manuscript has been lost.

12. Edward Bellamy, *The Duke of Stockbridge* (not published in book form until 1901, at New York), 77.

13. At twenty-one, Bellamy had written in his journal, page 8, "Were the ambition that spurs my labors one of the ordinary ones as for pelf or fame . . . I should be well content to let it go and earn my daily bread in some plodding business. . . . But I cannot turn my heart from the great work which awaits me. It is a labor none other can perform."

14. *Edward Bellamy Speaks Again*, 221.

15. Edward Bellamy, "How I Came to Write 'Looking Backward,'" *Nationalist*, I (May, 1889), 1.

16. *Edward Bellamy Speaks Again*, 223.

17. Edward Bellamy, *Looking Backward* (Boston, 1898), 85 ff.

18. *Ibid.*, 260.

19. *Ibid.*, 196.

20. *Ibid.*, 334.

21. John Bakeless, "Edward Bellamy," *Dictionary of American Biography*, II, 163.

22. Ibid.

23. Cyrus F. Willard, "The Nationalist Club of Boston," *Nationalist*, I (May, 1889), 16.

24. *Ibid.*, 24.

25. *Ibid.*, 25.

26. *Ibid.*, 24.

27. *Ibid.*

28. *Ibid.*, 26.

29. See *Nationalist*, I, *passim*; each issue carried a section devoted to club news.

30. *Nationalist*, I, 219.

31. *Ibid.*, 127.

32. *Ibid.*, 225.

33. *Ibid.*, and p. 172.

34. Edward Bellamy to Henry O. Houghton, October 17, 1889.

35. Cyrus F. Willard, "First Anniversary: A Retrospect," *Nationalist*, II (December, 1889), 39.

36. *Nationalist*, II (January, 1890), 75 ff.
37. *Ibid.*, II (May, 1890), 206 ff.
38. *Ibid.*, II (November, 1890), 289 ff.
39. Ficton also became the means of attacking Nationalism as well as spreading other utopian views. Arthur Vinton, *Looking Further Backward* (Albany, 1890) and J. W. Roberts, *Looking Within* (New York, 1893) were novels that attacked Bellamy's Nationalism. For a list of utopian novels in this period, see Forbes, "Literary Quest for Utopia," 188–89.
40. *Nationalist*, II (March to September, 1890).
41. *Ibid.*, II (April, 1890), back cover of this and succeeding issues.
42. *Ibid.*, II (October, 1890), 20.
43. *Ibid.*, 21.
44. Nicholas Gilman, "'Nationalism' in the United States," *Quarterly Journal of Economics*, IV (October, 1889), 65.
45. *Nationalist*, II, 68.
46. W. T. Harris, "Edward Bellamy's Vision," *Forum*, III (October, 1889), 202.
47. *Ibid.*, 204.
48. R. N. Roark, "Prof. Harris's Discovery," *Nationalist*, II (January, 1890), 59–61; Herbert Birdsall, "Prof. Harris's Lack of Vision," *Nationalist*, II (January, 1890), 61–63.
49. Emile De Lavelaye, "Two New Utopias," *Living Age*, CLXXXIV (February 15, 1890), 394.
50. Thomas W. Higginson, "Edward Bellamy's Nationalism," *Our Day*, V (April, 1890), 337.
51. Thomas W. Higginson, "Step by Step," *Nationalist*, I (September, 1889), 145.
52. Bellamy to Higginson, January 3, 1890.
53. Bellamy to Higginson, December 28, 1890.
54. William Higgs, "Some Objections to Mr. Bellamy's Utopia," *New Englander and Yale Review*, LII (March, 1890), 231–39.
55. *American Newspaper Directory* for 1891 (p. 323) gives the circulation of the *Nationalist* as "exceeding 3000"; on the Harvard copy of the December, 1889, issue of the *Nationalist* is stamped "This edition, 35,000."
56. *New Nation*, I (April 11, 1891), 172.
57. *Nationalist*, II (December, 1889), 33.
58. C. F. Willard, "News of the Movement," *Nationalist*, II (January, 1890), 75. Some looked upon Bellamy as another Harriet Beecher Stowe. One commentator said, "The leavening of America against negro slavery which was so largely brought about by the circulation of 'Uncle Tom's Cabin' is being duplicated in the present and future arousing of the people against industrial slavery with 'Looking Backward' as its inspiration."
59. Edward Bellamy to Horace E. Scudder, August 25, 1890.
60. "Excerpts from the Notebooks and Journals of Edward Bellamy," 3.
61. *New Nation*, I (February 14, 1891), 40.
62. Bellamy had tried to get the Boston Nationalists to do this in June, 1889, when he asked them, in a letter, to "advocate raising the age of compulsory education to seventeen with thirty-five weeks of school and support for poor children." Although the plan was unanimously adopted, there is no record of anything having ever been done about it.
63. *New Nation*, I (March 28, 1891), 137.
64. *Ibid.*, I (April 11, 1891), 168.
65. *Ibid.*, II (June 11, 1892), 370.
66. *Ibid.*, I (February 7, 1891), 29.
67. *Ibid.*, II (November 26, 1892), 698.

68. Anna L. Dawes, "Mr. Bellamy and Christianity," *Andover Review,* XV (April, 1891), 414.
69. W. H. Gardner, "The Pulpit and Social Questions," *New Nation,* I (January 9, 1892), 23.
70. *New Nation,* II, 23.
71. *Ibid.,* I (February 21, 1891), 67.
72. *Ibid.,* II (January 2, 1892), 11.
73. *Ibid.,* I (February 28, 1891), 76.
74. *Ibid.,* 80.
75. In April, 1891, when the clubs were yet quite active, the *New Nation* discontinued the practice of devoting a section to club news.
76. *New Nation,* I (April 25, 1891), 203.
77. *Ibid.,* I (March 14, 1891), 103.
78. *Ibid.,* 101.
79. *Ibid.,* I (March 21, 1891), 118.
80. *Ibid.,* I (May 30, 1891), 277.
81. *Ibid.,* 301. Hardly any succeeding issue of the *New Nation* was without some platform, either state or national, of the Populists.
82. *New Nation,* I (December 5, 1891), 716.
83. *Ibid.,* I (October 17, 1891), 584.
84. *Ibid.,* I (November 14, 1891), 662.
85. *Ibid.,* I (March 21, 1891), 126. It is not difficult to believe that Bellamy, nevertheless, favored the free coinage of silver, since he so heartily endorsed every section of the Omaha platform of the Populists. *Ibid.,* II (October 15, 1892), 632.
86. *Ibid.,* II (February 12, 1892), 98.
87. *Ibid.,* II (March 5, 1892), 145.
88. *Ibid.*
89. *Ibid.,* II (March 19, 1892), 183, reprinted from the *Michigan Patriot.*
90. *New Nation,* II (April 9, 1892), 233.
91. Frank B. Tracy, "Menacing Socialism in the Western States," *Forum,* XV (May, 1893), 332.
92. *Ibid.,* 334.
93. *New Nation,* II (October 22, 1892), 644.
94. *Ibid.,* II (November 19, 1892), 685. Bellamy was himself a candidate for the electoral college on the Populist ticket.
95. *Ibid.,* II (November 26, 1892), 697.
96. *Ibid.,* III (September 16, 1893), 428.
97. *Ibid.,* III (August 26, 1893), 401.
98. *Ibid.,* IV (February 3, 1894), 49.
99. *Ibid.*
100. *Ibid.,* 50.
101. "The Programme of the Nationalists," *Forum,* XVII (March, 1894), 81–91; and "How I Wrote 'Looking Backward.'"
102. Bellamy, *Equality* (New York, 1897), 157.
103. *Nation,* LXV (August 26, 1897), 170.
104. W. D. Howells, "Introduction," Bellamy, *Blindman's World* (Boston, 1898), xi.
105. William Heinemann, "The Book of the Month," *Review of Reviews,* XVI (August, 1897), 200.
106. John Clark Ridpath, "Is the Prophet Dead?" *Arena,* XX (August, 1898), 288.
107. W. F. Phillips, "Edward Bellamy—Prophet of Nationalism," *Westminster Review,* CL (November, 1898), 503.
108. Nicholas Gilman, "Bellamy's 'Equality,'" *Quarterly Journal of Economics,* XII (October, 1897), 76.

Notes to "James Boon, Free Negro Artisan"

1. Minutes of the Court of Pleas and Quarter Sessions for Franklin County, June 16, 1827.
2. The Minutes of the Court of Pleas and Quarter Sessions for Franklin County record Boon's age as twenty-one years in September, 1829. Since he was eighteen years old in June, 1827, his birthday must have fallen between June and September.
3. Minutes of the Court of Pleas and Quarter Sessions for Franklin County, September 13, 1825.
4. *State* v. *Boon*, "affray and assault and battery," Minutes of the Court of Pleas and Quarter Session for Franklin County, September 15, 1825.
5. *Laws passed by the General Assembly of North Carolina, 1825–1830* (Raleigh, 1831), 15.
6. Minutes of the Court of Pleas and Quarter Sessions for Franklin County, June 16, 1827.
7. Walter Clark (ed.), *The State Records of North Carolina* (Winston, 1905), XXIII, 581.
8. In 1838, when portions of the apprenticeship law were rewritten, the requirement to teach apprentices to read and write was confined to white wards, *Laws, 1838–1839.*
9. In this connection it is interesting to observe that the "X" mark of James Boon has been cut out of almost all of his papers which are in the North Carolina Department of Archives and History.
10. Minutes of the Court of Pleas and Quarter Sessions for Franklin County, September 16, 1829. A copy of this release is also in the papers of James Boon, North Carolina Department of Archives and History, hereinafter referred to as Boon Papers. "And set free" is an additional phrase on Boon's copy which was signed by the Clerk of the Court. It was doubtless used as an identification by Boon.
11. Minutes of Court Pleas and Quarter Sessions for Franklin County, March 13, 1835.
12. See the account of Boon's work for Benjamin Avery, July and August, 1834. Unless otherwise specified, the manuscript materials quoted hereafter are in the Boon Papers.
13. See Boon's account of work for D. Cosby, September 8, 1849.
14. For an account of Dunston's apprenticeship see Minutes of the Court of Pleas and Quarter Sessions for Franklin County, September, 1822.
15. *Ibid.*, March, 1826, and March, 1833. For a discussion of Boon's family connections, see pages 223–24, herein.
16. See, for example, Benjamin Jones to James Boon, Dr., June 10, 1839, and Carter Evans to James Boon, March 6, 1848.
17. Memorandum of March 9, 1841.
18. The bill for the work done by Hilley is dated August 23, 1848.
19. Collins' receipt for Boon's payment for their hire is dated February 2, 1850.
20. Mordecai's receipt is in the Boon Papers, September 1, 1850. See also Cosby & Company to James Boon, 1850.
21. See page 220, herein.
22. See, for example, James Boon to Tho. D. Fleury, June 28, 1839.
23. Bill for Mrs. E. R. Yarbrough, March 9, 1846.
24. Bill for Augustus Lewis, June 1, 1849.
25. James Boon to Augustus Lewis, March 22, 1847.
26. James Boon to Ballard, Harris, and Davis, April–May, 1849.
27. Very often, the bills merely indicated that work had been done and did not give an indication of the nature of the work performed.
28. William Haywood to James Boon, May 7 and 28, 1838.
29. A. L. Perry to James Boon, November 9, 1845.

30. Patterson and Dent to James Boon, February–December, 1848, March–September, 1849. Other stores at which Boon purchased materials were Stith and Co., Macon and Wilson, and F. and S. T. Patterson, all of Louisburg.
31. James Boon, Bought of James Anderson, April 29, 1848.
32. Receipt of Young Patterson to James Boon, March 28, 1840.
33. Augustus Lewis to James Boon, March 22, 1847, and March–June, 1849.
34. W. D. Powell to Mrs. Delia Herring, April 19, 1851.
35. James Boon to Vaughan, December 20, 1837. Boon usually charged his employers .25 per load for transporting materials to the job.
36. James Boon to W. T. Fentress, February 16, 1850.
37. James Boon to William Jeffreys, May 1, 1848.
38. James Boon to Augustus Lewis, March 22, 1849.
39. James Boon to Mr. Mead, October 8, 1849.
40. James Boon to Benjamin Jones, June 10, 1839.
41. William Mitchell to James Boon, January 6, 1840. There is a reference in the statement to work done by Mitchell during the previous June.
42. See page 217, herein.
43. See the tabulated wage scale in Guion Griffis Johnson, *Ante-Bellum North Carolina* (Chapel Hill, 1937), 70.
44. John Hope Franklin, *The Free Negro in North Carolina, 1790–1860* (Chapel Hill, 1943), 136 ff.
45. It is difficult to make any comparison between the wages of Boon's assistants and the prevailing wages. Seldom were they classified according to the type of work they were doing, and one must be content to observe that he made careful distinctions among them and that in all probability they too received less than the prevailing wage. An additional observation can be made, however, that whenever Boon hired slaves to work for him he always paid their owners one dollar per day per slave.
46. See the tax lists of Franklin County, 1840–1850. See also the Minutes of the Court of Pleas and Quarter Sessions for Franklin County, 1840–1850. Members of this and other firms for which Boon worked often filled public positions of trust and responsibility.
47. November 14, 1843.
48. December 2, 1847.
49. March 7, 1848.
50. Statement by Will O. Jeffreys, March 22, 1848.
51. Dabney Cosby to whom it may concern, October 27, 1850.
52. Will Plummer to Richard H. Mosby, October 8, 1839.
53. R. H. Mosby to Isacc Fanecon, Halifax, North Carolina, February 22, 1842.
54. Carter Evans to James Boon, January 20, 1848. For a long time, Wilmington had led the state in restricting the freedom of free Negroes. As early as 1785 free Negroes were required to register, secure a protector, and wear an arm band with the word *Free* on it. See Franklin, *Free Negro in North Carolina*, 59–60.
55. Carter Evans to James Boon, March 6, 1848.
56. March 22, 1848.
57. This is William Dunston, a free Negro carpenter, who had worked regularly with Boon in Louisburg and who worked on the Jeffreys job in Wilmington.
58. Carter Evans to James Boon, September 10, 1848.
59. James Boon to D. Cosby and Company, September 8, 1848.
60. See Registers Book No. 19, Wake County, North Carolina, 388. On August 31, 1852, Boon was referred to as a resident of Wake County.
61. Ballard, Harris, and Davis to James Boon, January to September, 1849.
62. Yarboro and Perry to James Boon, November 15, 1834.

63. Ballard, Harris, and Davis to James Boon, August to December, 1848.
64. *Ibid.*, January to September, 1849, and R. F. Yarbrough and Company to James Boon, January to October, 1849.
65. W. W. Jones to James Boon, April to June, 1849.
66. *William Mitchell* v. *James Boon*, January 6, 1840.
67. Patterson and Dent to James Boon, June 13, 1849.
68. Ballard, Harris, and Davis, August, 1848, to January 1, 1850. See also his accounts with R. F. Yarbrough and Company, January to October, 1849, for other illustrations of Boon's difficulties with merchants.
69. April 16, 1849.
70. January 1, 1851.
71. The Books of the Register of Deeds for Franklin County shed almost no light on the subject. They show disposition of property by Boon without showing acquisition.
72. See page 220, herein.
73. Richard Noble's recommendation of Boon, July 10, 1843.
74. Deed Record No. 28, Franklin County, North Carolina, January 2, 1843, p. 379.
75. Deed Record Book No. 31, Franklin County, North Carolina, July 4, 1855.
76. Contract between James Boon and W. H. Furman, February 8, 1848. Furman owned land adjoining Boon's property.
77. W. W. Jones to James Boon, February 18, 1850.
78. Receipt given to Wiley Clifton, April 7, 1840.
79. January 18, 1849.
80. January 22, 1849.
81. September 5, 1849. See also his note to Ballard, Harris, and Davis, August 19, 1850, and the one to John Skinner, January 28, 1851.
82. James Boon to Davis Young, Trustee, Deed Record Book No. 28, Franklin County, North Carolina, January 2, 1843, p. 379.
83. James Boon to James H. Yarbrough, Trustee, Deed Record Book No. 30, Franklin County, North Carolina, January 20, 1851, pp. 362–64.
84. James Boon to Charles G. Scott, Trustee, Registers Book No. 19, Wake County, North Carolina, August 31, 1852, p. 388.
85. It may be said, however, that in 1849 Boon's property was up for sale for debts according to a notice issued September 4, 1849. Apparently he satisfied his creditors' claims before the date of sale.
86. James Boon to Benjamin Avery, July and August, 1834.
87. James Boon to B. Hawkins, February 27, 1848.
88. *M. F. Sykes* v. *James Boon*, March 11, 1841. A similar judgment was rendered in the case of *Willy Jones* v. *James Boon* for $16.09, January 21, 1851.
89. Among these are receipts for poll taxes paid in Raleigh, for a blind mare which he purchased in 1849, for house rent paid for himself and for others, and for many other transactions. See his papers, 1830–1857.
90. William Jones to James Boon, November 4, 1840.
91. William Jones to James Boon, February 18, 1850.
92. William Jones to James Boon, August 14, 1840, and November 4, 1840.
93. William Jones to James Boon, December 26, 1850.
94. Sarah Boon to James Boon, November 27, 1849.
95. Sarah Boon to James Boon, July 11, 1850.
96. Contract between A. B. Humphrey and James Boon, December 31, 1851.
97. Deed Record Book No. 31, Franklin County, North Carolina, July 4, 1855, p. 663. The deed was not registered until January 30, 1857.
98. Sarah Boon to James Boon, November 27, 1849.
99. Sarah Boon to James Boon, July 11, 1850.
100. Yarboro and Perry to James Boon, November 15, 1834.

101. Myers and Baucum to James Boon, July 5, 1848. Boon also had a gold watch that was of sufficient value to be one of the items which he conveyed in a deed of trust in 1851. Deed Record Book No. 30, Franklin County, North Carolina, p. 363.
102. E. S. Harding to James Boon, March 13, 1850; J. Creech to James Boon, March 13, 1850.
103. William O. Green to James Boon, May 21, 1850.
104. D. Johnston to James Boon, July 5, 1848.
105. Boon sold two gallons to Lockward Alford on August 15, 1848. There is no record of his having received a permit to retail liquor from the county court.
106. W. W. Jones to James Boon, April–June, 1849.
107. October 27, 1850. There was agitation against the sale of liquor to free Negroes during this entire period, but a law preventing such sale was not enacted until 1859. Franklin, *Free Negro in North Carolina*, 80–81.
108. See the statement from Boon's physician, Willie Perry to James Boon, October, 1844, to January 18, 1851. Unfortunately, a part of the statement is mutilated and no light is shed on the condition of Boon's health after 1851.

Notes on "James T. Ayers, Civil War Recruiter"

1. This stout-hearted editor (for a short time) of the *Mattoon Gazette* preferred the reestablishment of slavery in Illinois to the extension of political and social equality to Negroes.
2. Records in the office of the Adjutant General of the State of Illinois, Springfield.
3. *Portrait and Biographical Album of McLean County, Illinois* (Chicago, 1887), 294.
4. *Ibid.*, 295.
5. Norman Dwight Harris, *The History of Negro Servitude in Illinois and the Slavery Agitation in that State, 1719–1864* (Chicago, 1904), 139.
6. Arthur C. Cole, *The Era of the Civil War, 1848–1870,* Volume III of *The Centennial History of Illinois* (Springfield, 1919), 220.
7. From the diary of James T. Ayers, hereinafter referred to as Diary. The pages are not numbered in the original manuscript.
8. Diary.
9. *Ibid.*
10. *Ibid.*
11. *Ibid.*
12. *Ibid.*
13. The reasons that prompted the President and his assistants to pursue this course of action are too well known to require recounting here. For an extensive discussion see Fred A. Shannon, *The Organization and Administration of the Union Army, 1861–1865* (Cleveland, 1928), and George W. Williams, *A History of the Negro Troops in the War of the Rebellion, 1861–1865* (New York, 1887).
14. Williams, *History of Negro Troops*, 90 ff.
15. Fred A. Shannon, "The Federal Government and the Negro Soldier, 1861–1865," *Journal of Negro History*, Vol. XI, No. 4 (October 1926), 574.
16. *Ibid.*, 575.
17. *The War of the Rebellion: A Compilation of the Official Records of the Union and Confederate Armies* (130 vols.; Washington, D.C., 1880–1901), Ser. III, Vol. III, p. 215; hereinafter cited as *OR*. Unless otherwise indicated, all citations are to Series III.
18. *OR*, Vol. III, p. 216.
19. Williams, *History of Negro Troops*, 115; *OR*, Vol. III, pp. 1178–79.
20. *Journal of Negro History* (October, 1926), 575.
21. Williams, *History of Negro Troops*, 120 ff.; *OR*, Vol. IV, p. 90.
22. Williams, *History of Negro Troops*, 125.
23. *OR*, Vol. IV, p. 90.

24. *OR*, Vol. III, p. 1191.
25. Diary.
26. *Ibid.*
27. It has been impossible to identify William F. Wheeler as an army officer.
28. Diary.
29. *Ibid.*
30. *Ibid.*
31. *OR*, Vol. IV, pp. 79, 85–86. It was perhaps this communication from Stanton that prompted General Thomas to appoint General Chetlain to recruit in west Tennessee and Captain Mussey in middle and east Tennessee.
32. *Ibid.*, 434.
33. *Ibid.*, 433–34.
34. *Ibid.*, 436.
35. Diary.
36. *OR*, Vol. IV, pp. 595–96.
37. *Ibid.*, 770.
38. Diary.
39. *OR*, Vol. IV, p. 768.
40. Diary.
41. *OR*, Vol. V, p. 662. Walter L. Fleming, *Civil War and Reconstruction in Alabama* (New York, 1905), 88, claims that many Negroes who enlisted in northern Alabama were credited to northern states. Instead of the official figure of 4,969, he claims that a conservative estimate of the Negroes who enlisted from Alabama would be near 10,000. By order of Provost Marshal General James B. Fry, the recruiting of Negroes was stopped on April 29, 1865. *OR*, Vol. IV, p. 1282.
42. Shannon, *Organization of the Union Army*, II, 162–63. Williams, *History of Negro Troops*, contains many examples of the Negro's gallantry during the war.
43. Diary.
44. *Ibid.*
45. *Ibid.*
46. Major General Richard J. Oglesby of Decatur, Illinois, had distinguished himself as a military leader in the early days of the war. As chairman, in 1861, of the state senate committee for the reorganization of the militia, he predicted that with the war at hand "the whole country . . . would rise *en masse*, and . . . volunteer their services . . . speedily and without delay." Cole, *Era of the Civil War*, 273, 328.
47. Diary.
48. *Ibid.*
49. *Ibid.*
50. *Ibid.*
51. *Ibid.*
52. On February 25, 1865, for example, Ayers, at the request of his commanding officer, conducted the funeral of one of the men in his convalescent corps. Ayers said, "I made some Remarks then sung 'and must I be to Judgement brought,' prayed with the Soldiers and we Piled the Earth upon Earth and Left our Strange Brother Soldier to take his Rest far here in the South." Diary.
53. *Ibid.*
54. *Ibid.*
55. *Ibid.*
56. *Ibid.*
57. *Ibid.*
58. *Ibid.*
59. *Ibid.*
60. *Ibid.*
61. *The Report of the Adjutant General of the State of Illinois* (Springfield, 1900), VI,

542, states that Ayers was "on detached duty, with a view to promotion in the U.S. Colored Troops."

62. Ms. in the War Department, Adjutant General's Office, Washington, D.C., dated July 29, 1865.
63. Diary.
64. *Ibid.*
65. *Ibid.*
66. *Ibid.*
67. *Ibid.*
68. *Ibid.*
69. From the pension files of Civil War veterans, No. W. O. 165,560 in the National Archives.
70. "Letters Received," 1865, U.S. Colored Troops, Recruiting, Adjutant General's Office, p. 334.
71. "Letter Book," Vol. I, U.S. Colored Troops, Adjutant General's Office, p. 314.
72. Surgeon General's Office, Record and Pension Division, October 28, 1868.
73. See the pension files of Civil War veterans, No. W. O. 165,560 in the National Archives. A copy of the license for this second marriage is in this file.
74. Diary.
75. *Ibid.*

Notes to "John Roy Lynch: Republican Stalwart from Mississippi"

1. See the *Journal of the House of Representatives of the State of Mississippi* (Jackson, 1870), 98–99, 155, 159, 415, 776–77.
2. *House Journal* (Jackson, 1871), 7, 12, 24, 25, 30, 34, 263, 756–57, 1042.
3. *House Journal* (Jackson, 1872), 3, 4, 9, 34, 333, 343, 863.
4. *Presidential Election, 1872: Proceedings of the National Union Republican Convention* (Washington, D.C., 1872), 9, 33.
5. Jackson *Weekly Clarion*, September 5, 1872.
6. John Hope Franklin (ed.), *Reminiscences of an Active Life: The Autobiography of John Roy Lynch* (Chicago, 1970), 99–106.
7. *House Journal* (Jackson, 1873), 2055.
8. *Ibid.*, 2057–58.
9. *Congressional Record*, 43rd Cong., 1st Sess., p. 74.
10. *Ibid.*, pp. 118–19; James G. Blaine, *Twenty Years of Congress: From Lincoln to Garfield with a Review of the Events Which Led to the Political Revolution of 1860* (2 vols.; Norwich, Conn., 1884–86), II, 515.
11. *Congressional Record*, 43rd Cong., 1st Sess., pp. 370, 766, 1121, 3770, 3990–91, 4445–46.
12. See, for example, *ibid.*, 44th Cong., 1st Sess., pp. 206, 321, 1203; *ibid.*, 47th Cong., 1st Sess., pp. 3946, 4531.
13. *Ibid.*, 43rd Cong., 1st Sess., p. 4955.
14. *Ibid.*, 43rd Cong., 2nd Sess., p. 947.
15. James W. Garner, *Reconstruction in Mississippi* (New York, 1901), 372.
16. *Hinds County Gazette*, October 25, 1875.
17. Quoted *ibid.*, October 12, 1875.
18. Jackson *Weekly Mississippi Pilot*, November 20, 1875.
19. During Reconstruction *black Republican* was an opprobrious term used by conservatives to describe Republicans who supported equal rights for Negroes.
20. *Hinds County Gazette*, January 31, 1877.
21. Natchez *Daily Democrat and Courier*, September 12, 1880.
22. Greenville *Times*, September 24, 1880.
23. Natchez *Daily Democrat and Courier*, September 30, 1880.
24. Jackson *Weekly Clarion*, October 20, 1880.

25. *Hinds County Gazette,* December 8, 1880.
26. Natchez *Daily Democrat and Courier,* December 21, 1880.
27. *Ibid.,* April 29, 1882.
28. *Ibid.,* April 30, 1882.
29. *Ibid.,* May 13, 1882.
30. Natchez *Daily Democrat,* September 2, 1882.
31. Raymond *Gazette,* November 1, 1882.
32. Natchez *Daily Democrat,* September 26, 1882.
33. *Ibid.,* October 3, 1882.
34. Quoted *ibid.*
35. *Ibid.,* November 3, 1882.
36. *Ibid.,* November 5, 1882.
37. *Ibid.,* November 17, 1882.
38. John A. Garraty, *Henry Cabot Lodge: A Biography* (New York, 1953), 78.
39. *Proceedings of the Eighth Republican National Convention Held at Chicago, Illinois, June 3, 4, 5, and 6, 1884* (Chicago, 1884), 6.
40. *Ibid.,* 22–23.
41. *Ibid.,* 23.
42. *Hinds County Gazette,* October 19, 1881.
43. Adams County Indirect Index to Land Conveyances, from 1789, Bk. PP., p. 298, Office of the Chancery Clerk, Adams County, Natchez, Miss.
44. *Ibid.,* Bk. QQ, p. 226; Bk. SS, pp. 435, 558; Bk. VV, p. 657; Bk. WW, p. 355; Bk. YY, pp. 36, 329, 569; Bk. ZZ, pp. 372, 638; Bk. 3-A, pp. 469, 757; Bk. 3-B, pp. 432, 547, 549, 679, 761; Bk. 3-C, pp. 580, 589, 661; Bk. 3-D, p. 260; Bk. 3-O, p. 657; Bk. 3-R, p. 215.
45. *Ibid.,* Bk. ZZ, p. 372; Adams County Land Deed Records, Office of the Chancery Clerk, Bk. 3-K, p. 348.
46. Index to Land Conveyances, Bk. UU, p. 444; Bk. YY, p. 36; Bk. 3-B, pp. 547, 549, 679, 761; Land Deed Records, Bk. 3-P, p. 723.
47. Index to Land Conveyances, Bk. 3-G, p. 495; Land Deed Records, Bk. 3-K, p. 371.
48. Index to Land Conveyances, Bk. YY, p. 569; Bk. 3-A, p. 469.
49. Land Deed Records, Bk. 4-P, p. 19.
50. In several of the transactions William Lynch is the grantor, the agent and attorney for John R. Lynch, or the plantation lessor.
51. Lynch discusses his legal career in Franklin (ed.), *Reminiscences of an Active Life,* 369, 502.
52. One must assume that Lynch conducted his business from his residence, since he is not listed at any other address in *Sullivan's Chicago Law Directory* (Chicago, 1934–35).
53. William L. Dawson to author, Tuskegee Institute, Alabama, February 19, 1968. Dawson was a member of the Lynch household for several years.
54. Chicago *Defender,* May 12, 1928.
55. *Proceedings of the National Conference of Colored Men of the United States, held in the State Capitol at Nashville, Tenn. May 6–9, 1879,* quoted in Herbert Aptheker (ed.), *A Documentary History of the Negro People in the United States* (New York, 1951), 723–24.
56. John R. Lynch, "Should Colored Men Join Labor Organizations?" *A.M.E. Church Review 3–4* (October, 1886), 165–67. For Lynch's role in promoting business cooperation in the effort to solve the problems of unemployment, see August Meier, *Negro Thought in America, 1880–1915* (Ann Arbor, 1963), 138.
57. John R. Lynch, *The Facts of Reconstruction* (New York, 1913), 11.
58. Lynch said he had received hundreds of letters complimenting him on his work. He does not indicate that any of them came from historians. John R. Lynch, *Some Historical Errors of James Ford Rhodes* (Boston, 1922), xiii.
59. Chicago *Defender,* November 11, 1939.

60. New York *Times*, November 3, 1939.
61. Chicago *Tribune*, November 3, 1939.

Notes to "The Land of Room Enough"

1. Robert F. Berkhofer, Jr., *The White Man's Indian: Images of the American Indian from Columbus to the Present* (New York, 1978), 116.
2. *Ibid.*, 83.
3. Winthrop Jordan, *White Over Black: American Attitudes Toward the Negro, 1550–1812* (Chapel Hill, 1968), 7.
4. *Ibid.*, 60–62.
5. The arguments are conveniently summarized in William S. Jenkins, *Pro-Slavery Thought in the Old South* (Chapel Hill, 1935). Excerpts from the principal writers are in Eric L. McKitrick (ed.), *Slavery Defended: The Views of the Old South* (Englewood Cliffs, N.J., 1963).
6. Jenkins, *Pro-Slavery Thought*, 249.
7. Quoted in William Stanton, *The Leopard's Spots: Scientific Attitudes Toward Race in America, 1815–1859* (Chicago, 1960), 34.
8. Jenkins, *Pro-Slavery Thought*, 249, 250.
9. McKitrick (ed.), *Slavery Defended*, 122.
10. These laws are discussed in John Hope Franklin, *Racial Equality in America* (Chicago, 1976), 24–26.
11. Berkhofer, *The White Man's Indian*, 175.
12. New York *Times*, September 11, 1977.
13. *Ibid.*, May 13, 1980.
14. Joel Dreyfuss, "Blacks and Hispanics, Coalition or Confrontation?" *Black Enterprise*, IX (1979), 23.
15. New York *Times*, May 12, 1980.

Notes to "The South and the Problem of Change"

1. The view of the New World as a liberating and regenerating force has been discussed by many writers. See the summary statement in David Brion Davis, *The Problem of Slavery in Western Culture* (Ithaca, 1966), 4–7.
2. This was among the indictments against the king that did not appear in the final draft of the Declaration of Independence. Carl L. Becker, *The Declaration of Independence: A Study in the History of Political Ideas* (New York, 1942), 180–81.
3. Davis, *Problem of Slavery*, 4.
4. "American Slavery in 1857," *Southern Literary Messenger*, XXV (August 1857), 85.
5. *Congressional Globe*, 35th Cong., 1st Sess., 961–62 (March 4, 1858).
6. *Ibid.*, 30th Cong., 1st Sess., Appendix, 43–44 (December 22, 1847).
7. *Annals of Congress*, 16th Cong., 1st Sess., 414 (February 15, 1820).
8. Guion Griffis Johnson, "The Changing Status of the Southern Woman," in John C. McKinney and Edgar T. Thompson (eds.), *The South in Continuity and Change* (Durham, 1965), 421.
9. Anne Firor Scott, *The Southern Lady: From Pedestal to Politics, 1830–1930* (Chicago and London, 1970), 4.
10. [Harriet B. Jacobs], *Incidents in the Life of a Slave Girl*, edited by Lydia Maria Child (Boston, 1861), 79.
11. Frederick Law Olmsted, *A Journey in the Seaboard Slave States* (New York, 1856), 18, 28.
12. John Thompson, *The Life of John Thompson, a Fugitive Slave* (Worcester, 1856), 31.
13. [Jacobs], *Incidents*, 49.
14. Lewis and Milton Clarke, *Narratives of the Sufferings of Lewis and Milton Clarke* (Boston, 1846), 20.

15. U.S. Bureau of the Census, *Negro Population, 1790–1915* (Washington, D.C., 1918), 208.
16. See, for example, James D. B. De Bow, *The Interest in Slavery of the Southern Non-Slaveholder* (Charleston, 1860).
17. Abel P. Upshur, "Domestic Slavery," *Southern Literary Messenger,* V (October 1839), 685.
18. Quoted in William S. Jenkins, *Pro-Slavery Thought in the Old South* (Chapel Hill, 1935), 291.
19. *Congressional Globe,* 35th Cong., 1st Sess., Appendix, 71 (March 4, 1858).
20. William Stanton, *The Leopard's Spots: Scientific Attitudes Toward Race in America, 1815–59* (Chicago, 1960); and Jenkins, *Pro-Slavery Thought.*
21. S. A. Cartwright, "Diseases and Peculiarities of the Negro," in James D. B. De Bow (ed.), *The Industrial Resources, etc., of the Southern and Western States* (3 vols.; New Orleans and Washington, 1853–1856), II, 322.
22. Quoted in Jenkins, *Pro-Slavery Thought,* 217–18.
23. Joseph H. Fichter and George L. Maddox, "Religion in the South, Old and New," in McKinney and Thompson (eds.), *The South in Continuity and Change,* 359–60.
24. A classic statement of the case is in Thornton Stringfellow, "The Bible Argument: or, Slavery in the Light of Divine Revelation," in E. N. Elliott (ed.), *Cotton Is King, and Pro-Slavery Arguments* (Augusta, Ga., 1860), 459–521.
25. *Ibid.,* 461, 496–97.
26. James Henley Thornwell, *The Rights and the Duties of Masters* (Charleston, 1850), 43–44.
27. George Fitzhugh, *Sociology for the South, or the Failure of Free Society* (Richmond, 1854), 222.
28. George Fitzhugh, *Cannibals All! or, Slaves Without Masters* (Richmond, 1857), 97–99.
29. Emma LeConte, *When the World Ended: The Diary of Emma LeConte,* edited by Earl S. Miers (New York, 1957), 90.
30. The convict lease system and peonage are among the forms of involuntary servitude discussed in C. Vann Woodward, *Origins of the New South, 1877–1913* (Baton Rouge, 1951), 212–15; George B. Tindall, *The Emergence of the New South, 1913–1945* (Baton Rouge, 1967), 212–13; and Stetson Kennedy, *Southern Exposure* (Garden City, N.Y., 1946), 48–77.
31. J. C. Wood to J. O. Wilson, secretary, American Colonization Society, February 9, 1903, American Colonization Society Records, Series I, Vol. 292, in Manuscript Division, Library of Congress.
32. Woodward, *Origins of the New South,* 226–27.
33. Scott, *Southern Lady,* 106–33.
34. *Congressional Record,* 49th Cong., 2nd Sess., 980 (January 25, 1887).
35. Scott, *Southern Lady,* 169–70.
36. Fichter and Maddox, "Religion in the South," 360.
37. Carter, *Southern Legacy* (Baton Rouge, 1950), 30.
38. William A. Mabry, *Studies in the Disfranchisement of the Negro in the South* (Durham, 1938); Vernon L. Wharton, *The Negro in Mississippi, 1865–1890* (Chapel Hill, 1947); and Paul Lewinson, *Race, Class, & Party* (London, New York, 1932) are among the many works that deal with the new legal status of Negroes in the postwar years.
39. John Hope Franklin, "History of Racial Segregation in the United States," American Academy of Political and Social Science, *Annals,* CCCIV (March 1956), 1–9; and Charles S. Johnson, *Patterns of Negro Segregation* (New York and London, 1943).
40. Bertram W. Doyle, *The Etiquette of Race Relations in the South: A Study in Social Control* (Chicago: 1937).

41. Wilbur J. Cash, *The Mind of the South* (New York, 1941), 183.
42. Woodward, *Origins of the New South*, 372–73.
43. Louis R. Harlan, *Separate and Unequal: Public School Campaigns and Racism in the Southern Seaboard States, 1901–1915* (Chapel Hill, 1958), 248–69.
44. See the communication from Caroline Patterson, president of the Georgia Association Opposed to Woman Suffrage, to Frank Clark, January 4, 1918, U.S. Congress, House of Representatives, Committee on Woman Suffrage, 65th Cong., 2nd Sess., *Extending the Right of Suffrage to Women: Hearings on H. J. Res. 200, Jan. 3–7, 1918* (Washington, 1918), 327.
45. Quoted in A. Elizabeth Taylor, *The Woman Suffrage Movement in Tennessee* (New York, 1957), 112.
46. Elizabeth C. Stanton *et al.* (eds.), *History of Woman Suffrage* (6 vols.; New York, 1881–1922), V, 463.
47. Wilma Dykeman and James Stokely, *Seeds of Southern Change: The Life of Will Alexander* (Chicago, 1962), 143–52.
48. The conservative character of southern churches is discussed in Kenneth K. Bailey, *Southern White Protestantism in the Twentieth Century* (New York, Evanston, and London, 1964), 1–24. For a discussion of the southern churches and race see David M. Reimers, *White Protestantism and the Negro* (New York, 1965), 25–50.
49. Tindall, *Emergence of the New South*, 204.
50. Quoted in Maynard Shipley, *The War on Modern Science: A Short History of the Fundamentalist Attacks on Evolution and Modernism* (New York and London, 1927), 174.
51. The fight is summarized in Bailey, *Southern White Protestantism*, 72–91.
52. Benjamin Quarles, *Black Abolitionists* (London, Oxford, and New York, 1969).
53. Gilbert Osofsky, *Harlem: The Making of a Ghetto: Negro New York, 1890–1930* (New York, 1966) and Allan H. Spear, *Black Chicago: The Making of a Negro Ghetto, 1890–1920* (Chicago and London, 1967) deal with white resistance to change in two northern cities.
54. Gilbert Osofsky, "The Enduring Ghetto," *Journal of American History*, LV (September 1968), 243–55.
55. Rayford W. Logan (ed.), *What the Negro Wants* (Chapel Hill, 1944). See also the "Publisher's Introduction" by W. T. Couch, in which he expressed disagreement with most of the contributors to the volume.
56. *Congressional Record*, 80th Cong., 2nd Sess., 4543 (April 15, 1948).
57. V. O. Key, Jr., *Southern Politics in State and Nation* (New York, 1949), 5.
58. Atlanta *Constitution*, July 27, 1948; Charleston *News and Courier*, July 28, 1948.
59. *Congressional Record*, 80th Cong., 2nd Sess., Appendix, 4654–55 (July 27, 1948).
60. Charleston *News and Courier*, August 5, 6, 1948.
61. *Congressional Record*, 84th Cong., 2nd Sess., 4515–16 (March 12, 1956).
62. J. Harvie Wilkinson III, *Harry Byrd and the Changing Face of Virginia Politics, 1945–1966* (Charlottesville, 1968), 113–54.
63. Paul M. Gaston, *The New South Creed: A Study in Southern Mythmaking* (New York, 1970).

Notes to "The North, the South, and the American Revolution"

1. David Ramsay, *The History of the Revolution of South Carolina, from a British Province to an Independent State* (2 vols.; Trenton, 1785).
2. For example, see Mercy Otis Warren, *History of the Rise, Progress, and Termination of the American Revolution Interspersed with Biographical, Political and Moral Observations* (2 vols.; Boston, 1805).
3. Jared Sparks, "Materials for American History," *North American Review*, XXIII (October, 1826), 276.
4. Michael Kraus, *A History of American History* (New York, 1937), 163–98. See also,

Sydney G. Fisher, "The Legendary and Myth-Making Process in Histories of the American Revolution," *Proceedings of the American Philosophical Society*, LI (April–June, 1912), 53–75.

5. George Bancroft, *History of the United States from the Discovery of the American Continent* (8 vols.; Boston, 1858), VI, 527–28, VIII, 462–75. See also, David D. Van Tassel, *Recording America's Past: An Interpretation of the Development of Historical Studies in America, 1607–1884* (Chicago, 1960), 110–20.

6. Charles G. Sellers, Jr., "The American Revolution: Southern Founders of a National Tradition," in Arthur S. Link and Rembert W. Patrick (eds.), *Writing Southern History: Essays in Historiography in Honor of Fletcher M. Green* (Baton Rouge, 1965), 40–41.

7. The quality of David Ramsay's works has been seriously challenged by one critic who charged Ramsay with plagiarism, among other things. Orin Grant Libby, "Some Pseudo Histories of the American Revolution," *Transactions of the Wisconsin Academy of Sciences, Arts, and Letters*, XIII (Madison, 1901), 419–25; and Orin Grant Libby, "Ramsay as a Plagiarist," *American Historical Review*, VII (July, 1902), 697–703. See also, Page Smith, "David Ramsay and the Causes of the American Revolution," *William and Mary Quarterly*, XVII (January, 1960), 52.

8. William Moultrie, *Memoirs of the American Revolution, So Far as It Related to the States of North and South Carolina, and Georgia* (2 vols.; New York, 1802).

9. Henry Lee, *Memoirs of the War in the Southern Department of the United States* (2 vols.; Phildelphia, 1812).

10. Mason L. Weems, *A History of the Life and Death, Virtues and Exploits of General George Washington* (Philadelphia, 1800); David Ramsay, *The Life of George Washington* (Baltimore, 1807); and John Marshall, *The Life of George Washington* (5 vols.; Philadelphia, 1804–1807).

11. *Southern Literary Messenger*, I (January, 1835), 591.

12. *De Bow's Review*, X (May, 1851), 599.

13. Lorenzo Sabine, *The American Loyalists or Biographical Sketches of Adherents to the British Crown in the War of the Revolution* (Boston, 1847), 30, 32.

14. Elwood Fisher, *Lecture on the North and South, Delivered before the Young Men's Mercantile Library Association of Cincinnati, Ohio, January 16, 1849* (Charleston, 1849); and Edward B. Bryan, *The Rightful Remedy, Addressed to the Slaveholders of the South* (Charleston, 1850), 87.

15. Lawrence Massillon Keitt, "Patriotic Services of the North and the South," *De Bow's Review*, XXI (November, 1856), 491–92; and Joseph Johnson, *Traditions and Reminiscences, Chiefly of the American Revolution in the South* (Charleston, 1851), 556.

16. Bryan, *The Rightful Remedy*, 47.

17. *Ibid.*, 46.

18. Augustus Baldwin Longstreet, *A Voice from the South: Comprising Letters from Georgia to Massachusetts, and to the Southern States* (Baltimore, 1847), 25.

19. Andrew P. Butler, *A Speech of A. P. Butler, of South Carolina, on the Bill Providing for the Surrender of Fugitive Slaves. Delivered in the Senate of the United States, January 24, 1850* (Washington, 1850), 11.

20. *Congressional Globe*, 34th Cong., 1st Sess., Appendix, 543 (May 20, 1856).

21. *Ibid.*, 627–28. See also Andrew P. Butler, "The South's Sacrifices in the Revolution," *De Bow's Review*, XXI (August, 1856), 197–98.

22. William Gilmore Simms, *The Sources of American Independence: An Oration, On the Sixty-Ninth Anniversary of American Independence, Delivered at Aiken, South-Carolina, Before the Town Council and Citizens Thereof* (Aiken, 1844), 22.

23. John W. Higham, "The Changing Loyalties of William Gilmore Simms," *Journal of Southern History*, IX (May, 1943), 210–23.

24. William Gilmore Simms, *The History of South Carolina, From its First European Discovery to its Erection into a Republic: With a Supplementary Chronicle of Events to the Present Time* (Charleston, 1840). More than half of the book treats the period from 1775 to 1783. See, especially, pp. 133–319.
25. William Gilmore Simms, "South Carolina in the Revolution," *Southern Quarterly Review,* XIV (July, 1848), 45–51, and (October, 1848), 261–337.
26. *The Pro-Slavery Argument; As Maintained by . . . Chancellor Harper, Governor Hammond, Dr. Simms, and Professor Dew* (Charleston, 1852), 243.
27. [William Gilmore Simms], *South-Carolina in the Revolutionary War: Being A Reply to Certain Misrepresentations and Mistakes of Recent Writers, In Relation to the Course and Conduct of this State* (Charleston, 1853), 2–9.
28. William P. Trent, *William Gilmore Simms* (Boston, 1892), 205.
29. Mary C. Simms Oliphant, Alfred Taylor Odell, and T. C. Duncan Eaves (eds.), *The Letters of William Gilmore Simms* (5 vols.; Columbia, S.C., 1952–1956), III, 454.
30. *Ibid.,* 456–58, 521–49.
31. New York *Tribune,* November 19, 1856. The New York *Herald* blamed the small attendance on "the unusual number and peculiar excellence of other places of attraction . . . and, to some extent perhaps, to the high price of the tickets," which were 50¢ per lecture or $1.25 for the three. New York *Herald,* November 19, 1856.
32. William Gilmore Simms, "South Carolina in the Revolution. A Lecture," in Oliphant, Odell, and Eaves (eds.), *Letters of William Gilmore Simms,* III, 521–22.
33. New York *Tribune,* November 24, 1856.
34. New York *Herald,* November 24, 1856.
35. New York *Post,* November 21, 1856. The New York *Times* called the lecture "eloquent and interesting" and said that William Gilmore Simms would always be listened to "courteously and respectfully. . . . These courtesies are the more creditable, because they are never reciprocated." New York *Times,* November 19, 1856.
36. New York *Post,* November 26, 1856.
37. Quoted in Trent, *William Gilmore Simms,* 224.
38. John Letcher, *Speech of Hon. John Letcher, of Virginia, on the Political Issues Now Before the Country* (Washington, 1856), 3.
39. *Congressional Globe,* 34th Cong., 1st Sess., Appendix, 655 (June 21, 1856).
40. *Proceedings at the Inauguration of the Monument Erected by the Washington Light Infantry, to the Memory of Col. William Washington . . .* (Charleston, 1858), 37.
41. Bryan, *The Rightful Remedy,* 46–47.
42. William H. Trescot, *The Position and Course of the South* (Charleston, 1850), 16.
43. James De Bow, "The South and the Union," *De Bow's Review,* X (February, 1851), 160.
44. Keitt, "Patriotic Services of the North and the South," 494. In an introductory note praising Lawrence M. Keitt's article the editor said: "Though we dislike such comparisons when they are provoked, it is not our part to shrink from them." *De Bow's Review,* XXI (November, 1856), 491. For additional statements in defense of the South's role in the Revolution, see Joseph Johnson, *Traditions and Reminiscences Chiefly of the American Revolution in the South* (Charleston, 1851); Robert Toombs, *An Oration Delivered . . . at Oxford, Georgia, July, 1853* (Augusta, 1853); John Randolph Tucker, *Address Delivered before the Phoenix and Philomathean Societies of William and Mary College on the 3rd of July, 1854* (Richmond, 1854); and Henry Wise, "Gov. Wise's Oration at Lexington, Va., 4th July, 1856," *Southern Literary Messenger,* XXIII (July, 1856), 1–19.
45. Letcher, *Speech of Hon. John Letcher,* 3.
46. Hiller B. Zobel, "Jonathan Sewall: A Lawyer in Conflict," *Publications of the Cambridge Historical Society,* XL (1964–1966), 131.

47. Benjamin Quarles, *The Negro in the American Revolution* (Chapel Hill, 1961), 43–50. The best account of the Cuffe episode is in an unpublished biography of Paul Cuffe by Sally Loomis.

48. Emory R. Johnson, T. W. Van Metre, G. G. Huebner, and D. S. Hanchett, *History of Domestic and Foreign Commerce of the United States* (2 vols.; Washington, 1915), I, 118. See also Eric Williams, *Capitalism and Slavery* (Chapel Hill, 1944), 80; and James Pope-Hennessy, *Sins of the Fathers: A Study of Atlantic Slave Traders, 1441–1807* (New York, 1968), 231–41.

49. Leslie H. Fishel, Jr., and Benjamin Quarles (eds.), *The Negro American: A Documentary History* (Glenview, Ill., 1967), 56.

50. John C. Fitzpatrick (ed.), *The Writings of George Washington from the Original Manuscript Sources 1745–1799* (39 vols.; Washington, 1931–1944), IV, 186.

51. David Ramsay, *The History of the American Revolution* (2 vols.; Lexington, 1815), II, 291; E. Merton Coulter, *A Short History of Georgia* (Chapel Hill, 1933), 136; Kenneth Coleman, *The American Revolution in Georgia 1763–1789* (Athens, 1958), 170–71; and John Hope Franklin, *From Slavery to Freedom: A History of Negro Americans* (New York, 1974), 91–92.

52. James Curtis Ballagh (ed.), *The Letters of Richard Henry Lee* (2 vols.; New York, 1911–1914), II, 242.

53. Simms, *Sources of American Independence*, 25.

54. George Fitzhugh, *Sociology for the South or the Failure of Free Society* (Richmond, 1854), reprinted in Harvey Wish (ed.), *Ante-Bellum Writings of George Fitzhugh and Hinton Rowan Helper on Slavery* (New York, 1960), 88–89.

55. For an account of Robert Toombs's visit to Boston, see John Hope Franklin, *Southern Odyssey: Travellers in the Antebellum North* (Baton Rouge, 1976).

56. *Liberator*, XIV (June 28, 1844), 103, quoted in Albert P. Blaustein and Robert L. Zangrando (eds.), *Civil Rights and the American Negro: A Documentary History* (New York, 1968), 111–12.

57. *The Works of Charles Sumner* (15 vols.; Boston, 1875–1883), II, 341, 359.

58. *Sarah C. Roberts* v. *City of Boston*, 59 Mass., 198 (1849).

59. *Acts and Resolves Passed by the General Court of Massachusetts in the Year 1855: Together with the Messages* (Boston, 1855), 674–75.

60. For example, see *Southern Literary Messenger*, XIX (October, 1853), 645–46; New Orleans *Daily Delta*, July 17, 1855, April 9, 1857; and Governor William McWillie's declaration in the New Orleans *Daily Picayune*, November 22, 1857.

61. See Raymond A. Bauer and Alice H. Bauer, "Day to Day Resistance to Slavery," *Journal of Negro History*, XXVII (October, 1942), 388–419; and Harvey Wish, "The Slave Insurrection Panic of 1856," *Journal of Southern History*, V (May, 1939), 206–22.

Notes to "A Century of Reconstruction History"

1. Nehemiah Levtzion, "The Long March of Islam in the Western Sudan," in Roland Oliver (ed.), *The Middle Age of African History* (London, 1967), 16–17.

2. Leo Africanus, *The History and Description of Africa* (New York, n.d.), III, 823–25; and Mahmoud Kati, *Tarikh El-Fettach*, edited by O. Houdas and M. Delafosse (Paris, 1913), 13–54.

3. See, for example, Christopher Hill, *Puritanism and Revolution: Studies in Interpretation of the English Revolution of the 17th Century* (New York, 1964), esp. Chap. 1; and David Underdown, *Royalist Conspiracy in England* (New Haven, 1960).

4. James S. Pike, *The Prostrate State: South Carolina under Negro Government* (New York, 1873).

5. See the very favorable comments by Henry Steele Commager in the introduction to a reissue of *The Prostrate State* (New York, 1935).

6. Robert F. Durden, *James Shepherd Pike: Republicanism and the American Negro, 1850–1882* (Durham, N.C., 1957), 214–19.
7. Joseph G. de Roulhac Hamilton, "William Archibald Dunning," *Dictionary of American Biography,* 3, pt. 1, p. 523.
8. William Archibald Dunning, *Reconstruction, Political and Economic, 1865–1877* (New York, 1907), 116, 120, 121, 213.
9. Walter L. Fleming (ed.), *Documentary History of Reconstruction: Political, Military, Social, Religious, Educational, and Industrial, 1865–1906* (New York, 1966), I, 267.
10. For some of the best examples of the work of Dunning's students, see Walter L. Fleming, *Civil War and Reconstruction in Alabama* (New York, 1905); and Joseph G. de Roulhac Hamilton, *Reconstruction in North Carolina* (New York, 1914).
11. Rhodes, *History of the United States* (New York, 1906), VII, 168.
12. Dixon, *The Leopard's Spots: A Romance of the White Man's Burden* (New York, 1902); *The Clansman: An Historical Romance of the Ku Klux Klan* (New York, 1905); and *The Traitor: A Story of the Rise and Fall of the Invisible Empire* (New York, 1907); and Bowers, *The Tragic Era: The Revolution after Lincoln* (New York, 1929).
13. Du Bois, "The Freedmen's Bureau," *Atlantic Monthly,* LXXXVII (1901), 354–65, and "Reconstruction and Its Benefits," *American Historical Review,* XV (1909–10), 781–99.
14. Lynch, *The Facts of Reconstruction* (Boston, 1913), preface, 92–99. This entire volume is reprinted in John Hope Franklin (ed.), *Reminiscences of an Active Life: The Autobiography of John Roy Lynch* (Chicago, 1970) xxvii–xxxviii. See also *Some Historical Errors of James Ford Rhodes* (Boston, 1922), xvii. The latter work originally appeared as two articles in the *Journal of Negro History:* "Some Historical Errors of James Ford Rhodes," II (1917), 354–68, and "More about the Historical Errors of James Ford Rhodes," III (1918), 139–57. Also see John Garraty (ed.), *The Barber and the Historian: The Correspondence of George A. Myers and James Ford Rhodes* (Columbus, Ohio, 1956), 29–38.
15. Alrutheus A. Taylor, *The Negro in South Carolina during the Reconstruction* (Washington, 1924), *The Negro in the Reconstruction of Virginia* (Washington, 1926), and *The Negro in Tennessee* (Washington, 1941).
16. W. E. B. Du Bois, *Black Reconstruction: An Essay toward a History of the Part Which Black Folk Played in the Attempt to Reconstruct America, 1860–1880* (New York, 1935), 713.
17. *Ibid.,* 724.
18. Paul Herman Buck, *The Road to Reunion* (Boston, 1937); Horace Mann Bond, *Negro Education in Alabama: A Study in Cotton and Steel* (Washington, 1939); and Vernon L. Wharton, *The Negro in Mississippi* (Chapel Hill, 1947).
19. E. Merton Coulter, *The South during Reconstruction* (Baton Rouge, 1947), xi, 86, 336.
20. W. L. Nunn, *Texas under the Carpetbaggers* (Austin, 1962), 19, 25n.
21. Thomas A. Bailey, *The American Pageant: A History of the Republic* (Boston, 1961), 475–76.
22. Joe Gray Taylor, *Louisiana Reconstructed, 1863–1877* (Baton Rouge, 1974), 49.
23. Joel Williamson, *After Slavery: The Negro in South Carolina during Reconstruction, 1861–1877* (Chapel Hill, 1965), 63. Also see Roberta Sue Alexander, "North Carolina Faces the Freedmen: Race Relations during Presidential Reconstruction, 1865–1867" (Ph.D. dissertation, University of Chicago, 1974).
24. For examples of such work, see Herbert G. Gutman, *The Black Family in Slavery and Freedom, 1750–1925* (New York, 1976); John W. Blassingame, *Black New Orleans, 1860–1880* (Chicago, 1973); and Carl R. Osthaus, *Freedmen, Philanthropy, and Fraud: A History of the Freedmen's Savings Bank* (Urbana, 1976).

25. Rembert Patrick, *The Reconstruction of the Nation* (New York, 1967); Kenneth M. Stampp, *The Era of Reconstruction, 1867–1877* (New York, 1965); and John Hope Franklin, *Reconstruction after the Civil War* (Chicago, 1961).

26. See, for example, A. A. Taylor, "Historians of the Reconstruction," *Journal of Negro History*, XXIII (1938), 16–34; Francis B. Simkins, "New Viewpoints of Southern Reconstruction," *Journal of Southern History*, V (1939), 49–61; Howard K. Beale, "On Rewriting Reconstruction History," *American Historical Review*, XLV (1939–40), 807–27; T. Harry Williams, "An Analysis of Some Reconstruction Attitudes," *Journal of Southern History*, XII (1946), 469–86; Bernard A. Weisberger, "The Dark and Bloody Ground of Reconstruction Historiography," *Journal of Southern History*, XXV (1959), 427–47; Vernon L. Wharton, "Reconstruction," in Arthur S. Link and Rembert W. Patrick (eds.), *Writing Southern History: Essays in Historiography in Honor of Fletcher M. Green* (Baton Rouge, 1965), 295–315; and John Hope Franklin, "Reconstruction and the Negro," in Harold M. Hyman (ed.), *New Frontiers of the American Reconstruction* (Urbana, 1966), 59–76.

27. For a discussion of the impact of the scientific study of history on research and writing, see W. Stull Holt, "The Idea of Scientific History in America," in his *Historical Scholarship in the United States and Other Essays* (Seattle, 1967), 15–28.

28. Fleming, *Civil War and Reconstruction in Alabama*, 523. Fleming knew better, for in another place—deep in a footnote—he asserted that Rapier was from Lauderdale, "educated in Canada"; *ibid.*, 519 n.

29. Loren Schweninger, *James T. Rapier and Reconstruction* (Chicago, 1978), xvii, 15.

30. Fleming, *Civil War and Reconstruction in Alabama*, 12. For an account of Yancey and other white southerners in the North to secure an education, see John Hope Franklin, *A Southern Odyssey: Travelers in the Antebellum North* (Baton Rouge, 1976), 45–80.

31. Fleming, *Civil War and Reconstruction in Alabama*, viii–ix; and John W. Du Bose, *Alabama's Tragic Decade, 1865–1874* (Birmingham, Ala., 1940). Du Bose's work is a collection of his newspaper articles published in 1912.

32. John W. Du Bose, *The Life and Times of William Lowndes Yancey* (Birmingham, Ala., 1892), 407–22.

33. Thomas McAdory Owen, *History of Alabama and Dictionary of Alabama Biography* (4 vols.; Chicago, 1921), II, 845–46, IV, 1335, III, 278. For a discussion of the problem of defining carpetbaggers in Alabama, see Bond, *Negro Education in Alabama*, 65.

34. Hamilton, *Reconstruction in North Carolina*, 663.

35. *Ibid.*, 666–67.

36. Beale, "On Rewriting Reconstruction History," 807–27.

37. See, for example, Coulter, *The South during Reconstruction*, and Bailey, *The American Pageant*, Chap. 24.

38. See C. Vann Woodward, "The Political Legacy of Reconstruction," in his *The Burden of Southern History* (New York, 1961), 107.

39. For some of the works that deal with these themes, see John W. Blassingame, *The Slave Community: Plantation Life in the Antebellum South* (New York, 1972); Euguene D. Genovese, *Roll, Jordan, Roll: The World the Slaves Made* (New York, 1974); Robert William Fogel and Stanley L. Engerman, *Time on the Cross: The Economics of American Negro Slavery* (2 vols.; Boston, 1974); Gutman, *The Black Family in Slavery and Freedom*; and David Brion Davis, *The Problem of Slavery in Western Culture* (Ithaca, N.Y., 1966), and *The Problem of Slavery in the Age of Revolution, 1770–1823* (Ithaca, N.Y., 1975).

40. A few who were associated with counsel for the plaintiffs have published some of their work. See, for example, Alfred H. Kelly, "The Congressional Controversy over School Segregation, 1867–1875," *American Historical Review*, LXIV (1958–59),

537–63; and John Hope Franklin, "Jim Crow Goes to School; The Genesis of Legal Segregation in Southern Schools," *South Atlantic Quarterly,* LVIII (1959), 225–35.

41. Michael Perman, *Reunion without Compromise: The South and Reconstruction, 1865–1868* (Cambridge, 1973); and Leon Litwack, *Been in the Storm So Long: The Aftermath of Slavery* (New York, 1979).

42. Thomas J. Pressly, "Racial Attitudes, Scholarship, and Reconstruction: A Review Essay," *Journal of Southern History,* XXXII (1966), 90.

43. J. R. Pole, "The American Past: Is It Still Usable?" *Journal of American Studies,* I (1967), 70–72.

44. Edward F. Sweat, "Francis L. Cardozo—Profile in Reconstruction Politics," *Journal of Negro History,* XLVI (1961), 217–32. For examples of other intraparty conflicts, see Robert H. Woody, "Jonathan Jasper Wright, Associate Justice of the Supreme Court of South Carolina, 1870–77," *Journal of Negro History,* XVIII (1933), 114–31; and Schweninger, *James T. Rapier and Reconstruction,* 75, 144.

45. Schweninger, *James T. Rapier and Reconstruction,* 114.

46. Franklin (ed.), *Reminiscences of an Active Life: The Autobiography of John Roy Lynch,* 101–102.

47. Thomas B. Alexander, *Political Reconstruction in Tennessee* (Nashville, 1950), 204–205, 240–41; and Taylor, *Louisiana Reconstructed,* 214.

48. Henry L. Swint, *Northern Teacher in the South* (Nashville, 1941); Bond, *Negro Education in Alabama;* and Robert Morris, "Reading, 'Ritin,' and Reconstruction" (Ph.D. dissertation, University of Chicago, 1976).

49. Irwin Unger, *The Greenback Era: A Social and Political History of American Finance, 1865–1879* (Princeton, 1965); George R. Woolfolk, *The Northern Merchants and Reconstruction, 1856–1880* (New York, 1958); Robert P. Sharkey, *Money, Class, and Party: An Economic Study of Civil War and Reconstruction* (Baltimore, 1959); and Osthaus, *Freedmen, Philanthropy, and Fraud.*

50. Gutman, *The Black Family in Slavery and Freedom;* Howard Rabinowitz, *Race Relations in the Urban South* (New York, 1978); John H. Cox and La Wanda Cox, *Politics, Principles and Prejudice, 1865–1866: Dilemma of Reconstruction America* (New York, 1963); and Thomas Holt, *Black over White: Negro Political Leadership in South Carolina during Reconstruction* (Urbana, 1977).

Index

Index

Index

Lee, Richard Henry, 380
Leopold II, 268, 273–74
Letcher, John, 376, 379
Lewis, Augustus, 210, 211, 213
Lewis, Julian, 299
Liberia, 161
Libraries and archives, 4–9, 288–89, 304–305
Library of Congress, 304–305
Lincoln, Abraham: during Civil War, 42, 69, 231, 234; and public morality, 72, 163–79; and colonization of blacks, 136; view of blacks of, 138–39; and patronage, 166–70, 176–77; importance of honesty to, 168; feelings of, about abuse of power of public office, 170–72; personal favors and, 172–73, 176, 177; attitude of, toward financial matters, 173–74; associations of, with business community, 174–75, 178; influence peddling and, 175–78; reelection of, 240, 241, 242; death of, 245–46
Lincoln, Benjamin, 376–77
Litwack, Leon F., 396
Locke, Alain, 145, 300–301, 302
Lodge, Henry Cabot, 260–61
Logan, Rayford, 52, 141
Longfellow, Henry Wadsworth, 268
Longstreet, Augustus Baldwin, 371, 379, 380
Lovejoy, Elijah, 227
Lucy, Autherine, 42
Lynch, John Roy: writing biography of, 182; early life of, 250; education of, 250–51; in Mississippi legislature, 252–55; campaign for U.S. Congress, 253–54, 397; in U.S. House of Representatives, 254, 255–60; and charges of election fraud, 257–59; as temporary chairman of Republican National Convention, 260–61; retirement activities of, 261–63; military career of, 262–63; comments on Congressional career of, 263–64; family of, 263; concern of, for position of blacks, 264–66; death of, 265; importance of, 265–66; *Reminiscences of an Active Life*, 265; *The Facts of Reconstruction*, 265, 388
Lynchings, 145, 149, 281, 361

McCary, William, 254
McClellan, George B., 241
McClernand, John A., 169
McCulloch v. *Maryland*, 125
McDuffie, George, 107, 114

McKinley, William, 263
Mackinnon, Sir William, 268
McQuigg, E. H., 126
McVeigh, Wayne, 419n28
Malcolm X, 287
Mantle, Burns, 17, 20
Marion, Francis, 369
Marshall, John, 125, 369
Marshall, Thurgood, 41, 287, 306
Mason, George, 94, 156, 336
Melbourn, Julius, 87, 88–89
Meredith, James, 287
Merrick, William, 105
Methodists, 86, 134, 228, 357
Mexican War, 105, 115, 342
Mexican-American Legal Defense and Education Fund, 344
Mexican-Americans, 341–47
Mexico, 104–106, 114, 115, 342
Miles, William Porcher, 62, 377
Miller, Kelly, 15
Mitchell, William, 210, 212, 217
Monroe, James, 136
Morality. *See* Public morality
Moravians, 74
Mordecai, George W., 210
Mordecai, Henry, 219–20
Morgan, Arthur, 181
Morphis, Sam, 84
Morris, George Sylvester, 399–400
Morris, Gouverneur, 336
Morris, Robert, 397
Morton, Samuel G., 335
Moss, James, 220
Motley, John L., 401
Moultrie, William, 369
Muhammad, Askia, 384–85
Mulattoes, 354–55
Mussey, R. D., 233, 234, 238–39

National Association for the Advancement of Colored People (NAACP), 16, 17, 18, 42, 51, 144, 286, 287, 306, 312–14, 345
National Urban League, 144
Nationalist, 192, 194–97, 204, 422n55
Nationalist Education Association, 194
Nationalist movement, 184, 190–205, 422n39
Nationalization News, 199
Native Americans. *See* American Indians
Nazism, 146
Negro History Bulletin, 45, 51
Negro History Week, 45, 51
Negroes. *See* Blacks
Nell, William C., 44